Rewards for High Public Office in Europe and North America

Anyone observing the recent scandals in the United Kingdom could not fail to understand the political importance of the rewards for high public office. The British experience has been extreme but by no means unique, and many countries have experienced political controversies over the pay and perquisites of public officials.

This book addresses an important element of public governance, and does so in a longitudinal and comparative manner. The approach enables the contributors to make a number of key statements not only about the development of political systems but also about the differences among those systems. It provides a unique and systematic investigation of both formal and informal rewards for working in high-level positions in the public sector, and seeks to determine the impacts of the choices of reward structures.

Covering 14 countries and drawing on a wide range of data sources, this work will be of great interest to students and scholars of comparative public administration, international politics and government.

Marleen Brans is Professor at the Public Management Institute of the Katholieke Universiteit Leuven, Belgium and Guest Professor at the Centre Montesquieu d'Etudes de l'Action Publique, at the Université Catholique de Louvain, Belgium.

B. Guy Peters is Maurice Falk Professor of American Government at the University of Pittsburgh. He is also an Honorary Professor at both Roskilde University Centre and at the City University of Hong Kong, and Distinguished Professor of Comparative Politics at Zeppelin University, Germany.

Routledge Research in Comparative Politics

Rewards for High Public Office in Europe and North America

Edited by Marleen Brans
and B. Guy Peters

LONDON AND NEW YORK

First published 2012
by Routledge
2 Park Square, Milton Park, Abingdon, Oxon, OX14 4RN

Simultaneously published in the USA and Canada
by Routledge
711 Third Avenue, New York, NY 10017

Routledge is an imprint of the Taylor & Francis Group, and informa business

British Library Cataloguing in Publication Data
A catalogue record for this book is available from the British Library

Library of Congress Cataloging in Publication Data
Rewards for high public office in Europe and North America / edited by Marleen
Brans & B. Guy Peters.
    p. cm. — (Routledge research in comparative politics ; 49)
Includes bibliographical references and index.
1. Public officers—Salaries, etc. 2. Civil service—Salaries, etc.
3. Government executives—Salaries, etc. 4. Comparative government.
I. Brans, M. (Marleen) II. Peters, B. Guy.
JF1661.R52 2012
331.2'166—dc23   2011043851

ISBN: 978-0-415-78105-3 (hbk)
ISBN: 978-0-203-12072-9 (ebk)

Typeset in Times New Roman
by Cenveo Publisher Services

Printed and Bound in the United States of America
by Edwards Brothers Malloy

Contents

Tables

Figures

Preface

Anyone observing the scandals in the United Kingdom during the Spring and Summer of 2009 could not fail to understand the political importance of the rewards for high public office. The British experience has been extreme but by no means unique, and a number of countries have experienced political controversies over the pay and perquisites of public officials. For example, even in Sweden, with its more consensual style of politics, the possibility of large increases in the salaries of Members of the European Parliament provoked significant public debate.

The rewards for high public office are not, however, just a political issue. They are also an important set of data for comparative political analysis. The levels of rewards, their changes over time and the comparison of different positions among themselves and with the private sector help us to understand the political system. The level of visibility of the rewards of office, and the availability of data to the public also provide interesting insights into political life and culture. These data can be seen as 'dependent variables' resulting from a number of factors in politics, as well as 'independent variables' explaining at least in part political recruitment as well as public cynicism about the public sector.

This volume builds on the earlier book (Hood and Peters 1994) on the rewards of public office in Europe and North America as well as a book (Hood and Peters with Lee) on rewards for high office in Asia and the Pacific. The present book covers the period from the early-1990s to the near present, and the information included can be compared directly with the earlier data for many countries. The present book also contains, however, chapters on several Central and Eastern European countries that have gained independence since the earlier volume on Europe, and which are experiencing many of the same political challenges over rewards as the other countries. For all countries, we examine the rewards offered to chief executives, ministers, members of parliament, top-level civil servants, and senior judges.

Each of the country chapters provide not only discussions of the monetary and visible rewards available to public officials, but will attempt to document the (sometimes extensive) informal rewards available. We cannot ascribe monetary values to many of these informal rewards, but we provide substantial information about their magnitude and nature. In addition to descriptive chapters about each of the countries, this book has a comparative chapter and a number of comparative tables that enable us to compare directly levels of rewards and changes in rewards.

In summary, this book addresses an important element of public governance, and does so in a longitudinal and comparative manner. The approach enables us to make a number of interesting statements not only about the development of political systems but also about the differences among those systems. It provides a unique systematic investigation of both formal and informal rewards for working in high-level positions in the public sector, and seeks to determine the impacts of the choices of reward structures.

The completion of this book has been aided by a number of opportunities for the authors to meet. Our first meeting was at the European Consortium for Political Research Workshops in Cyprus in 2006. Some of the authors also participated in a panel at the Nispacee Conference in Lublijana in 2006. Zeppelin University in Friedrichshafen, Germany provided generous support for an authors' meeting in early 2009, and the project has also been supported by the Dutch Ministry of the Interior (Nederlandse Ministerie Binnenlandse Zaken en Koninkrijksrelaties). Also, Karin Fleming helped with the preparation of the final manuscript by a detailed copy-edit.

Finally we should thank the authors for their continued involvement and their patience during the long process of putting this book together.

Marleen Brans
B. Guy Peters

Contributors

Shirin Ahlbäck Öberg is Associate Professor and Senior Lecturer in Political Science at Uppsala University, Sweden. Her publications include articles, books, and book chapters about monitoring and auditing.

Marleen Brans is Professor of Public Administration and Policy at the Public Management Institute of the Catholic University of Leuven. Her research interests include politico-administrative relations, policy analytical capacity of civil service systems, and interactions between government and civil society.

Dionyssis G. Dimitrakopoulos is Senior Lecturer in Politics at Birkbeck College, University of London. He has published widely on various aspects of the politics of European integration. His work has appeared in, *inter alia*, Political Studies, the Journal of Common Market Studies, and the Journal of European Public Policy.

Jean-Michel Eymeri-Douzans is Professor at the Institute of Political Studies (IEP) of Toulouse, France. His research interests include the study of governing institutions, comparative public administration, and politico-administrative decision-making.

Elisabetta Gualmini is Full Professor of Political Science at the University of Bologna and President of the Research Foundation "Carlo Cattaneo Institute". Her research interests deal with welfare and labour policies in comparative perspective and administrative reforms.

Jane Järvalt is a PhD student of public administration at the Tallinn University of Technology and Head of Human Resources at Nordea Bank Estonia. Her research interests include civil service, public management and strategic HRM.

Jan Kenter is Policy Expert Top-Level Rewards of the Dutch Ministry of the Interior in The Hague. He drafted the law on disclosure of top level rewards, in effect since 2006 and the bill restricting top level rewards (expected

January 2013). He is the Secretary of the public sector top level rewards committee (Dijkstal committee).

Erik Láštic, PhD. is a Lecturer at the Department of Political Science, Comenius University, Bratislava, Slovakia. His research focuses on the Slovak political system and its institutions, with a special interest in referendum experiences in Slovakia.

Per Lægreid is Professor at the Department of Administration and Organization Theory, University of Bergen. His research interests include: institutional changes of central government organizations, democratic governance, administrative reform, welfare state reforms, and administrative policy with a special focus on New Public Management and post-NPM reform initiatives.

Martin Lodge is Reader in Political Science and Public Policy at the Department of Government and the Centre for Analysis of Risk and Regulation, London School of Economics and Political Science. His research interests include the study of executive politics and regulation.

Jan-Hinrik Meyer-Sahling is Associate Professor of European Politics at the University of Nottingham. His research has focused on: civil service governance in Central and Eastern Europe, the Europeanisation of national political systems in Europe East and West, and the institutionalisation of political time in Europe.

Katja Michalak is Reader of Political Science and Public Administration in the Department for Public Management & Governance at Zeppelin University. Her research interests include Comparative Politics, Political Governance, Bureaucracy, Political Institutions, Democratization, and Political Psychology.

Gary Murphy is Associate Professor of Government in the School of Law and Government at Dublin City University and in 2012 Fulbright Professor of Politics at the University of Chapel Hill. He has written extensively on continuity and change in Irish politics, as well as on regulating lobbying.

Eoin O'Malley is Lecturer in Political Science in the School of Law and Government, Dublin City University. His main research interests are in the operation of cabinet government and prime ministerial power, both in Ireland and comparatively. He is currently undertaking research on the position of Taoiseach (prime minister) in Ireland.

Edward C. Page is Sidney and Beatrice Webb Professor of Public Policy at the Department of Government of London School of Economics. His research interests include: British and comparative public policy and administration, law-making, and bureaucracy.

Salvador Parrado is Professor of Public Administration and teaches at the Spanish Distance Learning University in Madrid. He works on comparative administrative systems, senior civil service and public management.

B. Guy Peters is Maurice Falk Professor of American Government at the University of Pittsburg, and Distinguished Professor of Comparative Politics at Zeppelin University (Germany). He is also co-editor of the European Political Science Review. His main interests include comparative public policy and administration, and American public administration.

Tiina Randma-Liiv is Professor and Chair of Public Management and Policy at Tallinn University of Technology. Her main research interests include civil service reforms, performance management, policy transfer, and small state administration.

Paul G. Roness is Professor at the Department of Administration and Organization Theory, University of Bergen. He has published numerous articles on public sector organizations and institutional change, using organization theory. His recent publications are on change and continuity in public sector organizations, and the autonomy and control of state agencies.

Katarína Staroňová is a Lecturer at the Department of Public Policy and Economy, Comenius University Bratislava, Slovakia, and a consultant on the issues of governance in CEE countries. Her research is in the area of policy-making processes and the capacity of central European governments, with specific focus on politico-administrative relations, public involvement in decision making and impact assessment.

Theo A. J. Toonen is Dean of the Faculty Technology, Policy and Management of Delft University of Technology. He is Chair in Institutional Governance and Public Administration at Delft University of Technology and Leiden University. His research interests are comparative public administration and bio-based governance.

Frits M van der Meer is CAOP Professor in Public Sector and Civil Service Reform at Leiden University. He has studied and published in the area of comparative public management and bureaucracy. In addition he is interested in administrative history and its implications for present day government and society.

László Vass is Professor and Rector at the Budapest College of Communication and Business. His research interest is government, public administration and management, and interest groups politics.

Edit Vassné Varga has been HR manager in different organizations at the Hungarian public administration. Now she is working as the Head of Human Resources Department of Hungarian Public Nonprofit Company for Regional

Development and Town Planning. Her publications deal with the performance management in the Hungarian public sector.

Bart Verbelen is affiliated research fellow at the Public Management Institute of the Catholic University of Leuven. He has conducted research on poverty alleviation by local governments, performance budgeting, and determinants of health care systems. His other research interests include comparative public policy, research methods, and evaluation.

1 Rewards for high public office

Continuing developments

Marleen Brans and B. Guy Peters

Governments depend upon employing high quality personnel to make and implement their decisions. Individuals who choose to go into politics, or the public bureaucracy, may do so out of a sense of duty, or because they believe the work will be interesting, or because they are able to work out their own psychological problems (see Duvillier, Genard and Piraux 2003; also Lasswell 1930). Or they may choose to work for the public sector because the rewards they are offered are at least adequate for their needs and match their preferences concerning the types of career and the mixture of rewards they would like to have.

Governments have a variety of ways in which they can reward their high officials. While most citizens might tend to think first about salaries and direct financial rewards, there are a number of other more subtle and less direct ways in which public officials can be rewarded, some of which may be at least as important in motivating employees as are high salaries. Further, some of the relative attractiveness of public office may be a function of the surrounding economy and society, so that the public sector may be able to provide a range of benefits for officials that are unattainable from the private sector. One obvious example is the respect in which civil servants traditionally have been held in some countries in continental Europe, in contrast to the disdain found in some Anglo-Saxon countries. For example, our first study of rewards in Europe found that rewards for German civil servants were governed in part by an 'alimentation' principle, meaning that civil servants had the right to a life-style befitting their important role as servant of the State.

The variation in the level and types of rewards offered to higher level public employees (RHPOs) is important in itself, but it can also be important as a means of understanding the dynamics within different political systems. The choices made by those political systems reflect underlying political, cultural, and economic patterns and can be used as a window to understand the internal politics of each country. Further, the reward structures found in the public sector at any one time reflect political choices, some of which may have been made decades or even centuries ago, while other patterns may be very recent reactions to rapidly changing circumstances in the present.

The above paragraph implies that RHPOs are rather similar for all types of office, but the variation among offices may be as important as the relative differences among countries. For example, in some democratic systems legislators are paid relatively poorly because it is assumed that good citizens should want to hold these offices, or there is a tradition of the social and economic elite holding office. On the other hand, civil servants may be paid well because they are the managers who are necessary to make the State run effectively. In other cases the politicians may be well paid and prevent other High Public Officials (HPOs) from being better paid than they are, using formulae to maintain the differentials among the groups.

It is not just the members of government who are concerned about the rewards being offered to public officials, members of the public are also concerned. To the extent that they are aware of the information, citizens make judgments about their governments on the basis of what 'bargains'[1] they make with officials over rewards. Citizens in democratic systems may assume that the formal rewards offered to participants in the public sector are sufficient and may be surprised when there is a range of other rewards – available during and after public employment – that can provide those employees with a much higher income as well as less tangible rewards.

Analyzing rewards

The present research on rewards of high public office in Europe is based on several previous studies (Hood and Peters 1994; Hood and Peters with Lee 2003). The first study addressed rewards in a number of European countries, with the data collection ending with 1991. This first book included papers on eight Western European countries, as well as the United States, and mapped the types of salaries and other rewards being offered to chief executives, members of parliament, top bureaucrats and judges in those countries. This research was undertaken for a period in which the New Public Management was perhaps not yet in full flower, and had not had the pervasive effects on rewards, at least for the bureaucracy, that it had by 2009. Further, although we did attempt to assess the range of benefits received by individuals in high public office, the conceptualization of those rewards was not as complete as that later developed in the Asia-Pacific study.

The second study included data from seven countries in Asia and the Pacific Rim. This study included a much greater range of economic circumstances, ranging from rather wealthy Commonwealth countries – Australia and New Zealand – to a poor but rapidly developing country – China. Likewise, most of the countries involved had a 'Confucian culture' while the two Antipodean countries were Westminster democracies. Hong Kong and Singapore are Asian countries but have been significantly impacted by their former British colonial masters. There were also huge variations in the amount and type of rewards offered to public officials, with Singapore paying some of the highest public salaries in the world, while the formal rewards of public office in China are very small.

In this second study of the rewards of high public office in Europe, a number of factors have been altered significantly, and hence the updated information should provide an even more interesting and useful picture of the nature and impact of rewards for public office. First, and most obviously, the number of countries in which it is possible to do this research has increased substantially, and with that increase the nature of the economic and political systems included in our 'sample' has also increased. With the fall of Communism in Central and Eastern Europe there are a number of additional countries that must make autonomous choices about rewards, and must do so in the context of political and economic transformation. These decisions are also made in the context of very different political and economic histories. This book comprises chapters on RHPOs in four post-communist countries: Estonia, Hungary, Romania, and Slovakia. Of the countries studied in the 1994 book, six (Belgium, France, Norway, Sweden, the UK, and the US) return in country chapters in the present book; one (Denmark) is present in the data for the comparative chapter. Next to the new cases from Central and Eastern European (CEE) countries, yet another four new cases are included in the chapters: Ireland, Italy, the Netherlands, and Spain.

As implied above, the New Public Management also has substantially greater influence over decisions about rewards than was true at the time of the first study of rewards in Europe. The idea of 'pay for performance' has much greater impact on the manner in which civil servants are paid in these countries than it did previously, and rather than thinking about clear categories of pay we need to consider ranges and the impact of bonuses on total rewards. This idea has yet to influence the manner in which political leaders are rewarded, but the increasing influence of performance management more generally is making apparent to citizens which government programs are performing the best, and perhaps therefore also which ministers are doing their jobs most effectively. In any case, this book demonstrates that 'pay for performance' schemes have changed pay differentials within the public sector, the patterns of which were remarkably similar cross-nationally in the cases covered in the first study, with political masters making more than their civil servants. Even if 'pay for performance' has not caught on with ministers, the introduction of performance pay for civil servants has sparked off some interesting games between the two sets of office-holders with decisions on rewards as ways to protect both power and status.

Finally, decisions about the rewards of high public office are increasingly being made in the context of citizen distrust of government and of political leaders. Somewhat paradoxically, given that the evidence is that most governments are delivering services more efficiently and working more effectively, and often in a more transparent manner as well, the level of citizen discontent continues to increase and citizen participation through conventional channels continues to fall. While certainly not the sole, or perhaps even a major, cause of this discontent, the sense that public officials are overpaid and/or are receiving large amounts of extra-legal income may fuel the fire of that discontent. Therefore, we do need to be even more concerned with the political environment of rewards than in the past.[2] Several of the cases in this book demonstrate how, at least, the perception of citizen distrust makes officials respond with changes to the level and structure of their rewards.

Table 1.1 Dimensions of rewards (based on Hood and Peters 1994)

Tangibility	Formality	
	Formal	*Informal*
Tangible	Salary	Post-government employment
Intangible	Medals	Respect

Dimensions of rewards

Our previous research has identified two major dimensions that help to classify and understand the rewards offered to high public officials (see Table 1.1). The first dimension is formality, or the extent to which the rewards of office are officially sanctioned and transparent. The most obvious example of this type of reward is a salary that is paid publicly according to formal rules. On the other hand, the rewards of public office may not be as formalized, and could be the result of the position that the person achieves in society and the connections that result from having a public career.

The other relevant dimension of rewards is their tangibility. Again, salaries are a very tangible reward, as are many of the benefits available to employees, such as pension rights and chauffeur-driven cars. Some of these benefits may be difficult to price, but they are very real and identifiable, and may be as important to attracting and retaining employees as are formal salaries. Other aspects of rewards are intangible, and are a result of the respect that may come from having held these offices. The line between tangible and intangible rewards may be difficult to maintain in practice, however, given that it is possible to convert that respect into more tangible benefits.

Table 1.1 shows the four major categories of rewards, along with an example of each. Almost all reward systems provide some or all of these rewards, although the balance may be different across different political systems. Salaries are the obvious example of a tangible, formal reward for public officials. Other formalized benefits and perquisites for office holders fall into this category, although many citizens may consider these benefits to be excessive, and to represent public officials 'ripping off' the system. At the other end of these dimensions are informal, intangible rewards, which are typified by informal patterns of respect and social privilege granted to public officials.[3] In some societies these benefits can be substantial, while in others – e.g. the US – the reaction may be one of disrespect rather than respect.

Informal, tangible rewards may be quite legal and appropriate, but often have a sense of illegitimacy to citizens, and hence they can be one of the sources of the growing disrespect of public officials. For example, it may be perfectly legal for a retiring civil servant, after a 'cooling off period', to take a position in a firm that does business with government and thereby earn much more than his public salary, but citizens see this practice as corrupt. Likewise a judge may retire from the bench and return to private practice, retaining the honorary title of judge and charging perhaps higher fees than an ordinary attorney. In our earlier study of RHPO in Europe we found that members of the *grands corps* in France often received financial benefits that were definitely off the books from their *corps* (Rouban 1994). The list of rewards could be extended easily, but the basic point is that these real yet informal rewards are often all too apparent to the public, and bring public service into disrepute.

Finally, the formal, intangible rewards are those that accrue to public officials but for which there is no monetary value. An example would be the 'gongs' given to senior public officials in the UK, with clearly understood 'entitlements' for certain types of awards. As was humorously pointed out in *Yes, Minister*, senior diplomats are virtually entitled to some degree of the Order of St. Michael and St. George. These rewards are in principle intangible, but they may indeed produce some real benefits for their recipients, and hence the boundaries among these categories may not be watertight, and clever actions by recipients may be able to convert the intangible into the tangible. That having been said, however, these dimensions appear to be a useful way to begin to think about the issue, and a way to begin to compare countries and offices.

The rewards game

Although it is partially correlated with the dimension of formality, another variable that can be used to typify rewards is their transparency. How obvious are the RHPOs to citizens, and hence how likely are they to provoke a sense that the HPO is 'ripping off' the system? For example, although many of the benefits offered to HPOs are formalized and legal their existence is often a source of envy and disdain. One example is the continuing American debates over what to do about a more universal health care program. The fact that Congressmen have an excellent health care insurance program yet seem incapable of adopting one for other citizens has not gone unnoticed.

Time is another aspect of the visibility dimension in analyzing rewards of high public office. In many reward systems the benefits of working for the public sector may come some time after having been an employee. For example, our study of rewards in Japan identified the importance of the *amakudari* system in which civil servants retire early from their surprisingly poorly paid positions in the public sector and become very well compensated directors of public and quasi-public corporations (Nakamura and Dairokuno 2003).[4] The *pantouflage* of French public servants is not dissimilar, although it occurs earlier in their careers. This way of rewarding public employees may be substantially less visible than rewards. The same also goes for part-time earning opportunities, where formal rewards are combined with incomes from remunerated professions, directorships, paid consulting and speaking assignments, and of course in some countries from multiple office-holding in central and local government.

This book devotes quite some attention to transparency. Several of the chapters show how the level of transparency in RHPOs has decreased since our first

Table 1.2 Strategies of transparency in the interaction with respectful or disrespectful citizens (adapted from Hood and Peters 1994)

	Top public officials' strategies	
Citizens' attitudes	*Transparent (rewards are published, visible, and easy to understand)*	*Opaque (rewards are not published, concealed, and complicated)*
Respectful	Rewards: visible Legitimacy: high	Rewards: invisible Legitimacy: high
Disrespectful	Rewards: visible Legitimacy: low	Rewards: invisible Legitimacy: low

research, at least for civil servants, given that the details of many pay for performance contracts are not made public. The outcome for politicians looks different though. Since the mid-nineties, several countries have introduced pay for ethics schemes on the rewards for politicians, such as caps on outside earning or transparency registers for multiple occupations.

In the political game surrounding RHPOs (Table 1.2) citizens and the HPOs (especially politically selected HPOs) have somewhat different concerns and different strategies. To some extent HPOs are better off if the extent of their rewards is not widely known, given that many citizens may consider that employees in the public sector are overpaid and underworked. On the other hand, if their rewards are initially not transparent and then do become public, the level and types of reward will appear to be even more suspect than would high levels of reward that are made public readily, unless pay-for-ethics schemes were a successful trade-off.

The extent to which a strategy of openness will work successfully, however, is in part a function of the initial level of respect of the public for the public sector. For populations who, in principle, respect government and its occupants the transparent strategy may work well. However, for less respectful populations the openness strategy may fail from the outset, and only confirm their worst suspicions. The danger is that assuming populations to be distrustful, and hence hiding rewards from them initially, may become a self-fulfilling prophecy and all cases will deteriorate toward low legitimacy and low respect.

Measuring rewards

The quantitative data appended to this book comprises the basic data needed to understand what has been occurring in the area of rewards for high public officials. This data enables us to compare rewards across countries, across categories of HPOs and across time to be able to understand the political choices made and the consequences of those choices.

This appendix identifies the quantitative data requirements for the project, but there is also a good deal of qualitative information that is important for understanding RHPOs. For example, we have not been able to assign a quantitative monetary value to perquisites available to HPOs such as cars or access to government-owned facilities, but they are still identifiable. The authors of the individual chapters have been as detailed as possible in identifying all perquisites of office.

Explaining patterns of rewards

In this book rewards for high public office are both a dependent and an independent variable. Most of the chapters focus on RHPOs as a dependent variable, reflecting a variety of characteristics of each country. There appear to be conomic, cultural, and political explanations for these patterns, all of which have some face validity, and a case can be made for the utility of each of these approaches. While we will not be engaged in formal comparative analysis attempting to confirm some explanations and to reject others, we will be able to gain some inklings of the relative explanatory capacity of these factors.

The cultural basis of rewards is very much related to the respect in which the public sector is held by the public. This dimension has been identified as important in a number of studies of political culture (Almond and Verba 1963; Norris, 1999), and certainly appears to be related to the willingness to pay higher rewards.[5] Everything else being equal, those political cultures that are less supportive of the public sector will be likely to have lower rewards for HPOs than will other political systems. The participatory nature of the culture may also influence the relative rewards given to different groups of HPOs, tending perhaps to reward elected politicians more generously than bureaucrats or judges. Finally, egalitarian cultures, such as the Norwegian and Swedish, are expected to provide relatively lower levels of rewards relative to wages in the economy than in other countries, while hierarchical cultures, such as the Belgian, French, and Italian, are expected to do exactly the opposite.[6]

Economic factors provide an alternative explanation for the patterns of rewards offered to HPOs. The most obvious hypothesis linking economic factors to rewards is that more affluent countries will pay their public employees more, and also may pay them more relative to the private sector. As societies develop economically it is easier for governments to tax, and therefore they can extract money for higher RHPOs. Having the Central and Eastern European countries in the 'sample' for the present book allows for better testing of this hypothesis than the more constrained level of economic variance found in the Western European countries. The relatively rapid change in these economies also provides a means of looking at the role of economic change.

Finally, political factors have an influence on the style of rewards for public officials. These effects are to some extent captured in the cultural variable, but there are other political explanations as well. For example, to the extent that the states involved have chosen to play a developmental role in their economy and society, they may tend to reward public officials, and perhaps especially bureaucrats, more handsomely.[7] More legalistic political systems may focus on rewarding judges particularly well, and ensuring that their status in the political process enables them to be effective arbiters. In addition, the adoption of more neo-liberal ideas about the role of government and civil servants in many of the countries may also be helping to shape RHPOs, often downward at least with respect to the remainder of the economy.

These hypotheses represent places at which to begin the analysis of the factors that shape patterns of rewards for public officials, but there are also a number of other factors that emerge in the analysis of the individual countries. Again, examining RHPOs in the context of change provides an especially powerful insight into the policy and management choices made by governments. The countries of Central and Eastern Europe continue their economic and political transitions, and management systems in Western European countries continue to change in response to both changing ideas and changing political circumstances, so that we should be able to assess a variety of dynamic elements influencing rewards.

The consequences of rewards

Governments have generally sought to recruit the 'best and brightest' to fill important roles in the public sector. In some cases they have been, and continue to be, successful in doing that, while in others the public sector may be populated by those who could not find better positions in the private sector or who are risk averse and do not want to subject themselves to the competition associated with the private sector. The question, therefore, is to what extent do the rewards being offered – both the level and the type – affect career decisions of individuals and persuade them to join and remain in the public sector?

Patterns of rewards may also affect the governance capacity of political systems beyond the simple ability to recruit high quality personnel into the public sector. In particular, to the extent that some portion of the rewards offered to high public officers involve movement in and out of higher paid positions in the private economy, the link between government and economy is rather obviously strengthened. This pattern of moving people to the private sector appears to have been functional for cases such as France and Japan, and is perhaps less successful for the US. But the extent to which public office also involves some part or future private office is potentially important for understanding the impacts of rewards.

As implied above, the choice of RHPOs by a political system can also affect the manner in which citizens and their public officials interact, as well as the legitimacy of the political system considered more broadly. There are certainly a large number of factors that affect political legitimacy, but the sense that public officials are being rewarded too well, and/or in inappropriate ways, can certainly contribute to the malaise in which many contemporary governments appear to find themselves. Therefore, understanding the broader political and social impacts of reward systems, and not just their impacts on recruitment and retention of HPOs, is important to recognizing the full range of consequences of these rewards.

Summary and plan of the book

The present book draws on previous experience and previous findings, and has a strong comparative foundation across time as well as across countries. Along with that strong foundation, the present research also provides a means of examining change in the RHPOs in a number of systems in response to rapid social, economic and political developments, as well as fundamental changes in the way in which many people in and out of government think about the public sector.

Perhaps the most important thing to recognize concerning this research on RHPOs is that the rewards of high public office are not merely formal systems of pay and perquisites. Rather, they reflect fundamental features of the political and administrative systems, and also have major political consequences. Therefore, we are engaged in an exercise that involves many aspects of comparative politics, and we are also attempting to understand the choices made by governments and the consequences of those choices for the governments themselves, as well as for the societies within which they function. This research therefore has many academic virtues, as well as a number of more practical applications.

The book starts with a cross-time, cross-country and cross-office comparative chapter, to be followed by the thick descriptions of individual country cases. First come the Anglo-Saxon cases of the UK, Ireland, and the US. Next the Scandinavian cases of Norway and Sweden, as well as the Netherlands are discussed, to be followed by chapters on RHPOs in four countries with a Napoleonic heritage: Belgium, France, Italy, and Spain. Then come the four CEE countries included in the study: Estonia, Hungary, Romania, and Slovakia. Also included is an overview of rewards for top officials in the EU institutions. In the conclusion, the main observed patterns and trends are summarized.

Notes

1 For a different view of bargains see Hood (2000).
2 The Australian (Painter 2003) and New Zealand (Gregory 2003) cases in the Asia-Pacific rewards book also demonstrated extremely clearly the need to be conscious of citizens and their perceptions when designing systems for rewarding public officials.
3 Some of these 'rewards' may actually cost the HPO money. Officials are frequently asked as board members of charitable and community organizations, requiring not just time but generally also a financial contribution.
4 The *pantouflage* of French public servants is not dissimilar, although it occurs earlier in their careers.
5 That having been said, the deferential 'Confucian culture' did not appear to have as strong a relationship in the Asian countries as might have been expected. Of these cases the Japanese research offered the clearest example of cultural influences.
6 These categories are derived from cultural theory (Douglas and Wildavsky 1982; Hood 1998), but also have more common sense meanings.
7 Again from the Asian experience the role of the State in Singapore is a clear example of this political style and consequence of extremely high rewards. For the European cases France may be the prototype (van der Eyden 2003).

References

Almond G.A. and S. Verba (1963) *The Civic Culture. Political attitudes and democracy in five nations* (3rd edn 1989). Newbury Park, CA: Sage.

Douglas, M. and A.B. Wildavsky (1982) *Risk and Culture: An essay on the selection of technical and environmental dangers.* Berkeley, CA: University of California Press.

Duvillier, T., J.-L Genard and A. Piraux (2003) *La motivation au travail dans les services publics.* Paris: L'Harmattan.

Gregory, R. (2003) New Zealand – the end of egalitarianism? In C. Hood and B.G. Peters, with G.O.M. Lee (Eds), *Rewards for High Public Office: Asia and Pacific Rim States.* London: Routledge, pp. 88–104.

Hood, C. (1998) *The Art of the State: Culture, rhetoric, and public management.* Oxford: Clarendon Press.

Hood, C. (2000) Relations between ministers/politicians and civil servants: public service bargains new and old. In B.G. Peters and D.J. Savoie (Eds), *Governance in the Twenty-first Century.* Montreal: McGill/Queens University Press.

Hood, C. and B.G. Peters (1994) *Rewards at the Top: A comparative study of high public office.* London: Sage.

Hood, C. and B.G. Peters, with G.O.M. Lee (2003) *Rewards for High Public Office: Asia and Pacific Rim States.* London: Routledge.

Lasswell, H.D. (1930) *Psychopathology and Politics.* Chicago, IL: University of Chicago Press.

Nakamura, A. and K. Dairokuno (2003) Japan's pattern of rewards for high public office; a cultural perspective. In C. Hood and B.G. Peters, with G.O.M. Lee (Eds), *Rewards for High Public Office: Asia and Pacific Rim States.* London: Routledge, pp. 105–118.

Norris, P. (Ed.) (1999) *Critical Citizens. Global support for democratic governance.* Oxford: Oxford University Press.

Painter, M. (2003) Rorts, perks and fat cats; rewards for high public office in Australia. In C. Hood and B.G. Peters, with G.O.M. Lee (Eds), *Rewards for High Public Office: Asia and Pacific Rim States.* London: Routledge, pp. 70–87.

Rouban, L. (1994) France: Political argumentation and institutional change. In C. Hood and B.G. Peters (Eds), *Rewards at the Top: A comparative study of high public office.* London: Sage, pp. 90–106.

van der Eyden, T. (2003) *Public Management of Society: Rediscovering French institutional engineering in the European context.* Amsterdam: IOS.

2 Rewards at the top

Cross-country comparisons across offices and over time

Marleen Brans, B. Guy Peters, and Bart Verbelen

The rewards offered to high public officials provide a window into the manner in which political systems function, and the underlying values that guide those systems. Looking at these rewards with a comparative perspective provides even more insight into governments because we can see the differences among the political systems as well as how they have changed over time. The data presented here focus primarily on the visible, tangible rewards offered to public officials, and hence are only part of the total rewards these officials receive. Despite that limitation, they do provide substantial insight into variations and trends in paying high public office as well as into variations between political systems.

In this chapter we will address a range of questions that will illuminate various dimensions of the basic puzzles of rewards of high public office. These range from very basic questions about who gets paid more to questions about the effects of several possible explanatory factors on the levels of rewards. In particular, we will ask whether the wealth of a country, certain institutional conditions, and the rise of the New Public Management (Christensen and Lægreid 2007) can explain the observed differences in rewards. We will conclude with a discussion of the importance of transparency and public knowledge of rewards in shaping the patterns of compensation and benefits offered to top public officials.

By examining the rewards for high public office across countries, across time and across a range of officials that are all employed at the top of the public sector, we will get a rather complete picture of rewards and the politics that are behind those rewards. Each of the country chapters contained in this book tells an interesting and important story about the pattern of rewards in that country, but the comparison in this chapter helps us understand the similarities and differences between the cases and offers some tentative explanations for rewards. By identifying which cases represent the norm and which are the outliers we can begin to understand the complex decisions that may go into making choices about how to reward officials in the most important public offices in these countries.

Who gets what? Patterns of rewards

The most fundamental question about the rewards of high public office is simply who gets what. There are substantial differences among the countries included in the analysis as well as differences, although in general not so significant, among the various types of public officials. It therefore pays individuals better to be employed in the public sector in some countries, and likewise in general it pays to have chosen certain occupations within government.

The data in Figures 2.1–2.3 show that, in general, rewards in the countries of Eastern Europe tend to be the lowest. This might be expected given relatively lower wages in these economies in general, but the contrast with other countries is significant. The Eastern European countries are followed by the Scandinavian countries and a number of continental countries. The relatively low levels of rewards in Scandinavian countries might be surprising, given their general affluence and the importance of the public sector in these economies. At the other end of the distribution of rewards being offered are the UK and the US, both of which tend to pay the best, on average, across the range of positions. Again, the relatively high levels of rewards in the US might be unexpected given the general anti-statism in the public sector, although the openness of many administrative positions to competition from the private sector may explain part of these higher rewards (see below). Also in the group of high wages we find the EU institutions, which generally pay their top officials more than member states do for comparable positions. A comparison between top public salaries in the UK and the EU institutions shows again that the UK is an outlier in Europe: the UK is the only European member state in our sample that pays top civil servants and judges better than Europe pays the top officials in the European Commission and the President of the European Court of Justice.

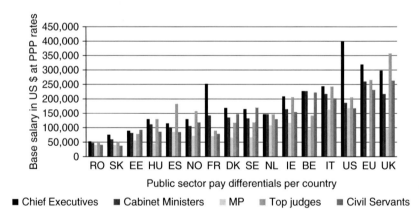

Figure 2.1 Who gets what? Top public sector base salaries in 2007, in US $ at purchasing power parity (PPP) rates.
    Note: For France, 2008 data are used due to incomplete series for 2007.
    For Romania, 2007 data are averages of figures for 2005 or 2006 and 2008.
    Slovak civil servants' pay is based on 2006 data. Up until 2009, MEPs were paid differently depending on their nationality. See the Appendix for notes on calculations for individual countries in the sample.

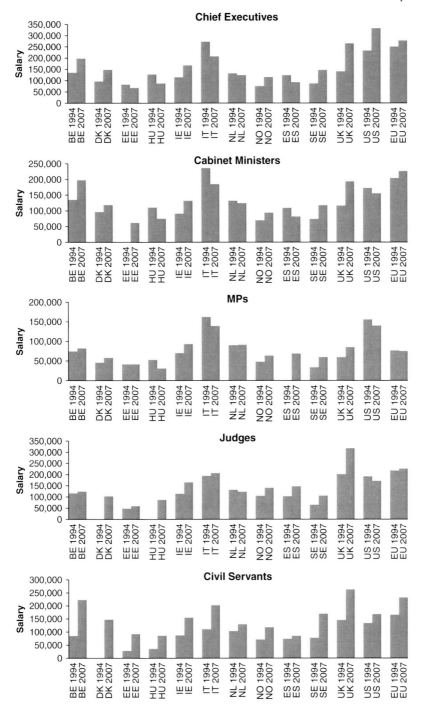

Figure 2.2 Winners and losers? Changes in base salaries, in US $ at purchasing power parity (PPP) rates at 2000 prices.

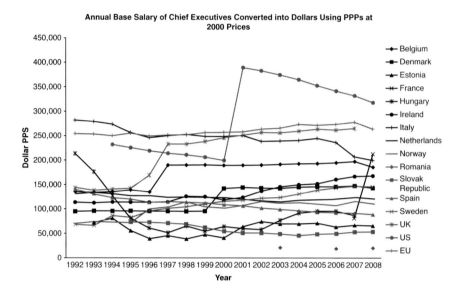

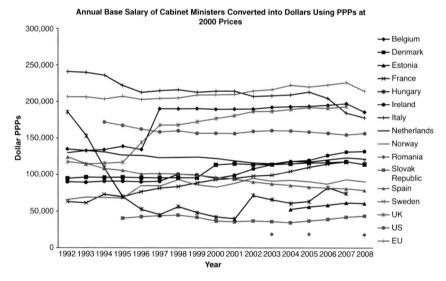

Figure 2.3 Changes in base salaries of top officials in US $ at purchasing power parity (PPP) rates, at constant prices of 2000
          Note: Gaps in series indicate missing data.

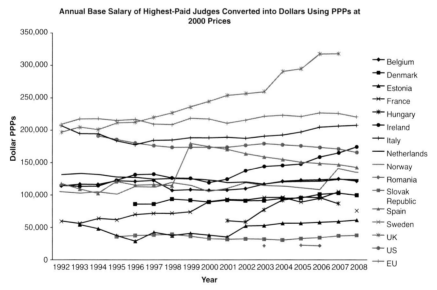

Figure 2.3 Cont'd.

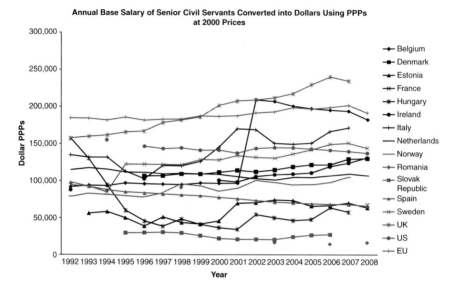

Figure 2.3 Cont'd

The countries of Continental Europe tend to be in the middle of the distribution of rewards, although Spain has had low and markedly declining levels of rewards for a range of positions when compared to other countries. The contrast between Spain and Italy is perhaps particularly interesting. Although both are Southern European countries in the Napoleonic tradition (Ongaro 2009) their patterns of rewards are significantly different. Italian rewards are substantially higher than those in Spain in all categories, and indeed Italian wages are relatively high even when compared to other Napoleonic countries, such as France and, at least for members of parliament (MPs), Belgium. We therefore need to consider the institutional factors, and other possible factors, that have generated rather different patterns in countries with substantial similarities.

When we compare rewards across the several positions in government there are also some clear winners and losers. The clearest losers are MPs. In most countries the rewards offered to MPs are lower than for other offices. At the other end of the distribution, chief executives tend to be paid the best, although ministers and civil servants also do well in some of the countries. This pattern is visible in countries who pay their MPs relatively little as well as in countries such as Italy, whose MPs are the most well paid in Europe. We will explore the factors involved in these differences below, but it seems that MPs are constrained in increasing their own salaries (whether legally or politically). Further, the civil service may be the group who are most directly in competition for employees with the private sector, so they may have their salaries driven up to be able to attract at least some of the 'best and brightest' in the society. That competition, combined with the managerialism of the past several decades, has tended to accelerate growth in the rewards of upper level civil servants in most countries.

Although there are some general patterns of rewards for the offices in the public sector, the different countries tend to reward the offices differently. Both civil servants and judges in the UK tend to be rewarded better than their counterparts in other countries. The US president is the best paid chief executive, although still the salary is rather low for the office often described as the most powerful in the world. Finally, Italian MPs tend to be better paid than other parliamentarians, and Belgian ministers are also among the best paid. These patterns reflect a number of institutional and political factors in all of the countries, and the logics involved in these differences will be discussed more fully in the individual national chapters.

The level of equality across the offices also varies between the countries. The reward structures in most Central and Eastern European countries are relatively equal. In the Eastern European cases the explanation may be in part cultural and in part the relative paucity of available assets that are producing wage compression. We would have expected the egalitarian cultures of the Scandinavian countries to have sustained relatively equal (and low) levels of rewards across the various offices, but Figure 2.1 shows more evidence to dispersion than expected from the egalitarian patterns observed in the early 1990s (Hood and Lambert 1994: 28). In the group of countries with egalitarian features, we now find the Netherlands with the most visible compression at the top. Also typical for this country, as well as for Belgium, is the equality in base salary for the prime minister (PM) and cabinet ministers. This testifies to the role of the PM as 'primus inter pares' or first among equals, typical for maintaining the balance in precarious coalition government. The most pronounced dispersion we find in the UK, where the rewards for different offices have become quite distinct. Other pronounced disparities we find in the presidential and semi-presidential systems of the US and France, mainly accounted for by the relatively high pay of the president, who is clearly not first among equals. If we discounted the payment to the president in the US, pay at the top would be rather compressed, which we would not expect from the market orientation of the American society as a whole. Overall, in most countries the richest High Public Official (HPO) is the chief executive. Unusual cases are found in the UK, Spain, and Norway, where the chief executives are topped by chief justices.

The above comparisons are drawn from figures on base salary only. The criterion which we have applied for 'base salary' is the same that was used in the 1992 study (Hood and Lambert 1994: 29). Base salaries refer to rewards that are routinely paid to HPOs in cash, without reference to particular circumstances or production of specific expense claims. Thus excluded are benefits in kind (such as houses, travel, or cars) and allowances paid on a reimbursement basis. Additionally, all kinds of tax-free expense allowances and premiums or bonuses that can vary per person are excluded. What are included, though, are such fixed, salary-based components as holiday pay, and end-of-year premiums. For maximum transparency on the boundaries of pay, the reader is referred to the appendix of the book, which provides the figures on which this comparative analysis is based, the office to which they pertain, and the definition of base salaries in different countries.

The total reward structure, including all kinds of allowances, benefits in kind, outside and post-service earning opportunities, may on the one hand upset the observed patterns to some extent. For instance, MPs in many countries may top up their income with all kinds of allowances, often tax-free, or with earnings from holding multiple offices or from private sector engagements. The individual country chapters in this book reveal particular features that are too unique and variegated to capture in cross country comparisons. On the other hand, the variations in the width and depth of add-ons to base salaries, as well as applicable tax regimes, may equally be reinforcing some patterns observed on the basis of salaries only. The strictly proportional tax regimes may keep the Nordic countries well separated from the US and the UK, who have more lenient tax regimes. Similarly, the relatively low taxes applicable to EU salaries keep these RHPOs safely at the top along the vertical axis. 'What you see is what you get,' is clearly a feature described in the chapters discussing rewards in Scandinavian countries, so we do not expect any substantial changes up or downward from including add-ons in the analysis of RHPOs in these countries.

Changes in rewards over time

As well as examining the distributions of rewards at the end of the time period under consideration in this study, we also need to understand the changes in these distributions over time. We should expect there to be a substantial amount of path dependence in these reward structures, given the difficulties in adjusting those rewards in highly institutionalized political systems. Despite that institutionalization and the substantial stability in the rewards provided, there also has been considerable change in several of the countries and some more gradual changes in all. There are some inertial factors operating but at the same time there are significant political and market pressures producing change.

Public sector officials in the UK tended to be the biggest winners in these changes. For all the types of UK officials being considered in this study there were gains, and to some extent substantial gains. The other winners over time seemed to be officials in the Scandinavian countries. The UK and Scandinavian countries were exactly the countries whose officials saw their salaries erode in the 1970s, and who had begun to make up for that in the 1980s (Hood and Lambert 1994). At least for the Scandinavian countries, the gains of the last two decades to some extent reflect something of a catch-up for countries in which the rewards historically had been extremely low by international standards, especially given the relative wealth of these countries. In Eastern Europe in turn, public officials tended to be losers, although the relatively shorter time period for these data as well as missing data make comparisons across time less meaningful than for the others.

In the 1994 study, among the different types of public officials MPs tended to be most vulnerable to pay erosion. In several countries, MPs suffered losses, although in many cases just relative losses, which appeared to be a consequence of the political difficulties these officials face in raising their own salaries. Legislatures have attempted to ameliorate these losses by creating automatic mechanisms (see below) that at least keep their salaries equal to inflation. Pay erosion for MPs is less of a trend in the last two decades, particularly when we exclude the Central and Eastern European cases in our sample, as well as Italy and the US. In most European countries MPs' formal salaries have improved. For some of these countries, the explanation lies with the introduction of 'pay for ethics schemes' (Hood and Peters 1994), whereby less visible rewards were traded for higher basic pay. This was the case in the Netherlands and Norway in the mid-1990s, and in Sweden in 2006. However, over time some clear losers have emerged. The biggest losses for MPs' pay were 16 percent in Italy and 12 percent in the US. Both these countries began with the highest levels, so there has been some convergence at least for this group of officials (see Figure 2.3).

The big winners over this time period have been the civil servants who may be less visible politically and who can also claim substantial expertise (whether in a policy field or in management more generally) in running public programs. Compared to most cases where improvements to top civil service pay have been gradual, the Belgian civil service has benefited from a strikingly abrupt raise, marking the radical modernization plans of the government at the time. Judges also have tended to come out as winners over this time period, although not as markedly as civil servants. These findings appear to indicate that some profes-sionalization, or depoliticization, of rewards has been occurring, as those groups who are the most clearly exposed to political pressures have been suffering the greatest relative erosion of their rewards (see Figure 2.3).

The rewards for chief executives displayed the most unusual pattern during this time period, especially in the US but also in several other countries. There has been some tendency to determine the rewards for the chief executive rather distinctly from those of other officials, so that there may be a large increase at once, then gradual erosion over time until there is another catch-up. For example, the rewards of the US president were lower than those in several other countries prior to the major increase that took effect in 2001[1], but since then the rewards have tended to decay. Although time series are unfortunately missing for the French case, the country chapter on France reveals the substantial increase of 162 percent of the French president's salary under Sarkozy (see also Figure 2.3).

Wealth and rewards

As we begin to explain comparatively the patterns of rewards offered to high public officials that we observe in these data, we will start with the simplest hypothesis: that richer countries will pay their public officials more. The logic is rather obviously that the more affluent countries will have the resources neces-sary to offer higher levels of reward and will therefore pay higher salaries.

Further, the public sector in more affluent systems may have to offer those higher rewards to be able to compete with salaries offered in the private sector.

When the data are examined during the most recent time period, for instance for chief executives in Figure 2.4, there is some support for this hypothesis. The least affluent countries – those in the Eastern European countries – clearly offer lower rewards than do the more affluent countries of Europe and North America. If, however, we remove the Eastern European countries from the analysis then the hypothesis appears weaker. In particular the Scandinavian countries are among the richest in this 'sample' but also offer relatively modest rewards to their top public officials. Also, the UK is not at the top of the gross domestic product (GDP) ladder for these countries but tends to provide among the most handsome salaries to public officials. This is also true for Italy.

If we examine the relationship between affluence and levels of reward over time the relationship looks perhaps even more suspect. The most obvious case that undermines the logic of affluence promoting higher levels of rewards comes from Norway. During the time period we are studying, the gross domestic product

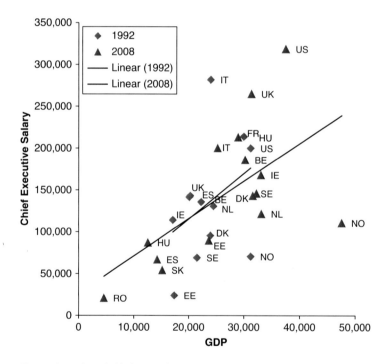

Figure 2.4 Plot of chief executive's pay against gross domestic product, (GDP) per head by country, 1992–1993 and 2007–2008 (in $ PPP at 2000 prices).
   Note: For years of missing data, the closest available year was taken: Estonia, GDP data of 1993; US, chief executive salary for 1994; UK and Hungary, chief executive salary for 2007 (see Appendix for details).

(GDP) of Norway increased dramatically, but the level of rewards increased only modestly. The level of rewards for MPs has remained particularly low when compared to the rewards offered in other countries despite the substantial rise in GDP. This indicates that political and institutional factors may be more significant than economic factors in explaining the level and development of rewards for high public office (RHPOs). Also odd is the fact that over time developments for Italian and Dutch chief executive pay is the reverse of what is expected, since with improvements of GDP, salaries have gone down.

The Norwegian case certainly appears to undermine the argument that wealth should be related to levels of reward for high public office, but there is also some evidence that rewards may indeed be related to economic growth. For example, rewards in Ireland and in some Eastern European countries increased along with the economic expansion in these countries. This increase in rewards was even true for positions, such as Irish MPs, that are more politically exposed.

Levels of GDP per head thus go some way to explain comparative RHPOs, but certainly not all the way. In most, but not in all, countries do HPOs have to gain from increases in GDP. Whether there is an effect on RHPO from the most recent economic and financial crisis is too early to tell, but there is no evidence in the last four decades that high public officials will suffer when the economy flounders. The relationship between wealth and top officials' pay seems to be unclear, and should be held against the possible effects of institutions, to which we now turn.

What role do institutions play in explaining rewards?

The evidence on economic explanations for RHPOs is mixed, so that any simple understanding of rewards based on wealth appears unsatisfactory. There can be several versions of a political explanation for those rewards, but the most significant of these are based on the nature of the government institutions responsible for making and implementing decisions about rewards. For the group of countries in this study the democratic nature of institutions may be especially important, given that the public in many countries is extremely skeptical about paying high levels of rewards to public officials. Thus the more capable democratic pressures can be channeled through the institutions of government the more likely salaries are to be suppressed. In turn, the comparatively generous rewards for most types of EU officials can be interpreted as a particular translation of the EU alleged democratic deficit.

We have already noted some of the consequences of these institutional factors for the rewards of high public office. The most noticeable is that legislatures are often incapable of increasing their own salaries and indeed may find it difficult to increase salaries for any public officials. We have already noted that MPs have tended to fare worse than other categories of officials during this time period, while salaries for the less visible officials, such as civil servants, have not created nearly as much political discussion, even though in many cases they are significantly higher.[2] It is striking to note that the most recent change in EU officials' rewards confirms this pattern. When in 2009, uniform salaries were introduced for Members of European Parliament (MEPs), who had hitherto been paid at the level of allowances of the member states' MPs, they were set at over three times less than salaries for other top EU officials.

One of the most important institutional transformations affecting the rewards of high public office has been the increasing depoliticization of the processes used to decide upon the rewards. As noted several times already, parliaments have considerable difficulty in improving their own rewards, and also encounter difficulties in increasing the rewards for other public officials. Therefore, in a number of the countries included in this study, mechanisms have been designed to remove the decisions from the political realm and to make the decisions more or less automatic (see Table 2.1 for examples).

One of the simplest forms for depoliticizing decisions about rewards has been to link those rewards for office to the average wages in the society. This has been the case in the Slovak Republic since 1993, and since 2002, also the rewards for all major Estonian public offices, except the higher civil service, are linked to average wages in the society. This mechanism has been to some extent a 'pay for performance' scheme so that if the government were successful in economic management then they would also be rewarded for that success. This was a reasonable plan but for part of the period in question the salaries rose so rapidly that the parliament had to act to reduce the rapidly increasing public salaries. In the Irish case the creation of a general wage settlement in the economy during part of this time period did not necessarily benefit public employees but it did depoliticize the decisions.

In other cases, the rewards for other offices are pegged to decisions made for one particular office; in Italy, for example, wages for parliament have been linked to those for the judiciary, who have traditionally been particularly successful in securing high rewards. The chapter on Italy describes the judges as a 'sui generis' class, the protection of whose independence has gone hand in hand with the endowment of special privileges. Magistrates have traditionally constituted a successful institutional lobby that remains independent of legislative and

Table 2.1 Depoliticization and reference points for top public sector pay

Formal and informal references points, or independent pay committees			
Formal reference points	*Highly integrated*	*Civil service*	France, Netherlands, Hungary
		Average wages	Estonia, Slovakia
	Disjointed	*Judges*	Belgium, Italy
		Civil service	Belgium, Spain
Informal reference points	*PM*	Netherlands, Spain	
	Private sector salaries	Estonia, Ireland, Belgium	
Independent pay committee	Norway, Sweden, UK, Ireland		

executive power, always claiming guaranteed independence, which in turn has direct repercussions on wage policy. In many cases, it is civil service salaries that serve as reference points for highly integrated pay systems. This is the case in France, the Netherlands, and Hungary, but also in the EU: top office remunerations are percentage-wise deviations from top civil service pay.

In other countries, the rewards system across different offices is characterized by sets of more loosely coupled reference points. In Belgium, MPs' salaries have traditionally been linked to those of state councilors, but their holiday pay and end of year premium have recently been coupled to the system applicable to civil servants. Also, in Spain the civil service reward structure has served as a loose model only, from which the rewards of other offices have departed.

What is also common in some cases is that wages are adjusted to rates of inflation so that officials maintain their purchasing power, as in the case of Congress in the US. In the case of Congress, the rewards are increased annually in relation to changes in the price level unless Congress acts to block the increase. This has enabled members of Congress to maintain their purchasing power and have the opportunity to appear self-effacing and almost noble if they should decide to deny themselves the rewards in any one year.[3]

Another means of depoliticizing how the RHPOs are determined is to use expert commissions that (presumably) make decisions on the basis of information about rewards for analogous positions in the private sector, as well as other factors deemed relevant. This method has been used in the UK in a variety of different guises. Similarly, in the US, before the system was made more automatic, the President's Pay Agent used expert advice to determine rewards. Several other countries have moved away from linkages to formal reference points to adopting suggestions from independent pay committees. In Norway, until 1991, the pay of executive politicians was linked to the pay of Supreme Court judges, with the PM making 1 percent more than the president of the Supreme Court, and ministers 1 percent more than Supreme Court judges. MPs' salaries were coupled with those of deputy directors general in ministries up until 1993, when all these offices' salaries were set on a certain step on the general pay scale. From 1996 onward, they were made subject to recommendations by an independent pay committee appointed by Parliament. We find a similar development in Sweden in the mid-1990s, when references to civil servants, and later judges, were removed for MPs' salaries, which together with ministers' salaries became subject to recommendations of the independent pay board.

Another institutional question that has arisen in designing systems of rewards has been referred to as 'pay for ethics'. That is, public officials have accepted formal or *de facto* agreements to have higher but more transparent rewards in exchange for not accepting as much outside remuneration, or as a trade-off for foregoing less visible allowances of all kinds. This model has been demonstrated, for example, in the 1991 agreement on pay for Congress in the US, and also has been institutionalized now in a number of the countries in Eastern Europe. In the Netherlands, Sweden, and Norway, expenses allowances for MPs' pay have been traded for higher formal salaries.

The development of rewards in Ireland, on the other hand, presents a rather different experience in attempting to institutionalize ethical concerns. In a period of rapidly rising incomes in the private sector in Ireland, the rewards for public office grew only modestly in comparison so that there was a sense that public employees, and perhaps especially political officials, should 'top up' their salaries from other sources. These sources appear to have included some that might violate any usual conception of ethical rewards within the public sector. Likewise, the stretching of parliamentary expenses by some MPs in the UK clearly appeared to have moved beyond acceptable ethical bounds.

The rise of New Public Management

The time period included in this study contained the rise of the New Public Management (NPM) as a widespread approach to governance and the public sector. Although the NPM has a number of different dimensions (Hood 1991) and interpretations, it has some definite implications for the RHPOs. In particular, the emphasis on using management techniques imported from the private sector has meant that there have been a number of attempts to impose 'pay for performance' in the public sector (see Perry, Mesch, and Paarlberg 2006).

The basic idea of 'pay for performance' is that individuals in government positions should be rewarded on the basis of their contributions to the success of their organizations, or the public sector more generally. This logic is impeccable within the domain of private sector management, but is very difficult to implement in government. While governments may be able to measure the performance of lower level personnel relatively easily, assessing the performance of top level civil servants whose tasks involve policy advice to ministers or managing large programs is more difficult. And how does one measure the performance of a legislator, or a judge? Interestingly, however, most programs of performance management have concentrated on the upper echelons of the public sector, especially the civil service.

Despite the seeming difficulties in implementing 'pay for performance' within the public sector, a number of countries have attempted to implement this approach in government, even given the special difficulties encountered for high public officials. For example, in Italy and Norway the governments have implemented contract systems for many public officials, and less extensive arrangements have been implemented in many other countries. In the less extensive systems of performance pay the system tends to offer bonuses to employees – usually civil servants – rather than providing more permanent rewards.

Given the somewhat vague nature of the NPM and its possible relationship to rewards in the public sector, it is not surprising that performance is interpreted rather differently in different settings. For example, in Estonia the general performance of the economy is considered to measure the performance of public officials. The vague nature of performance in the public sector can also be used to justify rewards to most employees, as in the case of Slovak Republic. In most other cases performance is measured by more conventional means and the rewards tend to be given to individuals rather than to groups of employees.

One of the more successful means of implementing 'pay for performance' has been to use performance contracts for higher civil servants and in some cases ministers. These contracts are in general private so that they become a less transparent means of increasing the levels of rewards for some officials. This mechanism for performance management has been used even in the Scandinavian countries to reward managers of major public enterprises or even in more conventional civil service positions. In less extreme versions of performance management the use of bonuses and salary increases provide rewards in ways that are not open to intensive public scrutiny.

Next to creating greater opacity, 'pay for performance' practices have in some countries upset the hierarchy embedded in formal reference points. In some cases this has strengthened the articulation of informal reference points in paying high public office. These are not laid down in laws and regulations, as the formal reference points are, but serve as benchmarks that signify standards and norms on what are acceptable and desirable pay differentials. In many countries, if not formally, the salary of the Prime Minister (PM) seems to function as an informal reference point, signaling the apex of the pay system at the top of public offices. This informal reference also functions as a standard to put caps on possibilities for certain offices to raise their rewards way above the chief executive's pay. In the Netherlands, for instance, bonuses for top civil servants are informally capped at 130 percent of the PM's salary.

Lifetime earnings for public employees

Another way of considering the institutional effects of the rewards offered to high public officials is to consider them from the perspective of lifetime income. That is, although the rewards for high public office in the short-run may be relatively meager, holding these positions may enable an individual to earn a much higher income after leaving office. In some cases, e.g. Japan and Korea (see Nakamura and Dairukono 2003, Kim 2003) this reward structure is very well institutionalized, with senior public servants often retiring to take lucrative positions as director in public and quasi-public corporations.

In the countries considered in this book this pattern is less formal, but in some cases it is no less institutionalized. Perhaps the clearest cases it is France with its pattern of *pantouflage*, meaning that after some years of service in civil service positions individuals 'parachute' into positions in the private sector. This opportunity is especially available for members of the *Grands Corps* because their contacts (as well as their general abilities) are useful to organizations in the private sector. Also, many politicians have a civil service background and, although the formal rewards of political positions may be little different from those of the civil service, the opportunities for informal rewards will be substantially greater. The chapter on France, however, points at a backlash of extensive *pantouflage* in recent years. Globalization and liberalization would have made private companies less dependent on government. At the same time, an ethics committee has started to check possible conflicts of interests when civil servants covet positions in the private sector.

Finally, in the US, and to a lesser extent in the UK, there is a well-established pattern of public officials – political as well as civil service – going into private firms or into lobbying activities after leaving office. The revolving door between the public and the private sector continues to revolve, but most of the traffic goes from government to the private sector (Maranto 2006). Indeed, there is some evidence that political officials may rationally specialize in certain policy areas while in office in the anticipation of higher incomes after leaving office (Parker and Parker 2009): for example, specializing in defense issues while a Congressman usually will produce a higher income after leaving office than would specializing in urban affairs or in social policy.

Transparency and the hidden iceberg of rewards

We have amassed a good deal of information about the rewards for high public office in these countries, but to some extent we are merely seeing the tip of the iceberg. We have been concentrating on the rewards that are visible, that are provided formally and generally, and that are taxable. These rewards are themselves substantial, but there are a number of less formal rewards, some with substantial monetary value, that are not identified so readily and which may be difficult to calculate in current monetary terms. Even in countries with high levels of transparency these rewards may not be widely known or understood, and if they do become visible to the public they may become the source of substantial political discontent, as citizens may believe they had been deceived.

This large iceberg of benefits hidden beneath the surface helps to emphasize the importance of transparency in rewards for the public sector. In addition to examining the levels of rewards for high public officials we also examined the level of transparency of those rewards and found substantial differences among the countries. At one end, Sweden, and close behind it the US, Norway, and the Netherlands, had high levels of transparency for rewards. In these countries all basic information about rewards is published and available online, with the exception of some information about performance contracts. Likewise, most of the information about benefits is transparent so that again citizens (or researchers) can find what the total rewards package is for officials, and in some cases, such as Sweden, this includes even credit card statements of ministers. Also, the structure of rewards for HPOs is rather straightforward so that what one sees is what they get.

At the other end of this transparency dimension both Belgium and France were amongst the least transparent systems included in the study, to the extent of great difficulties for the French case author to collect consistent times series. The process by which rewards are determined is at best opaque, and many of the rewards are not readily made available to the public. Belgian, and also Spanish, authorities are quite reluctant, for instance, to reveal exact figures regarding the payments to Speakers of the Houses of Parliament, who get substantial add-ons, whereas in the Netherlands and Scandinavian countries these premiums are visible, on top of being more compressed.

Perhaps reflecting some path dependency from their past, several countries in Central and Eastern Europe also have limited transparency in their provision of rewards. This is the case for Romania and the Slovak Republic. But Estonia and Hungary have moved to greater transparency.

Although there are marked differences in transparency in this set of countries, in all there are some benefits for working for the public sector that are not obvious and that are difficult to quantify. These less visible benefits range from various employment benefits, such as pensions, travel allowances and housing, that do have some monetary values to knighthoods and their equivalents. All of these benefits, even if highly intangible, do have some real value for the recipients but they may not be readily recognizable by the general public, and may be considered simply part of the rewards associated with any position.

Although we can characterize the level of transparency in general, we should also distinguish between passive and active versions of transparency. In active transparency, the information on public sector rewards, and indeed on other aspects of public sector employment (see Derlien and Peters 2008), is published or made readily available in other manners. Passive transparency, on the other hand, means that although the information on rewards may in principle be public, some form of action is required to obtain it, perhaps something as significant as filing a freedom of information request (as for Slovakia and Romania). Clearly passive transparency may not in reality create much real transparency for the public.

Amongst the most actively transparent reward regimes we find Sweden, Norway and the Netherlands, joined by Estonia and Hungary. In Sweden all government agencies operate under the principle of public access, a principle that has a long tradition (*offentlighetsprincipen*). This principle of public access means that the general public and the mass media are guaranteed an unimpeded view of activities pursued by the government. Information about wage levels and other rewards for all government employees are thereby readily accessible for everyone, and this transparency does invite coverage of rewards or perks for most HPOs. For instance on the parliament's website one can find a full account of all rewards (over time) in Swedish as well as in English. In Estonia, rewards for all categories of public office-holders are published in public acts. In the Netherlands, the 2006 'Act on publication of publicly financed top wages', which means that all salaries in organizations financed from public means in all sectors of government are published. Also, in Hungary there has been a recent move to active publications of rewards for public offices, mainly through law.

Several of the countries that have active transparency regimes governing rewards also deploy registers of part-time earnings or financial interests, for instance in Sweden, but also in Estonia where high public officials are held to reveal their personal wealth and source of income in the State Gazette.

In addition to the differences between active and passive transparency, it is important to note the differential movements in transparency for the various positions within the public sector. As noted above concerning the influence of

NPM on patterns of rewards, the increasing use of personal performance contracts for civil servants, as well as the general movement towards personalized rewards, makes determining levels of compensation for senior civil servants increasingly difficult. This move to individualization and variability of rewards for top civil servants means that bonuses and add-ons are not published in readily available sources. One not only needs to know the legal framework but also the reward policy and structure of each individual public organization. In spite of the openness and obligatory publishing, the underlying principles of top civil servants' rewards in Estonia, for instance, are neither transparent nor consistent. This declining transparency of the rewards of civil servants in part reflects the trade-off between the managerialist devotion to flexibility in rewards and the more political demands for transparency. On the other hand, there have been numerous political pressures to make the rewards for political officials (and especially those of parliamentarians) more transparent. This is the case for both already transparent regimes, such as the Scandinavian and Dutch ones, but also in traditionally more opaque regimes, such as in Belgium, France, and Italy.

In Italy, a move to transparency took off with the 'clean hands' policy in the period 1992–1994, following a serious system crisis. New attempts for greater transparency gained momentum in 2008–2009, when the Italian minister for Public Administration started a battle in favor of transparency. In Belgium, in turn, the 1995 revision of MPs rewards was crucial in rendering the system, at least partially, more transparent. France is an interesting case in that the disjointed moves to more transparency cover both politicians and senior civil servants. Since the early 2000s, bonuses for civil servants have been made public and subject to plans to revise them into performance pay schemes, and ministers' rewards have been reorganized to do away with the 'secret envelopes' controversies. Ministers would top up their salaries with about 50 percent from these payments. Indeed, at the end of the Jospin Premiership, in 2002, a scandal occurred when it was revealed that the unspent 'secret funds' were used by exiting PMs and ministers as 'black money' for financing political activities and also for highly controversial private expenditures.

Private sector mobility

The lifetime earnings model discussed above implies some mobility between the public and private sector, but the rewards of high public office may to some extent be shaped by opportunities available in the private sector. This openness is especially important in public administration, given that most other posts depend upon election or other more political forms of selection. In some governments the administrative system is open to recruitment from the private sector, while in others the career is generally closed. When the system is more open there is more direct competition so that wages might be expected to be elevated.

This openness to competition from the private sector has been one aspect of the reforms associated with the NPM, so that this may also be a major component of the differential growth of rewards for civil servants as contrasted to other top positions in the public sector. The UK is perhaps the clearest case of this mobility in the current collection of countries. After the adoption of the NPM ideology during the Thatcher years there has been substantial movement between the public and private sectors, and also rapidly increasing levels of rewards. The *post hoc* argument here is that the need of the civil service to be able to attract high quality personnel from the personnel market in the private sector implies that government will have to increase the rewards available. Yet in Belgium, the substantial raise in civil service top salaries was an explicit *a priori* component of reforming the civil service by opening top positions up to the market.

Summary and conclusions

The amount of rewards offered to high public officials, the manner in which the benefits are awarded, and the differences in rewards among officials within the same political system tell a great deal about how governments function. The public sector has a good deal of discretion in how they choose to reward their top officials and those choices do help to define the nature of the political systems. Although there is a great deal of convergence in many aspects of public administration in the European and North American countries in this study the pattern of rewards has remained highly divergent (compare with Hood and Peters 1994). There remain marked country profiles in pay differences between certain offices that can be traced back to the nature of coalition government, or to the strength of parliamentary assemblies. For instance, compression for members of the executive in the Netherlands and Belgium is typical for 'weak' Prime Ministers in coalition government, while the comparatively high level of pay for legislators in the US and Italy reflect the strong role of legislative assemblies in these otherwise highly different political systems. Pay differentials thus signal political power and hierarchy, and radical changes either do not happen or are seen to be a threat to the political system.

Other differences that persist relate to the composition of the overall reward structure for HPOs. The iceberg of add-ons to base salaries in some countries does not merely reflect strategies on the part of politicians to avoid public backlash over serving themselves. The composition of the iceberg is itself a reflection of concepts of representation. In countries such as France, Belgium, and Italy, MPs should not be detached, salaried professionals, but active elsewhere in society, be it in local politics or business. It should not come as a surprise that such income supplementation and opacity of rewards are sanctioned in the Nordic countries as well as in the Netherlands, where remainders of protestant culture have supported both transparency and compression.

The RHPOs represent the path dependence that has been central to the historical institutionalism (Steinmo 2008) so that the way in which countries decide to reward their top officials tends to persist. The interesting exception to that generality has been found in the countries of Central and Eastern Europe, which underwent significant managerial and political changes. In most other cases the changes over the years have been gradual and the basic patterns of reward tend to persist. This tendency has been seen perhaps most clearly in France and longer time series could make the comparatively highest pay raise for top civil servants in Belgium fade back into the previously dominant pattern.

Despite the general persistence of patterns of rewards there are still shifts in some rewards. The biggest shifts appear to have been in favour of some groups of officials, notably the higher civil service, as a result from the rise and resonance of managerialism in the public sector. Likewise, parliamentarians now have to expect greater transparency over their rewards, not only in terms of the structure of rewards, but also in terms of mechanisms that promote public scrutiny. Both sets of changes feature strongly in the country chapters that follow.

Notes

1 In general the salary of the president cannot be increased during his or her term of office, so this increase was given to George W. Bush upon taking office although it had been adopted earlier.
2 The most obvious case of the visibility of rewards for MPs has been in the UK where the misuse of parliamentary expense allowances created a major political scandal (see Lodge, this volume).
3 In 2011 Social Security recipients will not receive a cost-of-living increase because inflation was below the level that triggers increases. Congress will, however, receive slight increases.

References

Christensen, T. and P. Lægreid (Eds) (2007). *Transcending New Public Management. The Transformation of Public Sector Reforms*. Aldershot: Ashgate.
Derlien, H.-U. and B.G. Peters (2008) *The State at Work: Public Sector Employment in Ten Western Countries*. Cheltenham: Edward Elgar.
Hood, C. (1991) A public management for all seasons? *Public Administration*, 69:3–19.
Hood, C. and S. Lambert (1994) Mountain tops or iceberg tips? Some comparative data on RHPOs. In C. Hood and B.G. Peters (Eds) *Rewards at the Top: A Comparative Study of High Public Office*. London: Sage, pp. 25–48.
Hood, C. and B.G. Peters (Eds) (1994) *Rewards at the Top: A Comparative Study of High Public Office*. London: Sage.
Kim P.-S. (2003) The politics of rewards for high public office in Korea. In C. Hood and B.G. Peters, with G.O.M. Lee (Eds), *Rewards for High Public Office: Asia and Pacific Rim States*. London: Routledge, pp. 119–129.
Maranto (2006) *Beyond the Government of Strangers: How Career Executives and Political Appointees can Turn Conflict into Cooperation*. Lanham, MD: Lexington.
Nakamura, A. and K. Dairokuno (2003) Japan's pattern of rewards for high public office; a cultural perspective. In C. Hood and B.G. Peters, with G.O.M. Lee (Eds), *Rewards for High Public Office: Asia and Pacific Rim States*. London: Routledge, pp. 105–118.
Ongaro, E. (2009) *Public Management Reform and Modernization: Trajectories of Administrative Change in Italy, France, Greece, Portugal and Spain*. Cheltenham: Edward Elgar.
Parker, G.R. and S.L. Parker (2009) Earning through learning in legislatures. *Public Choice*, 141:319–333.
Perry, J.L, D. Mesch and L. Paarlberg (2006) Motivating employees in the New Performance Era, *Public Administration Review*, 66:505–514.
Steinmo (2008) Historical institutionalism. In D. Della Porta and M. Keating (Eds), *Approaches in the Social Sciences*. Cambridge: Cambridge University Press, pp. 113–138.

3 Rewards at the top in UK central government

Martin Lodge

'Look Tony, you've got a wife who earns a quarter of a million a year. I've got a wife who spends a quarter of a million a year.'
John Prescott, then deputy prime minister, protesting about a freeze on ministerial salaries.
> A. Rawnsley, 2001, *Servants of the People*. London: Penguin, p. 54.

'… and do you know what it is all about? Jealousy.'
> Sir Anthony Steen, MP, 21 May 2009

To say that rewards for high political office dominated British political headlines in late Noughties was arguably an understatement. Following the *Daily Telegraph*'s purchase of a leaked CD containing details of all members of parliament's expenses, the daily headlines throughout May and early June 2009 were dominated by stories ranging from the trivial to the outlandish and from the gaming of the rules to the outright fraudulent. As a result, the public was informed that among those costs which had been 'incurred wholly, exclusively and necessarily to enable [MPs] to stay from [their] only or main home for the purpose of performing […] duties as MP,' were demands for lavatory seats, fake house ornamentation, tree planting and pruning, moat cleaning, trouser presses, mole catchers, TV and sound systems, stainless steel dog bowls, food mixers, 'Maximus' love seats in deep moss brushed cotton, bed linen, pipe repairs underneath tennis courts, manure, and book cases. In an early leak, one then-senior minister, Jacqui Smith, was uncovered to have registered the back bedroom at her sister's London home as primary residence, thereby being able to claim a 'secondary residence allowance' (£116,000) for the family home (where her husband and children lived) in her constituency. More embarrassingly, she was also found to have (unknowingly) claimed for her husband's downloading of two adult films (£10 in total). Meanwhile, a number of peers were suspended after being accused of having requested 'cash for amendments.' Other MPs, including ministers, were accused of gaming the tax system by regularly 'flipping' their second home designation and using legal means of avoiding capital gains tax when selling their properties. Arguably more fraudulently, a small number of MPs were found to have claimed and received mortgage repayments although their actual mortgages had already been paid off.[1]

The political response to the ongoing expense saga was immediate.[2] One response was the forced resignation of the Speaker of the House of Commons, Michael Martin (the first such resignation in over 300 years). A second was the announced resignation of a large number of MPs (from across the political spectrum) that had faced constituency and party pressure to resign. This also included a number of cabinet ministers (including Jacqui Smith) as the expense saga became embroiled with wider upheaval of the Labour government that threatened the immediate future of Prime Minister Gordon Brown. Other politicians quickly repaid the criticized amounts.

A third, and most important in the context of this chapter, was the acceleration of announcements of internal reforms, especially a re-examination of earlier claims, further codification of expense rules that reduced the scope for claims to be made, the capping of certain claims, such as mortgages and rent, and the requirement to quarterly publish all expense chits. The government also proposed the creation of a 'Parliamentary Standards Authority' that was to be able to disallow claims, order repayment and impose penalties. These reforms were to await further proposals to be put forward by the Parliamentary Standards Commissioner, Sir Christopher Kelly, in autumn 2009 as well as wider constitutional reform debates. Overall, the emphasis on reducing parliamentarians' authority on determining their own pay regimes, as well as trends towards further codification and increased externalization of MP expenses followed the pattern over the last decade or two.[3]

Earlier examples of political responses to perceived public criticism of political rewards, included prime minister Gordon Brown's successful strong-arming of his parliamentarians into not voting for a pay rise that would go beyond that of other public servants (in particular, the police), although the rise had been advocated by the pay review body. At the same time (2008), the government announced that it was seeking legislation to abandon parliamentarians' freedom to vote on their own salaries, thus further endeavoring to divert public attention via institutional means.

The specific interest in 'allowances' and 'expenses' was initially raised in January 2008, when a backbench Conservative MP (David Conway) was revealed to have paid his sons for non-existent research assistance. This triggered further revelations about previously unknown parliamentary perks, such as the existence of a so-called 'John Lewis list' of goods that were accepted as legitimate expenses for parliamentarians requiring London accommodation.[4] Parties announced demands for their parliamentarians to 'come clean' over their expenses and two parliamentary reviews were asked to deliver 'root and branch' reform suggestions over disclosure requirements and perks in terms of living and office expenditures. By 2009, these proposals remained in disarray and awaited the Parliamentary Standard Commissioner's recommendations. This followed the government's failed attempt to limit the release of MPs' expenses under Freedom of Information legislation. As a result, 1.2 million receipts (at an approximate cost of £2 million) between 2004 and 2008 were to be released by July 2009 – and it was these leaked details that were obtained by the *Daily Telegraph* and caused the media storm in spring/early summer 2009.

Apart from allowances, interest regularly also focused on possibilities of outside and post-career earning opportunities. In early 2008 ex-prime minister Tony Blair joined J.P. Morgan, as part of a 'small handful' of jobs he wished to take, for an estimated £2 million per year package (the second being with Zurich insurance for an approximated £500,000). These part-time jobs complemented his memoir writing (under a £4.6 million deal), his speeches (rumored to bring in another £100–200,000 per engagement), his activities as an (unpaid) Middle East 'envoy', and his £3.19 million pension pot.

The bureaucratic domain did not escape controversy either. For example, the National Audit Office reported (in late 2007) that former civil servants had made a return of 20,000 percent on their shares from the privatization of QinetiQ, the former Defense Evaluation and Research Agency. In early 2008, the Department of Health's commercial director, Chan Wheelan, a US citizen, was criticized for receiving £185,000 plus bonuses, a civil service pension, two business class return flights to the US per year, a £35,000 relocation package, and an £8,400 per month housing allowance (*Financial Times*, 30 January 2008, p. 4). One year later, in February 2009, media attention turned to the 'hospitality list' for senior civil servants that listed invitations by various organizations to Wimbledon, football matches, arts and culture events, flower shows as well as numerous breakfast, lunch, and dinner invitations (among them the Confederation of British Industry, the National Eating Disorder Awareness Week or the Overseas Cemeteries Trust).[5]

The global economic meltdown meant that Cabinet Secretary, Gus O'Donnell, announced in February 2009 that he and his permanent secretary colleagues would selflessly abstain from taking their bonuses. Gordon Brown enquired into the abolition of MPs' final salary pension schemes. In the meantime, one bank chief executive suggested to MPs in a parliamentary committee hearing that 'people like you and me […] are on relative modest salaries' (Eric Daniels, Lloyds Banking Group chief executive, earned £930,000 in contrast to MPs on nearly £62,000) (*Financial Times*, 12 February 2009, p. 3).

In other words, rewards for high political office have hardly vanished from public attention over the past decade and were in fact at the heart of wider debates regarding constitutional reform. Notably, rewards for politicians and senior bureaucrats developed in distinct ways in the light of such public attention. In contrast to the increasing visibility of political rewards, the rewards for civil servants reduced in their transparency, given individualization of pay deals at the top and departmentalization for the rest of the ministerial bureaucracy and those working in executive or regulatory agencies. In addition, most bureaucrats at the top earned more than their political masters, while some chief executives of executive agencies also earn more than the most senior civil servant, the Cabinet Secretary. Figure 3.1 illustrates the various trends in the reward bargains during the period of interest in this volume. The rest of this chapter considers

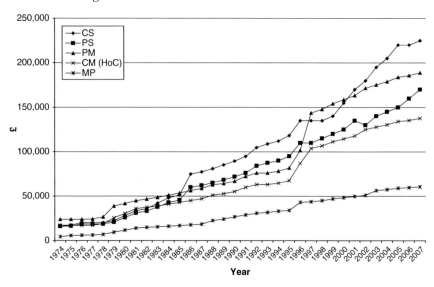

Figure 3.1 Rewards for high public office in the UK.
    Source: Senior Salaries Review Board, House of Commons Library.

bureaucratic and political reward patterns in turn, before considering the extent to which established theories of political reward apply to the British case in the past decade or so.

The political reward bargain: from club of gentlemen to league of eunuchs?

In earlier work, Christopher Hood (1994) pointed to three key features of the politicians' reward bargain at the national UK level. First, there was little evidence that political business cycles existed. Second, there was a consistent shift towards 'hiding' material rewards through substantial increases in expenses and allowances as well as through allowing for discretionary handling of supplementary sources of income. Third, Hood pointed to a growing pay discount for politicians, not only in relative terms, but also in comparison to top civil servants and the private sector.

Developments since the early 1990s broadly followed these patterns – but it would be difficult to suggest that the ongoing public pressure on political rewards had created a league of lowly paid eunuchs. One recurring in British political life has been the claim that political salaries should be linked to those of bureaucrats in order to allow for 'depoliticization.' Following an earlier policy (1988–1993) where parliamentarians had linked their pay to the rate increases received by the average of 'grades 5–7,' parliamentarians opted (in 1996) to link their pay to the mid-point of the annual increases of the senior civil service pay band.[6] At the same time (1996), MPs voted (against the wishes of the then-Conservative government and the Labour front bench) in favor of an increase of 26 percent in their salaries, as had been recommended by the Senior Salaries Review Body (Review Body on Senior Salaries 1996). It was the same constellation – a large number of MPs considering retirement or fearing their demise at the hand of the electorate and therefore more interested in reward than fearing party whips – that provoked the Labour government in 2008 to announce that parliamentarians were to vote on legislation that would end their ability to vote on their own pay increases. An earlier study of parliamentary pay had also found widespread support among MPs for abolishing their right to vote on their salary and to tie salary decisions to a basket of comparable salaries set by the Senior Salaries Review Board (see Review Body on Senior Salaries 2007b).

As illustrated in the introduction, most attention focused on allowances, whether these related to 'second homes,' office-expenditures or outside earnings. The qualitatively important changes over the past 15 years affected the way in which politicians could supplement their earnings. Following outcries over 'sleaze' that were associated with the final days of Conservative reign during the mid-1990s, ideas regarding the regulation of parliamentary (House of Commons) ethics became increasingly prominent (Kaye 2005). Part of this development was the rise in parliamentary salaries (in order to reduce 'temptation'), the emergence of a quasi-regulator for parliamentary standards, and a higher office allowance that was however granted on supposedly stricter conditions. The regime provided for the disclosure of outside earnings, mainly for the 'provision of paid parliamentary services' (i.e. advice on parliamentary matters and speeches), and the authorship of books and political speeches more generally.

The regime for office allowances was increasingly formalized. As Figure 3.2 indicates, 'office allowances' grew substantially, but on increasingly restrictive terms, for example expecting MPs to avoid using allowances to top up their own family income.[7]

In 2001, the Senior Salaries Review Board suggested a reform to the allowance system, and since 2004 some details of MPs were published on a parliamentary website. The changes to the allowance system represented a major attempt at regularizing parliamentary expenditures, mostly by reducing discretion (via the central provision of IT equipment and the codification of employment contracts), while still maintaining a differentiated set of additional sources of reward. Despite these attempts at codification and transparency, the practice of regulating parliamentary expenses proved to be more difficult. The second Commissioner for Standards in Public Life came to grief when challenging MPs over their parliamentary allowances. One Conservative leader's resignation (Iain Duncan Smith) was partly over (disproven) allegations regarding his wife's employment. And during the first media storm of 2008 over expenses granted for second homes in London, it was revealed that the list through which 'reasonable expenses' were assessed by the House of Commons validation clerks was kept secret as otherwise those rates (taken from the website of the department store 'John Lewis') would 'become the going rate.'[8] In other words, despite these attempts at

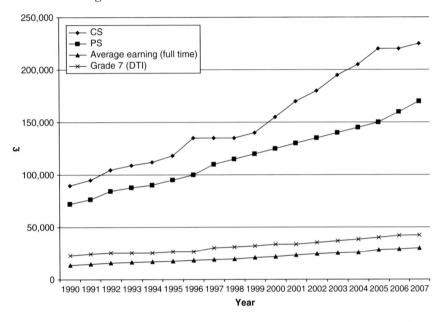

Figure 3.2 Senior bureaucrats in comparative perspective.
        Source: Civil Service Yearbook, First Division Association, Senior Salaries
        Review Board, Department for Business and Regulatory Reform (Freedom of
        Information request).

institutionalizing rules, discretion remained very much at the heart of parliamentary pay as parliamentarians continued to be in charge of their own rules, relying on a system of 'audit' of expenses.

Over the years, it was media scrutiny of expense claims that continued to embarrass parliamentarians (for example, leading to league tables regarding car miles claimed). Reflecting a view of the media as chief regulator of public conduct rather than relying on institutional means, it was argued that rather than the 'Advisory Committee on Business Appointments' exercising thorough and draconian oversight over politicians' and top civil servants' retirement to private sector occupations, this role should be played by the media through 'naming and shaming' (*Financial Times*, 22 February 2008, p. 2). In other words, while parliamentary debates largely evolved around the search for institutional devices, the facilitation of Tocquevillian pressures was widely seen as more effective in controlling supposed reward 'excesses.'

Politicians in government witnessed – at least formally – significant increases in their formal pay. However, Figure 3.1 only notes the agreed increases in earnings since the late 1990s as part of the overall increase for politicians that had been supported by the backbench revolt against their respective front-benches in 1996 (although suggestions were made that this revolt was 'tolerated').

However, as part of a policy to signal 'restraint', the incoming Labour government decided not to take the pay increase. As a result, between the 1997–2001 elections, cabinet ministers, apart from the prime minister, were on lower actual salaries than the leader of the opposition, William Hague, who decided to take the pay increase. The 'restraint' was lifted shortly after the 2001 election without attracting much public attention, although it was claimed that Labour ministers had 'saved' the country £2.5 million. Regardless of restraint, the pay reward for politicians in government became increasingly different to that of parliamentarians and suggested a growing hierarchy of pay reward that reflected seniority of post and a move away from a more compressed and supposedly mutuality based reward system.

In sum, the traditional reward bargain for parliamentarians – a low salary compensated by an informal system of allowances and other income sources – had increasingly moved towards one that was more, but still incompletely codified. Furthermore, the direction of travel in terms of political rewards was one of higher salaries – despite studies suggesting that parliamentarians earned about 88 percent of supposedly comparable public service and 85 percent of supposedly comparable private sector jobs. In addition, 'additional earnings' increasingly moved 'above' the waterline, thereby making them more open to outside scrutiny and criticism (but not external oversight), whether about the employment of family members or about the size of claimed car allowances. Such pay increases did not however necessarily change the availability of outside earning opportunities, with, for example, Conservative parliamentarians said to be receiving substantial earnings from directorships in non-listed companies.

The bureaucratic reward bargain: 'I will work harder'?[9]

Bifurcation (thus multiplication) was one key trend diagnosed for the higher civil service when examining the Public Service Bargain applying to UK central government in general (Hood and Lodge 2006, chapters 4 and 7) and similarly there was considerable diversification in reward patterns across Whitehall.

Trends

Following on from the experience of the 1980s, the first trend was the multiplication of pay bargains, with personalized pay deals for chief executives of the so-called Next Steps agencies and for the directors general of the newly formed regulatory agencies, leading the way for the introduction of a pay deal for permanent secretaries in 1996. In many cases, chief executives earned more than 'their' permanent secretaries (although these figures were not public and were not considered by pay review bodies). This bifurcation that emerged in the 1990s put substantial pressure on the pay bargain that applied to 'traditional' civil servants (in size and type) and motivated changes across Whitehall in the mid-1990s. Following ministers' rejection of proposals that civil service pay should be increased by 50 percent in the early 1990s, the then Conservative government considered whether to replace the tenure for senior civil service with (time-limited) New Zealand-type contracts.

The Senior Civil Service (SCS) was a response to these proposals (see Hood 1998: 446–447). In 1993, a report by the Efficiency Unit considered whether senior civil servants should be placed on contracts of an indefinite and rolling nature. The subsequent 1994 White Paper 'Continuity and Change' announced the creation of an SCS that was to operate a common reward system and to provide for a 'go anywhere' bureaucratic elite. Although contracts were supposed to be of an indefinite nature, it suggested that short-term contracts would be considered. By the time of the launch of the SCS in 1996, proposals had mutated into something more traditional: civil servants remained on indefinite contracts – although on explicitly individualized ones. While pay for the senior civil service remained 'government-wide' in order to allow for a 'mobile elite', all other pay grades were departmentalized – again borrowing an idea first trialed with executive agencies, namely departmental autonomy over pay. Permanent secretaries were provided with individual pay deals.

The 1999 White Paper 'Modernising Government' (Cabinet Office 1999a: chapter 6) contained a series of commitments towards pay that reinforced existing trends. One was the advocacy of greater flexibility in pay, linking reward more extensively to measured performance (in particular linking reward to public service agreement targets), a second was the endorsement of greater competition from outside and inside the civil service in terms of recruitment at an increasing number of levels in the bureaucracy and the third, support for short-term contracts. In this context, two further reports dealt with reform of the top civil service reward bargain. The report by Michael Bichard (then a high-flying permanent secretary) advocated greater non-consolidated performance pay elements in the overall reward bargain (i.e. pay components that were not pensionable or would be added to basic pay). Such a regime was to be monitored by the National Audit Office (Cabinet Office 1999b). A second review, led by a private sector finance director, suggested that incentives should play a greater role in central government operations, in particular in the light of greater pay flexibility that was to vary on counts of both region and performance (Matkinson 2000).

In 2002, these proposals were partly incorporated into a new pay policy for the SCS, with nine pay bands merging into (broadly) three and the political commitment to tackle 'underfunding' and a 'lack of transparency,' as well as to allow for market alignment and a 'robust' performance management and pay system (see SSRB 2007). Permanent secretaries and the cabinet secretary were placed outside these bands. The return to a three-layered hierarchy reflected the failure of an over-differentiated individualized system to provide for sufficient flexibility to allow for job mobility within and across ministerial departments, while it also reflected departmental problems in operating such a system.

Since 2002, two further types of bifurcation among reward bargains occurred. One bifurcation was a variation in pay between ministerial departments for the same pay grade. While these differences were not of a substantial nature, they were still seen as impacting on staff recruitment and retention across individual departments. A second type of bifurcation occurred within ministerial departments. Here, traditional public servants were said to be working at a considerable discount (averaging 22 percent) with 'externally recruited' colleagues (i.e. staff that had been recruited from outside the core civil service), despite being on the same grade (Senior Salaries Review Board 2006, 2007). In other words, the reward side, at first sight, revealed a decline in a clear hierarchical order in which seniority was linked to pay grade and a corresponding individualization of pay, within broad pay grades, that created a wider effect of diversification and multiplication.

Changing patterns?

The reward dimension of the traditional Whitehall bargain was defined by an exchange of services and skills for the provision of a secure material reward that included a (nominally non-contributory) pension. Salaries in the British civil service were traditionally seen as being lower than those in the private sector. Enhanced job security, a perception of underlying meritocracy and an attractive final salary pension scheme were regarded as tempting incentives for (risk averse) employees.

A further attraction was said to be a relatively stable expectation as to how high up in the organization one could reasonably expect to rise. The expectation was that promotion would occur approximately every six years during which three different 'jobs' were to be performed. While the job placement process was to some extent seen as near-random, there was nevertheless a belief in a 'system looking after' civil servants. And while guidance or even rules were never written down, clear understandings existed as to the type of positions that constituted a 'stairway to heaven', most of all to the position of the private secretary to the minister or 'bill work' (developing or drafting legislation).

The pay dimension was further characterized by *noblesse oblige*, namely a pattern of double imbalance. Under this system young entrants were to be paid relatively well (in relation to competitor private sector jobs) and then increasingly less so. Certain aspects of the reward bargain compensated for the material imbalance during civil servants' careers. First, there was the excitement from being involved in political decision-making. Second, there were further immaterial rewards, such as honors. Honors traditionally served two functions, one being the recognition of (high-level) seniority within the bureaucracy, the other being a 'compensation prize' for people having missed out on departmental promotions or who may have experienced particularly traumatic policy-making experiences. Third, 'double imbalance' was, for some, just an aspect of 'delayed gratification' in that the bureaucratic after-life was rich in earning opportunities (for those at the very top in particular). These earning opportunities were further enhanced by allowing civil servants to retire at 60 (at the latest), rather than at 65.

By the late 2000s, the traditional perceptions of the material reward – a respectable salary, a good pension and job security – were all said to have become undone. For new joiners, pensions had moved from a final salary scheme to one that relied on average earnings; pay at the top had increased substantially (although not in line with those private sector positions top bureaucrats liked to be compared with); and job security had been challenged by staff redundancy programs from the 1980s onwards.

There was considerable evidence to suggest some weakening of the traditional components of stable and predictable career progression and also evidence of a decline of the double imbalance pattern. The world of the stable career escalator (up to the position of the deputy secretary) came under considerable pressure by the early 1990s. The escalator arguably stopped at an earlier level as positions were increasingly opened up to internal and external competition. Moreover, the system was no longer seen to be 'looking after' people, instead it was said to have turned into a 'free for all'. As a result some civil servants reached higher levels more quickly than before, whereas others were left behind earlier and at lower levels and encouraged to leave – and a small number were sacked.

The further indicator of a decline in traditional understandings was the multiplication and diversification of rewards within departments and across top bureaucrats. Reward packages for agency chief executives were generally higher than those of their heads, the permanent secretaries of ministerial departments. While this could be seen as 'fair' in that chief executives had a higher 'risk surcharge' (seeing that they had to face the sack for failure in meeting performance targets and a less attractive pension deal), this bifurcation caused irritation and demands for increased pay among 'traditional' bureaucrats. There was, over the past 15 years, something of a convergence between the two types of employment, with top civil servants expected to compete for their new positions, permanent secretaries on individualized but rolling contracts and agency chief executives moving from fixed term to rolling contracts.

Similarly, there was considerable support for the argument that the traditional system of 'double imbalance' had weakened. As Figure 3.1 indicated, salaries at the top rose rapidly during the late 1990s and reduced wage compression. While politicians refused to grant the full extent of recommended pay rises and resorted to the staging of pay increases, these increases were nevertheless significant, outpacing many sectors in the economy (see Figure 3.3).

As Figure 3.3 shows, the ratio in pay for the cabinet secretary/grade 7 equivalent rose from 3.91 (in 1990) to 5.31 (in 2007), while the ratio of the salary for grade 7 equivalents to average earnings fell from 1.67 (1990 to 1.41 (in 2007). Moreover, there were also arguments that highlighted the decline in immaterial rewards for those at the top. First, it was argued that privileged access to political decision-making had become an increasingly contested territory with 'traditional' civil servants being shouldered to the side by a new type of political advisor. Thus, the role of permanent secretary was often no longer seen as solely that of a political *confidant*, but more of the chief administrator of a department.

The honors system also came under attack. In 1991, then Prime Minister John Major demanded a widening of the honors system to recognize special deeds

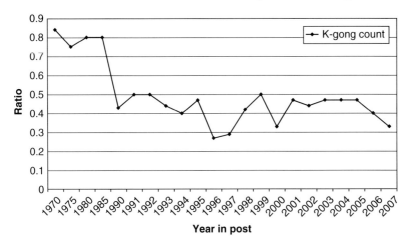

Figure 3.3 Permanent secretaries: K-gong count.
    Source: Civil Service Yearbook, *Who's Who, Who Was Who,* Nexis News.

rather than mere occupations. The total numbers of honors presented to civil servants returned, after an initial dip in totals, to their old pattern (Philips 2004). Nevertheless, the growing publicity surrounding 'gongs', especially following the rejection by artists and an alleged decline in civil servants' degree of appreciation, meant that the honors system was arguably less of a valuable commodity than before. In addition, it was said that the attractiveness of recruiting retired top bureaucrats to company boards had decreased, partly because of transparency rules, partly because of changing corporate governance demands.[10]

The supposed age of managerialist reform also brought elements of competition and pay individualization into British reward bargains. Such individualist understandings violated many conventions underlying 'club government' in Whitehall with its informal, but well-understood ranking system (see Hood *et al.* 1999). The idea of substantial weight being placed on 'performance' also potentially clashed with broader notions of the British civil servants as a 'serial loyalist' (i.e. someone who would work enthusiastically for any party in government). Performance-driven systems associated a bureaucrat with a political goal, thereby potentially undermining a civil servant's credibility to claim that she or he would be able to work enthusiastically for a different party in government (and a potentially contradictory policy).

One key element of this increase in individualist pay components was the use of performance bonuses. Starting with rather small performance bonuses in the 1980s, the granting of extra material rewards became increasingly institutionalized after 1991, although hardly at a significant scale, given that bonuses formed approximately 8 percent of the base salary (the equivalent in the private sector was between 26 and 57 percent). Performance pay was only approximately 4 percent of the departmental salary 'pot' with commitments regarding increases

of up to 10 percent being regularly postponed. Over 55 percent of all civil servants received some form of performance recognition, with performance assessment crowded in one particular performance grade (Matkinson 2000). By the late
2000s, attempts to deal with such grade inflation by forcing departments to utilize
'performance tranches' were seen as highly problematic and 40 percent of
SCS-type civil servants received pay awards lower than inflation (see SSRB
2007). In addition, performance assessment increasingly targeted wider (sometimes moving) government targets (especially those formalized in public service
agreements).

Similarly, 'open competition' was increasingly applied to lower ranks of the
bureaucracy (whereas in the past they were limited up to grade 7 at the most).
Permanent secretary positions remained (until the time of writing) a privilege for
'traditional' civil servants, despite regular calls for recruitment of 'real people' to
run government departments. Furthermore, since many of the top positions
granted to 'outsiders' involved individuals with public sector experience, figures
that suggested that between 27 and 43 percent of open competitions had gone to
external candidates should be treated with some caution.

The introduction of these components represented only one aspect of changes
in the overall reward dimension of the Whitehall bargain. They reinforced
an emerging style that emphasized an 'up or out' type of system (with
less emphasis on 'out'). There was little political interest in following the bureaucratic demand that increased visibility; blame-taking and reduced job security
were to be compensated by an increase in salaries (thereby also tackling the
bifurcation between externally and internally recruited senior civil servants) and
bonuses.

The move towards individualist and 'managerial' themes could nevertheless be
seen as far from transformative. Traces of the 'old' bargain's reward dimension
remained prominent. Hierarchy still mattered: ratios among the top three civil
service ranks remained broadly stable (Rimington 2008: 1112), and, regardless of
material reward, permanent secretaries still expected chief executives to come
to their offices. In addition, despite the increased amount of rivalry in terms of
promotion, the 'system' still arguably succeeded in generating the same sort
of civil servant progressing to the top – only at a faster speed.

Similarly, in relation to the potential decline of immaterial and post-career
rewards, when looking at the board membership of FTSE-listed companies, then
only an extremely select former civil servant group was highly connected in the
City, suggesting stability rather than an overall decline (or increase) (see
Jennings, Lodge, and Millo 2007). Looking at the 'after-life' of various generations of permanent secretaries as well as their 'honors' packages, does not reveal
any straightforward trend, although many of the significant developments might
have occurred below the absolute top. Figures 3.4 and 3.5 provide an overview
of the 'gong count' over the past decade and the ratio of permanent secretaries
that have pursued a post-career life somewhere in the private sector. The 'gong
count' reflects the ratio between those permanent secretaries with knighthood
status (a K-honor) to those without.

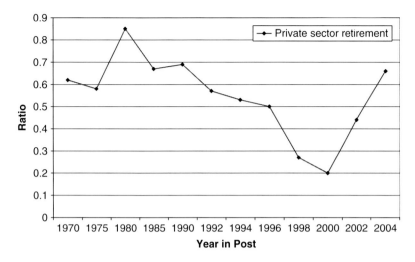

Figure 3.4 Permanent secretary private sector retirement.
    Source: Civil Service Yearbook, *Who's Who, Who Was Who*, Nexis News.

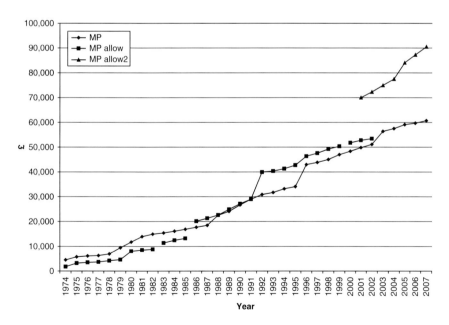

Figure 3.5 Parliamentary pay and allowances.
    Source: House of Commons Library.

Figure 3.5 suggests that there was a peak in terms of permanent secretaries finding an 'after-life' in the private sector during the early Thatcher years in the 1980s and a declining pattern since then – with a rise since the 2000s. The overall 'K-gong count' (Figure 3.4) suggests some broad stability throughout the 1990s, after a substantial downward shift that occurred sometime during the second half of the 1980s.

Furthermore, many of the absent ingredients of a 'full blown' move towards a more individualist 'performance pay' or 'private sector'-type reward dimension could be interpreted as a continuation of the traditional *noblesse oblige* pattern – although not necessarily as a matter of bureaucratic choice. A commissioned report by the Hay Group (2005) noted how salaries at the senior civil service level (and in particular at the higher level) had fallen behind those provided to public sector 'peers' (especially in local authorities). The 'real' civil service salary was below the lower quartile of the comparator job market, with pensions only competitive at the lower levels of the senior civil service. And while top bureaucrats were provided with better holidays and maternity provisions, they lacked, in contrast to the wider public sector, perks such as company cars and private medical insurance.

For others, the limited extent to which performance pay had been introduced was due to a political unwillingness to finance such a system, a departmental incapability to monitor and enforce a more individualized system that imposed tough conditions for awarding performance pay, while lacking clear objectives (see Towers Perrin 2006). It was therefore hardly surprising to witness a rapid rise in the 'cost free' membership of the senior civil service (in total numbers, from just 3,000 to well over 4,000) instead of the sort of pay rises that some parts of the top bureaucracy were advocating. In addition, the pay difference between 'internal promotions' and 'external recruited candidates' was seen by some as an explicit political statement from the center, while others argued that the pay differential was largely a result of budgetary allocations. A further indicator of the lack of interest in 'properly' financing a performance-related system on the lines of the private sector was the decision, in 2006, to alter the definition of 'market-facing' salary levels, away from mimicking private sector pay and towards a definition that emphasized the ability to recruit 'suitable candidates.'

Finally, the increased amount of rivalry and talk about performance introduced a degree of uncertainty that had been unknown in the past. This occurred in three main ways. One was that the criteria under which performance was assessed to qualify for performance bonuses were regarded as unclear and non-transparent (Senior Salaries Review Board 2005). The second was that it was not always clear whether the government would fulfill its promises in terms of providing rewards. The third effect applied to those bureaucrats operating on more explicit performance-related bargains, where pay was directly linked to the achievement of set objectives. Hitting formal targets did not always guarantee survival. Only a few public servants operating under this bargain publicly resisted their removal, regardless of whether the causes of the policy problem were directly associated with their organization or not. The seemingly voluntary falling on one's sword was allegedly compensated for by honors.

In sum, one trend has been a move away from an informal, yet somewhat predictable career 'escalator' and to some extent from a decline in the understandings that underpinned the idea of 'double imbalance'. However, this move away from old certainties generated greater uncertainty – uncertainty in terms of career progression in two senses. One was the uncertainty introduced by greater competition and rivalry and the decline of 'a system' that 'looked after' individuals, and uncertainty in the sense of a lack of transparency as to what the rules of the game were; thereby provoking the typically unquestioning civil servants' 'I will work harder' mentality.

Explaining reward patterns

According to the *Tocquevillian hypothesis*, democratic societies will not allow a high level of reward for political office. In many ways, Tocquevillian pressures were evident in the case of UK central government reward bargains – not just in terms of regular media headlines, but also in the argument that parliamentary expenditure and allowance had grown in such opaque ways to circumvent Tocquevillian pressures by keeping direct income levels relatively low. However, the political and bureaucratic reward bargains moved in different directions as a result of the external pressure on rewards. The political reward bargain moved towards a greater hierarchy *and* towards greater codification, while other hierarchical elements, such as attempts at instituting 'independent' pay reviews failed in the face of media criticism. In contrast, the bureaucratic reward moved towards a more individualist type of reward bargain, with bureaucrats not only faced with competition from inside and outside the public sector and performance-based assessments and pay elements, but also with an increased individualization of their reward package. Further support for the Tocquevillian hypothesis comes from wider trends in public sector pay. Those 'public sector professions' with highest support among the wider public were able to negotiate much better pay deals (such as doctors, teachers, and police) than the more powerful and more central top bureaucrats in Whitehall.

The *political business cycle* (rewards rise after elections) hypothesis receives only limited support. In the case of political rewards, the Labour cabinet granted themselves the pay rise after the 2001 general election, but such a decision was not repeated after other general elections. Substantial pressures for pay increases occurred *before* elections, that is, when the electoral penalty for such behavior could arguably be highest. But the motive (politicians wanting to obtain higher pay/pensions) requires specific opportunities. And this particular opportunity, in 1996, was the almost certain electoral 'death' of the Conservative government and the large number of parliamentarians facing retirement. That such a 'window of opportunity' does not necessarily lead to substantial pay increase for parliamentarians was witnessed in 2008 when a similar constellation (higher electoral uncertainty than at any time since 1997, large number of retiring parliamentarians) did not lead to a defeat of the government and opposition front-benches. Arguably, the conditions one year later, with an even larger number of MPs having announced their resignation or facing demands for their resignation at the next election, favored more far-reaching reforms.

In a context of high salience over political and bureaucratic reward, the idea that rewards would grow, particularly in their 'non-transparent' parts, should receive considerable support. Arguably, the patterns in bureaucratic pay, especially at the level of pay below that of permanent secretaries and the cabinet secretaries, became increasingly non-transparent with figures for departmental pay deals not being made available publicly. In addition, this reduced transparency went hand in hand with reduced compression and increasingly diverse and 'high' pay rewards at the top. On the political side, the traditional way in which politicians were remunerated 'non-transparently' continued despite growing codification. This included official residences, or the possibility to cash-in on ministerial experiences through the writing of memoirs, speeches and consultancy jobs. In contrast, while parliamentary allowances did increase significantly in the period under consideration, this came at the expense of growing codification and continued media interest. In other words, to some extent the iceberg of allowances had moved increasingly above the waterline.

Institutional explanations with their emphasis on routinization and the dominance of embedded standard operating procedures provides for some insight into changes on the bureaucratic side of the reward bargain. One example of new ideas being 'filtered' into existing norms and conventions was arguably the way in which ideas of contractualization were modified by the senior civil service into a system that was more akin to the traditional Whitehall bargain (namely indefinite tenure). Furthermore, the incentive system was nevertheless seen as producing similar outcomes for 'high flyers.' The existing pay structure, notwithstanding formalization, operated in the established 'informal' evaluation patterns that characterized the age of 'club government.' Similarly the return to a 'three level' hierarchy in the senior civil service was seen by many as a return to the 'institutional logic' of a functioning bureaucracy and away from over-differentiation under individualized contracts.

Attempts at depoliticizing pay for politicians by linking reward increases to those awarded to civil servants was a recurring theme throughout the past decade and a half or so. There was no major change to the institutional machinery illustrated by Hood (1994: 59) in that the government and parliament approved recommendations made by the Senior Salaries Review Body (previously called the Review Body on Top Salaries). The attempt at expertization did not take the politics out of reward, with governments regularly either 'ignoring' or at least only partially implementing the type of recommendations that had been made by the review board. Only in 1996 did MPs vote against the government and in favor of the review body's recommendations. A similar motivation – to take 'politics' out of allowances – was evident in the announcement to create a 'Parliamentary Standards Authority.'

A so far less widely explored institutional explanation of reward patterns focuses on contested logics and inherent instability. The attempts to address public pressure on political rewards by codification, whilst maintaining many trappings of previous 'club government' informality, was bound for inevitable break-down. The formalization made the conventions 'explicit' (in the form of expense receipts) and thereby open to the challenge. In a wider sense, therefore, the regulation of political reward exposed a pattern that was also considered by Michael Moran's discussion of the British regulatory state more widely (Moran 2003). Moran diagnosed an 'incomplete penetration' of the regulatory state's logic of synoptic control into traditional systems of informal control, which sowed the seeds for system break-down. Similarly, the regime governing political rewards sought to combine these two elements (codification and remaining informality), thereby leading to break-down and further demands at formalization and codification.

Conclusion

As the introduction to this chapter highlighted, political reward featured not just as a continuous presence on newspaper front page headlines, it also animated wider debates regarding political system change, in terms of rules of the game for parliament itself, but also more widely (such as renewed talk about electoral reform for Westminster elections). And the parlous state of the public finances also sowed the seeds for the next attack on the rewards for high political office, namely pensions. Both parliamentary and civil service pension systems came under renewed spotlight as private companies increasingly closed their final salary systems.

Over the past two decades or so, there has been a 'mirror image' development in the reward bargains that apply to politicians and senior bureaucrats as a result of Tocquevillian pressures. In the political system, despite attempts at codification and therefore with a greater possibility of outside challenge, practice still remained, until mid-2009 at least, very much in the hands of parliamentarians themselves. In the bureaucratic world, despite some continuation of traditional patterns, a growing emphasis on rivalry and uncertainty was combined with a decline in emphasis on *noblesse oblige* and stable career expectations. Individual contracts as well as pay decentralization to departments have also made reward bargains less transparent in the light of wider tendencies towards diversification and multiplication.

The argument that Tocquevillian pressures continue to apply to rewards for high public office, thereby keeping rewards 'low' with a relative decline in reward over time, receives some support when viewed in light of top private sector salaries. Nevertheless, there are further trends that add a distinctive flavor to this overall argument. One is the change in bureaucratic reward where top bureaucrats succeeded in substantially increasing their material reward over the past decade. Arguably the linkage between target-setting and performance pay was a political strategy to shift blame to bureaucrats in this age of public salience. Therefore the qualitative shift in particular towards rivalry could be seen as a distinct response to growing public distrust of politics – ending up however with the distinct reward bargain for bureaucrats with rivalry turning into something more akin to Russian roulette. In the political world, the veneer of increased codification and transparency, but based on the traditional understandings of discretion and 'gentlemanly good chap' conduct, provided the fertile ground for the developments of 2009. It meant that increasingly the political reward bargain had turned into an also uncertain world in that acceptable claims from the past became the burial ground of political ambition later.

Notes

1 Most famously, one MP (Sir Peter Viggers) had received £1,645 for a floating duck island and 'Stockholm' duck house. Google Maps revealed that the duck house had been removed, because, as Sir Peter suggested, it was 'never liked by the ducks.' A duck breeder commented that the duck house 'is just not suitable for ducks. The door is far too big. Ducks much prefer feeling snug … they like to squeeze through them and then they feel secure' (*Daily Telegraph*, 22 May 2009). The house designer shot back highlighting that the problem had been that the pond was 'minute … It was a long shot that ducks would occupy it. I find that ducks vote with their feet' (*Daily Telegraph*, 25 May 2009).
2 Within days, MP expenses were relegated to third place on the 'most read' list on the *Daily Telegraph* website, with the second place reserved for a story headlined 'Man complains his pizza has no topping – until he realizes it is upside down' (*Financial Times*, 15 May 2009).
3 Gordon Brown's initial proposals, first announced on YouTube (and causing much hilarity) on 21 April 2009, were vetoed by parliamentarians (http://www.youtube.com/watch?v=sBXj5l6ShpA, last accessed 1 June 2009).
4 http://www.timesonline.co.uk/tol/news/politics/article3330559.ece (last accessed 21 February 2009).
5 www.cabinetoffice.gov.uk/media/122200/hospitality_publication2007.pdf (last accessed 20 February 2009).
6 The earlier policy had to be abandoned due to changes in the civil service grades.
7 As a result, employment of family members was not prohibited *per se,* but pay was expected to reflect actual work. The employment of family members remained widespread until at least 2009.
8 For example, it was also revealed that one expense request for a fish-tank had been turned down (http://www.guardian.co.uk/politics/2008/feb/29/media.thebackbencher, last accessed 21 February 2009).
9 With apologies to Boxer from *Animal Farm*.
10 The breakdown of traditional conventions, namely that a decent pension would prevent former civil servants from revealing details of their relationship with politicians, was argued to be reflected in the publication of revelatory memoirs. In response to one former Washington ambassador's memoirs, measures such as confidentiality clauses and the automatic transfer of copyright to government were taken.

References

Cabinet Office (1999a) *Modernising Government.* Cm4310, London: HMSO.
Cabinet Office (1999b) *Performance Management.* London: Cabinet Office.

Hay Group (2005) *SCS Pay Market Comparability Study – Report.* London: Senior Salaries Review Body.

Hood, C. (1994) The UK. In C. Hood and B.G. Peters (Eds), *Rewards at the Top: A Comparative Study of High Public Office.* London: Sage.

Hood, C. (1998) Individualized contracts for top civil servants: copying business, path-dependent political re-engineering – or Trobriand cricket. *Governance.* 11(4): 443–462.

Hood, C. and M. Lodge (2006) *The Politics of Public Service Bargains.* Oxford: Oxford University Press.

Hood, C. *et al.* (1999) *Regulation Inside Government.* Oxford: Oxford University Press.

Jennings, W., M. Lodge and Y. Millo (2007) Loosening ties? Post-career trajectories among ministerial and bureaucratic elites in the United Kingdom. American Political Science Association Annual Conference, Chicago, 30 August–2 September 2007.

Kaye, R. (2005) Reluctant innovators: regulating conflict of interest within Washington and Westminster. In J. Black, M. Lodge and M. Thatcher (Eds), *Regulatory Innovation.* Cheltenham: Edward Elgar.

Matkinson, J. (2000) *Incentive for Change.* London: Public Services Productivity Panel. Performance Management. London: Cabinet Office.

Moran, M. (2003) *The British Regulatory State.* Oxford: Oxford University Press.

Philips, H. (2004) *Review of the Honours System.* London: Cabinet Office.

Rawnsley, A. (2001) *Servants of the People*, 2nd edn. London: Penguin.

Review Body on Senior Salaries (1996) *Review of Parliamentary Pay and Allowances.* Cm3330-I and II, London: The Stationery Office.

Review Body on Senior Salaries (2005) *Twenty-Seventh Report on Senior Salaries.* Cm6451, London: The Stationery Office.

Review Body on Senior Salaries (2006) *Twenty-Eighth Report on Senior Salaries.* Cm6727, London: The Stationery Office.

Review Body on Senior Salaries (2007a) *Twenty-Ninth Report on Senior Salaries.*, Cm7030, London: The Stationery Office.

Review Body on Senior Salaries (2007b) *Review of Parliamentary Pay, Pensions and Allowances 2007.* Cm7270-1/2, London: The Stationery Office.

Rimington, J.D. (2008) The value of the remuneration of high civil servants in Britain in the 20th century and its implications. *Public Administration*, 86(4): 1107–27.

Towers Perrin (2006) *Bonus Scheme Design and Effectiveness.* London: Office of Manpower Economics.

4 RHPOs in Ireland

Ratcheting pay in the public sector

Eoin O'Malley and Gary Murphy

Introduction

Ireland was for a very long time an anomaly; a stable democracy in North-West Europe with an economy more akin to a developing country. From the mid-1990s, however, Ireland underwent unprecedented growth, becoming one of the wealthiest countries in Europe. The ability of the state to attract talented individuals to work for it may have changed as economic growth caused the labor market to tighten when opportunities in the private sector arose. By early 2009, however, the Irish economy had encountered significant difficulties and rising unemployment and substantially decreasing taxation revenues placed enormous burdens on the public purse. In the context of pension levies specific to public sector workers in an effort to balance the public finances, the rewards to senior civil servants and politicians became highly politicized.

The ability to employ and promote competent and honest officials (be they politicians, bureaucrats or judges) is important, because as executive agents these officials are often afforded remarkable power, and the principals (citizens) have little control over them, except through politicians by way of regular elections. Politicians however have limited ability to select, direct, censure or remove bureaucrats and judges. As agents with access to state funds and decisions these groups face clear opportunities for corruption, especially in areas that are heavily regulated by the state (Gerring and Thacker 2005). Controlling the rewards of these three groups is one way citizens have to control the performance of their agents and incentivize certain types of behavior. As such rewards are central to accountability. In Ireland, as part of the shift to New Public Management (Hardiman and Mac Cárthaigh 2008), there was a decision to link public sector pay to that of the private sector. The rationale for this move might have been that it would expose those sheltered in the public sector to market disciplines (Garrett and Way 1999) and conversely ensure that there is no drain of talent to the private sector (O'Leary 2002). However, in practice this has caused some problems. The decisions on how to reward high public officials (HPOs) in Ireland are largely left to these groups, causing a likely conflict of interest. High levels of unionization in the public sector meant that there was a strong upward pressure on pay to all levels of the public sector (Hardiman 2006), but also made it difficult to shift pay downward to follow movements in the private sector, causing a type of ratchet effect.

In this chapter we look at the rules regarding pay and other rewards for the higher public officials in politics, the bureaucracy, and the judiciary. Before outlining the career paths of HPOs in Ireland, we introduce the Irish state system in which judges, bureaucrats, and politicians operate. Having described the ways in which decisions about rewards are made for HPO holders, we draw tentative conclusions as to the connection between rewards for high public office (RHPOs) and policy expertise, performance, and corruption.

The general context and career development

Politics

The Irish state was formed as a break away from the UK in the early 1920s and Ireland is a parliamentary democracy partly following the Westminster model, with a strong executive (O'Malley and Martin 2010), weak and inactive parliament with 166 TDs (MPs) who spend considerably more time on constituency issues than legislating (there is an extensive literature on the clientelist behavior of TDs, see Gallagher and Komito 2005). The fact that the Dáil sat for just 95 days in 2008 indicates that legislating is only a secondary aspect of their job. Ministers, who in practice all come from the Dáil, tend to be generalist in nature, and rely on civil service advice though are ultimately responsible for departmental actions. The government vote – the number of TDs in the government payroll – is significant. Up to 2010 there were 35 ministers (cabinet and junior) out of the government's parliamentary base of 85 TDs. Of the other 50, all but three have no other paid role as committee chair, vice chair or whip.

We can now think of politics in Ireland as a professionalized career (Gallagher 2003). TDs are more likely to come from occupations that expose them to the public on a daily basis and have reasonably flexible hours: so teachers, publicans, and doctors tend to be overrepresented in the Dáil. It was common in Ireland that many TDs would continue to practice their original profession, so those who were also barristers would continue to practice in the courts in the morning before going to the Dáil for the evening. Many politicians, even opposition front-bench spokespersons, were part-time politicians. Where, in the past, most TDs surveyed gave second occupations, now most describe themselves as full-time public representatives. As the idea of a safe seat is non-existent in Ireland the career is an insecure one, though turnover rates at about 20 percent are comparatively low (Matland and Studlar 2004). For ambitious TDs, being in government is important. The Dáil and its committees have little power, and parties are highly disciplined, so to achieve any influence over policy TDs need to be in government. A committee chairmanship is sought after only because it may allow an activist TD to increase his or her profile and because they receive a supplement to their salary (about €20,000 per annum).

Irish ministers are generalists, rarely having any technical expertise in the area they control. Though there have been cases where ministers for justice have been lawyers, ministers for education, teachers, and ministers for health, doctors, only once was an economist appointed minister for finance. So the selection of these ministers has more to do with the overrepresentation of certain professions in the Dáil than a decision to select an 'expert.' Taoisigh (PMs) have sole legal discretion in choosing ministers within strict constitutional limits, but in practice coalition and factional politics mean that party leaders of coalition parties select those ministers from their own parties, and Taoisigh find it hard to leave out of cabinet leaders of powerful factions (for a detailed discussion of the selection of ministers, see O'Malley 2006).

The civil service

The ethos and culture of the Irish civil service is very much like that of its British counterpart. Of the approximately 300,000 public servants (between a fifth and a quarter of the labor force), about 30,000 are civil servants. Two salient points of comparison with Britain are the civil service's tradition of non-involvement in party politics and its culture of secrecy. Irish civil servants, like their British counterparts, may not be a member of a political party. The Irish civil service also operates under a culture of secrecy that it would rather term as confidentiality. The position of the government is also protected by a tradition of limiting the amount of information the civil service is inclined to give, even when authorized to do so. A civil servant was allegedly sent a congratulatory memo from his superior for having confused a TD asking parliamentary questions (*Dáil Éireann*, Vol. 445, Col. 539, 2 September 1994).

One way in which the Irish civil service differs markedly from its British counterpart is in the background of the top civil servants. Unlike that of Britain where it is common for top civil servants to have an Oxbridge education, Irish civil servants are more likely to have been educated at a Christian Brothers' School (schools set up to provide an education to Catholics who could not otherwise afford one) and only more recently is it common that higher civil servants would have university degrees. The products of this education were 'intellectually able and hard working but rather narrowly practical in their approach' (Chubb 1992: 237) and the ethos of the Irish civil service was conservative. This apparently has the effect that the service tends not to promote initiative (Zimmerman 1997).

While the government can appoint anyone as a civil servant at any grade, the common entry route is through public, competitive exams at either administrative officer or executive officer level. In the past one's rise through the ranks, though ostensibly on merit, depended mainly on seniority in terms of years, and there was little discretion given to either ministers or civil servants to reward exceptional talent – jumping grade was very rare. Where there is now such a jump the appointment needs to comply with the code of practice of the Commission for Public Service Appointments (set up in 2004). Since 1984 higher levels of the civil service (Secretaries General and Assistant Secretaries General) are appointed by the government, but on the advice of the Top Level Appointments Commission (TLAC). The TLAC makes recommendations to the government that the government can choose to ignore. Up to then the next most 'senior suitable' available candidate was appointed, so progression through the ranks of the civil service was very slow, and there was a tendency towards conservatism. Now there is a set term limit (seven years) for SGs and they must retire by 60 (although this can and has been waived). In the past a civil service job was one of the most sought after jobs in Ireland. Its attraction lay in the fact that it is 'permanent and pensionable.' Apart from temporary political appointees, all civil servants are permanent and removing or even censuring them is difficult. In the Irish economic climate up to the 1990s there were few opportunities in the private sector, so for those who could not afford a university education, emigration, the church or the civil service was one's choice. Indeed T.K. Whitaker, one of Ireland's most eminent civil servants, told one of us that the only reason he applied for a job in the civil service was that there were no other jobs. Recently the attraction of such jobs has waned, although there does not seem to be a problem recruiting civil servants to the higher grades: whether there has been a drop in the quality of the candidates is unclear.

The judiciary

Within their own system senior Irish judges are thought among the most politically active in the world (Gwynn Morgan 2001). Since the 1960s senior Irish judges have taken a decidedly activist approach to the opportunities of judicial review, essentially reinterpreting the constitution to enunciate rights that are not specified in the constitution. This was encouraged by the leader of the government that appointed these early activist judges (Gwynn Morgan 2001: 12), but it is now the case that the courts provide a real constraint on government policy making by tending to guarantee the rights of individuals over the rights of parliament to make policy for the common good. The legal profession in Ireland is divided into two branches: barristers and solicitors; a distinction very few common law jurisdictions continue with. In Ireland, significant differences exist between the branches of the profession as they operate at present. Prior to 1995, solicitors were allowed to become District Court judges only; barristers alone were entitled to be appointed as superior court judges. On foot of the *Courts and Court Officers Act 1995*, solicitors are also now eligible to become Circuit Court judges, with the further possibility of 'promotion' to the High/Supreme Court.

While we see a de facto separation of powers in Ireland, the courts are subordinate to the Oireachtas. The Government (effectively a committee of the Dáil) appoints judges (who are often prominent members of a political party). Since 1995 there is a Judicial Appointments Advisory Board, which makes recommendations on senior appointments (except for Chief Justice of the Supreme Court and President of the High Court). These suggest seven names which the government can choose from, though the Government ultimately makes the decision.

Judicial appointments are permanent and there is no requirement for a judge to move up the ranks, so one's first judicial appointment can be to the Supreme Court, an occurrence that is not infrequent. Once in office, judges seem to act independently and there have been few if any cases where political bias was exercised (Byrne and McCutcheon 2001). Though judges are secure in their posts, the Oireachtas can censure and remove a judge for 'stated misbehavior or incapacity' (Article 35.4.1 Constitution of Ireland). This has never occurred, though there are cases of judges resigning following political pressure – but only after negotiating a deal on pension provision.

The pay of judges might be necessarily linked to that of barristers. However, as these are some of the most highly paid individuals in the country it would require a major pay increase to attempt to match these. As such most judges appointed to the bench are forced to take significant pay cuts. Another restriction is that judges cannot return to practice in the jurisdiction they served in, so the opportunities to move back are severely limited. Even with these disincentives, there does not seem to be a problem recruiting top barristers to take judicial positions.

Social partnership: public sector wage bargaining in Ireland

It was during a period of deep depression in the mid 1980s that the social partners (farmers, trade unions, and business interests) were invited to join in a governmental forum (National Economic and Social Council), to agree a joint strategy to overcome Ireland's dire economic difficulties. The forum's report *Strategy for Development* (1986) formed the basis upon which, in 1987 the new Fianna Fáil government and the social partners negotiated the *Programme for National Recovery* (PNR), which was followed by five other agreements. What made these agreements different from agreements of the 1960s onwards was that they were not simply centralized wage mechanisms but agreements on a wide range of economic and social policies such as tax reform, the evolution of welfare payments, and public sector pay (O'Donnell and Thomas 1998). One of the later pay agreements, *Partnership 2000*, negotiated in 1996 for the first time provided an integrated package of pay rises and tax cuts that enabled trade leaders to calculate the real value of the deal, in order to sell it to their members. This was followed by three further pay agreements the *Programme for Prosperity and Fairness, 2000–2003* (2000), *Sustaining Progress, 2003–2005* (2003) and *Towards 2016* (2006). However, within this framework it became increasingly difficult to reach a consensus as the union leaders were looking for an increased share of national wealth at a time when employers sought to reintroduce constraints. To that end the social partnership agreements stretching back to 1987 had evolved considerably from when the first agreement was developed strictly as a means of responding to a grave fiscal crisis. Later agreements evolved into a strategy for facilitating steady growth and the inward investment that fuelled such growth. Up to the economic crisis of 2008–2009, the very semblance of a threat from any of the social partners to withdraw from one of the agreements usually precipitated intense discussions to ensure that the demands of that particular sector were met without jeopardizing the remit of the agreements. However in February 2009 talks between the social partners to achieve savings in the public finances collapsed when unions refused to countenance a public sector pay cut.

While these pay deals covered all workers, in fact they had only patchy application in the private sector leading to complaints from unions representing public sector workers that growth in private sector wages outstripped that in the public sector. For this reason a system of benchmarking was set up to link grades in the public sector with equivalent jobs in the private sector. In return public sector workers were expected to concede to reforms of working conditions and practices, though these 'concessions' were of questionable value and seemed only to increase bureaucracy. The Public Sector Benchmarking Body reporting in 2002 recommended pay increases ranging from 2 to 27 percent, averaging at 8.9 percent for 138 pay grades. These are in addition to increases achieved through the partnership process. By 2008 economists had calculated in fact a pay premium of over 20 percent to working in the public sector (Kelly, McGuinness, and O'Connell 2008).

RHPOs in Ireland

For HPOs, while they receive pay increases due under social partnership agreements, many senior civil servants and politicians complained that their salaries had simply not kept pace with the private sector. Since 1969 the (appropriately named) Review Body on Higher Remuneration in the Public Sector has examined pay for members of the Government, Ministers of State, the Attorney General and the Chairman and Deputy Chairman of Dáil Éireann and Seanad Éireann, senior employees in the Civil Service, health boards, local authorities, non-commercial State bodies, Garda Síochána (police), and Defence Forces, as well as hospital consultants, university professors, and judges. It is an independent standing body of individuals from the private sector and trade unions supported by civil servants whose primary function is to advise the Government on the general levels of remuneration appropriate to certain top public service posts.

Its remit is to ensure the supply of suitably qualified candidates for posts in the public sector and as such a major consideration 'of public sector pay policy generally has moved … towards placing a greater reliance on benchmarking public sector salaries against the private sector' (Review Body 2000: 23). In its sixth general review, the Body argued

> that allowing pay rates at senior levels to fall significantly out of line with rates for comparable posts in the private sector will act, in the long term, as a disincentive to the development and retention of future top managers of high quality. In a modern and rapidly expanding economy, with high demand for the scarce supply of skilled and experienced personnel, it is not sufficient to rely on the commitment of senior managers to giving 'public service' as the principal means of retaining their services. The new economic realities mean

that exceptional public servants will have more opportunity to move from the public to the private sector.

(Review Body 2000: 23)

The method which the Review Body uses is to call for submissions from interested parties, and to retain a private consultancy firm (Hay Group) to provide information on rewards for equivalent salaries in the private sector. Exactly how the decision is made is unclear, and the Hay reports have been refused release under Freedom of Information legislation. The Review Body has decided that 'the appropriate benchmark for the groups covered by our remit was the lower quartile of private sector salaries and that, as a first step, salaries should be brought to 85% of this benchmark' (Review Body 2007: 26).

As Table 4.1 shows, the pay increases for HPOs have been significant. Let us take politicians as an example. In 1987, the outgoing Fine Gael/Labour Party government granted TDs a 19 percent salary increase. The unprecedented award was made on the recommendation of the Review Body and reflected the fact that Dáil pay had fallen well behind other sectors. For the first time, politicians pay would be linked with national agreements and they would automatically receive pay awards. Having done well out of the review in 1987, Dáil deputies looked for similar increases in 1990, which were rejected. In May 1996 the Review Body received a submission from an all party Dáil subcommittee seeking a 30 percent pay increase for deputies, the equivalent of an increase of IR£10,000 (€12,700) a year. With their claim based on the findings of a questionnaire sent to all deputies, the all-party submission maintained that a TD's basic salary was equivalent to €11.50 an hour. It said that deputies worked 70 hours a week when the Dáil was in recess, and 81 hours a week when it was sitting. Since 1991, the TDs

Table 4.1 Salaries of RHPOs in Ireland (selected years) and comparators

Year	TDs	PM*	Minister*	SGs	CJ	Mean CS**
1992	42,359	95,876	78,203	73,470	95,881	21,167
1996	43,640	111,125	88,900	96,739	128,270	24,321
2000	49,763	145,492	116,112	121,564	145,496	29,210
2005	88,556	252,352	195,189	180,302	240,405	41,463
2008	100,191	291,974	231,587	221,929	295,916	47,904
2008 as % of 1992	237	304	296	302	309	226
2008/2000	201	201	199	183	203	164

Source: CSO and Department of Finance
Notes: All values in euros (€)
* The figure for the Taoiseach and ministers includes the TD's salary (for Taoisigh it is always, though not necessarily, the highest salary due to long service increment):
** Average civil servant pay, and as such can be affected by differences in the composition of each grade.

stated, 'the workload has increased significantly. The number of committees has more than doubled and the frequency of meetings has increased substantially.' They acknowledged that Oireachtas members received a 'significant pay rise in 1992,' but, they stated in their claim, these pay increases were inadequate: 'In 1992, a TD's salary was equivalent to that of a principal officer (higher) in the Civil Service. Now, it is equivalent to that of an assistant principal officer (higher).' Ultimately their claim for what was basically a 30 percent increase was rejected and instead the Review Body recommended a 3 percent increase.

In early 2001 the Government accepted proposals for an increase in TDs' salaries to bring the annual pay of a member of Dáil Éireann up from €49,530 to €59,055. In addition, Ministers' salaries were being brought above €127,000. Senators received an even larger percentage increase, with their salaries rising by 31 percent from almost €31,750 to €41,275 annually. Salaries for Oireachtas members would in future rise automatically in line with increases for civil servants at principal officer (standard) grade, and thus come under the benchmarking arrangements. The Taoiseach's salary increased by over 22 percent from €145,415 to €177,800 per annum and Minister's pay rises from approximately €116,205 to €139,700. The report argued in favor of the increase for Ministers on the basis that 'the business of Government is now more complex and demanding than ever before' (Review Body 2000: 20). Economic, political and social changes had imposed 'enormous demands' on Ministers and 'current salaries … provide very inadequate compensation for the workloads borne by them.' In July 2005, the Cabinet approved a pay increase of 7.5 percent for ministers and senior civil and public servants arising out of an interim report. The salary of the Taoiseach (PM) exceeded €250,000, over double what it was in 1997. The Government has generally accepted and implemented the recommendations of the Review Body, although at times has found it politically necessary to forego ministerial rises. By the end of 2008 the Taoiseach's salary had risen to €285,000 and it was only the pressure of public opinion that led to the deferring of a further increase of €35,000 that had been recommended by the Review Body (2007).

In making its recommendation for RHPOs the Review Body makes comparisons to the private sector. Although little reliable data exist on senior private sector salaries, media reports indicate that salaries have increased dramatically for such positions. A survey in 2003 showed that there was an average annual pay rise of 17 percent for 70 executive directors of Irish publicly-listed companies. In 2002 the average basic pay of a CEO was €750,600, which when coupled with a pension provision rose to €1.1 m (*Sunday Independent* 4 May 2003). By 2008 the total remuneration of the CEO of AIB, Ireland's largest commercial bank was €2.1 m. However by 2009 with the collapse of AIB's share price, its chief executive said his annual income would be €670,000 and he would take no bonus. Such salaries and changes would still seem to dwarf those of the HPOs.

That one can compare competition for labour in the public and private sector in such a way is moot and some points need to be considered. These include the security of tenure for civil servants and the judiciary; the valuable pensions all three groups, politicians, judges, and senior civil servants receive, and the difficulty in calculating bonuses on the basis of performance. While it put no value on the security of tenure of HPOs, the Review Body report maintained that it would consider that 'the extent the value of public service superannuation [pension] arrangements should be offset against remuneration packages available in the private sector' (Review Body 2005: 20).

Pensions

One of the major attractions of work in the public sector is the state guaranteed pension. Public service pensions are very attractive because pay rises affect the pensions of those who are already retired. Pensions depend on number of years' service but for most of those with long service in the public sector the pension is half one's final grade salary. In 2007 the Review Body calculated the value of the pension at 15 percent of one's salary. Despite this assessment, Table 4.1 shows that significant increases in rewards were forthcoming. For TDs and ministers the operation of pension is different and depends on the number of years of service. In addition a retiring or defeated TD will receive a lump sum plus six, monthly severance payments based on years of service. A former deputy can then claim one's pension immediately. In order to qualify for a pension one must pay 6 percent of one's annual salary into the scheme. An example of one TD's pension arrangements illustrates how the scheme operates.

Alan Dukes, a TD of 21 years standing, lost his seat in 2002. He received €11,508 as a lump sum in severance plus payments of €4,315 per month for six months. He then started to draw his pension of €34,525 per annum. In addition, his 5½ years experience as a minister entitles him to 35 percent of a minister's salary (then €31,338). Ministers and TDs also receive a generous redundancy package, through in which former ministers are entitled to receive 75 percent of the ministerial salary for the first 6 months, 50 percent for the next 12 months, and 25 percent for the following 6 months. Generous pensions are not the only source of income for TDs, expenses are a controversial and significant way to top up one's salary.

Expenses

While for civil servants, expenses are covered on one's expenditure, ministers receive other benefits, such as a car and driver, during their term in office. Other ministerial expenses are paid directly by the state. The position that allows for the greatest increase in salaries is for parliamentarians. The expenses entitlement of TDs and Senators include a daily travel allowance of €61.53 for members who live within 15 miles of Leinster House. This is analogous to getting paid extra just for turning up for work. In 2009 those living more than 15 miles from the House were entitled to an overnight allowance of €139.67. They are entitled to a recently reduced 'mileage' allowance of 59 cent per kilometer up to 6,437 km and 28.5 cent per km thereafter. TDs can claim allowances for travel within the constituencies and to a range of grants for the constituency office, telephone, and secretarial expenses. In 2008 the operation of the Houses of the Oireachtas cost

€122 m. TDs salaries accounted for €18 m of this and TDs' expenses cost the State €11 m. One TD made claims of €93,880, almost matching his salary.

While these may seem reasonable given the expense of maintaining homes in both one's constituency and in Dublin, the way in which the scheme for expenses is operated allows TDs to effectively increase their salary. There is no requirement to provide receipts for one's expenses, and so one can claim for a full first-class plane ticket but travel in economy class. The necessity to sign in to claim one's daily or overnight allowances is just that. There is no need to actually do any work, and one can sign in any day, not just when the Dáil is sitting. One could therefore come into the Dáil just before midnight, sign in, wait a few minutes, sign in again and leave, though there are proposals to reform this. In the context of the economic downturn, the Minister for Finance was seeking cuts in the cost of running the parliament, and it is doubtful that any party would oppose such cuts.

Performance awards

Since 2001 senior civil servants can now receive performance bonuses 'rewarding excellence.' These are intended to incentivize civil servants to meet certain targets, and is consistent with the concept of 'managerialism' in the public sector (Hardiman and Mac Cárthaigh 2008). This idea was introduced on the recommendation of the Review Body. The awards are open to Assistant and Deputy Secretaries and the pool for awards is 10 percent of each grade's pay budget within the department. The maximum award is 20 percent of an individual's salary.

Performance targets are set by the Secretary General with the individuals, and various targets are weighted. The individual is then required to assess his or her own performance, which is then reviewed by the Secretary General. The Secretary General makes recommendations for the division of awards within his/ her own department. A Committee for Performance Awards (made up of civil servants and private sector executives) then assess the targets. In 2007 €2.7 m (10 percent of the relevant pay bill) was divided between 194 civil servants, with the top award being over €26,000 (Committee for Performance Awards Annual Report 2007: 11). The range of rewards awards exceeded the levels set by the committee itself, but remained at the 10 percent of pay limit. Questions remain about the appropriateness of targets, especially short-term performance targets, in the public sector and whether they are merely set with the goal of distributing all available funds in mind.

The rewards to Irish HPOs have increased dramatically in the last 15 years and this could be connected to the easing of the government's budgetary situation and the rapid economic growth. While most rewards are paid in the form of basic pay, for civil servants performance awards provide an additional source of income, and for TDs expenses potentially increase their incomes. For ministers and the Taoiseach the provision of a car and driver also add to the attractiveness of the position. For many top civil servants and politicians there are post-retirement rewards to look forward to other than one's pension. When former ministers or civil servants go on to work in the private sector it is usually to use their experience in the public sector, so arguably the public sector provides market-able experience as well as pay and pensions. Many become directors of private companies or get sinecures in the European Union. The rules preventing the take up of such posts are not stringent. Only the judiciary is prevented from returning to their previous profession and these must take a major pay cut on becoming HPOs. The argument that one needs to compete directly with the salaries of the private sector in order to guarantee the supply of good quality officials is ques-tionable. The example of the judiciary is a case in point. Frequently the highest earning barristers are willing to take up a position on the bench. Presumably financial reward is not their goal, so it must either be public service or the exercise of power that drives their choice.

Discussion: issues regarding the rewards for high public office

The rewards structure is important because it allows the control of HPOs. A number of issues are relevant. Do the rewards allow the recruitment and retention of suitably qualified people? Does the rewards structure incentivize appropriate behavior, quality, efficiency, and honesty? According to the Department of Finance, which incorporated the Department of the Public Service, there was no evidence of problems in recruitment or retention (Review Body 2007: 15). The significant policy failures evident from the collapse in the Irish budgetary posi-tion may be in part due to the dearth of skilled specialists in the civil service. One former Taoiseach recently reported that there were just three professional econo-mists working in the Department of Finance (*Irish Times*, 10 January 2009). One of the reasons for this is the common entry exam system leaves little room to employ people with the professional qualifications often required. As a way around this there has been an explosion in the number of agencies, as these are exempt from civil service employment rules. Current rules which stipulate early retirement for top civil servants by limiting their tenure (to seven years) probably also hinders the retention of highly skilled staff. A practice where former Secretaries General could remain in the service or are ineligible to draw a pension until a set retirement age might be more useful. There has been no indication that politics or the public sector was becoming unattractive, or that the increased salaries have attracted a new caliber of politician. Ministerial positions have been for many years highly sought after, but it may be less likely that one would refuse a place in cabinet – in the past some barristers refused to serve because they were afraid of the impact on their practice. The barrier of elected entry is probably the most significant constraint on hiring ministers with diverse skills and experiences.

When we think of rewards being used to incentivize appropriate behavior we may consider efficiency and initiative. While it is difficult to measure efficiency in the public sector, according to most observers including some former high ranking officials we interviewed, the Irish civil service is conservative and prone to blame avoidance. The performance rewards do not seem to have changed this, and they seem to have been used to distribute salary increases rather than reward excellence. As well as initiative, one might use rewards to encourage honesty. Two parallel tribunals have been investigating payments to politicians in Ireland since 1997. At one of these, the tribunal into planning corruption in County Dublin, Mr. Ray Burke, a long standing Fianna Fáil TD who was a minister on no fewer than six occasions, described TDs' salaries as so inadequate that fund-raising was an unfortunate fact of political life. He said that it left politicians open to allegations like those leveled against him and he urged the Tribunal chairman to consider this in his final report (Proceedings of the Flood Tribunal, 9 July 1999).

Murphy (1999, 2005) documents a number of cases of inappropriate payments to politicians and public officials. A number of politicians, most notably the former Fianna Fáil Taoisigh, Charles Haughey and Bertie Ahern, and Fine Gael Minister Michael Lowry have also shown to have received significant monies from private interests. All three were eventually forced to resign their offices but all three denied any impropriety in receiving such largesse. Yet can we categorically state that the receipt of large amounts of money was based on the lack of public monetary rewards and if there were significantly more rewards available, would these and other politicians not have felt the need to accept various monies? Of course we can never tell. While the salary scale is now far more generous, the sums involved in these cases would stretch an argument, that politicians and civil servants sought monies merely to 'top-up' their base salaries, beyond credulity.

Given increase in rewards and the falling trust in politicians, with 40 percent trusting the Dáil, and just 23 percent registering trust in political parties (Eurobarometer 61, Spring 2004), one might expect that there would be a reticence in awarding pay increases. Certainly the center-left government in 1996 (in advance of an election in 1997) suspended its own pay increases, and in the late 1980s a former minister made headlines and political capital by refusing to take his ministerial pension while he was still serving in the Dáil (this led to the reform of the ministerial pensions). Some left-wing politicians have raised the issue as a way of criticizing the government in 2008/2009 and rewards for public sector workers started to become a political issue. This led to cabinet ministers and top civil servants taking a voluntary pay cut.

The defense of the high increases up to 2008 is usually based on the independence of the process. However, the Review Body is chosen by government, and it reports to government, which ultimately makes the decision. Former civil servants and politicians have been members of the Body. For instance, it was chaired by Michael Buckley, who as a former senior civil servant would have benefited from increased pay as it is linked to his pension. Though this would probably be dwarfed by what he earned in his private sector position, the fact that one essentially had an insider making recommendations calls into question the independence of the process.

Overall the system seems to be all carrot and no stick. Incomes keep rising with questionable concessions to work practices or performance measurement. The pay budget for HPOs is small in the context of the overall state expenditure, and the principle that one pays one's decision makers well seems fair and logical. However, the rationale of linking pay to the private sector cannot be squared with the facts that pay in the public sector is subject to a ratchet effect where it can only go up, and where job, pay and pension security do not exist to the same extent in the private sector.

References

Byrne, R. and J.P. McCutcheon (2001) *The Irish Legal System*. Dublin: Butterworths.

Chubb, B. (1992) *The Government and Politics of Ireland*, 3rd edn. Harlow: Longman.

Gallagher, M. (2003) Ireland: party loyalists with a personal base. In J. Borchert and J. Zeiss (Eds), *The Political Class in Advanced Democracies*. Oxford: Oxford University Press.

Gallagher, M. and L. Komito (2005) The constituency role of Dáil deputies. In M. Gallagher and J. Coakley (Eds), *Politics in the Republic of Ireland*. London: Routledge.

Garrett, G. and P. Way (1999) Public sector unions, corporatism and macroeconomic performance. *Comparative Political Studies,* **32**(4): 411–434.

Gerring, J. and S.C. Thacker (2005) Do neoliberal policies deter political corruption? *International Organization,* **59**(1): 233–254.

Gwynn Morgan, D. (2001) *A Judgement too far? Judicial activism and the constitution.* Cork: Cork University Press.

Hardiman, N. (2006) Politics and social partnership: flexible network governance. *Economic and Social Review*, **37**(3): 347–374.

Hardiman, N. and M. Mac Cárthaigh (2008) Administrative Reform in a Liberal Market Economy. UCD Geary Institute Discussion Paper.

Kelly, E., S. McGuinness, and P.J. O'Connell (2008) Benchmarking, Social Partnership and Higher Remuneration: Wage Settling Institutions and the Public-Private Sector Wage Gap in Ireland. Dublin: ESRI Working Paper (270).

Matland, R.E. and D.T. Studlar (2004) Determinants of legislative turnover: a cross-national analysis. *British Journal of Political Science*, **34**: 87–108.

Murphy, G. (1999) A culture of sleaze: political corruption and the Irish body politic. *Irish Political Studies*, **15**: 193–200.

Murphy, G. (2005) Payments for no political response? Political corruption and tribunals of inquiry in Ireland, 1991–2003. In J. Garrard and J.L. Newell (Eds). *Scandals in Past and Contemporary Politics*. Manchester: Manchester University Press.

O'Donnell, R. and D. Thomas (1998) Partnership and policy making. In S. Healy and B. Reynolds (Eds). *Social Policy in Ireland: Principles, practice and problems*. Dublin: Oak Tree Press.

O'Leary, J. (2002) Benchmarking the benchmarkers. *ESRI Quarterly Economic Commentary* (Winter).

O'Malley, E. (2006) Ministerial selection in Ireland: limited choice in a political village. *Irish Political Studies*, **21**(3): 319–336.

O'Malley, E. and S. Martin (2010) The Government and the Taoiseach. In J. Coakley and M. Gallagher (Eds), *Politics in the Republic of Ireland,* 5th edn. Abingdon: Routledge.

Review Body, on Higher Remuneration in the Public Sector (2000) Report no. 38 to the Minister for Finance on the levels of remuneration appropriate to higher posts in the public sector. Dublin: The Stationery Office.

Review Body, on Higher Remuneration in the Public Sector (2005) Report no. 40 to the Minister for Finance. Dublin: Stationery Office.

Review Body, on Higher Remuneration in the Public Sector (2007) Report no. 42 to the Minister for Finance. Dublin: Stationery Office.

Sustaining Progress (2003) Social Partnership Agreement 2003–2005. Dublin: Stationery Office.

Zimmerman, J.F. (1997) The changing roles of the Irish Department Secretary. *Public Administration Review*, **57**(6): 534–542.

5 Rewards for high public office in the United States

B. Guy Peters

Any ambitious young person wanting to become wealthy early in his or her life should not plan to work for the federal government in the United States. The relatively low level of rewards offered to most public employees in the United States should be expected, given the low regard in which Americans hold government in general, and the federal government in particular. While public servants and some political leaders may be respected in many European and Asian (see Hood, Peters, and Lee 2003) societies, in the United States these officials are often considered necessary evils, and perhaps not even necessary. As a consequence of this general disdain for the public sector, pay and perquisites available to public officials are by no means commensurate with the responsibilities of those officials, and continues to fall behind the private sector. The Secretary of Defense, for example, manages the largest single organization in the world, public or private, but receives a salary of only $196,700, with relatively modest benefits when compared to managers in the private sector.

Our ambitious young person may not be able to achieve the goal of wealth early in a working lifetime, or even while working for government, but may be able to do so later in life. The higher rewards generally will come after leaving public office, although they will be at least the indirect result of having done public service. A number of political officials have moved from government into lucrative positions in lobbying firms (often thinly disguised as law firms), or have made millions from writing their memoirs, or earn thousands of dollars per speech to business organizations.[1] Having a former federal judge as a partner is often very attractive for any law firm, and they are willing to reward the former judge accordingly. Even public servants who leave office often can pursue lucrative careers in the private sector, although there are rules in place designed to prevent their working immediately for the firms which they regulated, or with which they contracted, while in government.[2]

This article will focus on rewards for officials at the federal level. To some extent the story would not be remarkably different were all levels of government considered, although some sub-national officials will be substantially better rewarded than are federal officials, other than the president. For example, public universities (mostly at the state level) are generally outside the pay systems that tend to provide relatively low levels of rewards, and top level professors and administrators earn salaries that are close to comparable with those paid by private universities, and at times higher than state governors.[3] Also, some state governments have moved further down the New Public Management road than the federal government, so that individualized contracts and merit pay may provide some state and local officials with substantial rewards for their involvement, eliminating standard civil service pay systems in favor of a wider and more lucrative range of rewards. In general, however, state and local pay systems tend to be even less lucrative than the federal systems.

The contemporary economic crisis makes the economic rewards of the federal government more appealing than they have been since perhaps the days of the New Frontier and the Great Society. Right now any job with a modicum of security is very desirable. The appeal, of course, as in those days may go beyond simple economics and includes some commitment to the program of the president. The federal government is now getting applications from more of the 'best and brightest' than at any time in recent memory, something that is crucial for replenishing the aging federal workforce.

Rewards in the federal government

Although we will be discussing the various rewards offered to high public officials in the federal government in their respective categories, one of the important institutional aspects of rewards is that they are to some extent linked. Given that constitutionally Congress is primarily responsible for public spending and shares responsibility for setting standards for the civil service with the president, this institution has been the central actor in setting pay for much of the rest of government, as well as for itself. In particular, members of Congress have not been comfortable with having members of the bureaucracy, or even political officials in the executive branch other than the president and vice president, earning more than they do. That principle has now been broken, given the rather severe disadvantage in which members of the executive branch were being placed by the barrier, although for much of recent history rewards for executives with very demanding jobs has been kept rather low. Further, although the ceiling of Congressional pay has been broken for the executives the rate of improving their rewards has been rather slow.

Given that politically it is extremely difficult for Congress to raise its own pay, it is difficult for federal pay to keep pace with changes in the remainder of the economy. The principal of comparability with private sector positions has been abandoned, being replaced by attempts to maintain comparability with movements in the society. Since the latter part of the 20th century the President's Pay Agent[4] has made an assessment of inflation rates in the economy and has recommended annual rates of salary increases. This method of adjusting pay has the virtue of relatively automatic adjustments with a minimum of political involvement, but has the disadvantage of merely maintaining the internal and external deviations of rewards from what salaries might be if high public officials were paid a market rate for their participation in the public sector.

The judiciary has been excluded from this linkage with Congressional salaries for most of its history, although it is now linked with the cost of living increments, and is the only group with a constitutionally protected salary scheme. That protection, however, extends only to forbidding any reduction in judicial salaries for sitting judges (a guarantee of their independence). That said, many judges have commented that slowly rising salaries during inflationary periods have amounted to a violation of that protection. Further, Chief Justice Rehnquist (2002; see also National Commission on the Public Service 2002) appealed a number of times during his tenure as Chief Justice for higher judicial salaries given that the increasing disparity between federal salaries and the salaries and fees available in the private sector was a major impediment to recruiting the 'best and brightest.'[5]

One important element of the personnel system in the United States that mitigates some of the potential negative impact of the low rewards available for public offices is that many positions that would be permanent public sector positions in most industrialized democracies are short-term positions in American government.[6] Although there is a career civil service, the upper two or three levels of executive organizations are appointed by the president or a cabinet secretary. The salaries for these positions are no better than for career positions, but most occupants do not remain in government for more than a few years. For many occupations, spending some time in Washington is almost necessary in order to learn the regulatory system and to develop important personal contacts. Thus, many individuals are willing to accept short-term economic losses for long-term gains.

The large number of positions of this type (approximately 4,500 in 2009) also presents a methodological problem for the study of public employment and rewards of office in the United States. If we do include these political appointees as the equivalent of higher civil servants then we will not be comparing individuals in similar functional positions in government. On the other hand, however, if they are included than we are really including political officials for whom the career opportunities and paths are markedly different than for most civil service systems. The obvious solution is to include both types of employees in the study (see below).

Historically the federal government provided good benefit packages that to some extent also helped to make the lower salaries received for the positions more palatable. For example, during the Reagan administration federal salaries were presumably set by a principle of comparability with the private sector (King and Peters 1994) and the President argued that federal salaries should be only 94 percent of private sector salaries because of the value of the benefits and the job security.[7] Those benefits have eroded significantly over the past 20 years. For example, a generous federal retirement system for civil servants has been replaced by Social Security, plus a small top-up pension based on earnings (the Federal Employee Retiree System) and paid for largely by employee contributions. Employees who entered the federal service prior to 1987 retained their older, more generous, retirement system. Further, the top political officials (especially

Congress) still have a very good retirement system with no apparent intention to reduce those benefits.

The benefit package is perhaps especially important for the federal executives who are only in Washington for a short period. One study (Light 2006) of the contemporary difficulties in attracting good people to jobs in Washington pointed out that the simple fact that government pays relatively little of the relocation costs of its new employees is a major deterrent for people who may want to move a family to the (extremely) expensive Washington, DC metropolitan area. Private firms, on the other hand, almost invariably pay full moving costs, and often make adjustments for housing costs.[8] To the simple costs of moving must be added other costs of living in Washington, such as private schools for the children.[9]

Changes in rewards in the United States

With some understanding of the political and institutional background of rewards for high public office in the United States, we can now turn to an examination of the data. The data for salaries and for most formal benefits are taken from official sources. Some of the other information is derived from more journalistic accounts of how public employees are able to add to their total income, in almost all cases after they leave the public service. Although unsubstantiated, these anecdotes are almost certainly true, given the rather modest rewards received by talented people in DC.

Personnel covered

Most of the choices of the personnel included in this study are easy. The president, cabinet secretaries (the equivalent of ministers), Congress, and the Supreme Court justices are obvious inclusions. The major question is who are the top civil servants in this system? The positions at the top of administrative pyramids in government that in other democracies are held by career public servants are in the United States held by political appointees. There is a career public service, and members of the Senior Executive Service (SES) hold extremely responsible positions, but they do so under more political supervision than in other systems. Therefore, we will present data for both Executive Schedule V positions, the lowest level political appointees, and for top SES positions. We might also have included federal district judges along with Supreme Court justices, but these salaries tend to be closely linked and most benefits are the same. Relatively little additional information would be gained by including the additional group of judges.

Tangible formal rewards

The principal formal tangible reward for high public officials in the United States is their salary. Table 5.1 presents data for salaries for the six officials that we have included in this study, beginning in 1994. Table 5.2 converts these nominal

Table 5.1 Salaries for high public officials in US dollars (nominal values)

	President	Cabinet Officer	ES V	Top SES	Congress[1]	Supreme Court[2]
1994	200,000	148,400	108,200	115,700	133,600	164,100
1996	200,000	148,400	108,200	115,700	133,600	164,100
1997	200,000	148,400	108,200	115,700	133,600	164,100
1998	200,000	151,800	110,700	118,400	136,673	164,100
1999	200,000	151,800	110,700	118,400	136,673	167,900
2000	200,000	157,000	114,500	122,400	141,300	173,600
2001	400,000	161,200	117,600	125,700	141,300	178,300
2002	400,000	166,700	121,600	130,000	150,000	184,400
2003	400,000	171,900	125,400	134,000	154,700	191,300
2004	400,000	175,700	128,200	158,100[3]	158,100	194,300
2005	400,000	180,100	131,400	162,100	162,100	199,200
2006	400,000	183,500	133,900	165,200[4]	165,200	203,000
2007	400,000	186,600	136,200	168,000	168,000	205,800
2008	400,000	196,700	139,600	172,200	172,200	208,100

Notes:
[1] Additions for being Speaker of the House or President pro tem of the Senate.
[2] The Chief Justice makes a somewhat larger salary, although the differential varies.
[3] For agencies with Certified Performance Appraisal system. Maximum of 145,600 in agencies without such a system.
[4] $152,00 without appraisal system.

salaries into real levels of reward, using 1994 as the base year for prices. These deflated figures provide a better sense of how rewards relate to changes in the economy. Further, we will relate these levels of rewards to changes in rewards for all employees and for white collar and professional employees in the United States to determine how well federal rewards are keeping up with those in the private sector. The answer is, in general, not very well.

The rewards offered to the individuals performing extremely responsible tasks in the federal government are not very generous, and in real terms have been eroding, if slightly, in many cases. For example, in real terms the salary offered to a cabinet secretary in 2008 is approximately 7 percent less than in 1994. The large increase in pay for the President, which began with President George W. Bush in 2001,[10] has moved the Chief Executive well ahead of his earnings in 1994 (the $200,000 salary was first given to President Nixon in 1969, and by 2001 its purchasing power was reduced by over half).

Congress has begun to address the problem of the effects of price changes on salaries by linking their own salaries, and therefore those of cabinet secretaries, other members of the Executive Schedule (ES) and most civil servants, to changes in the Consumer Price Index. This change occurred as a result of the 1989 Ethics Reform Act, the so-called 'Pay for Ethics' legislation. After a series

Table 5.2 Salaries for high public officials in US dollars (real values, 1994 = 100)

	President	Cabinet Officer	ES V	Top SES	Congress	Supreme Court[1]
1994	200,000	148,400	108,200	115,700	133,600	164,100
1995	199,453	144,358	105,253	112,549	129,961	159,630
1996	188,857	140,132	102,172	109,254	126,157	154,958
1997	184,672	137,027	99,908	106,833	123,361	151,524
1998	181,818	138,000	100,636	107,636	124,248	149,182
1999	177,936	135,053	98,478	105,338	121,595	149,377
2000	172,117	135,112	98,537	105,336	121,601	149,398
2001	334,728	134,895	98,402	105,188	118,242	149,205
2002	329,489	137,315	100,164	107,084	123,558	151,894
2003	322,061	138,406	100,966	107,891	124,557	152,138
2004	313,725	137,804	100,549	124,000	124,000	152,392
2005	303,490	136,646	99,697	122,989	122,989	151,138
2006	298,941	137,139	100,071	123,463	123,463	151,713
2007	292,748	137,201	100,102	123,703	123,703	151,727
2008	279,345	136,983	99,898	123,435	123,485	151,489

Note: [1] The Chief Justice makes a somewhat larger salary, although the differential varies.

of scandals over honoraria offered to Congressmen for speeches while in office, this legislation limited these (often very handsome) informal rewards in exchange for automatic cost-of-living adjustments that would go into effect unless blocked by Congress. Politically, the use of the cost-of-living adjustments enables Congress to keep its salaries, and those of other employees, at least even with costs without having to make very (politically) expensive votes to do so.

The recommendations for these annual changes are made by the Federal Salary Council, which is composed of experts appointed by the President. The recommendations for basic levels of change are relatively straightforward, with the real difficulties coming for area-based adjustments, especially for expensive areas such as California, Alaska, and Hawaii.[11] To prevent Congress from having to vote for their own pay increases, the legislation designed the process so that the increases occur automatically unless Congress acts to block them. Further, Congressional pay is not in the appropriation act that funds the legislative branch but rather in the appropriations act covering the Department of the Treasury and a number of independent agencies, thus making the pay increases even less visible.

Raising the President's salary in 2001 (legislation passed in 2000) was more politically visible, and involved a good deal of debate over how much officials were worth. The answers from the public would not have pleased the president, or anyone interested in government in the United States. In a Pew Foundation survey citizens at the time were willing to see that the president may need a raise, but most approved of a modest increase such as $25,000 or $50,000, not the doubling to $400,000 finally approved. That raise was substantial, but its purchasing power has been eroded by approximately 20 percent since the time it was adopted.

The United States government has done little that could be classified as New Public Management reforms, despite having a strong market ideology, especially under the current Republican leadership. There is little, for example, in the way of merit pay for members of the civil service, although the members of the SES do have some relatively minor opportunities to earn annual bonuses. First, the base rates of pay are higher in agencies that have developed an approved mechanism for assessing their employees' merit. In addition, the individual members of the SES can earn up to 35 percent of their annual salary as a bonus if they are designated as a Presidential Distinguished Executive.[12] Lower level bonuses are also available through the Performance Review Board.

The possibilities for bonuses, and the existence of various grades within the Senior Executive Service, provide a range of possible rewards to these top level civil servants. Table 5.3 shows the range of financial rewards – salaries plus bonuses – over time for SES members. There can be a variation of as much as 200 percent across members of the SES. These rewards remain available if the SES member takes a position as a political appointee under ES pay rules. Very few civil servants will actually receive these top level rewards, but for the few who do the rewards are substantial, and can actually exceed those available to cabinet secretaries. The data also point to the seemingly surprising finding that

Table 5.3 Range of SES salaries including bonuses in US dollars

	Minimum	Maximum (without bonus)	Maximum (with bonus)
1994	92,900	115,700	156,200
1995	92,900	115,700	156,200
1996	94,800	115,700	156,200
1997	94,800	115,700	156,200
1998	99,200	118,400	159,800
1999	102,300	118,400	159,800
2000	106,200	122,400	165,200
2001	109,100	125,700	169,700
2002	113,000	130,000	175,500
2003	116,500	134,000	180,900
2004	104,927	158,100	213,400
2005	107,550	162,100	218,800
2006	109,808	165,200	223,000
2008	114,468	172,200	232,470

the members of the SES – senior bureaucrats – have actually done better in tangible rewards than have any other group, excluding the president. Even without the bonuses, their rates of pay have been moving ahead faster than most other groups, and noticeably faster than their nominal bosses in ES positions. This disparity to some extent represents the need to keep senior managers in government, as well as the perception (now to some extent altered) that most ES employees would come to Washington for other reasons, and salary would not matter so much.

As noted, some of the employment benefits associated with high public office have been eroding for some time. Health benefits and some other basic benefits remain adequate, comparable to those offered by large private employers, and are available to virtually all public officials. The most noticeable change in benefits has been in retirement benefits, especially for the civil service, as described above. Further, like most Americans, employees in the federal government have been facing increasingly complex choices about health insurance, and some other components of their benefit package. The availability of multiple choices for coverage may provide the employee some sense of choice, but also may produce a great deal of frustration.

Although retirement coverage for most employees has been somewhat reduced, Congress has developed a more generous retirement system for itself and a few other groups in the federal government, which provides 70 percent better benefits. This is but one of many special benefits that Congress has developed for itself and its staff. For example, Congress is able to hire a large number of staff members both in DC and in their home districts, and with little oversight on the qualifications of these staff a number have been members of the family or close political allies.[13] They also have substantial office expense allowances, such as mailing, that critics argue are being used for personal gain, or to subsidize the political campaigns of incumbents.[14] Members of Congress also receive substantial travel benefits so they can spend almost every weekend in their home district engaging in political fence-mending, as well as in raising campaign funds.

Congress is the only one of the groups of government elites included in this study with so many special benefits, in part because they control legislation and public spending and therefore are able to write these benefits into law. The president does have huge perquisites while in office, but these are more associated with the conduct of the office than with personal benefits. There is, of course, the White House as a residence, Air Force One and a fleet of limousines for transportation, and a personal entourage for scheduling and to do virtually whatever the president wants. The president also receives a non-taxable (taxable until 1979) expense allowance for entertaining, travel, etc.

The pension benefits offered to the president and vice-president are also generous, and like Congressional benefits are much better than those of other federal employees. For example, President Clinton now receives a pension of $151,800 plus $150,000 for office expenses. Had she not been elected to the United States Senate, Hilary Rodham Clinton would have received a pension of $20,000 as a former First Lady. Presidents also receive protection from the Secret Service for at least 10 years after they leave office and most also receive an appropriation from Congress for a presidential library.[15] These benefits are substantial, especially given the opportunities that former presidents have for earning money in more informal ways (see below).

Tangible informal rewards

As intimated above, the most significant informal, tangible reward for high public officials is the ability to move from their public roles into lucrative private positions after completing public service. These movements through the revolving door to the private sector are to some extent regulated by law (the Ethics in Government Act) and by regulations issued by the Office of Personnel Management (see Revolving Door Working Group 2005). These regulations are designed to ensure that federal employees do not go to work immediately for the firms with which they have been doing 'business' or which they have been regulating while in government. There are, however, a number of reasons that enable the Office of Personnel Management or even the individual agencies with which an employ had been working to justify permitting an individual to evade these regulations, and indeed they are frequently avoided. In particular, the Department of Defense has been very liberal in granting exceptions from the general restraints on employment.

Civil servants and executive branch officials tend to be more controlled in how they spend their life after leaving government, at least for the first several years, by the Ethics in Government Act, among other legislation. Members of Congress, however, have had fewer such constraints. Many of them have gone to work immediately as lawyers and lobbyists in the firms along the K Street Corridor that is at the heart of the lobbying activities in Washington. The scandals surrounding the lobbying activities of Jack Abramoff and his associates are producing substantial public and political reactions. New legislation from the spring of 2006 is designed to restrict the activities of Congressmen for two years after they leave public office and to prevent them from becoming lobbyists with their old colleagues almost immediately. The initial spate of concern about controls over Congressmen has waned somewhat, as popular attention has been diverted to other issues, but if any legislation does emerge there may be no free lunches for Congress anymore, and certainly no free golf junkets.

One way of understanding what happens to executive branch officials after they leave office is to look at what the members of the last Clinton Cabinet did (Table 5.4). In most cases we cannot identify exactly what salaries these officials are now receiving, but it almost certainly is more than they earned while they were in Washington. That is certainly true for the President himself. In addition to the pension he now receives, he earns very large speaking fees – $9.5 million in 2003 (from Senate Financial Disclosure Form of Hillary Rodham Clinton). Further, the advance of royalties for his political autobiography was in the millions (10–12) of dollars, as was that for Hillary Rodham Clinton ($8 million). This is but one example of the rewards earned by a president who was far from liked by the business community. For former presidents, such as Bush Sr., the

Table 5.4 Careers after leaving Cabinet for selected Clinton Cabinet members

	Cabinet post	*Current*
Madeleine Albright	Secretary of State	Professor, Georgetown University
LawrenceSummers	Secretary of Treasury	President, Harvard University (Resigned)
William Cohen	Secretary of Defense	CEO, Cohen Group, Lobbyists
Bruce Babbitt	Secretary of Interior	Lawyer, Lobbyist
Alexis Herman	Secretary of Labor	Human Resources Director, Coca Cola; Numerous Boards of Directors
Andrew Cuomo	Secretary of Housing and Urban Development	Candidate for Attorney General, State of New York
Rodney Slater	Secretary of Transportation	Lobbyist, Lawyer
Bill Richardson	Secretary of Energy	Governor, State of New Mexico
Togo West	Secretary of Veterans Affairs	Chair of minority development Corporation

economic rewards from being on boards of corporations, etc. have been at least as large or larger.

The one category of high public official who do not tend to capitalize as much on their fame and contacts have been justices of the Supreme Court. While 'ordinary' federal judges often retire from the bench and resume lucrative private practice, justices from the Supreme Court tend to remain on the court until very late in their lives, and often die in office. Further, they have been very reticent about writing autobiographies or otherwise commenting on their lives and work for profit. Two recent justices have broken that mold somewhat. The first, Sandra Day O'Connor has written a memoir of her life (although hardly as lucrative as those of the Clintons) and is now teaching law. Also, Justice Antonin Scalia has received large speaking fees and expensive trips from businesses, creating demands that he recuse himself from some cases before the Court.[16]

In addition to the opportunities to earn salaries and other rewards after leaving office, Congress in particular has had the opportunity to 'earn' rewards, such as trips and golf weekends, while still in office. In some cases these junkets are paid by public funds, for example when members of Congress go on fact-finding tours to the Caribbean in January. Other trips have been paid for by lobbyists and corporations, which is one of the issues at the heart of the current discussions of lobbying reform. It has become clear that the role of money in political life is at times abusive, but the way out of the problem is still unclear.

We should also point out that there are some costs associated with having been a high public official. As well as often receiving a good deal of money on the basis of past service and contacts, the former official may also be expected to be a major contributor to both political campaigns, and to charities and other civic activities. While these activities will rarely if ever impoverish the former official they are real obligations that may reduce the seemingly immense rewards achieved by some officials after leaving office. Further, the loss of privacy may be seen as a real cost for former political leaders.

Intangible formal rewards

Pomp and circumstance for high public officials are present in all governments, and the United States is no different. Certainly the office of the President of the United States is surrounded with a large number of intangible benefits associated with the office, and which to some extent continue even after a president leaves office. Congress has also a range of perquisites that have little financial value, but still have value for the recipients of that special treatment. Likewise, the Supreme Court has created an aura around itself that provides it prestige perhaps even greater than the real power they have in the political system. That aura was to some extent dissipated by their involvement in the 2001 decision concerning the Bush–Gore election, but the formal trappings of their power and respect remain in place.

Civil servants have few, if any, of these rewards, and indeed often receive disrespect rather than respect from the public. It is difficult to identify any particular intangible benefits that are available to career public servants, other than the personal satisfaction that may come from doing their job well and from contributing to the well-being of their country.[17] Likewise, the political appointees in the executive branch, whether Cabinet Secretaries or lower level appointees, will receive rather little in terms of intangible rewards as a result of their service. For the 'in and outers' in government (Maranto 2005) they may receive financial and career benefits in the long-run, but they will not receive a great deal of support in the short-term. Their rewards may not be nearly as great as those of politicians, but they will be there for many, especially if they live within the Beltway.

Intangible informal rewards

In a society that does not confer a great deal of respect on public officials, whether in or out of office, this category of reward is perhaps less significant than in many other countries. The respect that public officials might expect is more often replaced by cynicism, especially for officials who have been able to mobilize a lucrative career after leaving office. To a great extent the respect and even affection that former officials are able to garner has been based more on personal attributes than on their holding a public office. For example, although Jimmy Carter is still cited as one of the least successful presidents in modern history, his career after leaving office has earned him immense respect and a Nobel Prize. Bill Clinton has been able to rehabilitate his image somewhat with work for development in the Third World and relief after natural disasters. The jury is, of course, still out on George W. Bush, but he may have further to go than the other presidents.

Some former participants in the public sector do receive substantial informal rewards, although rarely of much real economic value. Certainly members of the armed forces generally are more respected after their service than are the civilian members of the public sector. Likewise, having been a judge, Senator, or even a member of Congress does provoke some respect, although certainly not to the extent that is true in many other societies. Like so many other aspects of the public sector, Americans tend to be schizophrenic about public employees, disliking them in general but respecting them as individuals.

Summary and conclusion

Public employees in the United States are not the highly respected representatives of the State that we would expect to find in a European or Asian society. While many young Americans may grow up wanting to be president, or perhaps a member of Congress or a judge, few if any grow up thinking about being a civil servant. The individuals who do work for government are almost always proud of what they do in office, and satisfied with their careers (SES survey 1999), but at the same time generally would not advise young people to embark on a career in government. This somewhat dismal view of their own profession may change as more and more people have come to recognize that, in contradiction to Ronald Reagan, government is not the problem and it just might be part of the solution.

The rather conservative bent of American government for the past eight years, and in many ways since the election of Ronald Reagan, has reduced the modest respect for the public sector that had existed. That said, however, this period has led to institutionalizing some agreements about formal salaries and wages that did not seem possible before that time. Civil servants may be no more respected than they had been, but they are being treated somewhat better economically than they were in the past.

The early evidence is that President Obama will not be willing, or able, to do a great deal to improve their lot further, but this may not be due to a lack of respect for public employees. The president is facing real fiscal problems and may not be able to provide the necessary resources for employees. Also, freezing public salaries, which would only save the President little money, could be a political move that potentially could have important symbolic value in a society that still is not very positive concerning the public sector.

Notes

1 Colin Powell can now earn almost as much for one speech as he made in a year as Secretary of State. Bill Clinton likewise makes much more than his presidential salary for most speeches.
2 Rules on the 'revolving door' were reinforced during the Carter administration, but there are also ways around these rules that enable former public officials to go to work in the private sector, for firms whom they had worked with while in government, almost immediately after leaving office. President Obama has moved quickly after taking office to strengthen these rules.

3 For example, the president of my own University earns well over $400,000 while the Governor of Pennsylvania earns a salary of less than $200,000.
4 This is an almost mythical body comprising representatives from OMB, the Department of Labor, and the OPM.
5 The argument was that a newly minted lawyer in a major Wall Street firm would earn as much or more than a federal judge. The salaries offered to federal judges ($203,000 for the Supreme Court, 150,000 for District Court judges) a year appear handsome when compared to the average income in society (roughly $38,000) but compared to many other lawyers they are very modest indeed – the average pay for lawyers in private practice nine months after completing law school is already over $80,000.
6 The number of appointed positions has been increasing as presidents want to be able to exercise greater control over the executive branch (Light 1995).
7 The 6 percent figure for benefits appeared to have no factual basis but was simply a figure that President Reagan pulled out of the air.
8 Lower level jobs in the federal government do receive area based pay, and an elaborate system is in place to attempt to adjust for differences, but this is not applicable to the higher levels of the federal government, perhaps simply because most of them are located in one place.
9 President Obama has, after much controversy, placed his daughters in a private school in the District.
10 This was not Republicans rewarding one of their own; it was decided not to increase the salary of a serving president, although the fact that Bill Clinton was that serving president did not help to make the case for the increase to what was then a Republican-dominated Congress.
11 Very few of the high public officials included in this article live outside the Washington, DC area so these adjustments are of little importance here.
12 These are relatively rare, approximately one per department per year.
13 For example, several Congressmen who have been forced to resign over the past several years have hired family as staff, and Tom DeLay was able to get lucrative consulting deals for his wife.
14 Incumbents tend to be reelected at an extremely high rate, and again critics argue that they are able to use some of their allowances to subsidize their political careers. Bigger subsidies, however, may come from their use of spending programs to provide benefits to their constituencies.
15 Given the continued animus of the Republicans toward him, President Clinton has yet to receive an appropriation for his library.
16 In an act of personal bravery Justice Scalia also has been on hunting trips with Vice President Cheney.
17 As is true for most public servants, those motivations are important for SES members, as evidenced in surveys of their attitudes to the job.

References

Hood, C. and B.G. Peters (1994) *Rewards at the Top: A comparative study of high public office.* London: Sage.

Hood, C., B.G. Peters and G.O.M. Lee (2003) *Rewards for High Government Office in Asia and the Pacific.* London: Routledge.

King, D.S. and B.G. Peters (1994) The United States. In C. Hood and B.G. Peters (Eds). *Rewards at the Top: A comparative study of high public office.* London: Sage, pp. 145–165.

Light, P.C. (1995) *Thickening Government.* Washington, DC: The Brookings Institution.

Light, P.C. (1999) 'Raising the President's Salary, Evidence to House Committee on Government Reform', 24 May.

Maranto, R. (2005) *Beyond a Government of Strangers.* Lanham, MD: Lexington.

Rehnquist, W.H. (2002) Statement Before National Commission on the Public Service, 15 July. <http://www.supremecourtus.gov/publicinfo/speeches/sp_07-15-02.html>.

Revolving Door Working Group (2005) *A Matter of Trust.* Washington, DC: Revolving Door Working Group.

6 Rewards for high public office in France

Still the century of privileges?

Jean-Michel Eymeri-Douzans

Introduction: framing the map of the French context

In his memoirs, a former Minister for Finance (Arthuis 1998) tells this story: when taking office in 1995, he asked for full information about the real rewards of top civil servants. One year later he received a single page of figures, without official headers, printed on special paper from the secret services that prevents it from being copied. Conclusion of the parable: 'The only true state secret in France is the amount of administrative elite wages.' Such a lack of transparency must be seen in light of French reluctance to openly discuss revenues or money. As de Tocqueville (1856) demonstrated, one of the numerous 'French paradoxes' is the mix of a 'passion for equality' and/but a 'love for privileges.' In such a culture, it is unsurprising that opacity traditionally applies to politico-administrative elites' rewards, which tend to be organized more as privileges guaranteed to status groups than as proper rewards for individual achievements. Some recent changes are occurring, though, due to the trans-national influence of the New Public Management (NPM) on rewards for the administrative elite, while tradition remains unchallenged for politicians.

For a better understanding, a few French peculiarities should be recalled. France is an ancient nation, where the State was not supposed to serve but to rule society. 'State Power' has enjoyed for centuries a higher prestige than the power of money – a relation that is rapidly changing since the 1980–1990s. France had been so far a society driven by the *logique de l'honneur* (d'Iribarne 1993): national 'heroes' were political leaders, civil servants, and intellectuals rather than entrepreneurs. Money had never been the main pursuit, and wealth was no more than tolerated. However, two centuries after the 1789 Revolution and its 'abolition of privileges,' French society remains, to a large extent, aristocratic in practice. The *bourgeoisie*, this typical French social group, much wider than the Anglophone 'upper class,' is still alive (Pinçon and Pinçon-Charlot 2003). Belonging to the *bourgeoisie* is not mainly a matter of money: it is a matter of heritage, education, selective diplomas asserting one's belonging to 'the best and the brightest,' a shared *ethos*/art of living, and having a prestigious, respectable occupation, including high public office.

As a consequence, and differently from other EU countries where the civil service attracts middle-class people (except UK and Germany), there is a long tradition for the *bourgeoisie* to direct their children towards administrative careers. It is common to find top officials in the Ministry of Finance whose fathers were highly paid CEOs, and prefects whose fathers were wealthy lawyers. Moreover, some administrative 'dynasties' also exist.

Such a traditional belonging of the majority of State officials to the *bourgeoisie* (Birnbaum 1977, Suleiman 1979, Charle 1987) has determined three main features of the French reward system from the nineteenth century until recent innovations: (1) Differently from other countries where civil servants eventually become top civil servants after successful careers (Dreyfus and Eymeri-Douzans 2006), the French dominant group of *hauts fonctionnaires* is composed of a few happy 'high flyers' recognized as an *élite de la République* (Charle 1987), from the beginning of their career and quickly brought to the top by virtue of their initial elitist recruitment via *grandes écoles* (Bourdieu 1989, Suleiman 1979, Eymeri-Douzans 2001); (2) Using salary scales, career speed, opaque bonuses and privileges, those in power have unsurprisingly guaranteed to these *hauts fonctionnaires* a standard of living that maintains their rank; (3) Mobilizing generous provisions on 'statutory positions' (secondments, position 'at leave,' *hors-cadre*) as a strategic resource, *hauts fonctionnaires* developed since the 1870s a collective out-placement system, called *pantouflage* (Charle 1987b). This system gives mid-career civil servants who cannot expect further promotion, or have already reached the top, the possibility to move into better paid executive positions within public agencies, state-owned companies or private firms, without resigning (a 'parachute' comeback remains possible for 15 years or so). These traditional features have been subject to recent changes due to societal transformations and reforms driven by public criticism (see part 1 below).

For politics, the situation is different. In the mid-nineteenth century, the first generations of elected politicians were composed of patricians, landlords, businessmen or top civil servants – and were described as *les notables* (Jardin and Tudesq 1973). After the 'republicanization,' the social background of elected politicians changed. From 1875 to 1958, Parliament and the Government were populated by upper-middle class, university graduated professionals: lawyers, notaries, medical doctors, chemists, plus university professors and numerous secondary school teachers among socialist MPs, etc. There were very few businessmen and no longer top civil servants. The newcomers could not live *for* politics without living *on* politics. For decades, they increased 'parliamentary indemnities,' facing opposition from the press, clergy, trade unions, etc. Such resistance is one reason for the secrecy surrounding MPs' earnings, and also for the development of more hidden privileges, whose accumulation has given the impression that 'the political class' (a pejorative but ordinary phrase in France) lives in a world apart. Such opinion has even increased under the Fifth Republic, a regime that has both enhanced the prestige of 'State Power' and attracted into politics many *hauts fonctionnaires* with a higher social background and more technocratic profile than post-War politicians (part 2).

'Rewards' or privileges of top civil servants: the means to maintain rank

Our thesis is that, for centuries and until recent reforms, the level and nature of rewards for high public office (RHPOs) (tangible and non-tangible) in France have not been designed to 'reward' individual performance but are a dependent variable of the positioning of our administrative elite on the social ladder. The rewards of French top officials have been collectively managed to make sure that they could maintain their rank, in two respects: within the administrative world, to maintain the 'distinction' between their aristocracy and the rest of public servants; in society at large, to maintain their belonging to the *bourgeoisie*.

Basic salaries: the visible part of the iceberg

The salary of any civil servant is composed of:

- A *traitement indiciaire brut*: gross basic salary;
- A small *indemnité de résidence* (1 to 3 percent of the gross basic salary);
- A family supplement (up to 100 €/month for 2 children, 260 €/month for 3 children, plus 180 €/month per additional child);
- Opaque adds-on and bonuses, called *primes*, now under complete reform.

The 'net salary' is the addition of these four elements minus social contributions (health, pension) which amount to 17 percent of the gross basic salary, whereas income tax is paid *ex post*.

According to the Civil Service Act, there is one *grille indiciaire générale* (overall pay scale), which mentions two interrelated lists of coefficients: *indices bruts* (IB), used for hierarchical classification of the various corps and grades, and *indices majorés* (IM), which are the concrete figures used to calculate the exact basic salaries for each level. The formula is simple: *traitement indiciaire brut = indice majoré × value of the point d'indice*. The *point d'indice*, a key feature of French administrative culture, is an amount in euros, increased each year after negotiations with the unions. For 2008, its value is 4,57 €/month. For instance, the minimum gross salary (see below) is: IM 290 × 4,57 € = 1,325 €/month. The scale of *indices bruts* initially adopted in 1946 goes from IB 100 to IB 1015: the range between the lowest and highest salaries was a 1-to-10 range. However, decades of negotiations between unions and governments eager to please 5 million voters (plus families) have produced the *indices majorés* scale, which has upgraded the real bottom of scale to IM 290 while downgrading the top to IM 820, thus reducing it to a 1-to-3 range. However, the administrative elite did not accept such flattening: in 1957, another salary scale was created, significantly named *grille hors-échelle* (an oxymoron meaning 'out-of-scale scale'). This had been explicitly designed for *hauts fonctionnaires*: it only mentions letters, from A to G, whose equivalence in real money remained secret until 1982, when the new socialist government made it public (see Table 6.1).

Table 6.1 Hors-échelle scale (1 October 2008)

Grades	Gross basic salary/month (€)	Net basic salary/ month	Grades	Gross basic salary/ month (€)	Net basic salary/ month (€)
HE A1	4,026	3,341	HE C1	5,096	4,229
HE A2	4,186	3,474	HE C2	5,205	4,320
HE A3	4,401	3,652	HE C3	5,320	4,415
HE B1	4,401	3,652	HE D1	5,320	4,415
HE B2	4,588	3,808	HE D2	5,562	4,616
HE B3	4,835	4,013	HE D3	5,804	4,817
HE BB1	4,835	4,013	HE E1	5,804	4,817
HE BB2	4,963	4,119	HE E2	6,033	5,007
HE BB3	5,096	4,229	HE F	6,257	5,193
			HE G	6,860	5,693

A comparison between the minimum basic salary at IM 290: 1,325 euros and the top HE G basic salary of 6,860 euros shows a range of 1-to-5. There is no *corps* whose members start their career within the *hors-échelle* scale: it is reached progressively. But elite *corps* recruited through École Normale Supérieure (ENA) and *Polytechnique* can reach it much quickly and climb much higher than ordinary Group-A corps, such as secondary schools teachers, who can only reach HE A3 at the end of their career. Basic salaries for *hauts fonctionnaires* are modest at the beginning, but increase rapidly. For civil administrators, who represent half of ENA alumni, the apparent modesty of the HE B3 maximum should be qualified by the fact that their usual career consists of ascending, 10 years after ENA, to the 'executive positions' of ministerial departments' hierarchy, which have yet another salary scale, equivalent to that of grand *corps* (see Table 6.2).

No career path ends in HE F and HE G; these highest salaries being reserved for a few dignitaries: Vice-President of the Council of State, Presidents of the Court of Auditors and Court of Cassation, five-star generals acting as Supreme Headquarters Chiefs, etc.

Hauts fonctionnaires are unsurprisingly the main beneficiaries of the *hors-échelle* scale. However, other A-group public agents can also gain access to it: 43,330 civil servants are thus benefiting from that scale, half of them being teachers and academics. Such an enlargement was not within the plans of the administrative elite, who since the 1970s had another strategy: playing with the hidden part of the iceberg through constant increases of *primes*.

Primes: the hidden part of the iceberg now under scrutiny

Egalitarianism is a French core value, but as practical people the French love privileges. The history of RHPOs is a perfect illustration: the *hors-échelle* scale was

Table 6.2 Salary scale peculiar to executive *emplois fonctionnels* within ministerial departments

Emploi fonctionnel	Echelon	Cumulated seniority	Indices majorés	Net basic salary/month (€)
Sous-directeur	1st echelon	–	IM 731	2,772
	2nd echelon	1 year	IM 820	3,110
	3rd echelon	2 years	HE A3	3,652
	4th echelon	4 years	HE B3	4,013
Chef de service	Single échelon	–	HE BB3	4,229
Directeur/ Directeur général	1st echelon	–	HE C3	4,415
	2nd echelon	3 years	HE D3	4,817
	3rd echelon	6 years	HE E2	5,007

created in 1948 as a hidden privilege for administrative elites only, but was slowly democratized. In reaction, top officials have invented a new instrument to maintain the financial gap between them and 'the others': an opaque system of generous *primes*, whose total now represents one-half of the net real salary of high public officers. French *primes* have very little in common with 'performance-related pay' implemented through the NPM. Several features reveal their nature:

- *Primes* are not rewarding individuals but are collectively distributed to all the civil servants belonging to the same *corps* or ministry.
- There are 300 kinds of *primes*: each *haut fonctionnaire* enjoys an incredible and inconsistent set of 10 to 20 *primes* accumulated over time, some of them meaningless, such as the one for bicycles and shoes of *Génie Rural des Eaux et Forêts* (IGREF) engineers.
- Compared to performance-related bonuses, which are published in order to be incentives, *primes* were kept totally secret until recently.

Only recently has one comparative table of figures including the *primes* been made public. Even if the table uses mean salaries and does not enter into detail, it gives precious indications on the distortions between the 'official' basic salaries scale and the real global net salaries (see Table 6.3).

The table shows how the system of *primes* benefits *hauts fonctionnaires*, State engineers and the Judiciary, over academics and teachers. But these are only mean figures: for *primes* inequality has always been the rule. For instance, the all-powerful Ministry for Finance has always paid much higher bonuses than other ministries: Bercy directors general have real net salaries including *primes* ranging from 110,600 euros to 130,600 €/year (9,216 € to 10,883 €/month), whereas prefects do not earn more than 8,000 €/month. Such differences explain the long-lasting opacity of the system.

Table 6.3 Mean basic gross salary, *primes* and global net salary including *primes* of some significant categories of civil servants (per year)

	Gross basic salary (€)	Primes		Global net salary (€)
		Amount (€)	Age (%)	
Management:	32,879	16,433	50	43,083
– *Emplois de direction*	58,249	33,673	61	82,319
– civil administrators	43,744	23,940	55	58,925
– administrative attachés	31,132	13,125	42	38,091
Grand corps engineers	41,244	24,848	60	57,604
Judiciary judges	43,961	22,175	50	57,548
Army officers	29,903	16,912	57	42,977
University full professors	52,840	4,991	9	49,585
Secondary school teachers	28,350	2,425	9	26,244
Administrative secretaries (B-group)	22,503	6,383	28	24,710

Source: Rapport annuel sur l'état de la fonction publique 2007–2008, p. 528.

Such bitterly criticized unfairness led, since 2000, to a policy of 're-foundation' (67 decrees, 163 *arrêtés*) in order to simplify *primes* and make them transparent and fair. *Primes* in other ministries than Finance have thus been raised (+25 percent for Social Affairs, +50 percent for the Judiciary, 2000–2007). More recently, the NPM promotion of performance-related pay has influenced French decision-makers. To avoid confrontation with hostile unions, the tactic was to start at the top: since 2004 as a pilot, fully deployed in 2006, directors general benefit from a new performance-related bonus (6 percent to 16 percent of their total wages). Since Sarkozy's arrival, a more radical project is under adoption: a single *Prime de fonctions et de résultats* (PFR) to replace all existing ones. This individualized PFR will be twofold: half related to the level of the position currently occupied, half related to the performance of the agent (assessed annually). The implementation of PFR to administrative attachés is occurring in 2009–2012. The generalization to all A- and B-Group administrative agents is due to follow later. A slow move has thus started from an inherited conception of *primes* as corporatist collective privileges to a renewed conception of bonuses as partly individualized rewards. Such a move is congruent with current debates on the opportunity to replace the system of *corps* by a *fonction publique de métiers* (Silicani 2008). However, this new policy is still in its infancy, and its sustainability is highly dependent on the future political context.

'Small privileges' and other 'increasing returns'

High public officials can enjoy several other privileges and retributions, which are not accessible to the average civil servant and help them maintain their rank within the *bourgeoisie*. Without being exhaustive, and going from the most generic to the most peculiar, it is worth mentioning:

- Decorations: all *haut fonctionnaires*, when eligible in terms of seniority, are given decorations, a sport practiced for decades since many ministries have their own order ('Academic Palms,' 'Agricultural Order for Merit') with 3 grades (knight, officer, commander). Around 20 years into a career, they vie for the Order for Merit, and then can hope to become a *chevalier de la Légion d'Honneur*, the most prestigious order, with its 5 grades until the Grand Cross, the secret objective of the highest French dignitaries.

- Entering the *Who's Who in France* and some prestigious clubs: Gaining access to the prestigious yearbook considered as 'the repertoire of French elites' is a matter of vanity, but can also be useful for career reorientations or matrimonial strategies, since having one's biography in *Who's Who* is an efficient way to be recognized as a VIP. Not all *hauts fonctionnaires* are mentioned: political appointees are there (prefects, ambassadors, directors general, *ministerial cabinets*), whereas a selection of grand corps and other corps are included. A happy few also gain admittance into very prestigious (British style) clubs, some more connected with business, such as the *Automobile Club* or *Club de l'Union interalliée*. Others, such as *Le Siècle,* are more open to other sector elites (media, non-governmental organizations (NGOs)).

- Chauffeured official cars: Several thousand chauffeured cars are at the personal disposal of many public officers (prefects, ambassadors, rectors, directors general within central ministries, etc.) 24 hours a day.

- *Vie de château*: Prefects, like ambassadors, are high representatives of 'the State': the Prefecture are impressive palaces, where the prefect has the right and duty to reside and organize regular receptions to demonstrate 'the magnificence of the State.' This makes for a rather special life, allowing them to save the greater part of their salary (invested in countryside mansions for after retirement and maintenance of the same style of living).

- Some cheap apartments in Paris: There are thousands of accommodations that come with the job, which mainly benefit medium rank servants (elementary school directors, etc.), as well as prefects and ambassadors. A *haut fonctionnaire* in Paris has to pay for his accommodation. However, the central Bank of France, which owns hundreds of nineteenth century impressive buildings in the most expensive parts of Paris, rents out large apartments far below the market price to VIPs, among whom politicians and a few civil servants can be found.

- A few odd bonuses: In some cases, the ethics of RHPOs are highly controversial. Two examples: the numerous French *cabinets ministériels* (private offices of ministers) are populated with 75 percent of career civil servants, placed under secondment and still paid by their original units. In addition, they get a *cabinet* indemnity. For decades, these amounts were paid out of 'secret funds' allocated for financing intelligence services, distributed each month in small envelopes of cash money to the ministers' advisors, with a request not to declare these 'secret' bonuses for taxation. A second, pre-modern custom benefits the *Trésoriers-payeurs généraux* (head tax administrations in the provinces): they receive an extra bonus consisting of a small percentage of the taxes levied within their area.

However, the most decisive advantages of the administrative elite will be mentioned in the following section.

The major 'rewards': quick take-off, careers at the top, and pantouflage

The main privilege, and source of rewards, of the administrative elite relates to the high speed of their careers: high-flyers are not running a race *against* the clock but *with the help of* the clock. Careers of the most brilliant ENA alumni who join the *grand corps* are almost incredible. After a few years within the Council of State, or Financial Inspectorate, they are seconded to a variety of interesting positions. Between ENA+6 and ENA+10 years, they often enroll into a ministerial cabinet. Then, around the age of 42–44, if they do not opt for *pantoufage*, they are easily appointed as directors general. Until the age of 68, they can thus enjoy a long-lasting 'career at the top,' an alternation of executive responsibilities, such as director of *cabinet* of a minister, head of a public agency, director general again within another ministry, followed by a return to their original *grand corps*, and a final appointment as chairman of an inter-departmental committee or regulatory authority. Of course, all these positions offer a HE D/HE E salary, plus generous *primes*, a large office, a secretary, a chauffeured car, etc. What the professional life of these 'careerists-at-the-top' is about is to maintain their 'directorial' rank for life – and empirical data shows that they usually succeed.

The careers of the majority of ENA alumni, civil administrators, are less impressive but not slower. They have a quick 'first career' that enables them to be *sous-directeur* around the age of 38. Lots of them stop there, a few become *chef de service* (deputy-DG) or, when politically supported, director general, before the age of 43 on average, and usually for 3–5 years. The executive management of French ministries is thus younger, constantly moving, and with a quicker turnover than elsewhere in Europe. Civil administrators around 45–48 leave their ministry to start a 'second career' in various branches of the public sphere: appointments within ministerial inspectorates general, or as financial controllers (HE D and HE E salaries); secondments as directors general of one of our hundreds of public agencies (*établissements publics*), etc.

'Second careers' are also a major opportunity for those who are discontented with their income to move to business: traditional *pantouflage* has involved on average 15–20 percent of our top civil servants over the past decades. It must be understood as a result of the *grandes écoles* system: the State extracts from each generation the 'best and the brightest,' who are then attracted into public administration. These brilliant people work within the State during a first career that quickly brings them to the top. Then, at mid-career, a proportion of them are re-injected into business and civil society to join the executive staff of major firms, NGOs, etc. This movement ensures close inter-relations between State and business elites in France, which is a key factor in understanding our State *dirigisme* over economy and society (Kuisel 1984). However, *pantouflage* had its golden age in the 1980s, when a strong privatization policy was implemented. Since then, three new parameters have provoked a backlash. First, the liberalization/globalization of the French economy has strongly reduced the dependency of business on the State, making it less useful to hire expensive State officials whose social networks have become less crucial. Second, several *hauts fonctionnaires* who became CEOs of banks or companies proved to be terrible managers who led them close to bankruptcy. Last but not least, anti-corruption legislation was enforced in the 1990s that requires all civil servants aspiring a position in business to obtain the authorization from a 'Commission for Ethics' that controls possible conflicts of interests. As a result, *pantouflage* has not disappeared, but is less frequent and more individualized than in the past.

In conclusion, the most salient question French *hauts fonctionnaires* have to deal with in the nearest future seems to be this: will the French administrative elite, whose power and prestige as a status group has been correlative to the one of the State for decades and even centuries, be able to adapt enough to a changing world so as to reproduce its own privileges for a new generation?

Privileges of top elected politicians: a ticket for a life apart

In France, 500,000 citizens hold an electoral mandate – a result of the vast number of 36,000 municipalities, each having its own municipal council and mayor. These municipal officials receive small 'indemnities' while maintaining their principal occupation – they are not professionalized politicians, as are mayors of large cities. Even the 4,200 *conseillers généraux*, elected governing bodies of our 100 *départements* (provinces) are usually amateurs. The situation is different for the presidents (and some vice-presidents) of *conseils généraux* and regional councils (22 regions). These urban and regional higher officials have been given lots of powers and comfortable revenues since the decentralization process initiated in 1982. For consistency with the other chapters, these wealthy mayors and presidents will not be considered anymore, but the reader must bear in mind the French tradition of 'cumulating mandates,' two familiar archetypes being the *député-maire* (both MP elected in a given constituency and mayor of the main city within it) and the senator-president of a *Conseil général*. Such usual *cumul* of mandates means that national politicians are often locally elected politicians, and thus have several sources of revenue, within the limits of a so-called 'overall ceiling', defined as the amount of the basic indemnity of MPs $\times$ 1.5 = 8,100 €/month. The ceiling is often reached, seeing that second offices are held by 94 percent of MPs and 90 percent of presidents of regions and *conseils généraux*.

Members of parliament: the core of the 'political profession'

In France, becoming an MP is the major step to professionalizing into politics, and sitting in Parliament as long as possible is a main criterion for a reputed 'successful' political career. Being MP for decades is also the most efficient way for politicians to maintain their belonging to a 'golden' world offering a standard of living which they would be unlikely to obtain in any other occupation accessible to them.

The French National Assembly is more powerful than the Senate as an institution, but the mandate of senator is much more comfortable. Our 577 *députés* are elected by direct majority voting within constituencies every 5 years, and their mandates can be interrupted by a dissolution, whereas the 322 senators are indirect representatives, elected by local and regional politicians. That is the reason why the Senate is populated by old politicians who enjoy in Luxembourg Palace a quiet career end, the majority being former *députés*.

The 'parliamentary indemnity' of a *député* comprises:

- basic indemnity: defined as the mean between HE A1 and HE G of the *hors-échelle* scale, subject to social contributions and to the income tax;
- 3 percent residence indemnity;
- 25 percent indemnity *de fonction*, not subject to contributions nor to income tax.

The net parliamentary indemnity amounted to 5,177 €/month in 2008 (only 3,700 euros taxable).

In addition, each *député* receives an 'indemnity for mandate charges' of 6,223 €/month, freely usable without rendering accounts: since all major charges generated by the activity of MP are paid in addition, this envelope is an extra income used for personal cars, clothes, restaurant and cultural activities, presents, etc. Moreover, each *député* is entitled to 8,000 €/month to employ 1 to 5 contractual collaborators ('parliamentary assistants'). MPs are free to employ whom they want, where they want (in Paris, in the constituency). It often happens that a *député* employs his wife, or his other preferred sexual partner. Each *député* has a small two-room office, free phone-internet communications from the Assembly and from four other fixed lines wherever in France and two high-tech mobile phones, and free normal mail without quantitative restrictions. They can travel free in 1st class trains all over France and have a right to 40 free round-trip flights between Paris and the constituency. Last but not least, each *député* can benefit from a 10-year 76,000 euro loan with a minimal interest rate of 2 percent (less than inflation) to buy an apartment in Paris (new loan for each re-election).

For senators, rules and amounts are comparable. The indemnity is higher (lower contribution for pension): 5,850 €/month in 2008 (only 3,700 euros taxable). The envelope for mandate charges is the same, whereas the amount for 1 to 3 parliamentary assistants is smaller (6,750 euros). Elderly senators with a reduced activity often employ a youngster from their family (children, grandchildren, nephews, nieces).

Unlucky MPs who are defeated at elections are not abandoned: until 2007, they were entitled to receive for six extra months their net indemnity of 5,177 euros. Just before leaving power, President Chirac and his majority, in total silence from the opposition and the media, decided to add a 0 to the 6: exiting MPs, for the time they do not find new occupations (being a local politician is not considered an occupation) and up to the maximum limit of 60 months, receive 5,177 €/month. Moreover, former MPs enjoy comfortable pensions. The scant information available is the following:

- One single mandate gives a right to a small 1,500 €/month pension, provided the MP paid double contributions.
- The maximum amount of the full pension is 5,600 €/month and is reached after four mandates (20 years), consecutive or not.
- Pensions are paid from the age of 55 (a fraction can be paid from the age of 50).
- Widows of MPs get a 'reversion pension,' which is much higher than the half-pension allocated to civil servants' widows. Former MPs' orphans below the age of 24 (if students) also get a pension – a costly custom, since politicians often marry twice and have children late in life.

In conclusion, French MPs have a comfortable standard of living that is much higher than the rather modest official 'salary' of 5,100 to 5,800 €/month suggests. When taking into account all their privileges plus their frequent other mandates, the equivalent real income necessary for a senior executive working in a private company would probably go up to 18,000 euros, which is infrequent in France. Moreover, such salaries are impossible to reach while exerting the initial occupations of the vast majority of French MPs – half of them being civil servants, among them a lot of secondary school teachers, and very few being businessmen or lawyers. Thus, parliamentary politics remains undoubtedly a good solution for those individuals to enjoy a standard of living much higher than the one to which their own social/occupational background would have entitled them, had they not entered politics.

Ministers and Prime Ministers: a temporary vie de château

French ministers enjoy an all-expenditures-paid life within the most impressive 18th Century palaces of the Saint-Germain quarter of Paris, confiscated from Princes' families after the Revolution: *Hôtel de Matignon* for the Prime Minister, *Hôtel de Castries*, etc. But this golden life comes rather late, and does not usually last long. The constant right-left change-overs since 1981, and the habit taken by our long-lasting Presidents to change their Prime Ministers and renew their governments if they become unpopular (roughly every 3 years), generates rapid turn-over. As a consequence, a politician who is neither a key 'unavoidable' party leader nor a close friend of the President is lucky enough to be a minister for a 3-year period, which is the average of the recent decades. Even though President Sarkozy has appointed a few very young ministers, precise surveys show, on average, that ministers are around 49 years old when they are first appointed, and engaged in politics for two decades or so (Joly 2005).

What is their income during that exceptional period? Until 2002, French ministers used to be paid a main 'indemnity' equal to the basic salary of top civil servants of the highest grade of the *hors-échelle* scale, HE G, plus various adds-on; as a result, a minister used to earn a gross 7,800 €/month, and the lowest rank secretaries of state (junior ministers) 6,800 €/month. In addition, they could keep for themselves a part of the 'secret funds' envelope, thus raising their net real income to a total of 9,000 to 10,000 €/month. But, at the end of the Jospin Premiership, a scandal occurred when it was revealed that the unspent 'secret funds' were used by exiting Prime Ministers and ministers as 'black money' for financing political activities and highly controversial private expenditures. PM Jospin, hence, decided to get rid of the 'secret funds' envelopes to ministers. As a consequence, ministers suffered a downsizing of their real incomes: in 2002 a new law raised and reorganized ministers' revenues (see Table 6.4).

Moreover, all expenses relating to their official activities and everyday life are paid from the ministries' budget. As to their accommodation, a scandal occurred in 2005, followed by the dismissal of Minister Hervé Gaymard, who had chosen not to live in the ministerial official apartment within the Ministry but instead rent a 600 m² luxury duplex nearby Champs-Elysées, the rent of which amounted to 14,000 €/month, paid for by public budgets. French people discovered that quite often our ministers, claiming they dislike their official residence, generate extra expenditures by renting expensive all-furnished flats in upper-class quarters. A limitative regulation was thus issued: ministers can continue to benefit from this highly questionable system provided they restrict to an 80 m² flat + 20 m² for each child. However, this remains a very costly privilege, since French governments

Table 6.4 Revenue of French ministers (since 2002)

	Gross basic in demnity/month (€)	Allocation for special charges (no taxation) (€)	Annual gross income (only 60% subject to taxation) (€)
Prime Minister	20,206	6,037	314,916
Minister	13,471	6,037	234,000
Secretary of state	12,124	6,037	217,932

are numerous, the turn-over of ministers is frequent, and each new minister makes his/her own choices.

The Prime Minister and family have three residences with all necessary cooks, domestics, gardeners and guards: one large apartment within the *Hôtel de Matignon* (the PM offices), a beautiful mansion called *Pavillon de la Lanterne* within the vast park of Versailles castle, nearby Paris (which serves as the family house), and, farther in the countryside, the castle of *Champs-sur-Marne* (used for weekends).

All in all, French ministers, who spend nothing to enjoy such a life, can save no less than 400,000 € free of tax in a 3-year period as a minister: this is not a fortune, but well invested in real estate or bonds, it can generate substantial extra-revenues for the rest of their lives. Former Prime Ministers also save money on cars, since they get a chauffeured car for life.

After leaving government, former ministers retain their salary for six months, and usually return to their mandate as an MP (automatic reintegration, since 2008). They have no pension rights as former ministers. Their only non-tangible privilege is the mention on all documents, after their name, of their status as *ancien ministre*, plus a strong habit to be called *Monsieur le ministre* for life. Since they are around 53 years old (on average) when leaving office and have already had 'a life in politics,' they tend to remain professional politicians, very often cumulating an MP mandate and a Presidency of region and/or Mayor of a large city. For example, former PM Chaban-Delmas was the mayor of Bordeaux for 40 years and a long-lasting President of the National Assembly; former PM Barre was MP and mayor of Lyon; former PM Mauroy was the mayor of Lille; former PM Raffarin is a senator. A few others, having civil service backgrounds, are appointed to highest State dignities such as President of the Court of Auditors (Joxe, Seguin) or to the Constitutional Council (Veil, Debré). No more than a quarter of former ministers, usually those who were not professional politicians, manage to get top executive highly paid appointments within public agencies or companies. Very few, and only belonging to the right-wing, join private companies. It is noticeable that some CEOs of major firms who are picked up to become 'non-political' ministers for Economic Affairs fail to return to comparable n° 1 positions in business afterwards.

All in all, being an elected politician in France, provided one succeeds in following the cynical recommendation from President Mitterrand 'What is important in politics is to last long,' is a rational strategy for someone who wants to live beyond his/her means, or at least to live in a world of privileges that s/he could not have afforded on the basis of the income generated by his/her initial occupation.

The French President: a 'republican monarch'

Maurice Duverger usually qualified the Fifth Republic as a 'republican monar-chy.' Such qualification perfectly suits the financial rewards of the Presidency: it

---

The case of Jacques Chirac, '(P)resident of the Republic'

Mr. Chirac was born to a modest middle-class family. On his accession to the Presidency in 1995, after 30 years as an elected politician, his fortune amounted to 1.5 million euros, a figure which positions him among the first percentile of the wealthiest tax payers. Without going into detail, President Chirac owns a nice apartment in Paris (he never lived there, it is generating 30,000 €/per year revenue), a magnificent small 16th century castle with a vast park, nine hectares of wood in Corrèze countryside, plus a 570,000 € portfolio of shares and bonds. How did Jacques Chirac manage to accumulate such amounts?

- As regards incomes, the *cumul* of mandates is the answer: when he was not a minister or Prime Minister, Mr. Chirac was an MP, the Mayor of Paris, and *conseiller general.*
- As regards spending, the key enrichment factor is the all-expenses-paid system: since 1967, when he first became a minister, Jacques Chirac has always lived within public palaces, either as a minister, Prime Minister or Mayor of Paris (a 1,000 m² flat within the City Hall, where he lived with family without paying anything for it, neither for food nor beverages, for two decades). Since 1970, Mr. Chirac has not even had a car: he is always chauffeured in official cars.

As a result, Mr. Chirac was a wealthy man when entering the Elysée, and the accumulation process continued during his 12 years in office.

---

is republican since the President receives a rather modest personal salary (in comparison to some foreign heads of state, or CEOs of major companies). It is monarchical since the President enjoys the life of a king, and almost no-limit spending to ensure the grandeur of French State (which is legitimate) but also to satisfy his own caprices.

As for the official salary, French Presidents used to get 7,084 €/month (in 2007), which was in line with the former system for ministers but had not been upgraded since the 2002 reform, the reason being that French Presidents always had other revenues due to former activities. For President Chirac, the total amounted to:

Presidential basic net indemnity:	7,084 €
Pension as former MP:	5,300 €
Pension as former Mayor of Paris:	2,280 €
Pension as former *conseiller général*:	2,130 €
Pension as former member of the Court of Auditors:	2,896 €

(where he worked 5 years only, just after ENA)
Total: 19,690 €

The situation of President Sarkozy, who is much younger, was a self-employed lawyer, and had to finance his divorce, is rather different. Thus, he asked the Parliament to pass a new act that entitles him to get a net indemnity equivalent to the double of the highest salaries of the Civil Service: 19,331 €/month since 2008.

Since all the expenses of the President are paid from the Presidency budget, this reward, while subject to income tax, simply comes in addition to his fortune: when considering President Mitterrand stayed 14 years in office, and President Chirac 12 years, one can estimate that the two latest Presidents increased their fortune by 1.5 million euros at least during their mandates. President Sarkozy will do almost as good if he is re-elected for a second term.

As regards the monarchical style of living of French Presidents, some figures and examples: the Presidency each year receives a constantly increasing 112 million euro budget (2009), out of which 70 million goes towards the salaries of the 1,000 advisors (but bodyguards, Republican Horse Guards, numerous domestics, and chauffeurs are paid on other budgets). Out of this budget, which escapes any serious scrutiny, 1.6 million euros are devoted to the personal expenses of the President and his family (food and wines, shirts and ties, mobile phones). In addition, the first lady gets her clothes for free from grand couturiers. As for accommodation, the President can use up to seven different locations:

i The official apartments and the beautiful park of the Elysée Palace;
ii Next to the Palace, the more cosy, *Hostel de Marigny*;
iii A whole building on the banks of the river Seine, on Quay Branly, divided into vast apartments distributed to his family and friends (for 14 years, President Mitterrand hosted his mistress and illegitimate daughter, Mazarine Pingeot, here);
iv The large castle of Rambouillet (100 km from Paris), which is located in a wide forest where the 'presidential hunting,' a tradition dating back to king Louis XIV, occurs every autumn;
v The more family-style castle of Souzy-la-Briche (15 minutes from the Elysée by helicopter), bought under President Mitterrand who wanted a weekend resort;
vi A small 18th century *folie* in a wonderful park nearby Paris, *Pavillon de Marly*, where Giscard d'Estaing used to enjoy late after-theatre suppers with beautiful actresses;
vii The fortress of Bregançon, on the French Riviera, with the single private beach in France, ideal for sunny escapades.

The President – who has at his constant disposal a cortege of official cars, two large, specially-equipped airbus A 319 airplanes (modest equivalents of

Air Force 1), four small Falcon jets, and two high-tech helicopters always ready for take-off on Villacoublay military base – can travel freely in France and abroad, bringing with him a court of friends, servile advisors, efficient bodyguards, and domestics. For 'security reasons,' travel arrangements are kept secret when they are not official: President Mitterrand liked to travel incognito to Italy or Egypt with a legitimate 'false' passport … but on real public money. The monarchical culture of secrecy applies also to the sensitive matter of the President's health, within the Val-de-Grâce hospital, where Presidents go when they need surgery or treatments. Such secrecy made it possible for President Pompidou to die in office when the Nation did not know he was ill, and for President Mitterrand, who developed a fatal cancer one year after coming to power, to remain in office for 14 years, his doctors issuing annual medical bulletins stating he was in perfect condition. To sum up, a French President is treated as a king … and tends to behave like one.

What happens when the time has come to leave? The regime kindly looks after former Presidents – an easy task since there are very few: only Valéry Giscard d'Estaing has enjoyed a very long life as a retired President; as for Jacques Chirac it is too early to say. A former President receives, from the time he leaves office, an 'annual donation' equivalent to HE E: 5,007 € net/month. In addition, being a life member of the Constitutional Council, he receives the salary (HE F) of 5,193 € net/month. A former French President thus receives a comfortable 10,200 € net/month for life. In addition, a vast apartment in Paris is rented and equipped in order to be his offices, with two full-time secretaries and a team of chauffeurs-bodyguards all along with an official car at his constant disposal.

The only former President who has had a long after-mandate life is Valéry Giscard d'Estaing, who continued to be active in politics. Six years ago, his official incomes were:

Pension as former President:	4,884 €
Salary as Member of the Constitutional Council:	5,068 €
Pension as a former Finance Inspector General:	4,387 €
MP + President of Auvergne Region: ceiling of	7,754 €
'Indemnity for mandate charges' as MP:	5,553 €
Total:	27,646 €/month

Since President Giscard d'Estaing benefited from MP privileges, it is obvious that this patrician from a rich family has become richer since he left the Presidency. As for President Chirac, his income is lower since he is retired (17,000 €/month), but his new accommodation is strongly criticized: the family of his close friend, tycoon and former Lebanon Premier, Rafic Hariri, is 'temporarily hosting' him for free in a 7-million euro luxury 15-room apartment on the banks of the Seine, in front of the Louvre, completely furnished with antiques.

Conclusion

The study of RHPOs in politics and administration in France leads to one overall conclusion, which raises several issues. The main conclusion is self-evident: the French administrative and political elites have managed so far to organize for their own benefit a world apart, full of privileges, in which these associate-rivals comfortably live together without any serious feeling of culpability or corruption.

The issues and derived questions are the following: how and why does a country that had a Revolution two centuries ago remain such a 'paradise' for politico-administrative elites? Why do French voters/tax-payers criticize that situation in their ordinary discussions but remain collectively so docile and do not rebel politically? How and to what extent do the growing cross-border transfers of international models (going from NPM aspects about individualized HRM, performance-related pay, etc., to issues relating to transparency and ethics in public life) create conditions for major changes? In such an evolving environment, will French politico-administrative elites be clever enough to accept and organize themselves to adapt, modernize and limit their rewards and privileges so as to maintain the legitimacy of their dominant position?

References

Arthuis, J. (1998) *Dans les coulisses de Bercy. Le cinquième pouvoir*. Paris: Albin Michel.
Birnbaum, P. (1977) *Les sommets de l'Etat. Essai sur l'élite du pouvoir en France*. Paris: Le Seuil.
Bourdieu, P. (1989) *La noblesse d'Etat*. Paris, Ed. de Minuit.
Charle, C. (1987a) *Les élites de la République 1880–1900*. Paris: Fayard.
Charle, C. (1987b) Le pantouflage en France vers 1880–vers 1980. *Annales E.S.C.* 5: 1115–1137.
DGAFP (2008) *Rapport annuel sur l'état de la fonction publique 2007–8*. Paris, La Documentation française.
d'Iribarne, P. (1993) *La logique de l'honneur*. Paris: Le Seuil.
de Tocqueville A. (1856, new edn 1967) *L'Ancien Régime et la Révolution*. Paris: Gallimard.
Dreyfus, F. and J.-M. Eymeri(-Douzans) (Eds) (2006) *Science politique de l'administration. Une approche comparative*. Paris: Economica.
Eymeri(-Douzans), J.-M. (2001) *La fabrique des énarques*. Paris: Economica.
Eymeri(-Douzans), J.-M. (2005) La machine élitaire. Un regard européen sur le 'modèle' français de fabrication des hauts fonctionnaires. In H. Joly (Ed.) *Formation des élites en France et en Allemagne*. Paris: CIRAC.
Jardin, A. and A.-J. Tudesq (1973) *La France des notables*. Paris: Le Seuil.
Joly, H. (2005) Les élites politiques: regard croisé sur le cas français. In H. Joly (Ed.) *Formation des élites en France et en Allemagne*. Paris: CIRAC.
Kessler, M.-C. (1986) *Les grands corps de l'Etat*. Paris: Presses de la FNSP.
Kuisel, R. (1984) *Le capitalisme et l'Etat en France*. Paris: Gallimard.

Pinçon, M. and M. Pinçon-Charlot (2003) *Sociologie de la bourgeoisie*. Paris, La Découverte.

Silicani, J.-L. (2008) *Livre Blanc sur l'avenir de la fonction publique*. Paris: Ministère de la Fonction publique.

Suleiman, E. (1979) *Les élites en France. Grands corps et grandes écoles*. Paris: Le Seuil.

7 Rewards for high public office

The case of Italy

Elisabetta Gualmini

Paying the state's elites in Italy: a two-binaries wage system

In the summer of 2007 a bestseller titled '*La casta*' ('The caste system'), written by a well-known journalist of a prestigious national daily (*Il Corriere della Sera*), triggered a hot public debate. It presented a very disenchanted and skeptical picture of the waste and irrational expenditures related to politics: the privileges of MPs, the revenues in terms of houses, luxury goods, and offices, the multiplication of useless administrative committees at different territorial levels, highly-paid ministerial consultancies, and huge reimbursements to political parties.

The book is not a scientific text but it contains reliable data on rewards for MPs and members of regional and local governments that hit straight to the heart of the Italian citizens. Perhaps for the first time the issue of the 'costs of politics,' not without some exaggerations and misunderstandings, entered Italian media and newspapers forcefully.

It is in fact not particularly easy for common citizens to get access to information and statistics on the rewards for high public office. While the base salary of MPs is published on the related website, supplementary allowances and benefits are not. As for top public managers, the National Accounting Office (*Ragioneria generale dello stato*) provides online data from recent years but does not publish historical series. Finally for judges, ministers and prime ministers, one needs formal authorization in order to get information.

This chapter analyzes the salary dynamics of top public managers (in particular top bureaucrats in central administration) for the period 1992–2007. A comparison will be drawn with two other important political and administrative elites: judges and policy makers (MPs, Ministers, and Prime Ministers).

In Italy there is a different method of payment for these categories. Salaries for the majority of top civil servants (except for university teachers, senior members of the armed forces and the police, and magistrates) are subject to collective bargaining (introduced in 1993, drawing lessons from the private sector), while salaries of judges and politicians are regulated by law, which for MPs means 'self-regulation.'

However, notwithstanding structural differences, these two systems have gradually produced similar results in terms of salary levels. Magistrates and politicians have historically benefited from very high salary levels since the pressures to increase wages from the respective lobbies have been compelling and powerful. Top public managers also (especially in the state sector) enjoy high levels of pay, due to the upward effects from decentralized bargaining, exercised since 1993, which has allowed negotiating supplementary allowances. The contract system, which was introduced to freeze and control wage dynamics in the public sector in strict connection with inflation trends, has not had the expected results.

Senior public sector managers' salaries have obviously not risen at the same rate as those of magistrates or politicians due to the unrivalled self-regulatory power of the latter two categories, but they have certainly surpassed the salaries of managers whose wages are not subject to collective bargaining (cf. Figure 7.2).

The New Public Management (NPM) related idea of introducing the private-contract system into the public sector has thus produced a paradoxical effect. 'Pay for performance' schemes, deliberately aimed at bringing greater efficiency and rationality to the regulation of civil service's income policies, have enabled additional salary to be modeled flexibly, and have hence tended to lead to an increase in overall pay.

I hypothesize that this result is more the product of actors' strategies and goals, than of economic ideas and NPM rhetoric. The introduction of the 'contract system' has given trade unions a wider space to press for wage increases. Governments complied with that strategy in return for an extension of political appointments; and top civil servants could finally enjoy higher autonomy and better rewards through the system of variable allowances and incentives negotiated both at the decentralized level and within their individual contracts.

The salary system of top civil servants

Background

Italy is a unitary but highly decentralized political system, based since 1993 on a quasi-majority electoral system. Until the institutional turmoil of 1992–1993, the so-called 'Transition' from the First to the Second Republic, Italy was governed by highly unstable multi-party coalitions, characterized by the leading role of the Democrazia Cristiana, allied time and again with three or four different parties. The corruption scandals of the early nineties, which caused the turnover of almost the entire parliamentary class and the arrival of new political forces, like the Lega Nord party and Berlusconi's Forza Italia, produced a severe political crisis with direct impacts on the policy making process and the contents of public policy.

The 'technical governments' (Amato, Ciampi, and Dini) between 1992 and 1995, free as they were from party vetoes, were able to introduce structural reforms in several policy fields: health, labor market, state finance, pensions, and public administration. Due also to the exigency to reduce the public deficit for entering the European Monetary Union, the public sector underwent continuous screenings and revisions for downsizing, more efficiency and better service quality, as well as the introduction of managerial instruments and techniques

(Ferrera and Gualmini 2004). As for public administration, the original ministerial-bureaucratic model was literarily turned inside out in the attempt to correct – at least according to the reform texts – the pathologies of the past (see further).

The Italian bureaucracy has historically represented an emblematic example of the Weberian model (Freddi 1989, Mortara 1990). A very centralized state apparatus, protected and disciplined in all its branches by an excessive legislative production, went arm-in-arm with an administrative class almost impermeable by external challenges, with a hesitant attitude to innovation and change, low *esprit de corps* and a professional career mainly based on seniority and tenure. The 'classical' Italian bureaucrats – as they were depicted by the mainstream comparative literature (Aberbach, Putnam, and Rockman 1981) – perceived themselves as subordinated to politicians with whom, however, they did not refrain from creating exchange and sometimes clientelist ties (Cassese 1984).

The salary system was strictly regulated by law, until 1993. The organization of careers and wage policies was decided by the parliament or the government, and advancements from one level to another were granted by automatic seniority increments. Such a system encouraged immobility: Top executives were civil servants who had climbed all the rungs of the bureaucratic career ladder (which means that they were invariably rather old) and who could receive, once they had reached the eligible age, a pension related to the last 10 or 5 years' average earnings. Professional training was mainly based on job experience, an effective merit system was lacking and dismissals were basically non-existent. Trade unions protected the employees' social rights but did not take part in regulating the management of rewards.

This 'special status model' for the civil service could not hide from the profound transformations Italy faced in the early 1990s: European integration, market globalization and domestic political innovations put bureaucracy literary under siege. To this 'revolution' we now turn.

The 1990s and 2000s intense cycle of reforms: a new profile for Italian top bureaucrats?

The changes to public sector management made since the beginning of the 1990s were inspired by the New Public Management movement, which was already widespread internationally and on the political agendas of most European countries. The dominant idea, embraced enthusiastically both by center-left and center-right governments, was to adopt private sector management techniques to transform civil servants into true public managers (Hood 1991, 1999, Flynn and Strehl 1996, Lane 1997, Peters and Pierre 2001, Pollitt and Bouckaert 2004). Executive management, positioned at the very apex of the civil service apparatus, was to be the point of departure for this company-style revolution designed to penctrate every single branch of the state bureaucracy.

Even if change has been discontinuous and far less radical than was previously expected, several innovations took effect: (1) the introduction of the 'bargaining or contract system' for civil servants' and top public managers' wages (more than

3.5 million people; (2) the strengthening of top bureaucrats' responsibility for performance and the introduction of instruments for performance management and evaluation; (3) the review of the system of recruitment in favor of openness towards the outside world; and (4) the extension of political appointments ('spoils system') for top civil servants.

The first innovation is probably the most important. In 1993, legislative decree no. 29 introduced collective bargaining for negotiating civil servants' and 2nd grade executives' wages. In 1998 a further legislative decree (no. 80) completed the reform extending the contract system to 1st grade public managers as well (the so-called 'full privatization' of the civil service). The special public law regime was replaced by negotiations between trade unions and a newly-instituted agency representing public administration (ARAN – *Agenzia nazionale di rapp-resentanza delle pubbliche amministrazioni*). Bargaining takes place at two different levels: the national one, where general rules for career organization, economic treatment, social rights etc. are negotiated, and the decentralized one where training activities, 'pay for performance' incentives and allowances are decided (Bonaretti and Codara 2001, Bordogna 2002).

In the case of top management, national wage bargaining takes place on an 'area' basis (eight areas[1]), whereas for the rest of the personnel it takes place on a sector basis (*comparti*).

In addition to the national and decentralized agreements, an individual contract is provided for both first and second grade executives, where ad hoc conditions related to the office and financial incentives are further specified.

The reforms of 1993 and 1998, brought together in a single bill – no. 165/2001, constitute a genuine watershed; trade unions gained a relevant role in income policies' regulation for the large majority of public servants (except for the 'special' categories like judges, university professors, the armed forces, and the police).

The contract system was passed with a very explicit goal: to curb and rationalize upward income policies for the public sector and to link them to the expected inflation rate. But after a few bargaining sessions it became clear that the system was not able to pursue its original aims, mainly because of the upward effects of decentralized agreements on supplementary salary. This is why in January 2009 a new social agreement was signed by the IV Berlusconi government and national trade unions (with the exception of the more leftist trade union, CGIL): the linkage between salary and productivity was strengthened, the duration of contracts was unified both for the public and the private sector (three years), the role of centralized collective bargaining was weakened in favor of decentralized levels and the calculation of the inflation rate was linked to specific European standards fixed by an independent agency. It is still too early to say if this new agreement will produce results; the fact that it has not been signed by the biggest Italian union may hamper its implementation.

The second innovation, one of the greatest challenges over the past 15 years, is the introduction of the 'culture of control and evaluation' in the public sector, directly connected to public managers' responsibility. The clearer separation of competencies between the administrative and political spheres increased the autonomy of the executives in managing human, financial, and instrumental resources and their accountability for results. In 1993, specific evaluation units (*Nuclei di Valutazione*) were established within each administration and put in charge of evaluating the results achieved by individual managers, using standardized methods and parameters. In 1995 a system of performance management was formalized (*controllo di gestione*), which allowed public managers to control the ongoing performance of each administrative unit and the related process of goal attainment. In 1999, reform no. 286 revised the entire system of audits within the public sector, distinguishing among four categories, from legal auditing to evaluation procedures; from performance management to strategic control, the latter of which was meant as an overall control on the organization against its general mission. Finally, in March 2009, a delegation law formulated by the Ministry for the Public Administration Renato Brunetta further promoted the culture of evaluation and transparency focusing on external control instruments such as civil auditing and public reviews, and establishing a new national body for the evaluation of the entire public sector performance.

Another important reform targeted the system of recruitment to senior levels of civil service management. There are now two main channels of access to senior management posts: one, in which candidates have to sit a competitive exam organized by the individual administrations, is reserved for internal candidates with a degree and at least 5 years' seniority; the second, for graduates not currently employed in public administration, also involves a competitive exam, organized by the Higher School of Public Administration (*Scuola Superiore di Pubblica Amministrazione*). Selection is followed by a training period with a public administration body, after which trainees may be directly recruited to a managerial post (such candidates should account for at least 30 percent of all posts). As well as rejuvenating internal management, the reform has also raised the percentage of managers on temporary contracts for specific professional tasks (the percentage of such 'freelancers' among top-level management may vary from 5 percent to 10 percent of total staff, while in the case of 2nd-level management this percentage varies from 5 percent to 8 percent). This opens management positions to persons who do not necessarily come from the public sector, but who have the necessary skills and know-how to do a professional job within this sector for a given period before moving on.

The last innovation worth mentioning is the extension of political appointments among top civil servants (starting from 1998 for 1st grade public managers and from 2002 for 2nd grade executives). This system – which in the minds of decision makers was connected to both greater autonomy for public managers and the (expected) higher mobility – stipulates that political appointments for both 1st and 2nd grade managerial posts are to lapse 60 and 90 days, respectively, after a new government has been formed. The minimum duration of posts was first abolished and then reintroduced, in 2005, at 3 years, while the maximum term of office was reduced to 3 and 5 years, respectively. The main (and positive) goal of the reform was to strengthen the fiduciary relation between politicians and top bureaucrats in order to pursue greater effectiveness in terms of policy implementation. In practice, however, the new rules unquestionably produced greater politicization of public management and increased the overall precariousness of executive posts, even though the 'Americanization' of Italy's state bureaucracy has not been the case. The latest available figures reveal in fact a limited utilization of political appointments: as far as central ministries' management (Area I) is concerned, out of a total of 449 posts assigned, 23.2 percent of senior civil servants were not reconfirmed (Boscati *et al.* 2005). Furthermore, those who were not reconfirmed did not, in fact leave the civil service, but were given 'research' posts and were allowed to retain their job titles. In addition, a further impediment to the system has been introduced by a decision of the Constitutional Court (no. 161/2008) which declared some forms of 'automatic' turnover unconstitutional since they would contradict the constitutional rules about impartiality of public servants, thus limiting the use of political nominations to the very top of the administrative career.

In conclusion, policy change during the 1990s and 2000s has been intense, and for the first time has given the impression that administrative reform is able to act as a real 'constituent policy' (Lowi 1972, Capano 2000), in that new rules of the administrative game (involving actors, apparatuses, functions, and processes) were established and were discontinuous from the past. The policy design behind legislative texts was inspired by the doctrine of managerialism and meant to revise and weaken the dominant legal and bureaucratic administrative culture. The effective results, as we will argue later, are not fully congruent with expectations, or rather the final picture is a blurred one. Change has been pervasive especially in the field of internal public administration instruments and techniques, whereas such features as top management culture, performance and output control, and public services quality still need improving. Moreover, profound differences persist among areas of the country and different sectors of the public administration.

The development of rewards for HPOs: 1992–2007

We can now turn to the development of wages of top civil servants in comparison with other political and administrative elites, both in absolute and relative numbers (Tables 7.1 and 7.2).

The gross annual salary of Directors General in 2007, considered as the sum of base salary and supplementary allowances, appears to be higher than the one of MPs and Supreme Court Judges (at the apex of their careers): €173,400 against €140,448 for MPs and €150,683 for the Court of Cassation judges. Only the salaries of Ministers, the Prime Minister and the top categories of magistrates (President and 1st President of the Court of Cassation) are higher.

The comparison with the private sector is also interesting. 1st grade public managers earn much more than the average of their private sector's colleagues: in 2007, €173,400 against €114,712.[2] Even when we consider the economic sectors in which private managers' wages are higher, Credit and Insurance

Table 7.1 Annual salary of different types of HPO, 1992–2007 (in euros)

	1992	1995	1998	2001	2004	2007
Prime Minister	166,918	184,893	206,789	219,903	234,234	209,614
Cabinet Minister (also MPs)	142,784	160,128	177,700	189,174	204,184	186,558
Member of Parliament	94,514	110,604	119,712	127,716	144,084	140,448
1st grade Public Manager (Director General)	79,729	81,105	98,011	149,348	145,824	173,400
2nd grade Public Manager	59,344	49,643	65,317	63,088	65,744	80,517
1st President of the Supreme Court	122,094	132,900	151,011	166,347	187,666	208,499
President of the Supreme Court	113,605	123,660	140,985	154,781	174,617	194,002
Supreme Court Judge	88,238	96,048	109,274	120,220	135,627	150,683
Court of Appeal Judge	78,603	85,560	97,342	107,093	120,817	134,230
Tribunal Judge (3 years of seniority)	68,968	75,072	85,410	93,966	106,008	117,776
Private Sector's Executives*	62,400	71,929	79,040	94,653	104,325	114,712

Source: Conto Annuale – Ministry of Economics, various years.
Note: *INPS – National Institute for Social Security.

(€138,853 in 2007), Commerce (€135,148), and Extractive Industry (€121,589), the wage gap is still considerable.

For 2nd grade civil servants, amounting to 2,876 in 2007 against 361 Directors General in the ministries' sector,[3] rewards are quite different. Not only is their salary less than half of their superiors; their supplementary allowances, including 'pay for performance' schemes, are much more limited compared to chief executives. The result is that even tribunal judges at the beginning of their career (i.e. with only 3 years of seniority) earn more than 2nd grade state's public managers (€117,776 against €80,517). Private managers' salaries too significantly exceed those of 2nd grade public executives, which means that the majority of public managers earn much less than their private colleagues while the contrary is true for the very apex of the bureaucratic career.

What immediately stands out from Table 7.1 is the extraordinary high level of pay for judges, who represent in Italy a category *per se* in the civil service, excluded from the contract system. This corresponds to the tradition of safeguarding the independence of magistrates and endowing them with special privileges.

Table 7.2 Relative increases and wage differentials of the various categories, 1992–2007

	1992	*1995*	*1998*	*2001*	*2004*	*2007*
Prime Minister	2,81	3,72	3,17	3,49	3,56	2,60
Cabinet Minister (also MPs)	2,41	3,23	2,72	3,00	3,11	2,32
Member of Parliament	1,59	2,23	1,83	2,02	2,19	1,74
1st grade Public Manager (Director General)	1,34	1,63	1,50	2,37	2,22	2,15
2nd grade Public Manager	**1,00**	**1,00**	**1,00**	**1,00**	**1,00**	**1,00**
1st President of the Supreme Court	2,06	2,68	2,31	2,64	2,85	2,59
President of the Supreme Court	1,91	2,49	2,16	2,45	2,66	2,41
Supreme Court Judge	1,49	1,93	1,67	1,91	2,06	1,87
Court of Appeal Judge	1,32	1,72	1,49	1,70	1,84	1,67
Tribunal Judge (3 years of seniority)	1,16	1,51	1,31	1,49	1,61	1,46
Private Sector's Executives*	1,05	1,45	1,21	1,50	1,59	1,42

Source: Conto Annuale – Ministry of Economics, various years.
Note: *INPS – National Institute for Social Security.

Political analyses of the Italian judicial order have highlighted the unique characteristics and operation of this 'lobby' (Guarnieri 1992, Guarnieri and Pederzoli 2002, Zannotti 1989, 1995). Magistrates have traditionally constituted a successful institutional category that remains independent of legislative and executive power, always claiming guaranteed independence, which in turn has direct repercussions on wage policy.

The most distinctive indication of this independence was given by the inclusion in the 1948 Constitution of the Higher Council of the Judiciary (HCJ). This ad hoc body, in operation since the 1950s, exercises exclusive power over appointments, transfers, promotion and disciplinary measures. Over time, judges have not only managed to free themselves from the strictures of the civil service career, but as a result of their appeals and rulings, they have also managed to obtain a series of automatic pay increases that Parliament has failed to stop. In other words, 'magistrates have made their own salaries.' Considering that the judiciary features so-called 'open roles' (unlike the 'closed' roles in the rest of the civil service), whereby promotions are given regardless of the number of posts available, the impact of such measures is clear to see.

In the 1980s, when confronting runaway inflation caused by the oil crisis, neither the Parliament nor Government were much inclined to grant pay rises. Therefore, the magistrates decided to use their own institutional channels to better themselves. That is, they resorted to court rulings to get the increases they were asking for. Given that court rulings cannot create new laws but only confirm or implement existing ones, the answer was to extend pay increases from one category to another. In 1998, following the above-mentioned 'privatization' of senior civil servants, Law no. 488 provided for a mechanism whereby magistrates' pay increases were calculated on the *overall* pay of senior civil servants, including supplementary pay, which is the part of overall salary that varies the most. The introduction of this law came after pressure from the National Association of Magistrates, and it meant that magistrates had managed to exploit the more positive effects of civil service reform, despite not being directly involved therein, without damaging their independence.

As for policy makers, ministers who are also MPs cumulate two salaries; this is why they earn more than their parliamentary colleagues (€186,558 vs. €140,448). Prime Ministers add 50 percent more to the salary of a cabinet minister.

As for judges, the most significant part of the salary of politicians is established by law. For MPs, the law is also published on the Chamber of Deputies and the Senate's respective websites, thus reflecting a certain degree of transparency. Nevertheless, on top of basic pay (the so-called 'monthly allowance') there are various additions, such as a *per diem* allowance, lump-sum expenses, and health and insurance allowances, that inflate the basic salary and about which there is far less transparency (partly due to the complex calculations). For senators and MPs, a law introduced in 1948 established a salary of 65,000 lire plus a daily allowance of 5,000 lire for each day of presence (this allowance was reduced to 3,000 for politicians residing in Rome). However, since pay increases could be decided by the Executive Councils, the system was changed (Salvi and Villone 2005). Hence, Law no. 1261 of 1965 (still in force) linked MPs' basic pay to the maximum overall gross pay of those magistrates acting as presiding judges at the Court of Cassation. In 1993 this ratio was reduced to 96 percent of the magistrates' gross pay and, more recently, as is visible in Table 7.1, the 2006 Finance Bill reduced parliamentary allowances by a further 10 percent.

The monthly basic pay of MPs in 2008 is €11,704, on top of which they are paid a monthly allowance of around €4,000. If we multiply these figures by 630 + 321 (the number of MPs and senators, respectively) we get a total figure of €14,934,504 a year. MPs also receive numerous expense allowances for paying their assistants, to support electoral duties in their constituencies, or to cover such expenses as national and international travel and telephone (up to a maximum of €4,150 per annum for senators, and €3,098.74 for MPs). Furthermore, MPs may use the Italian railways, motorways, ferries or airlines free of charge. On top of these benefits, which are very difficult to monitor and which are utilized by the political parties or by single individuals, politicians are also eligible for a series of health, insurance and pension benefits. As for pensions, both MPs and senators receive a 'life annuity' from the age of 65 (or 60 if they have served during more than one legislature) for which they have paid in contributions; this annuity varies from 25 percent to 80 percent of gross pay (80 percent if they have served during six legislatures). As Salvi and Villone (2005: 37) point out, an MP who has served during three legislatures receives a pension equivalent to 55 percent of his/her allowance. That is, approximately, €6,865 a month, or €1,650,000 over 20 years, based on a total of €240,606 in contributions by the MP. Other citizens do not enjoy similar privileges. Indeed, if private citizens were to pay in the same amount as the MP over 15 years, their pension would be seven times smaller than that of an MP!

In Table 7.2 we can track increases in rewards. The data have been standardized with reference to the lowest level of salary (the one of 2nd grade public executives) in order to make intra-annual comparisons.[4] It is thus possible to observe how wage differentials among the categories have varied during the period considered, within a series of comparable figures (without a deflator's support).

Starting from top bureaucrats, we can see that in 1992 the wage gap between 1st grade and 2nd grade executives amounted to 0.34, whilst 15 years later, in 2007 it turned to 1.15 (having more than tripled!). This confirms that, right from the introduction of the contract system in 1993, decentralized bargaining has accelerated wage increases during all the selected years.

The wage gap for politicians has been more volatile in the course of the years. The wage differential between 2nd grade public managers and MPs was 0.59 in 1992 and 1.23 in 1995. It went down to 0.83 in 1998, increased again in 2001 and 2004 (1.02 and 1.19), and then decreased in 2007 (0.74, coming back to the level of 1998 more or less). The same oscillating dynamic can be noticed for Ministers (and consequently for Prime Ministers), whereby the ups and downs of salary levels are observed in the same years as for MPs and where the 2007 wage gap is even lower than the one of 1992. Unlike 1st grade public managers, politicians have thus reduced their wage differentials with respect to 2nd grade public managers in the course of the time.

As for judges as a whole, a still different trend has to be highlighted. Wage differentials have widened from 1992 to 2007 for all the career levels, but there has been a sensible slowdown in 1998.

Finally, the wage gap between the private and the public sector, considering 2nd grade public managers, favours private CEOs. In 1992, the differential was very low (0.05); in 1995 it rose to 0.45, in 2004 to 0.59 and in 2007 it slightly diminished (0.42), remaining, however, still significant.

To sum up, we can thus argue that, with the exception of the very top categories of the judiciary (1st President and President of the Supreme Court) and of the executive political class (Ministers and Prime Minister) – a very small group of people – the wage differential between the two levels of top bureaucrats is the highest.

To this purpose, it is important to look at Figure 7.1 where the executives' wages are broken down between base and supplementary allowances.

What is really striking is the soaring growth of supplementary wages of Directors-General, which surpasses the base salary. It amounted to 16,055 euros in 1992 and reached 109,891 euros 15 years later, while the base salary rose from €63,674 to €63,161 in the same period. Supplementary allowances are mainly rank and status allowance (*indennità di posizione*) and result and performance allowance (*indennità di risultato*). Figure 7.1 shows that decentralized bargaining has played a very important role in the negotiation of central ministries' top civil

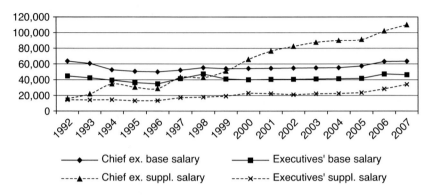

Figure 7.1 1st grade and 2nd grade public managers' salary growth, in the central ministries sector: base and supplementary salary, 1992–2000.
Source: Ministry for the Economy, Conto Annuale, various years.

servants' earnings and, more exactly, is at the basis of the displayed upward
dynamic. This effect is much less evident for 2nd grade public managers, whose
supplementary wage rose from 14,549 in 1992 to 28,406 in 2007, remaining
below the basic salary.

It should be added though, that the high level of supplementary salaries (and
thus of the whole salary) of ministries' top civil servants is not the rule in other
sectors of the public administration. Figure 7.2 shows the level of overall annual
wages for the different categories of public managers, with reference to the year
2007.

The comparison with the school sector is particularly striking, where the one
top managerial level is located much below colleagues in the ministries. In fact,
school managers earnt, in 2007, one-third (€59,642 per year) of what ministerial
managers earnt (€173,400 per year) Also in the healthcare and the university
sectors (referring to the bureaucratic career) and in regional and local governments pay levels are considerably lower.

It is now time to draw some general conclusions on the dynamics observed and
to look for plausible explanations.

Conclusion: HPO rewards, the 'narrative' of New Public Management and the strategies of actors

In general, our analysis indicates a general increase in wages, above the level of
inflation for 1992–2007 brought about by the 'contract system' (3 percent on
average) and more than in the private sector (cf. Table 7.2.). This is particularly
true for the state's sector (ministries and central agencies), for two reasons: trade
unions have been able to play a more cohesive and stronger role and supplementary allowances have been historically more consistent here than in other sectors
where the contract system was introduced.

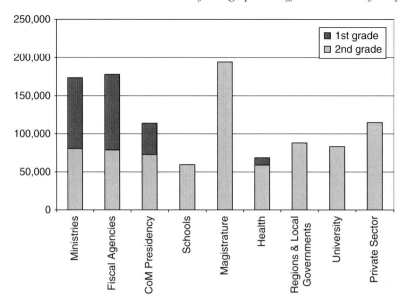

Figure 7.2 1st grade and 2nd grade (where existent) public managers' salary in different public sectors, 2007.
Source: Ministry of the Economy, Conto Annuale, 2008.

The intense cycle of administrative reforms of the 1990s and 2000s has brought about a more flexible method of bargaining rewards which produced more differentiated levels of pay.

The adoption of collective bargaining following the 1993 reforms, designed to tie pay increases to the programmed inflation rate, and to control pay rises, led to the kind of wage regulation that characterizes the private sector. In fact, there has been an overall stabilization of basic salaries, accompanied by an increase in additional salary (supplementary allowances and benefits). But this latter (variable) part of pay, negotiated at the decentralized level, has grown faster than expected and beyond the very logic of control and efficiency which was at the basis of its foundation.

How should these results be interpreted?

In the first place, we think that the NPM narrative is not the main explanatory factor. Economic ideas have not been able to pervade the public sector in a systematic and profound way, but only very selectively. When some suggestions like contracting out, outsourcing, and new HR management styles have been effectively introduced in the public sector; other instruments like control and evaluation, and personnel cost freezing have not worked very well. The NPM rhetoric has functioned as an intervening variable, which has influenced the 'periphery' of the administrative culture without really affecting its 'core.'

Italy's administrative reform can thus be identified as a 'pragmatic and contingent process of innovation' (Wright 1994), which answered to the domestic pressures to revise the public sector – together with other important policy fields – during the period of the institutional transition and technical governments, and to the external constraints connected to the entry into the EMU (Capano 2000, Gualmini 2003, Capano and Vassallo 2003, Capano and Gualmini 2006, Gualmini 2006).

As for wage regulation, this is only one part of the public sector's modernization strategies that has prevailed over the macro-rationale of reform. The remarkable increase of supplementary salaries (and thus of salaries as a whole in the last 15 years) seems the rational 'compromise' or 'arrangement' among the goals and preferences of three sets of distinct collective actors: trade unions, politicians, and top bureaucrats actors' goals.

Trade unions, mainly referring to the ones representing top civil servants (DIRSTAT – *Sindacato Nazionale dei Funzionari Direttivi, Dirigenti e delle Alte Professionalità della Pubblica Amministrazione*), supported the introduction of the contract system because of the extension of the bargaining role they had envisaged. They followed a specific 'membership logic' seeing in the reform the opportunity to protect the interests and to improve the benefits of their members. Even though the government's annual budget bill establishes rigid financial limits for national collective bargaining, in decentralized negotiations unions are much freer from legal constraints and can play the bargaining game, pushing up their claims for earning increases.

As for politicians, a more complex strategy has to be revealed. The 1992–1993 governments had very specific goals to pursue, in order not to be left out from the European Monetary Union (thus 'losing face' in front of the public opinion). No alternatives were available except for taking matters in their hands and resolutely restructuring the public sector. The contract system was one of the instruments of this process of 'forced' reorganization and modernization. It was perceived as both participatory and flexible, and as a way to control upward wages. More than a political logic, an efficiency and instrumental logic was the one surrounding the governments' action since they were playing for high stakes both in the international arena and in the domestic one.

Finally top bureaucrats, who in the Italian context had historically been marked by a weak intra-professional organizational culture and a passive attitude (Cassese 1999), saw in the new tools brought about by the reform (individual contracts and 'pay for performance' schemes) an opportunity to 'raise up their head,' to expand their role and resources and to enjoy more financial benefits. Counting on specific 'intangible assets' like expertise and high technical knowledge, they could play a part in the game negotiating on their own their working conditions within individual contracts and thus extending their power (Quaglia 2005). In exchange for that, in a tit-for-tat logic, they had to accept a higher degree of instability and precariousness compared to the past, which however in a 'protected' environment such as the one of the Italian public administration seemed in any case not too unfavorable to them.

In conclusion, the adoption of collective bargaining for the regulation of senior civil servants' economic and working conditions (the so-called 'privatization' of the public sector), resulted in higher rewards for top public managers, and was more the result of actors' strategic interests and goals than of the deliberate adoption of international management paradigms.

Notes

1 The 'areas' are as follows: Area I – Enterprises and Ministries; Area II – Regional and Local Administrations; Areas III & IV – Healthcare; Area V – Schools; Area VI – Tax Authorities and non-financial public bodies; Area VII – Research & the Universities; Area VIII – the Premiership. Cf. Carinci and Mainardi (2005).
2 This figure refers to the average value for all the categories of the private sector (Agriculture, Industry, Services, etc.), corresponding to 133,059 private managers in 2007. Data on private managers have been made available by INPS, the National Institute for Social Security.
3 In the whole public sector Directors General amount to 5,000 whilst 2nd grade executives amount to 40,000 (Conto Annuale – Ministero del Tesoro, 2008).
4 I thank Dr. Nereo Zamaro of the Italian National Institute of Statistics (ISTAT) for this methodological suggestion.

References

Aberbach, J.D., R.D. Putnam and B.A. Rockman (1981) *Bureaucrats and Politicians in Western Democracies*. Cambridge, MA: Harvard University Press.

Bonaretti, M. and L. Codara (2001) *Ripensare il lavoro pubblico*. Soveria Mannelli: Rubettino.

Bordogna, L. (Ed.) (2002) *Contrattazione integrativa e gestione del personale nelle pubbliche amministrazioni. Un'indagine sull'esperienza del quadriennio 1998–2001*. Milan: F. Angeli.

Boscati, A. *et al.* (2005) Dirigenza Area I. In F. Carinci and S. Mainardi (Eds) *La dirigenza nelle pubbliche amministrazioni*. Milano: Giuffré, Tomo I, pp. 5–304.

Capano, G. (2000) Le politiche amministrative: dall'improbabile riforma alla riforma permanente? In G. Di Palma, S. Fabbrini and G. Freddi (Eds) *Condannata al successo? L'Italia nell'Europa integrate*. Bologna: Il Mulino, pp. 153–198.

Capano, G. (2003) Administrative traditions and policy change: when policy paradigms matter. The case of Italian administrative reforms during the 1990s. *Public Administration*, 4: pp. 781–801.

Capano, G. and S. Vassallo (Eds) (2003) *La dirigenza pubblica: il mercato e le competenze dei ruoli manageriali*. Soneria Mannelli: Rubbettino.

Capano, G. and E. Gualmini (Eds) (2006) *La pubblica amministrazione in Italia*. Bologna: Il Mulino.

Carinci, F. and S. Mainardi (2005) *La dirigenza nelle pubbliche amministrazioni*. Milano: Giuffré, Tomo I.

Cassese, S. (1984) *Il sistema amministrativo italiano*. Bologna: Il Mulino.

Cassese, S. (1999) Italy's Senior Civil Service: an ossified world. In E.C. Page and V. Wright (Eds), *Bureaucratic Elites in Western European States*. Oxford: Oxford University Press, pp. 55–64.

Ferrera, M. and E. Gualmini (2004) *Rescued by Europe? Social and labour market reforms in Italy from Maastricht to Berlusconi*. Amsterdam: Amsterdam University Press.

Flynn, N. and F. Strehl (Eds) (1996) *Public Sector Management in Europe*, Harvester Wheatsheaf: Prentice Hall.

Freddi, G. (1989) Burocrazia, democrazia e governabilità. In G. Freddi (Ed.), *Scienza dell'amministrazione e politiche pubbliche*. Rome: NIS.

Gualmini, E. (2003) *L'amministrazione nelle democrazie contemporanee*. Roma-Bari: Laterza.

Gualmini, E. (2006) I ministeri. In G. Capano and E. Gualmini (Eds) *La pubblica amministrazione in Italia*. Bologna: Il Mulino, pp. 57–86.

Guarnieri, C. (1992) *Magistratura e politica in Italia*. Bologna: Il Mulino.

Guarnieri, C. and P. Pederzoli (2002) *La magistratura nelle democrazie contemporanee*. Roma-Bari: Laterza.

Hood, C. (1991) A public management for all seasons? *Public Administration*, **69**(1): 3–19.

Hood, C. (1999) *The Art of the State*. Oxford: Oxford University Press.

Lane, J. E. (Ed.) (1997) *Public Sector Reform. Rationale, Trends and Problems*. London: Sage.

Lowi, T. (1972) Four systems of policy, politics and choice. *Public Administration Review*, **4**: 298–310.

Mortara, V. (1990) *Introduzione alla pubblica amministrazione italiana*. Milano: F. Angeli.

Peters, B. G. and Pierre J. (2001) *Politicians, Bureaucrats and Administrative Reform*. London: Routledge.

Pollitt, C. and G. Bouckaert (2004) *Public Management Reform. A Comparative Analysis*. Oxford: Oxford University Press.

Quaglia, L. (2005) Civil servants, economic ideas, and economic policies: lessons from Italy. *Governance*, **4**: 545–566.

Salvi, C. and M. Villone (2005) *Il costo della democrazia*. Milan: Mondadori: 26.

Stella, G.A. (2007) *La Casta*. Milano: Rizzoli.

Wright, V. (1994) Reshaping the state: the implications for public administration. *West European Politics*, **3**: pp. 102–137.

Zannotti, F. (1989) *La magistratura, un gruppo di pressione istituzionale. L'autodeterminazione delle retribuzioni*. Padua: Cedam.

Zannotti, F. (1995) The judicialization of judicial salary policy in Italy and the United States. In C. Neal Tate and T. Vallinder (Eds), *The Global Expansion of Judicial Power*. New York: New York University Press, pp. 181–203.

8 Rewards for high public offices in Spain (1990–2009)

Incremental changes following the pattern of the civil service

Salvador Parrado

Introduction

In 2006 the Spanish Congress made the historical decision to publish the salaries of the members of the national parliament (MPs) for the first time in the 30 years of democracy. At least two possible interpretations could explain the introduction of some transparency at this late stage. On the one hand, this transparency measure launched by the president of the Congress fitted the overall strategy of good governance practices launched in 2005 by the Prime Minister, Rodríguez Zapatero, in order to address the declining levels of citizens' trust in public authorities. On the other hand, publishing MPs' salaries, considered to be the lowest among parliamentarians of the former EU-15 country members, could pave the way for a substantial reform of the reward system. The last two presidents of the Lower House had tried to raise salaries after changing political color in parliament. This resembles the economics of politics analysis in which the political business cycle helps to explain reward system changes. However, public opinion has frustrated any attempt to raise parliamentarians' salaries. Instead, incremental pay increases of MPs have been linked to the payment system of civil servants since the early democratic times, and several allowances have allowed for more substantial increases.

The blog of Rafael Estrella, Spanish Ambassador in Argentina and former MP from the socialist party (1979–2006) who decided to publish his salary and also his assets before the measure was decided, illustrates the controversy. He had received in December 2005 2,820 euros as a basic salary (taxed at 27 percent, i.e. €716.4), 1,645.05 euros (tax-free) per diem costs to compensate for monthly living expenses when in office, as his official residence was outside Madrid, in Granada. Furthermore, as speaker of a commission he obtained 1048.73 euros (also taxed at 27 percent = €283.2) monthly. In his blog, Mr. Estrella further claims that 1,645.05 euros do not cover the living costs in Madrid, and that after 25 years in politics he has not become wealthier, according to his property tax declaration. The real purchasing power of MPs would have decreased by 30 percent in the last 10 years and the salary of Spanish parliamentarians would rank the lowest in the former EU-15.

While this account is relevant by itself, the 151 reactions that his disclosure in the blog produced within the first six months are also illustrative. Most readers congratulated the parliamentarian for his transparency. Yet, many criticized his opinion on the comparatively low salary level. Critics came from different milieus and sectors: those receiving the compulsory minimum inter-professional salary; civil servants working in different levels of central administration and even the head of an American corporation sales department based in Madrid, who also disclosed his salary. Only one message out of 151 genuinely expressed surprise and disagreement with such a low salary. Although these opinions are not representative, in absence of systematic surveys, they illustrate the feelings towards rewarding politicians.

Public outcries over salary increases of politicians take place in a system in which trust in the political class and in specific institutions is not very high. Recent official surveys (2007 and 2006) from the CIS (Centre for Sociological Research) (barometer numbers 2633, 2672, and 2700) show that around 70 percent of interviewees believe that politicians do not worry much about people's problems and around 68 percent consider that those in power are always looking after their personal interests. Trends in public confidence in different institutions are also in decline in Spain according to the World Values Survey in 1981, 1990, 1995, and 2000. More than half of interviewees did not trust Parliament (with peaks of 69 and 60.1 percent of distrust in 1990 and 1995, respectively); 55 percent did not trust the civil service and the distrust in political parties grew from 32.8 percent in 1990 to 69.9 percent in 2000.

Those opinions hinder discussions about open salary increases of politicians and civil servants. Therefore, any reward negotiation should be expected to be secret. Three features will be further analyzed in this chapter. First, rewards have increased incrementally in relation to the Consumer Price Index. It is less visible that the current salary structure for high offices in the executive, the legislative and the judiciary has been shaped by that of civil servants, which also lacks transparency, probably as a consequence of the transition to democracy with a dominant role played by top civil servants. Institutional path dependence has played a role in how the salary has evolved. Second, parts of the reward system lack transparency, even when published in the official Gazette. Many decisions to increase transparency in the reward structure of public authorities are more related with the control of the Treasury on public expenditure than with the decision to enhance the transparency of rewards. Third, rewards for high public office (RHPOs) are lower than in most other European countries of a similar economic level. It is less widely known that disparities among different Spanish HPOs contradict principles of hierarchy (top political appointees having higher salaries than cabinet ministers and the Prime Minister himself) or shows sharp differences between powers as the president of the Congress receives almost double the salary of the Prime Minister.

This chapter examines the rewards system of the top offices in the executive, the judiciary and the legislative at the national level. Cultural theory, economic-of-politics and institutionalism will be used to understand the development of rewards.

Rewards for the executive and the judiciary

Salary levels and pay differentials

The civil service reward structure has served as a loose model, from which different non-transparent strategies in each group have departed. MPs, being unable to reform the system, have increased the share of rewards that are tax-free or less open to scrutiny. Top civil servants and political appointees have achieved a rise in the variable parts of the salary either through individual post allowances or through collective performance bonuses within ministries. For judges, a more managerial system with bonuses tied to the achievement of objectives has been in operation since 2003 and includes higher basic salaries than those of civil servants. Finally, the Prime Minister (PM), Deputy Prime Ministers (DPM) and cabinet ministers (CM) have witnessed increases at a faster pace than the rest of the executive, and transparency of their rewards has been enhanced. Their salaries have risen by 3 percent while the salary increase of civil servants and political appointees has been capped at 2 percent, as the expected or (wished by the government) annual inflation rate. This differential has only begun to diminish the gap between secretaries of States and the members of the government. At the same time, however, political appointees have been able to hiddenly bargain post allowances with which they enjoyed a 3 percent increase, while increases for the rest of the civil servants are capped at 2 percent.

Within the executive, there are four distinct groups of high public offices with some blurred borders and differences in expected salaries. Political executives are the government members like the PM, DPMs, and cabinet ministers. Political appointees fall into two groups. One group consists of policy advisors placed in *cabinets ministerieles*, not discussed in the chapter, and the second group comprises the three levels below cabinet minister: Secretary of State (SSt), Under-Secretary (U-S) and the equivalent Secretary General (SG) and Director General (DG). Almost all appointees are replaced after a change of government, although this is not compulsory. Finally, top civil servants are those placed in levels 28, 29, and 30. The borders are blurred because level 30 civil servants, under-secretaries and directors general are appointed outside the merit system. For these groups, different reward systems are expected because of their distinct potential conflicts of interest during and after office, and competitiveness patterns with private sector salaries.

Table 8.1 exhibits pay differentials for different HPOs in 2008. There is not an evident link among RHPOs of different groups of officials or between RHPOs and the average wage or the minimum inter-professional salary. As was culturally expected, the salaries of the Supreme Court representatives are higher than that of the PM. The relevance of a legalistic culture has fostered the increase of salaries of magistrates above executive salary levels. However, it is more difficult to understand that the President of the Lower House (PC) earns almost twice the amount of the PM or three times the salary of an ordinary MP. Even in the ministerial hierarchy some secretaries of State have higher salaries than cabinet

Table 8.1 Salaries of HPOs (in euros)

	2008	Pay differentials among top levels of each sector (PM =100)
Political executive		
Prime Minister (PM)	91,982.00	100.00
Deputy PM	86,454.00	93.61
Cabinet Minister	81,155.00	86.66
Political appointees		
Secretary of State (SSt)	97,524.4	105.68
Under-Secretary (U-S)	86,313.1	93.43
Director general (DG)	74,475.9	76.49
Career civil servants (top levels)		
Level 30 – (L-30)	68,050.0	64.83
Level 29 – (L-29)	63,848.0	55.94
Level 28 – (L-28)	59,712.9	45.96
Judiciary		
Supreme Court President (SCP)	146,342.5	137.15
Supreme Court Magistrate (SCM)	117,497.6	121.72
Legislative		
President of Chamber (PC)	188,172.0	151.12
MP	68,706.6	66.12
Private sector (data for 2006)		
CEO	178,572.2	151.0
Highest (Commercial Top Executive)	141,329.9	138.1
Lowest (Quality Top Executive)	81,264.7	92.3

Sources: For executive, annual budgetary laws 1990–2008; instructions from Ministry of Treasury 1990–2008; for Parliament, Congreso de los Diputados (2008); for private sector Watson and Wyatt Data Services (surveys of 2002–2005). (1) Seniority: 15 years of service have been considered for each post inholder, except for cabinet ministers and prime ministers. Political appointees receive seniority if they have civil service status, which applies to around 80 percent of post inholders. (2) For post allowance: highest values have been considered. (3) For PRP: average was given for 2005 by the Ministry of Treasury. Other years have been worked out considering the percentage of public employees' increase in salaries of 1 percent.

ministers or the PM himself, which cannot be explained by individualized contracts typical of more market-based administrations.

Rewards for top civil servants

The reward system was devised in 1984 and some of its principles were extended to political appointees and the Congress. Civil servants' salaries are characterized by the role played by trade unions and the link between salary increases and economic policies.

Salaries are unilaterally determined by the state through legislation, while adjustments are negotiated by public employees' unions and the Ministry of Public Administration. Pay increases are mechanistic and adjusted by the forecast annual rate of inflation. Civil servants, whose pay is negotiated centrally, and contractual staff, whose salary is negotiated at the levels of individual ministries, benefit from trade union negotiations. Top civil servants, with low trade union membership, also benefit from negotiations, but their salary has been eroded over time, as they do not think trade unions voice their specific concerns (Ortega 1992).

The Ministry of Treasury has always favored the connection between collective agreements and the general economic policy. This connection was applied, for instance, before the convergence with the euro-area by cutting off the link between public servant salaries to the cost of living and by even freezing pay increases (see Figure 8.1). In years of high economic growth, pay increases still stick at a distance (average of 1.14 percent below) to the cost-of-living index. At the beginning of the financial and economic crisis, salary increases are still pegged to the forecast annual rate of inflation. During the bonanza years, improvements were applied for all public employees in contribution to pension schemes, and a higher extra month's salary that was paid twice a year.

Salaries of top civil servants and political appointees have eroded in real terms. Public servants have lost an annual average of 1.14 percent of purchasing power since 1990 while top private managers (CEO and department executives) have gained 1.3 percent since 1998. This loss has induced top civil servants to develop at least two rather opaque alternative reward strategies. These strategies are not individualistic, as a more managerial culture would suggest. In terms of cultural theory, the strategies are rather hierarchist.

On the one hand, civil servants have upgraded specific positions with better post allowance entitlements and have gained more privileged access to perform-ance-related rewards. On the other hand, the agencification of some organizations (e.g. the Tax Agency created in the early 1990s) and recent grants of autonomy since 2007 have fostered some secrecy and salary increases. Parrado and Ruiz (1997) argued that the autonomization fostered salary increases in the Tax Agency, while salary levels in other semi-autonomous bodies like Social Security remained the same. A similar trend would be expected for the newly created agencies, although their salary position depends on their particular negotiations with the ministry of Economy and the Treasury.

As in other countries (see Christensen 1994 for Denmark during the 1980s), Spanish top civil servants have upgraded specific salary levels by increas-ing the variable and individual part of the payment, as any budget-maximizing public choice theory would predict. At the same time, institutional constraints make difficult a total individualization of salaries as the increase of the variable parts is achieved for a whole group of civil servants within the same level, ministry or category. Therefore the strategy has been more hierarchist than individualist.

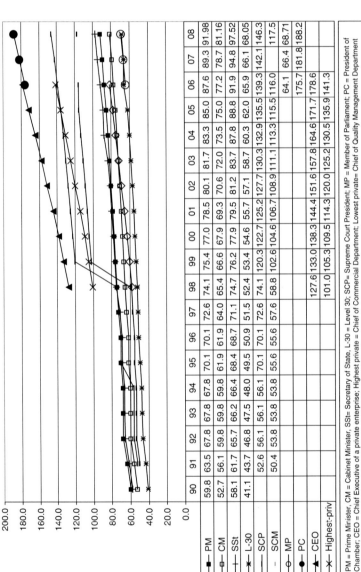

	90	91	92	93	94	95	96	97	98	99	00	01	02	03	04	05	06	07	08
PM	59.8	63.5	67.8	67.8	67.8	70.1	70.1	72.6	74.1	75.4	77.0	78.5	80.1	81.7	83.3	85.0	87.6	89.3	91.98
CM	52.7	56.1	59.8	59.8	59.8	61.9	61.9	64.0	65.4	66.6	67.9	69.3	70.6	72.0	73.5	75.0	77.2	78.7	81.16
SSt	58.1	61.7	65.7	66.2	66.4	68.4	68.7	71.1	74.7	76.2	77.9	79.5	81.2	83.7	87.8	88.8	91.9	94.8	97.52
L-30	41.1	43.7	46.8	47.5	48.0	49.5	50.9	51.5	52.4	53.4	54.6	55.7	57.1	58.7	60.3	62.0	65.9	66.1	68.05
SCP	52.6	56.1	56.1	56.1	56.1	70.1	70.1	72.6	74.1	120.3	122.7	125.2	127.7	130.3	132.9	135.5	139.3	142.1	146.3
SCM	50.4	53.8	53.8	53.8	53.8	55.6	55.6	57.6	58.8	102.6	104.6	106.7	108.9	111.1	113.3	115.5	116.0		117.5
MP																	64.1	66.4	68.71
PC																	175.7	181.8	188.2
CEO									127.6	133.0	138.3	144.4	151.6	157.8	164.6	171.7	178.6		
Highest-priv									101.0	105.3	109.5	114.3	120.0	125.2	130.5	135.9	141.3		

PM = Prime Minister; CM = Cabinet Minister; SSt= Secretary of State; L-30 = Level 30; SCP= Supreme Court President; MP = Member of Parliament; PC = President of Chamber; CEO = Chief Executive of a private enterprise; Highest private = Chief of Commercial Department; Lowest private= Chief of Quality Management Department

Figure 8.1 Nominal salaries of HPOs, 1990–2008 (in thousand euros).

Sources: For executive, annual budgetary laws 1990–2006; for Parliament, Congreso de los Diputados (2007); for private sector Watson and Wyatt Data Services (surveys of 2002–2005). (1) Seniority: 15 years of service have been considered for each post inholder, except for cabinet ministers and prime ministers. Political appointees receive seniority if they have civil service status, which applies to around 80 percent of post inholders. (2) For post allowance: highest values have been considered. (3) For PRP: average was given for 2005 by the Ministry of Treasury. Other years have been worked out considering the percentage of public employees' increase in salaries of 1 percent.

The structure of the Spanish civil service reflects a mixture of post and career systems; the career is reflected in the basic salary and the seniority bonus, which is a fixed amount granted every 3 years of service. The guaranteed allowances, like the rank or level allowance, reflect the personal grade and/or the level of the administrative post. At the lower administrative level, the fixed salary proportion becomes more prominent, 50 percent of individual reward, while this is just 30 percent for top levels. This fixed part is centrally determined for civil servants.

Bargains on the variable part of the rewards are determined individually and also collectively for civil servants of the same level, and they disguise the effects of the routine increase of public sector pay. First, individual salaries can still vary to a certain extent through the effect of 'add-ons,' which are negotiated for specific posts. The post is relevant for determining the variable parts of the salary. These bonuses are not linked to individual performance and they are fixed for the specific position irrespective of who occupies it. If the incumbent gets promoted, s/he retains her/his salary, seniority and level allowance but not post allowance. The post allowance, depending on the particular features of the post, and the individual or performance-related payment (PRP) allowance are negotiated by each ministry and the CECIR, a commission composed of representatives from the Ministry of Public Administration (MAP) and the Ministry of Economy and the Treasury. This ministry publishes an annual list of most common amounts of post allowances. The work of the commission is not transparent and it is difficult to ascertain what criteria help to increase the salary attached to a specific post. In fact, in spite of an overall two percent capping of post allowances, three percent has been annually recorded in the last 5 years, according to one official from the ministry of Economy and the Treasury. Negotiations allow for differences of post allowances among ministries, and the *corps* (notaries, diplomats, civil administrators, finance inspectors, etc.), who used to control pay determination before the 1984 legislation, play a less a relevant role now. Before 1984, they also had access to extra rewards coming from user charges on public services. In the present system, the *corps* are still relevant when negotiating post allowances for specific positions but their bargaining power also depends on the negotiating power of individual ministries. Post allowance represents at least a third of the monetary rewards for top civil servants.

Second, individual allowances from PRP are not transparent. PRP allowances also depend on negotiations between individual ministries and the ministry of Economy and Treasury. In theory, each ministry has 6 percent of total payroll at its disposal to distribute among 'best performers.' Except for some agencies that practice performance assessment, in most public organizations, this amount is allocated in equal shares for each administrative or political appointee level. The proportion of PRP for posts above level 28 and political appointees is between 11 and 15 percent of total rewards, i.e. the distribution of the 6 percent of the payroll benefits more either top civil servants or political appointees who are in charge of distributing the PRP bonus. The allowances promote civil servants in an informal way as their formal career is very short (Parrado 2004) and those organizations with lower post allowances are disadvantaged for career promotion.

The political executives

The salaries of *political executives* have undergone incremental routine increases that resulted in eroding the salary levels of the PM, Deputy PMs (DPM) and cabinet ministers (CM) in relation to the economy and to political appointees. Bonuses that have been included in the payroll of other political appointees, like PRP, are not available to PM and ministers. This can explain higher salaries for some State Secretaries and lower for ministers and even the PM (see Table 8.1).

Little 'extras' have helped political executives to overcome the tight schedules imposed by systematic pay reviews. This strategy assumes that high public officials will try to maximize rewards over their entire lifetime, considering that their appointment is not for life, like for judges of the Supreme Court. Political executives and appointees normally finish their official position at a relatively early age. The recent democratic presidents, Suárez, Calvo Sotelo, González and Aznar, left the PM office in their fifties and this is true for more than 70 percent (see projection from Parrado 1998, 2004) of political appointees. None of the abovementioned PMs remained in politics, rather they developed private activities. Deferred rewards come either as non-contributory pensions, better public pension schemes than most or better (or at least good) rewarded positions in public or private enterprises after their public office.

There are several little 'extras' of HPOs. The PM enjoys free housing, transport and other commodities for him and his family during his mandate. His salary is not competitive with any other HPO of equal status or even lower status, but former Prime Minister Felipe González justified this in a newspaper interview: 'you manage to save most of the salary, as food, accommodation and travelling is provided for free.' PMs have not been publicly concerned about the level of their income, although the post office appointments involving high salaries of former Prime Minister Aznar have raised some criticism. Salary increases attached to the consumer price index, like for the rest of public employees, are applied to the PM, whose salary consists of a single figure without further internal distribution of the reward structure. After their mandate, political executives and secretaries of State enjoy two years' salary of 80 percent of their rewards in office, a pension for life and security services during a fixed period of time.

The political appointees

The internal composition of political appointees' salaries has changed while the final figure has incrementally increased in nominal, but not in real terms. At first, the salary of political executives and appointees was not transparent, as it appeared as a single figure without further detailed distribution among different allowances. The members of the government still have a lump sum, while more transparency has been introduced for political appointees.

The salary structure for political appointments has been depoliticized by adopting the civil service framework. This strategy seems to fit into an overall strategy of downgrading the former political profile of under-secretaries and directors general and entrusting them with more administrative roles. However, it is odd to use the same structure for secretaries of State, considered junior ministers with high political profiles and belonging formally to the government in a wide sense, i.e. they are quasi-political executives.

The introduction of transparency and the specification of the salary structure appear to be also connected to the privatization of public enterprises throughout the last two decades. Political appointees used to receive tax-free extra allowances for being board members of an unlimited number of public corporations. These extra earnings are still at the disposal of political appointees with the limits of two boards per appointee according to the Code of Good Governance (*Código del Buen Gobierno* 2005). As the number of public corporations decreases through privatization, individual bonuses and fixed post allowances should compensate for the loss of extra earnings. Thanks to PRP, total earnings of secretaries of State are set slightly above the salary levels of political executives, unless cabinet ministers have other extra resources that official sources do not reveal. The increase in transparency of political appointees' reward structure contradicts the expected trend advanced by Brans and Peters in the introductory chapter.

Political appointees face the hardships of a relatively constraining conflict of interest system. They cannot work during the next two years after their office in private market jobs related to their official duties. Non-contributory pensions are not at the disposal of directors general and undersecretaries. Further, there are no posts in public enterprises for all of them, as the number of privatized public utilities has grown over the years. Many of the political appointees return to a downgraded position in the civil service with lower salaries.

In sum, there are no deferred rewards for political appointees as the chances that a political appointee could get into the European parliament, an Embassy or private industry are not very high. Thus, a 'life-time earnings model' appears less viable for these officials than for many others.

The judges

Judges, like the rest of civil servants, have had a similar reward structure with fixed components and variable post allowances. The 2003 Act that linked a substantial part of pay to performance was motivated by a concern with the functioning of the judicial system and their low productivity. The amount of salary devoted to bonuses was fixed in law rather than having flexible arrangements between the judiciary authorities and the individual judges. This system does not apply to Supreme Court magistrates, who experienced leap increases in 1994 and in 1998 (see appendix).

Alongside the pay increase, legislation emphasized a stricter incompatibility regime for judges and magistrates so that they could exclusively focus on their tasks instead of devoting their time to parallel activities, like conferences and lecturing.

The working environment of magistrates was also improved and they started to work in court instead of going home to write their sentences.

Interpretation

According to the framework devised by Hood and Peters (1994) and also the introductory chapter of this book for understanding reward structures, the institutional account better explains the evolution of the rewards system for the executive and judiciary, in spite of their differences. The most plausible explanation lies on routinization of mechanical increases of basic payments and routine caps on flexible parts of the salary. The introduction of PRP has not placed a premium on individuals achieving targets because performance has been neither measured nor rewarded in most organizations, except for magistrates, whose earning increases have escaped routinization at some point.

The privatization of public corporations and the difficulties in attracting managers from private enterprises to public office have induced some changes in the earnings of secretaries of State as well as some little extras that should compensate for the lost of public corporations board membership. Thanks to this, the salary position of secretaries of State is better off than that of ministers and the PM. However, they have a weaker relative position in regard to their private counterparts (see Table 8.1).

The arguments of economics-of-politics, which rely on political business cycles producing an increase of rewards after elections, cannot be sustained with the data. In line with this rational choice approach, however, bureaucrats have tried to get advantages in the reward system by reviewing post allowances and allocating PRP bonuses, which are less visible. In some cases, like the Agency for Tax Administration, the greater freedom for managing human resources has allowed more leverage in setting higher salaries.

Finally, the prediction of the cultural theory that rewards would move from the hierarchist to the individualist quadrant does not apply. There is a hierarchist tradition with salary levels ranked by 'levels' of post allowances. PRP bonuses are also bargained by taking into account administrative levels. These implicit collective bargains would entail a communitarian perspective whereby top officials get the best rewards collectively. Therefore a combination of hierarchy and community would better explain how rewards are structured in the Spanish executive.

Rewards for politicians from the legislative

The salaries of the MPs refer to parliamentarians of the lower house (*Congreso de los Diputados*) and the upper house or territorial chamber (*Senado*) as they are established at the same level. The lower chamber with 350 members of parliament and the *Senado* are almost monopolized by the two biggest parties that have taken up at least 80 percent of the seats in the last 25 years. The left (*Izquierda Unida*) and nationalist parties from the regions make up the rest.

Longitudinal data for MPs' salaries since 1990 are lacking. However, in interviews with MPs who were at the Parliament since early democratic times, it seems that MPs' salary was always established in relation to civil service salary limits. During the socialist government initiated in 1982, an MP earned between 660 euros to 900 euros monthly and had few resources to do their job (see *El País* 4 January 1983). Parliamentarians had to share offices in the Congress building and the 202 members of the socialist parliamentarian group had only four personal assistants for all of them. The hardships of parliamentarians were obvious and, although they had autonomy to set their salary levels, a sharp increase without pegging it to anything recognizable for the public would not be acceptable. Therefore, Peces Barba, president of the Lower Chamber at the time, a civil servant himself from the professorial *corps*, proposed to establish the civil service as a model.

Similarly to Germany (Derlien 1994), the first legislatures were filled with civil servants who came from top ministerial echelons. Besides, the management of Congressional affairs was left to public employees with civil service status, to whom the centralized payroll for ministries also applied. Legal officials from the Congress and civil servants of a high prestigious *corps*, helped establish the salary level of early democratic times and to link it to the basic salary level of directors general (see appendix). However, over time MPs have lost the pace with directors general, and their salary is lower than the rewards for level 30 civil servants. Earning increases of MPs were adjusted to the percentage established in the annual budgetary law for civil servants. MPs' income is taxed like every normal citizen's income. As civil servants and political appointees have at their disposal post allowances and PRP bonuses, their marginal increases have been favored in comparison to MPs due to individual or collective bargains. However, MPs have obtained supplementary allowances associated to the various parliamentary committees.

MPs that come from outside the capital receive compensation costs, amounting to 1,700 euros monthly, for living in Madrid, to pay for accommodation and other expenses. At Madrid prices, a decent reasonable one room-flat in the Congress neighborhood is difficult to rent for less than 1,200 euros per month. Many MPs choose to share a flat. Still others prefer to commute by plane or train every day during Congress' session period, as transportation costs between Madrid and MPs' residences are free. Besides, it is not uncommon that MPs receive their salary through the bank account of their political parties, who deduct affiliation quotas and more. For instance, a socialist MP in office during the nineties declared that the party usually took between 100 and 120 euros monthly from each member.

MPs have also some add-ons once their mandate has expired: better pension schemes after 7 years in office when meeting particular requirements and compensation pay after the dissolution of the House when not re-elected. Other perks recently added to MPs include a notebook and a mobile phone (with outgoing calls covered by the House) as parliamentary sessions are announced through e-mail or text messages. MPs also receive a maximum of 200 euros monthly for taxi expenses in Madrid; the average taxi fare oscillates between 10 and 13 euros.

MPs complain that their salaries are comparatively low in relation to European counterparts, that the compensation for expenses hardly covers their costs and, besides, that they do not have the means (i.e. personal assistants) to undertake their legislative tasks. MPs from the largest parties in the House (Conservative Party and Socialist Party) have on average one personal assistant for three MPs. Some committee chairs may share a personal assistant with the chair of another committee. Minority parties are a bit better staffed in the House, as there is one personal assistant for every two MPs.

In comparison, central administration directors general have chauffeured cars according to rank, assistants and, depending on the ministry, they can enjoy a flat. So, overall rewards for MPs and directors general are no longer the same.

Unlike civil servants, MPs negotiate salary levels among themselves without public scrutiny. This would facilitate an increase in their own pay as public choice theory would predict, but they have not done it so far. MPs have followed two less visible strategies to improve their earnings. First, they have increased tax-free per diem allowances. Second, each MP is (vice)-chair of at least one of the many parliamentary committees, which involves extra allowances. Nevertheless, pay increases have not been radical, as they cannot easily be hidden in the Congress' budget, and would hence cause public criticism.

Interpretation

Recent successive presidents of the Lower House have pushed for a sharp increase in MPs' salaries voicing it publicly, but the outcry has thwarted those initiatives. The use of non-taxable allowances has not been enough to compensate the 'service' of MPs and a recent measure for enjoying full retirement pension after 7 years, a scheme five times more generous than the 35 years for normal employees has also raised public concern. Equally controversial was the compensation payment introduced in 2000 for the period between the dissolution of the Houses and the formation of a new Chamber after elections (*El País* 19 January 2000).

The conditions for substantially increasing the parliamentarians' payroll included secrecy of deliberation on salary figures, comparatively low salaries with regards to other European Parliaments, and loss of purchasing power. The rewards have not evolved as the economic-of-politics account would suggest. In fact, the reward structure has evolved routinely in institutional terms, and the rent-seeking behavior has only been present in per diem allowances and more generous pensions after office.

Comparison with the private sector

RIIPOs compared to other managerial occupations in Spain and to inflation rates over time appear ungenerous. This trait has been steady since the early 1980s. Gutiérrez-Reñón and Labrado-Fernández (1988) noticed four basic trends in public pay: (1) salaries in the private sector are higher than in the public sector for jobs with similar content and responsibilities; (2) in the first range of jobs with less responsibilities, job content and salary increase accordingly; (3) in the range of civil servants at levels 29 and 30, the rather small salary increases do not relate to an increase in technical difficulty and responsibilities; (4) in the range of directors general, the increase of responsibility does not correspond with a salary increase.

The average salary of the Spanish CEOs (see Table 8.1) is higher than the wage of the President of the Chamber, the highest salary in the public sector. The lowest executive ranks (normally Customer Relations Manager or Quality Manager) almost equal the salary of the secretaries of State, while the rest enjoy salaries well above the earnings of the secretaries of State. Furthermore, public sector salaries are on average 1.14 percent lower than the inflation rate while salaries for private Spanish executive positions are on average 1.3 percent higher than the inflation rate. Finally, the perquisites of executive positions such as cars, restaurant vouchers and life insurances are significant when compared with their counterparts in the public sector.

As public sector salaries cannot compete with private enterprise payment for high rank officials, there has been a process of 'agencification' in the Spanish system since the budgetary law of 1991, and the recent 2006 Act whereby more than 30 agencies, National Airports Association, Post, Tax Agency among others, have been created to operate under private law. This shift allows agencies to contract personnel for top positions and to fix different salaries for staff. Agency salaries can theoretically compete with private enterprise payments. However, the consequences for rewards of the 'agencification' process still remain to be seen.

Conclusion

Institutional accounts of routinization and mechanistic application of bargaining procedures between trade unions, the ministry of public administration, and the ministry of treasury explain the development of the reward system for all Spanish HPOs. As bureaucracy preceded democracy (cf. Derlien 1994 for Germany), the civil service reward structure shaped salary in other positions. As a consequence, only civil servants have the incentives and the means to hold a political appointment and a parliamentarian seat because the system plays a role in the bureaucratic career in a wide sense. Low salaries have largely prevented outsiders from entering the government or parliament.

Distrust of citizens towards politics and bureaucracy has thwarted any attempt to improve the reward structure for HPOs. There are signs of hidden bargains that try to ameliorate the salary system, but those attempts have not improved their relative position in relation to the private sector.

Nominally speaking, there are some relevant elements of NPM in the Spanish system: soft agencification and the introduction of PRP since the early eighties. They have entailed less transparency in how top civil servants and political appointees top up their salaries. These amounts do not change dramatically the position of these officials in comparison with private sector executives.

The introduction of shy NPM practices does not account for a change from hierarchist to a more individual practice in rewards for high public offices according to the predictions of the cultural theory.

References

Christensen, J.G. (1994) Denmark: institutional constraint and the advancement of individual self-interest in HPO. In C. Hood and B.G. Peters, *Rewards at the Top. A Comparative Study of High Public Office*. London: Sage, pp. 70–90.

CIS (Centro de Estudios Sociológicos) (2006) Estudio 2633. Barómetro de enero de 2006.

CIS (Centro de Estudios Sociológicos) (2007) Estudio 2700. Barómetro de abril de 2007.

CIS (Centro de Estudios Sociológicos) (2007a) Estudio 2672. Barómetro de enero de 2007.

Derlien, H.-U. (1994) Germany: the structure and dynamics of the reward system for bureucratic and political elites. In C. Hood and B. Guy Peters, *Rewards at the Top. A Comparative Study of High Public Office*. London: Sage, pp. 166–186.

Gutiérrez-Reñón, A. and M. Labrado-Fernández (1988) *La experiencia de la evaluación de puestos de trabajo en la Administración Pública*. Madrid: Ministerio para las Administraciones Públicas (MAP).

Hood, C. and B.G. Peters (1994) Understanding RHPOs. In C. Hood and B.G. Peters, *Rewards at the Top. A Comparative Study of High Public Office*. London: Sage, pp. 1–24.

Ortega, L. (1992) La reforma de la alta burocracia en España. In *Revista Sistema*, **107**, pp. 5–20.

Parrado, S. (2004) Politicisation of the Spanish Civil Service: continuity in 1982 and 1996. In B.G. Peters and J. Pierre (Eds), *Politicization of the Civil Service in Comparative Perspective. The quest of control*. Routledge: London, pp. 227–256.

Parrado, S. (1998) Controlling the access to the Spanish summit (1938–1991). In J.C.N. Raadschelders and F.M. Van der Meer (Eds), *Administering the Summit*. Bruselas: Instituto Internacional de Ciencias Administrativas, Cahier d'Histoire de l'Administration, vol. 5, pp. 115–131.

Parrado, S. and J. Ruiz (1997) The path of quality in a Spanish autonomous agency. In *Public Productivity & Management Review*, **21**: 56–69.

9 Rewards at the top in Belgium
Uneasy struggles with transparency and variability in paying public office

Marleen Brans

This chapter discusses the material rewards for national politicians and civil servants in Belgium. Until the mid-nineties, the developments of the structure and level of these rewards were relatively stable, reflecting the professionalization of both classes, as well as a persistent uneasiness with the transparency of rewards. Since the mid-nineties, two major changes took place. First, MPs adapted their reward structure in an effort to remove recurrent controversies. Second, top civil servants in the Federal Administration took a premium when a Belgian translation of the New Public Management (NPM) doctrine radically changed the status and rewards of the top rank of the administration. Both of these changes comply with cross-nationally observed trends, where *pay for ethics* schemes for politicians seek to rebuke allegations of sleaze, and *marketization* increases top civil servants' salaries to a level that is competitive with private sector managerial positions. Yet, the translations of these trends should not be taken at face value. The Belgian MPs' move to transparency was highly ambiguous, reflecting a reconciliation of income protection for everyone with diverse political principles of parliamentary pay. The premium for top civil servants from NPM, in turn, suffered a severe political backlash, demonstrating the partisan translation of global public sector reform in a national context.

Parliamentary pay: an ambiguous move to transparency

When Belgian MPs revised their rewards in the mid-1990s, they did not do so with the intention to improve them. The revision was a response to a longstanding controversy of the fiscal regime that came to be questioned by the tax administration and politicized by a party in opposition. The revision started in 1989 and concluded in 1996, although the installation of registers of mandates and income dragged on until the mid-2000s. Its outcome presented a move towards transparency and was presented as a concession to citizens. The move was ambiguous, though. It resulted from extensive party compromises, not only in terms of divergent interests, but also in terms of actors' preferred models of representation. The following sections present the development of MPs' rewards into a highly controversial structure, and the dynamics of their subsequent reform (Brans 1999).

MPs' rewards

Although parliamentary pay in Belgium came to include several indirect salary-linked benefits, the reluctance to call it a salary has persisted over time. Originally, the 1831 Constituents intended to categorize pay for representatives' *traitement*, or remuneration. But this term was quickly abandoned in favor of *indemnité* in French or *vergoeding* in Dutch. When pay was introduced for senators in 1921, and when a differentiation between representatives and senators was sought, the label of *indemnité* survived for representatives. Senators' pay was constitutionally laid down as a mere reimbursement of expenses. This way, both categories remained remote from the concept of 'remuneration'. This labeling was meant to prevent allegations of political careerism in the House and to suggest a continuation of disinterestedness in the Senate. However, pay quickly came to include indirect benefits that are usually associated with salaries. The first such benefits for representatives were, in fact, already made possible under the 1920 Constitutional revision: pensions. In addition, allowances of representatives were subjected to income tax. In 1926 (Circulaire n° 14382, confirmed by subsequent circular letters), only half of representatives' allowances came to be considered as a reimbursement of expenses. The other half was considered as professional income, and subsequently liable for taxation. These two salary related regulations were made applicable to senators' pay later on. Pension schemes were made compulsory immediately after the war and senators were taxed from 1959 onwards. From the mid-1960s, when senators and representatives' pay converged, they came to include other salary-related benefits: holiday pay, end of year premium, social security schemes. The level of pay was eventually explicitly linked to salaries, and also to mechanisms that are generally applicable to salaries: indexation and wage restraint measures.

Admittedly, some typical salary-related benefits remained absent from parliamentary pay structures: seniority raises or guarantees against dismissal. These two benefits sit ill with predicaments of representative democracy itself: equality between members of the legislature (one (wo)man, one vote, one pay) and the inherent condition of subjectability to elections. Apart from these restrictions, it can be safely said that parliamentary allowances, for both representatives and senators, now have the character of 'temporary remuneration' for work. The reparation of expenses, therefore, is replaced, largely because expenses have increasingly been offset by intrinsic office rewards. At the eve of the 1995 revision, MPs' pay structure comprised the following formal elements:

- basic allowances, including holiday pay and end of year premium; 50 percent exempt from income tax;
- free travel on public transport and car travel allowances;
- intrinsic office rewards: office facilities, postal franchise, photocopies, free drinks and subsidized meals, insurances, assistance and staff facilities;
- special allowances for intra-parliamentary leadership positions;
- pension scheme and a one-year severance pay.

As to informal rewards, it should be mentioned that few restrictions applied to part-time earning opportunities, which – given the number of MPs that hold multiple offices and private occupations together with their parliamentary office – provided a major source of income (De Winter and Brans 2003). For the period 2003–2009, 82 percent of the members of the federal chamber combined their office of MP with a local mandate (Put and Vanlangenakker 2010).

Opaque structure and non-public decisions

As established by the 1920–1921 Constitutional revisions, the reward structure of representatives and senators was relatively transparent. The sum of allowances was stipulated, as was the right to a free travel pass. For the House of Representatives a pension scheme was provided and also a special allowance for its Speaker. For the latter benefits, the Constitution did not mention concrete sums or levels. Subsequent modifications to basic allowances, their fiscal treatment, the extension of intrinsic office rewards, and special allowances turned the overall reward structure into a rather messy and opaque one. Three features of MPs' rewards blurred the transparency of formal rewards as laid down in the Constitution: the 50 percent tax exemption, the range of intrinsic office rewards and the system of special allowances. The tax exemption, had it been legally established, could, in fact, have been regarded as a transparent feature of MPs' rewards. It was indeed meant as a reimbursement of expenses. As such, it was a simpler way to offset members' professional costs than compensating them through all kinds of expense allowances on top of basic allowances. In addition, the exemption was the only reward – apart from the constitutionally settled ones – that had some basis in written regulation available from outside the legislature: the circular letters of the Minister of Finance. Its main principled problem was its discordance with the Constitution. In practice, it also allowed for double (ab)use of deducting professional expenses. The gradual expansion of intrinsic office rewards and expense allowances further hurt the transparency claim of the exemption. Their range was extensive. No single public account listed what they amounted to in taxpayers' money. We cannot tell from the budgets, for instance, to what extent members' meals in the parliamentary restaurants are subsidized or how much they consume in drinks. Neither can we calculate how much travel allowances, occasional expense reimbursements or office furniture amount to. Only assistance can be estimated, since the budget lists the personnel expenses of assistants. Also the system of special allowances for parliamentary leadership positions, such as the Speaker, Vice-Speakers, Questors, parliamentary secretaries and parliamentary group leaders, adds to the opacity of the reward structure, although it is, in fact, a clear and understandable one once information is obtained.[1] The special allowances range from 15 to 72 percent of the parliamentary allowance, and were also tax-exempt until 1996. They provide substantial add-ons to the ordinary backbenchers' allowances, making, for instance, the Speakers of the Senate and the House the best paid public officials.

It was possible to broadly reconstruct the reward structure of Belgian MPs, through recourse to a range of separate documents, more confidential than public, and with the help of the Financial Services of the Houses. It is clear that citizens at large have a hard time working out how much their MPs exactly receive. Active transparency is low; passive transparency is conditional.[2] Rewards in kind are difficult to estimate, and even some cash rewards are concealed in lump sums under single budgetary headings. The Belgian reward structure was thus characterized by a lax audit and disclosure regime for expense-allowances and non-cash job perks. It got even less transparent when including outside earning opportunities. Up until 1999, no registers listed members' outside earning activities. They could be indirectly studied by calculating their financial impact upon members' total reward packages. This proved too time-consuming a job for a researcher, let alone for citizens at large.

For more than 70 years, decisions on legislative salaries and other benefits were 'depoliticized'. They were removed from the ordinary political process to make them immune to cross-party competition and public scrutiny. First, this was done through linkage, with allowances automatically following the salaries of magistrates at the Council of State. Other decisions were made in small, non-transparent intra-parliamentary decision-making units, which facilitated consensual decision-making and even allowed for bypassing the Constitution.

Until 1921, there was still some concern about having the exact sum of the allowances and other benefits inscribed in the Constitution. However, constitutional orthodoxy was abandoned after 1921. Occasionally, it was proposed to bring the Constitution in accordance with reality, or at least to formally enable the legislature to change the reward structure through delegation and special majority laws. But overall, decision-making was characterized by constitutional bypassing. Up until the revision in 1995, rewards were not settled by laws, the second highest norms in legal hierarchy.

Reward decisions in the Belgian parliament are typically taken by the Bureaux of the Houses, prepared and implemented by the College of Quaestors, which is composed on the basis of political proportionality. Decision-making in these units is characterized by low publicity of debate and low active and passive transparency. Documents and minutes of meeting of Bureaux and Colleges of Quaestors are not public. They are not subject to the law on publicity of government proceedings or to archival law. And they are not equally distributed among ordinary backbenchers, which would otherwise increase transparency.

Also, the annual budget approval is traditionally surrounded by transparency lowering devices and, moreover, is characterized by strong mutual autonomy of the two houses versus the executive. The grants to the Senate and House are part of the government's draft budget, but they do not fall under the government's authority. The sums and their distribution are solely decided by the legislative chambers. In addition, it is part of tradition for the two houses not to control, debate or pass judgments on each other's budgets. Finally, the public budget only lists the general grants. The detailed budget is generally not distributed.

1996 Revision: games between MPs, administration, parties, and press

Prior to its revision, the Belgian reward structure was vulnerable to public controversy in several respects. Its most controversial component was the tax exemption. The legal and constitutional ambiguity of this tax exemption received particular salience in the course of tax inspectors' industrial action for better pay conditions. In the period 1988–1990, multiple disputes arose between individual legislators and their tax inspectors over the treatment of party contributions and electoral expenses and the non-application of the 1926 circular letter. Specifically, parliamentary leadership positions were targeted, culminating in the non-application of the exemption to the income of the Speaker of the House. At first, disputes were dealt with internally. Individual MPs filed complaints with the Minister of Finance. On occasion, the Speakers of the House and Senate intervened on their behalf. In the wake of the 1988 tax reform, the legal ambiguity of the exemption was complemented with allegations of double standards, which presented MPs' fiscal regime as an unwarranted privilege. The leader of the Flemish Liberals picked up on these controversies and, with his legislative proposal, the issue became fully politicized and widely covered in the parliamentary press. The first common response of legislators simply sought to clarify the fiscal regime and end disputes. Shortly afterwards, it meant to redress the legal ambiguity. The need to counter the *double standards* controversy became stronger after the results of the 1991 elections, the interpretation of which urged MPs to redress their public image. A second catalyst came in 1993–1994, with the disclosure of several corruption scandals. The same dynamics also characterized a decision on another reward component that appeared early on the agenda of the revision. An absenteeism scheme, which makes MPs lose part of their income when frequently absent, was at first an answer to the common annoyance of parliamentary group leaders over the continuous absence of certain members and to their concern to meet the quorum at meetings. Initially penalizing absence was focused on disciplining MPs in order to improve internal organization. Only gradually, and with a first boost after the 1991 elections, did the expectation of the absenteeism scheme as an external *trust-inducing measure* gain significance. Other elements of the reward structure got drawn in along the process of the revision. Controversies over part-time rewards and allowances for parliamentary leadership positions were mainly articulated by the Greens. Large differences in pay sat ill with the Greens' egalitarianism and their view on parliamentary office as an independent professionalized occupation.

After initial public party competition over MPs' rewards, the traditional parties (Liberals, Socialists, Christian-Democrats) quickly *agreed to agree.* The search for an effective cartel had to prevent electoral bidding, and the inclusion of the Greens was to foster a broad consensus that extended beyond the majority, and with it, beyond allegations of *business as usual.* Moreover, participation in and the location of the debate were organized in such a way that consensual decision-making was facilitated. At the same time, the Extreme right was ostracized and not given a chance to exploit the issue. Preparatory meetings took place *extra muros*, exemplary of the diplomacy character of decisions, which is typical for Belgian consociationalist politics, and a *serenity deal* was meant to insulate the talks from media attention (by preventing leaks). In the Walloon village of Gesves, it was decided that the principle of the reform should be *ni plus, ni moins*, meaning income neutral. After this consensus, agreement was sought within the Parliament, but not without several intermediate rounds of informal negotiations, issue linkage and package deals.

The bulk of the revision was, thus, prepared outside the formal institutionalized decision-making bodies of Parliament. Due legislative process was preceded by 5 years of informal negotiations. Intermediate publicly presented deals consisted of interim agreements and confirmations of the political will to move ahead with the revision. Formal decisions were prepared in numerous intra-Chamber and inter-Chamber informal working groups, the characteristic features of which are low publicity of debate, limited numbers of participants and the incidence of *extra-muros* meetings. The usual competencies of formal internal decision-making bodies, such as the College of Questors, were bypassed, to be restored only after the approval of the bills and the 1995 elections. Constitutional reform as an option was ruled out from the start.

Interesting here is the sequencing of informal decision locations and the intermediate formal ones. The joint use of informal and formal decisions can be looked at in terms of Becquart-Leclercq's (1989) structuralist distinction between a symbolic mode of politics, which embodies the idealized image of society, and the operational mode of politics, which embodies the rules of the game as applied, the implicit codes and the accepted tactics. On the operational level, informal meetings offered participants the opportunity to discuss the revision of rewards in terms of efficiency, practical feasibility and functional necessity, but were less focused in terms of legality and legitimacy. The characteristic low publicity of these meetings, re-enforced by the *serenity* deal, protected participants from public backlash over their positions. It offered parties the opportunity to defend their reward structures in terms they would not dare use in public. It also provided a forum where political deals could be struck and co-operation be *bought* by linking other issues to the revision. The intermediate public decisions served the symbolic code of politics. The public debate was conducted in terms of legitimacy and legality, and the revision was presented as a move to greater transparency and to a closer assimilation between citizens and politicians. We find clear evidence of this in the different discourses of public and non-public documents. The public documents typically refer to the *ni plus* (not more) principle of the Gesves deal, whereas non-public documents emphasize the *ni moins* (not less) principle.

MPs' rewards after the revision: character, structure and level?

The 1996 revision did not alter the character of pay, it only partially altered the components of MPs' pay structure, and as to the level, income neutrality was clearly the structuring principle. The tax exemption was abolished, and replaced by a tax-free allowance. Also, the generous leadership allowances were brought under the same regime. The expense allowances were set at exactly the same level of the simulated fiscal loss of taxing basic allowances. This was the so-called *ni plus, ni moins* principle. At the same time, the revision introduced a number of *trust inducing measures*, which would help to justify the revision to the broader public. The measures included the penalization or absenteeism scheme (rejected by the Senate, though), and a halfhearted commitment to install registers of means and offices, the implementation of which was delayed until 2005 due to the lack of enabling legislation.

Supporting the position of the traditional parties, the revision temporarily countered the Greens' pressures for caps on multiple office-holding, or an improvement of post-service rewards, which did not materialize until several years later, in 1999 and 2002. Caps on outside earning now apply only to public offices, of which MPs can take up one executive office or two other public offices (e.g. board of public company). The combined income cannot exceed 1.5 times the parliamentary allowance. Severance pay has been improved in two ways. The maximum has been raised from 2 to 4 years, and one gets 2 years after 15 years of service, instead of after 24 years.

As to the level of pay, income neutrality was the leading principle of the reform, with the exception that frequently absent representatives will suffer a pay cut. The pay differentials show how MPs did not improve their income, and we know that the average fiscal loss is neutralized by the expense allowance.

Safe from controversy?

Of the strategies MPs can choose to deal with controversy over their rewards (Hood 1995), *asceticization* was clearly the Greens' project. The other partici-pants, due to rival concepts of representation and vested political interests, did not follow it. The abolition of fiscal privilege without compensations and caps on outside earnings would moreover have lowered material comfort too substan-tially, which was not desired by the majority of participants, particularly not when pay-offs in terms of citizens' appreciation were not guaranteed. The *pay for ethics* strategy was briefly followed during the intra-chamber negotiations. The Flemish Liberals, temporarily joined by some majority parties, supported an income rise accompanied by trust-inducing measures. The penalization scheme designed in Gesves was quite severe. The Secretariat of the working group's proposal to incorporate a range of intrinsic office rewards in the general expense allowance equally fits the *pay for ethics* strategy. The demands on co-operation of this strategy, however, appeared too heavy. The consensus was too fragile and the fear of electoral bidding too strong. Parties did not dare to meet the challenge to uniformly defend raising basic allowances, or defend the tax exemption. As one Flemish Socialist respondent put it: 'The political class has no uniform iden-tity. The debate could hence not be conducted in terms of the independence of parliamentary office.'

The Greens opposed pay raises for ideological reasons, and the Flemish Socialists were weary of them because they feared electoral backlash. Both the process and the outcome of the revision show features of the *devious approach*. In the search for an effective cartel, the *serenity* deal and the multiple informal decision-locations all served to ease collective action problems. The dual use of formal and informal decisions allowed for a public presentation of the revision as an income-neutral move towards greater transparency and a closer assimilation between MPs and citizens. At the same time, it served to protect the level and structure of rewards. As to the outcome, the revision removed one controversial element of the reward structure, but replaced it by another potentially controversial component. Despite some necessary give and take, the revision did not fundamentally alter the level of material comfort MPs enjoy. It compensated fiscal loss and left the range of intrinsic office rewards untouched. Neither did it fundamentally hurt MPs' part-time earning opportunities, since incompatibilities were removed from the agenda. It even slightly improved travel allowances and did not rule out future increments. Transparency was only partially increased by settling the principles of the revision by law and rendering, if not the level, at least the sources of part-time earning visible through registers. Although applicable to leadership allowances, the revision failed to disclose their system. The details of the total reward structure are still not easily accessible, and the decision location is kept behind the closed doors of Bureaux and Colleges of Quaestors.

Admittedly, legal and constitutional controversy over MPs' fiscal regime has been countered. Controversy in terms of *double standards* has not. Although settled by law, the fiscal regime does not fully comply with regulations that apply to ordinary citizens. For ordinary citizens within the same fiscal category as MPs, general expense allowances and travel allowances are not tax-free. Although the penalization scheme has introduced the principle of *no pay without labor*, it is still potentially controversial. The extent of its application is not transparent and exemptions are internally decided. Its limitation to plenary sessions does not structurally restrict outside-earning practices. Allegations that MPs are overpaid, since they are professionally active outside parliament, remain possible. The registers of offices, however, do restrain allegations of conflicts of interests, but the registers of means are a weak instrument to protect MPs against allegations of sleaze. Special leadership allowances have been made dependent upon performance, and their fiscalization has put an end to their *black pay* character. Their opacity, however, carries potential roots for controversy. Overall, the revision has left the reward structure and its decision location still quite opaque, which makes it continuously vulnerable to allegations of sleaze and self-serving attitudes.

NPM and top civil servants' premiums

In the first study of rewards for high public offices (RHPOs) (Hood and Peters 1994), the reward system for Belgian top civil servants was described as on the one hand rather strictly regulated, and on the other hand as blurred by an opaque bonus system, by service in *ministerial cabinets* as stepping stones to higher positions, and by a system of informal politicization.

In the following 15 years, the senior civil service has been radically transformed and rewards were revised, following an international trend to private sector managerialist doctrine. Pay at the top was improved and greater variability exists, although not fully intended. Those with the highest pay checks have, to a large extent, been recruited from former members of *ministerial cabinets*, confirming the latter's function as stepping stones to higher office. Yet, the details of recruitment at the top do not confirm outright politicization, but a blending of the Belgian political system's need for political control with the recruitment of high caliber people at the head of government services. To our present knowledge, the existing bonus system has not been explicitly addressed by any reform yet.

Ambitious (Copernican) reform of the Federal Civil Service

Higher pay for top civil servants was introduced as part of a broader reform project, of which competency management was characteristic for a modernized human resources policy (Brans and Hondeghem 2005). In February 2000, after a new purple-green (composed of Social Democrats, Liberals and Greens) government had been formed, the Minister of the Civil Service in conjunction with the PM launched a plan to modernize the federal administration, adopting principles of the international NPM agenda. The press quickly called it the 'Copernicus plan', a label which the Minister keenly adopted, since it corresponded with the government's ambitious discourse on modernization.

The astronomer Copernicus had caused a revolution in showing that not the earth but the sun was the center of the universe. Similarly, the Copernicus plan was to convert the Federal administration from a closed, rigid bureaucracy into a modern, customer-oriented organization with the citizen at its centre instead of the administration. The central catalysts for this Copernicus change were to be the radical revision of the organizational structure, the strengthening of the administration's managerial and policy roles, and the introduction of a modern human resources policy. Copernicus would also radically change the status of senior civil servants, in terms of both the conditions of appointments and rewards.

To understand the nature and rewards of the new administrative top, one first needs to grasp the organizational changes made under Copernicus. The traditional ministries became Federal Government Services (FGS), and Secretaries-General were replaced by Chairs of the Management Committee. Directors-general no longer preside over the old-fashioned 'Administrations' but over Operational Directorates. Copernicus also introduced a number of new structural interfaces, such as the policy board, and policy units. The policy board is presided over by the Minister and is responsible for a number of managerial tasks as well as for assisting the Minister in drafting and monitoring the execution of his or her policy programs. At the same time, each FGS is endowed with a new policy formulation

unit, in charge of the co-ordination and integration of policy advice and evaluation. The introduction of these units was to coincide with the radical substitution
of ministerial cabinets with strongly reduced personal secretariats, and the transfer of the tasks of those cabinets to the administration (Brans, Pelgrims, and
Hoet 2006, Brans and Steen 2006). This latter component of the plan was later
omitted.

New managers on contracts: purge, pay, and politicization

The modernization of the human resource management (HRM) function was one
of the main pillars of the Copernicus reform of the early 2000s. A modernized
HRM would break with traditions in which recruitment and staff selection were
very centralized and rigid, and remuneration rewarded only grade and seniority.
Many changes were implemented. The central recruitment secretariat was transformed into a modern selection agency, Selor. Personnel planning was introduced. The old evaluation system was replaced by development circles. The old
grading system was replaced by functions, with function weighing as a new
perspective on remuneration. Copernicus also adopted the international trend
towards competency management, although in the course of its implementation
this got watered down, with competency measurement being substituted by
certified education matched with straightforward salary raises.

As to top functions, the changes introduced by Copernicus were far-reaching.
Copernicus radically broke with at least two traditional features of the Belgian
civil service: the career system and the relatively low status of top officials.
Whereas the traditional top civil servant climbed slowly to the top, the Copernicus
recruitment allowed for swift ascension. Both the chairs of the federal government services and the degrees directly below were appointed by mandate or
contract, on the basis of modern style assessments. The chairs of the management
committees were put on 6-year contracts, the term of which exceeds legislative
terms by two years. An exception was made for the PM's Chancellery, whose
chair serves 4 years, which is justified with reference to the strong political character of this office. The rewards of office also changed. The salaries for the very
top – the chairs of the management committee – more than doubled (see jump in
Figure 9.1). Pay differentials within the administration widened, whereas also the
distances between top public sector offices changed remarkably. People at the top
of the administration started earning more than 2.5 times an MP's base salary,
and even slightly more than a Minister. Admittedly, the administrative top does
not benefit from the kind of untaxed expense allowances, as do Ministers and
MPs, and cannot combine several incomes, as their outside earnings are restricted
by incompatibility rules.

To some extent, these changes to pay differentials induced subsequent changes
in MPs rewards. Directly following the improvements for the top of the administration, MPs (modestly) improved their annual holiday pay to align with the
system applicable to federal civil servants (see Figure 9.2), although their salaries
are in principle linked to another office (Members of the State Council).

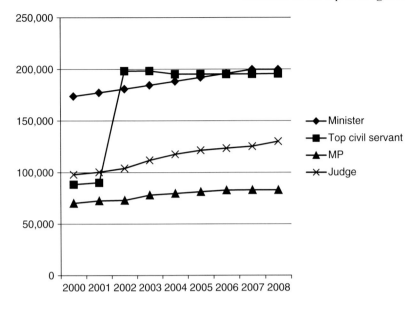

Figure 9.1 Pay differentials 2000–2008 (nominal annual salaries in euros inclusive of holiday pay and end of year premium; top civil servants on Copernicus pay).

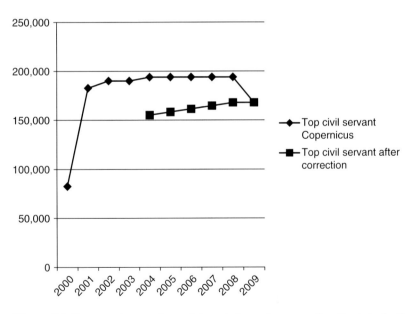

Figure 9.2 Downward correction of top civil service pay after the introduction of Copernicus 2000–2009 (nominal annual salary in euros in euros without holiday pay and end of year premium).

Moreover, the pay rise for top civil servants was perceived to be upsetting the differentials beyond what was acceptable. Two years after Copernicus had revolutionized top civil service pay, the managerial pay rise was corrected downwards by about 30 percent for new appointees at the apex of the administration. In addition, the salaries for those appointed before 2004 were no longer adapted to keep up with inflation, which made ministerial pay move back up the pay ladder to again surpass the administrative top by 2009. Eventually, the post-Copernicus pay correction was made applicable to all appointees, whether or not appointed before 2004. While this restored the pay differentials back to the traditional ones with ministers at the top, top civil servants were still making twice as much as before managerial reform.

The Copernicus HRM policy recruited the heads of the 13 federal government services on the principles of competency management. At the same time, however, we can discern a persistence in the need of ministers for political control over the administration. Copernicus was about to abolish *ministerial cabinets*, which had long been the traditional locus to combine political control with professional administration. The details of the Copernicus recruitment also bring about some evidence of the politicization of appointments, but conclusions on this point need to be qualified (Brans, Pelgrims, and Hood 2006).

The heads of the 13 federal government services were appointed in 2002. All candidates went through external assessment procedures, but in the end, it was the Ministers who selected from among the top ranked candidates. All five incumbent secretaries-general with an affiliation to the Christian Democrats (who were not represented in the purple-green government coalition) were removed from the top of the administration, whereas the three secretary-generals with a socialist label managed to hold on to their positions. However, this operation cannot be equated with a complete purge. Of course, the press was quick to make allegations of new and expensive forms of politicization (Knack 2002), but the evidence is not unequivocally supporting this position. First, although the purple-green ministers removed incumbent Christian-Democrats from the top of the administration, they recruited two new Christian-Democrats. Second, partisan preferences of new top officials did not always coincide with those of the minister who appointed them. Third, even if political criteria surfaced in the final decision, the choice was likely to be between equally competent candidates. At the very least it could be plausibly argued that members of ministerial cabinets were probably just as good managers and leaders as the other applicants that survived the assessments. But they may have additional competencies that the frameworks did not test for, competencies that Ministers seem to appreciate. The appointment of two new candidates associated with the Christian Democrats, one of whom served as a head of ministerial cabinet, suggests that the positions are not entirely filled on the basis of partisanship. More generally, it is striking to note that four new chairs are former heads of ministerial cabinets under the present coalition, and one was a deputy head. The new director of the Central Recruitment Agency (Selor) was also a cabinet head – this position was included in the appointments arithmetic to maintain a 50-50 balance between the Flemish and francophone language groups at the federal level. Only two new chairs were recruited from outside the government, which puts the official argument behind the doubling of pay somewhat into perspective. In principle, the substantial salary increase was meant to attract managers from the private sector to the top of the federal administration. In practice, they radically improve the status and rewards of career civil servants and members of the ministerial bureaucracies (Brans and Hondeghem 2005).

Variability and equality: clash between tradition and trend

The Copernicus modernization of the human resources function and the recruitment and rewards at the top put strong emphasis on flexibility and differentiation (Hondeghem and Depré 2005), yet they did not carry so far as to introduce variable pay at the top. At the start of the reform, it was suggested to weigh the jobs of the new chairs of the management committees. Yet, having heavyweight and lightweight top managers in terms of pay and competencies involved the threat that the same might be applied to the portfolios of Ministers. The cabinet thus rejected the principle of variable pay for the very top. It did, however, allow for variable weights for managers below the chairs, such as the directors-general.

The resistance against variable pay is even more visible in the traditional articulation of values, such as equality, legality, and objectivity, by the first new coalition to follow the Copernicus legislature. Several of the HRM Copernicus changes were watered down or reconsidered. Competency measurements were substituted by certified formation, several aspects of the HR function were recentralized and the rewards for top offices were reduced. But the chairs of the management committees, and their sub-top on contracts appointed before 2004 all maintained for about 5 years a personal retainer from having been the right person at the right time of public sector reform. In 2008 the first contracts expired, and several managers were not reinstituted. In absence of published data on severance pay and re-integration allowances, we cannot judge the post-service rewards of the Copernicus experiment.

It is safe to say that even the corrected pay meant a substantial improvement of the status and rewards of managers of the federal administration. In the absence of recent data on average, mean and percentile managerial pay in the private sector, we cannot pass a balanced judgment on the current width of the pay gap between the public and private sectors. What we do know, however, is that rewards for the top of the federal service are far out of reach of what managers of semi-public and public companies earn, ranging from 445.000 euro for the CEO from the National Railways (NMBS), 900.000 euro for the CEO of the National Postal Services (De Post) and more than 2.5 million euro for the CEO of Belgacom (Telephone and Communications) (figures 2006).

The transparency and level of rewards for these CEOs, and the idea that their pay level should be linked to their companies' performance, has been recently discussed in Parliament, but with a half-hearted commitment from those who do not want a spill-over of the debate to other public offices, confirming, once again, the uneasiness over transparency of rewards for public office in Belgium.

Conclusion

With this chapter we hope to have demonstrated that rewards for high public office are worth studying beyond the mere satisfaction of curiosity over other people's pocket books or the easy adoption of populist critique. Rewards for public office are interesting, dependent variables in political science and public administration, both comparatively and over time. They serve as indicators of the characteristics of political systems and public sector developments over time.

In the last 15 years, two major developments of public sector pay in Belgium occurred. Both developments comply with internationally observed trends, such as the debate on standards of public life for politicians, and the marketization of the public sector. In a major revision, MPs sought to redress recurrent controversies over what were perceived as special privileges. Once conflicts with the administration and party competition firmly anchored the revision in the agenda of the Parliament, MPs made the revision look good to citizens. They did not improve their rewards, but spent much time to make sure they did not suffer from the revision either. The decisional aspects of the revision all testify to the fact that MPs act rationally over their rewards, both amongst themselves and vis-à-vis citizens. But the outcome of the revision also shows the partisan nature of the eventual outcome, which honor the majority parties' preferred model of representation. Parties do not just further their members' material interest, but their preferred concepts of representation, which in Belgium still allow for extensive involvement of MPs in civil society and in multiple public and private offices. The analysis also shows the uneasiness of the Belgian political class with the transparency of their rewards. Researchers still have a hard time reconstructing the different components of the reward structure, so citizens at large have a lot of difficulty accessing the information on their representatives' earnings. Making rewards public and information easily accessible remains an ongoing challenge.

The top civil service pay also has changed. The public sector reform that took off at the turn of the millennium was meant to revolutionize HRM in the federal administration. Although many of the reform components suffered severe political backlash and were overruled by the successive coalition government, the status and rewards for the top of the administration have changed for good. The position of many of the top managers is now contractual and their eventual pay rise is substantial. To some extent, rewards at the top for civil servants have become more variable, while clear links with performance pay have not taken off. Variability and performance pay in Belgium, certainly at the Federal level, sit ill with the remainders of a civil service culture that favors equality and legality, and with the partisan defenders of these principles. At the same time, the ambitions of the HRM reform and the actual implementation of recruitment at the top has re-invented traditional mechanisms of political control that are vital in a vulnerable political system and that have always rewarded those that play key roles in it.

Notes

1 It is one of the rewards on which information is little accessible. The budget of the Chamber for instance lumps the different allowances together with child benefits and travel allowances.
2 The conditional character of passive transparency is exemplified by the way in which information was provided by the *Questuur* of the Chamber. The overview of rewards was explicitly restricted to oral information.

References

Becquart-Leclercq, J. (1989) Paradoxes of corruption: a French view. In A.J. Heidenheimer *et al.* (Eds), *Political Corruption: A handbook*. New Brunswick: Transaction Publishers, pp. 191–212.

Brans, M. (1999) *Public office – private rewards. The dynamics of material rewards systems for legislators*. Firenze, EUI, PhD thesis.

Brans, M. and A. Hondeghem (1999) The senior civil service in Belgium. In E.C. Page and V. Wright (Eds), *Bureaucratic Elites in Western European States*. Oxford: Oxford University Press, pp. 120–146.

Brans, M., C. Pelgrims and D. Hoet (2006) Comparative observations on tensions between professional policy advice and political control in the Low Countries. *International Review of Administrative Sciences*, **72**(1): 57–71.

Brans, M. and A. Hondeghem (2005) Competency frameworks in the Belgian governments: causes, construction and contents. *Public Administration*, **83**(4): 823–837.

Brans, M., C. de Visscher and D. Vancoppenolle (2006) Administrative reform in Belgium: maintenance or modernization? *West European Politics*, **29**(5): 979–998.

Brans, M. and T. Steen (2007) From incremental to Copernican reform? Changes to the position and role of senior civil servants in the Belgian federal administration. In E. C. Page and V. Wright (Eds) *From the Active to the Enabling State. The Changing Role of Top Officials in European Nations*. London: Palgrave MacMillan, pp. 63–80.

De Winter, L. and M. Brans (2003) Belgium: political professionals and the party state. In J. Borchert and J. Zeiss (Eds) *The Political Class in Advanced Democracies. A comparative handbook*. Oxford: Oxford University Press, pp. 44–66.

Hondeghem, A. (2002) Competency management: the state of the art in the public sector? In S. Horton *et al.* (Eds), *Competency Management in the Public Sector*. Amsterdam: IOS, pp. 173–180.

Hondeghem, A. and M. Parys (2002) Competency management in Belgium: the Flemish and federal governments on the move. In S. Horton *et al.* (Eds), *Competency Management in the Public Sector*. Amsterdam: IOS, pp. 49–64.

Hondeghem, A. and R. Depré (Eds) (2005) *De Copernicushervorming in perspectief. Veranderingsmanagement in de federale overheid*. Brugge: Vanden Broele.

Hood, C.C. (1995) The politics of fasting and feasting. In F.F. Ridley and A. Doig (Eds), Sleaze: *Politicians, private interest and public opinion*. Oxford: Oxford University Press.

Hood, C.C. and B.G. Peters (1994) *Rewards at the Top: A comparative study of high public office*. London: Sage, pp. 190–201.
Knack: 32(2002) 50: 20–4.
Put, G. and I. Vanlangenakker (2010) The extent of multiple-office holding in Belgium and its underlying reasons. Paper Politicologenetmaal, Leuven, 2010: 23.

Documents Chamber – Senate

KvV. Questuur. Service Des Affaires Generales. Finances, Economat (1989) *Historique du Mode de Calcul du Montant Imposable de l'Indemnité Parlementaire.* Brussel.
KvV. Questuur. Dienst Algemene Zaken. Financiën en Huisbestuur (1990) *Regl. Regl8N-il 10 09 1990. Voordelen toegekend aan de leden van het Bureau, de Questoren en de Fractievoorzitters die in het Bureau zetelen – Aanpassing ingevolge de wijzigingen van de parlementaire vergoeding. Mededeling overeenkomstig de beslissing van het Bureau dd 05 07 1979.*
KvV. Questuur (1994a) *Syntheseverslag van de advies\voorstelgroep "Algemeen Statuut van het Parlementslid".* Brussel, 26 April 1994.
KvV. Questuur (1994b) *Eindverslag van de advies\voorstelgroep "Algemeen Statuut van het Parlementslid". Detaillering van de principes overeengekomen tijdens het conclaaf the Gesves op 2 en 3 mei 1994.* Brussel, 24 mei 1994.
KvV. *Verslag namens de Commissie voor de Comptabiliteit.* (1995–1996), 30 January 1996.

10 Rewards for high public office in the Netherlands

Frits M. van der Meer, Jan Kenter, and Theo A.J. Toonen

Introduction[1]

Comparing individual earnings provides ample opportunities for discussion in a traditionally mercantile state like the Netherlands. In 2005, the media reported extensively on pay increases and bonuses awarded to CEO's of Dutch energy providers. Directors of the (still) publicly owned energy providers were granted large productivity bonuses while household energy prices had risen sharply and raises in the public sector were kept to a bare minimum. Public condemnation of this self-enrichment followed, and MPs raised questions to the responsible ministers. This case was not the first and only eruption of public and political indignation. In 2004, the media, informed by a departmental whistleblower, reported that civil servants of the department of Education, Culture and Sciences were awarded, or awarded themselves, substantial pay increases on unclear grounds. In April 2006, public discontent turned against severance payments to top civil servants after these were exposed by the National Audit Chamber. Earlier, in 2001, it was revealed that some top public officials received higher paychecks than the Prime Minister himself. This occurred primarily in the semi-public sector, which includes publicly funded hospitals, universities, state-owned energy enterprises and independent agencies. The public and political outcry led to the launch of a state advisory committee on rewards and legal position of the administrative and political top, the Dijkstal Committee for short (*Adviescommissie beloning en rechtspositie van de ambtelijke en politieke topstructuur*). The Committee's findings were more or less adopted in full by Cabinet Balkenende III in 2006 and presented to Parliament. Nevertheless, a parliamentary majority needed for the rapid implementation of the new plans could not be found so close to the next elections (January 2007). The parliamentary debates were delayed until fall 2008.

Internal inconsistencies in the justification principles of the Dutch system of rewards for high public office (RHPOs) help to explain current difficulties. The system of public personnel management has experienced a profound change from being a classical bureaucracy to a more New Public Management (NPM) inspired system (see Demmke 2004, 2005) – a transformation from an approach centered on public service and public interest towards a more businesslike, performance-oriented approach. In this chapter we argue that the classic doctrine was not substituted. A novel dominant principle of justification was introduced adjacent to it. The principles are used simultaneously, creating a conflict with possibly damaging consequences.

In line with the earlier publication by Hood and Peters (1994) and the introduction to this volume by Brans and Peters, we examine Dutch rewards primarily at the national level. Included in our discussion are: political officeholders, MPs, the chief judiciary and top civil servants. HPOs in other parts of the public sector are included when relevant for our discussion of the national reward system. The structure of this chapter is as follows. The first section presents a general overview of the structure of the Dutch public sector reward system, and touches upon the ever-increasing private 'fringe' of the public sector as a contextual factor. Section two addresses existing arrangements with respect to HPOs, while section three examines the current debate on remuneration for HPO and the different directions arguments are taking. This is followed by section four with an attempt to explain the dynamics behind the structure of and decision making on RHPOs. The final section presents our overall conclusions.

Public officials and their personnel system in the Netherlands: the context

Over the last decades, a central aim of governmental human resource management (HRM) policies has been to create a more flexible reward system open to the 'needs of modern times' (Dijkstra and van der Meer 2000). Emphasis on principles of seniority and status was reduced, with increased attention on a direct connection between pay, output, and performance. Performance related pay (PRP) was considered crucial for attracting and retaining professional staff (Committee Van Rijn 2001). NPM overtures were omnipresent in the official policy doctrine, yet in practice results proved difficult to realize. Several studies on central government HRM policies revealed the absence of definite and lasting results (BZK 1999, van der Meer and Toonen 2005), mainly due to lack of managerial attention and budgetary problems. Managers are chiefly responsible for their primary targets and less for adequate HRM performance. Likewise HRM funds are limited in view of the wide-ranging ambitions.

Over time, the Dutch RHPO system has become highly integrated, unified and standardized. The Dijkstal Committee's recommendations enforce this tendency towards centralization. The high level of integration and standardization involves close interconnections of the RHPO for top civil servants, political officeholders, MPs, and the Judiciary. Parallel treatment, however, often stops at the type and size of bonuses and allowances that each category enjoys (Committee Dijkstal 2004). Semi-public organizations like hospitals, non-profit health care organizations, public housing corporations, independent agencies, and the majority of publicly owned enterprises are exempt from this integrated system. Rewards for CEOs of these organizations and the steep increases in compensation are reasons for the rewards issue ranking high on the political agenda. Ironically, in some cases, for a number of independent agencies, a separate legal (often private) form was chosen in order to achieve a more flexible and generous reward system.

While the RHPO system at the central government level has remained highly integrated since the 1980s, the centralized system of pay negotiations between the government and unions was abolished in 1993. This 'sectoralization' created 13 separate government sectors: the central government, defense, the judiciary, the police, the provinces, the municipalities, water boards, education, higher professional education, professional and adult education, universities, academic hospitals, and research institutions. The ministry of Home affairs arranged pay policy negotiations with trade unions for each policy sector. Pay policies were adopted after an agreement was either reached or determined by the central government alone. Over time, a more open system of bargaining developed together with a system of independent arbitration (Pivot 2000). This development is part of the ongoing processes of 'normalizing' the legal status of civil servants and labor relations in the public sector. Normalization thus means convergence between public labor law and private labor law: with the private sector considered the example to be followed; civil servants will thus become employees, which is a highly contested issue (see Dijkstra and van der Meer 2005). The Minister responsible in 2008 presented a white paper in which she emphasized the importance of maintaining a special status for civil servants at least at the national level (Ministry of the Interior 2008).

An additional goal of this decentralized system of pay negotiations was creating more intergovernmental flexibility in employment (Dijkstra and van der Meer 2000). After the 1993 sectoralization, a vast array of organizations representing governmental employers sprung into existence (van der Meer and Roborgh 1993). Several organizations cooperated across sectors to strengthen their position. In response, the government recognized or designated intermediate organizations to administer pay negotiations. Government employers and the intermediate organizations organized themselves in an overarching employer organization: the Association of Government Employers (VSO). In addition to the decentralized structure, individual governments are responsible for regulating the position of their workforce and the development of HRM policies (Dijkstra and van der Meer 2000).

From the establishment of parliamentary democracy in 1848, Dutch politics has been characterized by its coalition government. The central government is headed by a relatively weak cabinet led by a PM, who is formally the first among equals. While formal compartmentalization persists, enhanced interdepartmental coordination mitigates its negative effects. Political coordination is reinforced by expanding cross connections between different ministerial policy fields. The PM's power is dependent on the incumbent's personal talent, and less on formal powers of the office. Administrative coordination is supported by current centralization tendencies. The creation of a single internal labor market, problems of deficient inter- and intra-ministerial mobility, and failed HR management supported the tendency to centralization.

Senior staff since the 1990s, and all civil servants in central government since 2001, are no longer employed by the individual ministries but appointed in 'the general service of the state' (Arbeidsvoorwaardenovereenkomst sector Rijk 2000–2001). Changing one's job within central government does not imply that one should first resign from government; a civil servant remains 'in the service of government.' This is a fundamental challenge to the once-dominant orientation of the Dutch central government employment system. From a practical HRM perspective the consequences are, however, limited. The implementation of HRM policies is managed by the departmental personnel units.

The same is not the case for the senior level civil servants from the position of senior policy directors. For those staff members the *Algemene Bestuursdienst* (Senior Executive Service, ABD) was created in 1995. The main purpose of this Senior Executive Service was to create a centralized managerial career system for core departmental policy units, with the exclusion of the Foreign Office, the Defense Ministry (the military part) and the executive agencies. Over time, to serve senior civil servants at the very apex of the administration, an elitist inner group was formed within ABD, called the Top Management Group (TMG). Members of the TMG are typically HPOs, such as directors general, inspectors general and secretaries general. Their appointment is guided by a bureau of the ABD (the relevant personnel unit) and formally executed by the Home Office Minister in consultation with the minister of the department with the vacancy. Since early 2006, the TMG members, about 70, are formally employed by the department of Home Affairs. Beside the TMG, there are other top civil servants in the ABD that fit the HPO description. First, we include members of the very top of the Foreign Service (the top ambassadors) and the military officers in the Defense department. In addition, we include top judicial personnel (judges and prosecutors in the Dutch Supreme Court and Courts of Appeal).

Rewards paid for high public office

The RHPOs are part of an integrated public sector reward system that operates as a framework for all public sector actors within the decentralized system described above. At present civil service arrangements govern to a large extent the structural context for the rewards for other HPOs. The primary source of the reward system is the Civil Service Act of 1929, which defines the civil service and operates mainly as a framework law. Its main purpose is to ensure that decentralized governments are enacting appropriate regulations, including rewards. The decentralized general regulations contain many provisions but many of the detailed matters are regulated with by-laws and other provisions. Civil service legislation is thus highly flexible but, to say the least, not very transparent. For our purposes bylaws, such as the Algemene Rijksambtenaren Reglement (General regulations for central government civil servants ARAR) and its related pay regulation (Bezoldigingsbesluit Rijksambtenaren BBRA 1984) for central government, are the most important. Comparable regulations are in force for the other decentralized sectors. All these pay regulations have a similar structure. The standard system distinguishes six functional groups with group I being the lowest and VI the highest. The functions are classified by criteria including education, experience, nature of the job (van der Meer and Raadschelders 1999). Based on these six functional groups, a system of salary scales attaches a particular function to a scale. The basic scale system reaches from 1 to 18 and each scale consists of a number of pay increments. Civil servants in levels 16 and above work mainly in the core bureaucracies and are members of the ABD. There is an additional category outside the basic system that is relevant to our analysis. It is within this scale that TMG members reside, and the relevant scale is 19, although it consists of a fixed amount of money without any pay increments.

In addition to top ABD civil servants, ambassadors of the Foreign Service are paid according to these scales. In some cases, they are paid at the level of Deputy Minister. Military personnel, the ranks lieutenant general to general, are also at level 19. The top of the Judiciary, i.e. the president and attorney general of the High Court, is positioned at level 21. All the scales mentioned here are referring to a so-called base rate. In addition to the basic salary, bonuses and allowances can be added. The allowances are essentially the same as for the remainder of the civil service (holiday pay, end-of-year payment, child allowance, etc.), but bonuses are different. The secretary general receives a fixed management bonus of 5 percent on top of his salary. In addition, a performance bonus was introduced in 2002 (BBRA 1984; art. 22 a and b). This bonus is theoretically unlimited but informally capped at 130 percent of a minister's salary, the ceiling of which has not been broken by any civil servant so far. The Dijkstal report *Over dienen en verdienen* (Serve and Earn 2004) mentions that the variable bonus in 2002 reached on average 15.5 percent on top of the standard pay for top civil servants working at level 19. Departmental ministers have the power to award the bonus based on performance contracts. There is a tendency for the size of bonuses to increase in accordance with the pay grade (Dijkstal Committee 2004). In addition, top civil servants that have been recruited from outside the civil service receive additional attraction fees.

For ministers and deputy ministers two scales, 21 and 20, were added to the general scale system. The foundation of the legal position of political officeholders in the central government is to be found in the *Wet Rechtspositie Ministers en Staatssecretarissen* (Act on the legal position of ministers and deputy ministers). As mentioned earlier this is exactly the same position as some senior ambassadors as well as judges and the public prosecuting office. However, when revising the public sector salary system in 1981 the then-center-right cabinet Van Agt–Wiegel argued that the salary of the PM should be the top salary of the public sector salary system, including the local, regional and central political rewards. This should also apply to the semi-public sector. This principle of unified top reward remains dominant today. However, its support eroded through a combination of labor relations sectoralization and implementation of NPM oriented administrative personnel policies and management reforms.

In the 1981 revision the pay difference between top civil servants and political officeholders was calculated at around 9 percent. Nevertheless over the years the differential has decreased. According to the Dijkstal Committee the pay differential was 6.6 percent in 2004. Similarly, the Minister of Home Affairs wrote in 1976 that the pay quote – the level of the highest salary divided by the minimum wage in the public sector – would ideally be situated around 8.5 percent. At present, this quote amounts to a factor of 7.6 (Dijkstal Committee 2004). Thus we can conclude that the basic salaries of political officeholders have been leveled down similar to what is general practice in the public sector when compared to private sector earnings (see below). Particularly in the 1980s and early 1990s salary harmonization was popular in some parts of the political spectrum. The government was to set the example. In accordance with the then-dominant political feeling more emphasis was put on raising salaries in the lower income brackets. An additional explanation can be found in the fact that the most powerful civil service union, ABVA/KABO, has their strongest representation in the lower grades of the civil service. Unions looking after the interests of middle and higher civil servants have only slowly gained strength, and still remain relatively weak due to the low unionization rate of senior staff members.

After 1981 no fundamental alterations were made to the salary structure for the political officeholders in central government. Their basic salary has changed and is changing according to the rate and levels customary for the central government. However, a problem arises. The coupling of the civil servants and the political officeholders' salaries only pertains to the basic salaries, including regular allowances like holiday pay and the end-of-year payments, and not to pension rights (APPA 1969), redundancy payments, and expense allowances. Prior to 1999 expense allowances were untaxed, after this date a fixed amount has been paid (see Table 10.1).

The rewards for political officeholders and top civil servants have gradually grown apart and the latter have overtaken the former. Many pay increasing arrangements applicable to the civil service are not extended to political officeholders. First, political officeholders do not receive performance bonuses, bonuses that for top civil servants amount to 15.5 percent of the average salary, not to mention the structural 5 percent bonus for the Secretary General. Jokingly it has been suggested to introduce performance pay for political officeholders and let Parliament decide. Although these ideas have not been forwarded in earnest, they are reminiscent of the now outdated possibility for Parliament to express its displeasure over the performance of a particular Minister by reducing one guilder from his salary, which

Table 10.1 Fixed yearly expense allowance, 2009 (in euros)

Prime Minister	15.213
Minister Foreign Office	15.213
Other ministers	7.607
Deputy ministers	6.331

was considered equal to a motion of no confidence. Second, the reductions of weekly working hours from 40 to 38 in 1985 and to 36 in 1997 were not compensated for in a comparable reduction in income but increases were moderated. In reality, the 36-hour working week is a notable concept in respect to the much higher actual working hours of top civil servants and political officeholders. Recently, central government civil servants were given the opportunity to extend their working hours in exchange for financial compensation amounting to an 11 percent salary increase. Political office holders do not have formal working times and were therefore exempted from the reductions and from financial compensation. Together with other measures this causes the growing differences in gross earnings, currently adding up to 30 percent, and a change in income rankings (see Table 10.2).

Even though ministers are at the apex of the unified salary system their relative income position eroded in comparison to top civil servants. Ministers' and deputy ministers' salaries are lower than those of the top management group. The erosion of the salaries of ministers and deputy ministers relative to the Secretary General is indicated in Table 10.3, which provides information on base salaries during the period 1970–2004.

The situation for political officeholders in central government becomes even bleaker when compared to salary changes in the broader public sector and earnings of private sector workers. Of all functions mentioned in Table 10.4, changes to the Minister's salary have been the smallest. Pay rises in the lower civil service grades have been more substantial. Pay rises were most notable in the private and semi-public sector. As the figures pertain to basic salaries only the picture would become even darker when we include the bonuses. These observations inspired the Dijkstal Committee's proposal to overhaul the system, discussed below.

The reward system for MPs is also connected to that of civil servants. The arrangements for salaries of members of the Second Chamber are laid down in the Constitution (article 62). MPs decide on the pay arrangements by qualified majority voting. Over the last decades MPs' base salary is coupled to scale 16 (€87,847 in April 2006). Originally, this coupling in 1991 followed considerations that MPs' work was of equal weight as that of provincial board members, located at grade level 16. To the annoyance of MPs, shortly after their coupling to level 16, provincial board members moved up to level 17, resulting in continuing appeals to upgrade the basic salary of MPs.

Table 10.2 Average rewards to central government officials (salaries including allowances, bonuses, merit pay, etc., 2002)

Title	RHPO (€)
Secretary-general	132.585
Director-general	121.068
Minister	120.336

Source: Dijkstal Committee: Over dienen en verdienen 2004; Kerngegevens (burgerlijk) overheidspersoneel 1970–. Appendices BBRA 1984.

Table 10.3 Basic salary of Ministers, Deputy Ministers, and Secretaries general (excluding 5% SG allowance)

Year	Minister	Deputy Minister	SG
1970	49.455	40.617	32.880
1975	62.299	53.823	53.110
1980	80.196	70.671	68.390
1985	81.648	74.935	68.753
1990	86.430	81.039	75.984
1995	99.248	93.066	87.260
2000	108.851	102.060	95.697
2005	122.109	114.540	107.451
2010	133.825	125.608	117.910
Index			
1970	100	100	100
2010	271	309	359

Source: Dijkstal Committee 2004; Kerngegevens burgerlijk overheidspersoneel 1970–. Appendices BBRA 1984.

Table 10.4 Changes in wage indices for public and private sectors, 1970–2004 (1970 = 100)

	1970	2004
Minister	100	247
Deputy Minister	100	282
Queens Commissioner	100	315
Secretary General	100	327
Civil servant (middle ranking)	100	400
Civil servant (junior high)	100	362
Civil servant (senior high)	100	387
Members of the judiciary	100	290
Vice president of the Council of State	100	286
Contract earnings private sector	100	456
Contract earnings private sector (including incidental awards)	100	601

Source: Dijkstal Committee 2004.

Compared to the base salaries of a Minister, a Secretary General or a Director General, MPs' base salaries are low. On top of the *schadeloosstelling* (indemnity) – a traditional term indicating that it is not really a salaried job – MPs receive various expense allowances for traveling and housing. They can, however, choose to be fiscally treated as civil servants. In that case they get a fixed allowance. The speaker of the Second Chamber and political party leaders receive additional bonuses depending on the size of their party. External activities are allowed to a certain extent. When extra earnings exceed the maximum, excess money is deducted from the *schadeloosstelling*. MPs also have to register their extra parliamentary activities.

The reward system came under pressure due to public concerns about the self-enrichment of public officials and political apprehension over permanent civil servants bypassing the political top in rewards. This was followed by the Dijkstal Committee and their reports, which are discussed in the next section.

Renewing the reward system for high public office: the Dijkstal reports

The Dijkstal Committee proposed to reinstate the capstone position of the PM's salary. The old unified structure should be replaced by a parallel civil service and political structure with the PM's salary at the apex. The PM should be awarded a 10 percent bonus on top of his basic ministerial salary. Ministers will be awarded a 30 percent pay raise in order to offset earlier lost pay raises. An additional 20 percent raise should be added at a later stage given developments to the labor market. A raise for deputy ministers would be in place as well, whose salary should amount to 90 percent of the minister's salary. These changes would not be applied to other grade 20 and 21 offices, such as members of the Council of State, the National Audit Chamber, the National ombudsman and Members of the Judiciary and top diplomats. The implications for the civil service system are restricted to the level 19 pay scale in which three salary bands were included (see Table 10.5). There would be 'lighter and heavier' Directors General positions, respectively levels 19.1 and 19.2, with a corresponding differentiation in income. Ninety percent of their income would be fixed and 10 percent performance related, and at the discretion of the Minister this could amount to 20 percent for exceptional performances. The variable part is decided by the Secretary General assisted by an advisory committee. Level 19.3 was reserved for the Secretaries General, incorporating the 5 percent performance bonus, thus omitting any variable component in their salaries.

The connection between the political reward system and the top management group was prolonged while political and administrative pillars came into existence. The political pillar would include the lower and regional governments.

Table 10.5 New salary bands within level 19 as proposed by the Dijkstal Committee

Function	Minimum	Maximum
Director-general (1)	103.021	114.696
Director-general (2)	114.696	127.008
Secretary-general (3)	141.588	

Source: Dijkstal Committee 2004.

In its 2005 report *Advies beloningsverhoudingen politieke ambtsdragers* (Advise on pay differentials political officeholders) a new classification was made (Table 10.6).

Finally, an external advisory board advises on structural changes in the system every four years. In the meantime, salaries of political HPOs would follow the pay agreements for central government civil servants.

The government took over the main recommendations of the Dijkstal Committee and presented draft legislation to Parliament in the spring of 2005. As to the publically contested pay of the CEO's of energy and social housing corporations, the Cabinet had to admit this was out of their control, and made a moral appeal to the respective boards. For salaries in central government itself, the cabinet considered the 20 percent extra market related pay increase on top of the 30 percent already proposed less 'opportune.' The differentiation within level 19 has also been rejected (BZK 2004). Given the early stages of the debate, solid conclusions are difficult, but the signs are not favorable. In the early stages of parliamentary discussions, political parties collided. In 2006, the leader of the social democratic PVDA, Wouter Bos, declared that a 30 percent raise was too much, and other, mainly leftwing parties, made similar objections. With elections only a year away and the government, amidst a climate of economic austerity, quite unpopular, the prospects for raising rewards for political office-holders were bleak. During the parliamentary proceedings on remuneration for MPs, it was suggested to have rewards for politicians decided by an independent institution, like the Chamber of Accounts. In the final coalition agreement between the CDA, the PVDA and the CU (a smaller confessional

Table 10.6 New pay levels of political officeholders and Members of Parliament as proposed by the Dijkstal Committee in euros and in relation to the ministerial base rate (put at 100%)

Function	Monthly wages (€)	Related to ministerial wages (%)	Rise to present situation (%)
Prime Minister	13.474	110	43
Minister	12.249	100	30
Deputy Minister	11.024	90	25
Queens commissioner	10.411	85	11
Mayor of large cities	10.411	85	11
Chairman Waterboards	8.574	70	10
Municipal board member	8.574	70	3
Provincial board member	7.349	60	2
Member of Parliament	6.737	55	1
Municipal councilor (large cities)	2.450	20	31
Provincial councilor	1.225	10	30

party) of 2007, it was indeed decided that such a committee should advise minis-terial salaries. The parliamentary debate on the so-called Dijkstal laws concluded in fall 2008.

In addition to the central government pay schemes, there are also plans to cap and regulate top rewards in other public and 'semi-public' organizations, with independent agencies and universities with ministerial salaries as the point of reference.

Towards an explanation of the Dutch RHPO system

In the introduction, Brans and Peters forward three explanations for varying patterns of RHPO decision making, i.e., economic, cultural and political explana-tions. What sense do they make in the Dutch case?

Our analysis shows that the Dutch RHPO system is highly standardized. The basic salary constitutes the largest part despite the existence of variable components. The implementation of the Dijkstal Committee's recommendations would not change this. On the contrary, civil servants' PRP would be integrated in the system. The ministers' salary will constitute the salary cap. Differences between ministerial and top civil servants pay are rather small. In addition, the system has been made more transparent. In March 2006 the 'Act on publication of publicly financed top wages' (*Wet Openbaarmaking uit Publieke middelen gefinancierde Topinkomens*) became operational. Salaries in organizations financed by public means in all sectors of government are now published. Transparency decreases the possibility of rent seeking and thereby is expected to improve public attitudes to politicians and other government officials. The formal reward system is highly depoliticized and rather technical. The desire to avoid public discussions on government salary levels underlies this approach. Nevertheless this strategy induces rigor and thereby constitutes an obstacle when an overhaul is needed. Fundamental change in the system is complicated by party political dynamics coinciding in a game centered around who is most frugal with public money. The 1981 integration of political and civil service systems into a combined salary system was rather successful in neutralizing party political conflict because the bureaucratic system was taken as a starting point.

Even more interesting is the government's attitude towards rewards for top civil servants. During the early 2000s, government documents stressed the impor-tance of raising government salaries in line with the private sector. Extra income should be related to explicit performance targets according to the 'best new public management principles.' Recent discussions and the Dijkstal report re-emphasize the primacy of politics and the public interest dimension of public employment (2004). The title of its 2004 report is telling in this respect: 'To Serve and Earn.' It represents the two conflicting sets of principles for finding justifications for the size of RHPO. Politicians, the popular media and citizens use these different criteria when judging the height of rewards for civil servants and political officeholders.

On the one hand, civil servants and politicians should deliver. Top civil servants should demonstrate clear results on the basis of a measured performance. Politicians, in turn, should also deliver and, in their case, live up to their promises. As argued above, several management instruments and philosophies have been imported from the private sector. Just rewards are understood here as rewards in accordance with demonstrated performance. The different natures of the public and private sectors, as well as the lack of adequate standards, complicate comparisons of rewards. This implies a level of autonomy or shielding from public vision when making pay decisions. The bureaucratized version enables parties to do so by awarding bonuses. Yet, the prowling eye of the media and the transparency of formal regulations make this difficult, particularly when changes to the system are contemplated.

On the other hand, the dominant idea of political and public nature of public employment and the reward system is in force. The general view holds that public sector employees are working for the public interest and should be frugal with public money. In addition, it is considered an honor to work for and in the public interest. The latter might not be a general view, given the low regards of government nowadays, but it is held by top civil servants themselves. Given this situation, according to the second perspective, increases in salaries of top civil servants should be checked and definitely should not surpass ministerial rewards. This also refers to employees in other parts and levels of government including the semi-public sector. The real problem in the Dutch debate on RHPOs is that both sets of criteria are simultaneously employed, and hardly ever weighted against each other.

Conclusion

Since the inception of the Civil Service Act of 1929 and the issuing of the *BBRA* the civil service pay system has been standardized. The initial absence of performance related bonuses made the system transparent and highly bureaucratic. Rank, scale, and the principle of seniority influenced pay levels at the top, which were determined through a negotiation process in which the central government had the final say. The latter meant that particularly during periods of economic austerity pay levels were the outcome of central government budget decisions. In the 'bad old days,' before 1945, it was argued that government employment effectively meant poverty combined with tenure. The honor of serving the public interest should be the motivating force. The dominant structure for rewarding civil servants was an integrated salary system with some allowances added to the base rate but without any serious variations. Since the 1980s the political reward system has been unified with that of the civil service.

Since the 1980s some important modifications to the civil service pay system have been made. The most important was a shift in perspective from a more bureaucratic oriented personnel management system towards one based on NPM principles. Included in this was the so-called normalization process involving convergence of public sector and private sector conditions, including social security schemes and pay negotiations. It also involved decentralization of labor negotiations in which a more equal position was envisaged. The introduction of flexible reward policies was of key importance, such as additional pay increments and bonuses. Yet the degree of flexibility should not be overestimated, since the average size of the bonuses is 15.5 percent of the basic salary. An important conclusion is that within government departments a standardized reward system is in operation. Some flexibility has been added in recent years but that level is still fairly limited compared to the situation at the top. Given the decentralization of labor negotiations and settlements, similar conclusions can be drawn for rewards for high public officeholders in the judiciary, military and the Foreign Service.

Developments in the rewards of executive politicians and MPs demonstrate a similar tendency towards standardization. On top of the 18 scales of the standard system, levels have been added for the senior civil servants (19), ministers (21), and deputy ministers (20). This system could easily create the mistaken idea that ministers and deputy ministers are considered civil servants. The coupling also applies to MPs, whose level 16 salary equals that of a deputy director and director. The reasoning behind this unified RHPO system is that it depoliticizes a controversial issue.

Discussing RHPOs is a popular topic and it is often used for party political gains. The latest round of political debates led to the installation of the Dijkstal Committee to find a solution to growing discrepancies between rewards to political and administrative officeholders. When the committee proposed to raise the salaries of ministers by 30 percent during the next cabinet period, public opinion turned against it. The Netherlands are currently in the middle of heated debates on rewards in the public sector. The level of intensity is rather new, although discussions on pay raises for politicians have always run high. The reasons are partly found in declining levels of trust in politics and the civil service since 2002. The lack of confidence in the politico-administrative system as a whole and the perceived austerity of government economic policy are not favorable conditions for salary raises. Moreover, the maneuvering room is limited, since new measures have increased transparency.

We have argued that the current debate on RHPOs is complicated by the conflicting coexistence of two dominant principles of justification. In relevant policy documents (often too slavishly underwritten by public administration experts) we have noted a change from a classical bureaucratic to a more New Public Management system. In short, this involves the change from a system organized around public service concepts towards a more businesslike performance-oriented approach. In this chapter, we have argued that the classic public sector approach was not so much replaced, but accompanied by the NPM based one. Both sets of appraisal are applied at the same time with some damaging consequences. Top public officials should perform and be paid accordingly, but also serve the public interest and take gratification from that service.

Note

1 The authors would like to thank Veerle van Doeveren for her valuable support.

References

Adviescommissie beloning en rechtspositie ambtelijke en politieke topstructuur (Committee Dijkstal) (2004) *Over dienen en verdienen*. Den Haag: BZK.

Adviescommissie beloning en rechtspositie ambtelijke en politieke topstructuur (Committee Dijkstal) (2005) *Advies beloningsverhoudingen Politieke ambtsdragers*, Den Haag: BZK.

Algemene Bestuursdienst (1996) Plan van Aanpak. Den Haag: ABD.

Algemene Bestuursdienst (1997) *Verslag van werkzaamheden* 1995/1996 (Progress report 1995/1996). Den Haag, ABD.

Algemene Bestuursdienst (1999) *Verslag van werkzaamheden 1998* (Progress report 1998). Den Haag: ABD.

Algemene Bestuursdienst (2001) *Verslag van werkzaamheden 2001* (Progress report 2001). Den Haag: ABD.

APPA (Algemene Pensioenswet Politieke Ambtsdragers) 1969.

Arbeidsvoorwaardenovereenkomst sector Rijk 2000–2001 (General labor agreement Central government 2000–2001).

Bekke, H.G.J.M., T.A.J. Toonen and J.L. Perry (Eds) (1996) *Civil Service Systems in Comparative Perspective*. Bloomington, IN, Indiana University Press.

Bekke H.G.J.M. and F.M van der Meer (Eds) (2000) *Western European Civil Service Systems*. Cheltenham: Edward Elgar.

Bossaert, D. and C. Demmke (2003) *Civil Services in the Accession States. New trends and the impact of the integration process*. Maastricht: EIPA.

Centraal Plan Bureau (CPB) (2005) *Reële contractloonstijging op de lange termijn*. Den Haag: CPB.

Demmke, C. (2004) *European Civil Services between Tradition and Reform*. Maastricht: EIPA.

Demmke, C. (2005) *Are Civil Servants Different because they are Civil Servants? Who are the civil servants – and how?* Maastricht: EIPA.

Commissie aanpak arbeidsmarkt knelpunten collectieve sector (Committee Van Rijn) (2001) *Investeren in mensen en kwaliteit (Investing in people and quality)*. Den Haag: BZK.

Dijkstra, G.S.A. and F.M van der Meer (2000) The Dutch civil service system. In: H.G.J.M. Bekke and F.M. van der Meer (Eds.) *Western European Civil Service Systems*. Cheltenham: Edward Elgar.

Dijkstra, G.S.A. and F.M van der Meer (2005) De positie van de ambtenaar meer buitengewoon dan normaal. In: *De Staatscourant*: 6-6, 25 October.

Eindrapport Interdepartementaal beleidsonderzoek effectiviteit personeelsmanagement rijksdienst (2001) *Rijk met personeel: naar een effectiever personeelsmanagement in de rijksdienst (Rich with personnel: towards a more effective personnel management in central government)*. Den Haag: BZK.

Hood, C. and B.G. Peters (1994) *Rewards at the Top. A comparative study of high public office*. London: Sage.

Kabinetstandpunt effectiviteit personeelsmanagement (2001).

Ministerie van Binnenlandse zaken (en Koninkrijksrelaties), *Kerngegevens (bezoldiging) overheidspersoneel 1970–2004*. Den Haag: BZK.

Ministerie van Binnenlandse Zaken (en Koninkrijksrelaties), *Mensen en management in de rijksdienst (People and management in central government)* 1997–1998. Den Haag: BZK.

Ministerie van Binnenlandse Zaken (en Koninkrijksrelaties), *Vertrouwen in verantwoordelijkheid*, Den Haag, 1999 (Trust in responsibility). Den Haag: BZK.

Ministerie van Binnenlandse Zaken (en Koninkrijksrelaties) (1999) *Management- en personeelsontwikkeling Rijksdienst.* Den Haag: BZK.

Ministerie van Binnenlandse Zaken (en Koninkrijksrelaties) (1999) *Nota Management en personeelsontwikkeling (White paper on Management and personnel development in central government).* Den Haag: BZK.

Ministerie van Binnenlandse zaken en koninkrijkrelaties & Rijksarchiefdienst Pivot (2000) *Overheidspersoneel: arbeidsverhoudingen. Een rapport institutioneel onderzoek op het deelbeleidsterrein. Arbeidsverhoudingen bij het overheidspersoneel in de periode 1945–1995* (1997), Den Haag: Pivot.

Ministerie van Binnenlandse Zaken (en Koninkrijksrelaties) (2001) *Investeren in het personeelsbeleid van de rijksdienst: personeelsbrief.* Den Haag: BZK.

Ministerie van Binnenlandse Zaken (en Koninkrijksrelaties) (2002) *Rijk aan voorwaarden. Een onderzoek naar secundaire voorwaarden bij de sector rijk.* Den Haag: BZK.

Ministerie van Binnenlandse Zaken (en Koninkrijksrelaties) (2004) *Kabinetsstandpunt Adviescommissie beloning en rechtspositie ambtelijke en politieke topstructuur.* Den Haag: BZK.

Page, E.C. and V. Wright (Eds) (1999) *The Role of Senior Officials in a Service State.* Oxford: Oxford University Press.

Page, E.C. and V. Wright (2007) *The Changing Role of the Senior Civil Service in Europe*, London: Palgrave (forthcoming).

Peters, B.G. and J. Pierre (2001) Civil servants and politicians: the changing balance. In B.G. Peters and J. Pierre (Eds), *Politicians, Bureaucrats and Administrative Reform*, ECPR Studies in European Political Science. London: Routledge.

Peters, B.G. and J. Pierre (2004) *The Quest for Control. The politicisation of the civil service in comparative perspective.* London: Routledge.

Pollitt, C. and G. Bouckaert (2004) *Public Management Reform: A comparative analysis.* Oxford: Oxford University Press.

Sprengers, L. (Ed.) (2006) *Heeft de ambtelijke status nog toekomst.* Den Haag: CAOP.

Steen T.P.S., C.F. van den Berg, F.M. van der Meer, P. Overeem and T.A.J. Toonen (2005) *Andere overheid in het buitenland: Inrichting van de centrale overheid. Een internationale vergelijking.* Den Haag: PAO.

Steen T.P.S., C.F. van den Berg, F.M. van der Meer, P. Overeem, and T.A.J. Toonen (2005) *Modernisering Governments in other Countries: International comparison of change processes in central government.* Den Haag: PAO.

van der Meer, F.M. (2002) *Civil Service Reform in Western Europe and the Rise of the Enabling State.* Paper presented during the Paul van Riper Symposium at ASPA conference Phoenix, AZ, March 2002.

van der Meer, F.M. (2004) Dutch government reform and the quest for political control. In B.G. Peters and J. Pierre (Eds), *The Quest for Control. The politicisation of the civil service in comparative perspective.* London: Routledge.

van der Meer, F.M. and J.C.N. Raadschelders (1999) The role of Senior Officials in The Netherlands. In V. Wright and E.C. Page (Eds) *The Role of Senior Officials in a Service State.* Oxford: Oxford University Press.

van der Meer, F.M. and R.J. Roborgh (1993) *Ambtenaren in Nederland. Omvang, bureau-cratisering en representativiteit van het ambtelijk apparaat.* Alphen aan den Rijn, Samsom H.D. Tjeenk Willink.

van der Meer, F.M and T. Toonen (2005) Competency management and civil service professionalism in Dutch Central Government. *Public Administration,* **83**, 839–852.

van der Meer, F.M. and F. van Nispen (2000) The market for civil servants in the Netherlands. In A. Morton *et al., Serving the State,* vol. 2, Ashgate.

van der Meer, F.M. and J.C.N. Raadschelders (2006) From the active to the enabling state: the changing role of the senior civil service in Dutch national government. In E.C. Page (Ed.), *The Changing Role of the Senior Civil Service in Europe.* London: Palgrave, London (forthcoming).

Velthoven, J.H., E.C.B. van Ettinger, J.A. Konst, M. de Rijke and P. van Polanen, *Rechtspositie van politieke ambtsdragers. Rapport beloning van hogere ambtenaren bij het rijk, TK* 2004–2005, 28479, nrs. 17–18.

11 Rewards for high public office

The case of Norway

Per Lægreid and Paul G. Roness

Introduction[1]

Norway has a long and strong egalitarian tradition affecting rewards for high public office (RHPOs). In this chapter the underlying question is why, in a country as rich as Norway, have RHPOs been so low compared to those in comparable countries? In the last two decades, attempts have been made to introduce greater differentiations in salaries. We discuss these efforts at reforming the salary systems for high public offices, focusing particularly on the attempts to introduce performance-based salaries for top civil servants. From the beginning of the 1990s onwards, New Public Management (NPM) had greater influence on decisions about rewards, both directly by reforming the salary systems and indirectly by structural devolution.

This chapter will focus on formal and tangible dimensions of rewards offered to high public officials through salaries. In the civil service, placement on a salary scale has traditionally been determined by position, but for the last two decades performance criteria and market pressure have been given higher priority. In Norway, like most other Organization and Economic Co-operation Development (OECD) countries, productivity and results-oriented elements have been introduced into the civil service pay system (OECD 1988, 1996, 1997, 2005a, 2005b).

We will first outline the Norwegian salary system for top civil servants, cabinet ministers, members of Parliament, and senior judges, emphasizing contextual features and the main reforms and changes during the last two decades. We will have a closer look at attempts at reforming the salary structure of top civil servants. Data on the actual development of salaries for all four groups since the early 1990s are then presented in a separate section, where some long time trends also are included. The conclusion is also mainly focused on reforms in top civil servants' pay.

The Norwegian salary and pension systems for HPOs

The general context

Norway is a small unitary, parliamentary, and multiparty state. Since the early 1970s, it has mainly been ruled by minority governments, and since 1994 it has been connected to the EU through the Economic Area Agreement. In a comparative perspective, it has a strong democratic tradition, has high per capita income and public finances are good due to the oil revenue. It has relatively strong collectivistic and egalitarian values, is consensus-oriented, and has low levels of internal conflict and well-developed corporatist arrangements. The civil service unions are strong in Norway, and it also has a comprehensive and universal welfare state. Its economy is open and dependent on exports. The relationships between parliament, ministers, and agencies are based on the principle of ministerial responsibility, meaning that the minister is responsible to the parliament for all activities within his or her policy area – in the ministry as well as in subordinate bodies. Political control over the civil service has, however, been passive, allowing the executive substantial leeway. Norway is characterized by a high level of mutual trust and shared norms among political and administrative leaders. The level of trust in public institutions is higher than in most other countries (Norris 1999). Surveys of political support for national government and parliament nearly always accord Norway a leading position. Until the mid-1990s, Norway was a reluctant reformer (Olsen 1996), but later Norway has become a more eager reformer, and structural devolution has become a main reform tool (Christensen and Lægreid 2003).

The pay for state employees is essentially decided in a collective bargaining system involving strong civil service unions. This system has developed gradually since the 1920s. In 1948, a general, standardized national pay scale, which left little room for flexibility, local autonomy and individualized benefits, was introduced. It covered all state employees, including top civil servants. During the 1980s, demands for individualized pay, adaptation to market pressure and productivity gains gradually became key words in the pay policy ideology, and some adjustments of the pay system were implemented (Lægreid 1995).

On the one hand, Norway has a political culture that is supportive of the public sector, has a good financial situation and, during 1995–2005, was more willing to adopt NPM ideas, all factors which might enhance high rewards for high public offices. On the other hand, it also has a strong egalitarian culture, powerful civil service unions and a consensus-oriented policy style which will tend to provide relatively lower levels of rewards.

Prior to 1990, salaries of top civil servants in Norway were determined through negotiations between civil service unions and the state as employer in a system characterized by an egalitarian wage policy, central control, standardization, permanent positions, and standardized salaries. In combination with the strong egalitarian norms of Norwegian society, this tradition resulted in low top civil servant salaries compared with other countries. Indeed, the salary table for Norwegian state employees was one of the most contracted of all the OECD countries. A survey of 10 OECD countries in 1991 revealed that the salary level for top civil servants was lowest in Norway (Hood and Peters 1994).

Reforms since the early 1990s

In the early 1990s, an attempt was made at revising the state salary system comprehensively, in accordance with the principles of performance management. The main objectives of these reforms were a better recruitment and increased efficiency within the individual state agencies, through restructuring toward less centralized control, less standardization and fewer collective agreements. While the national pay scale and the collective bargaining system were kept in a slightly modified form, in the general wage agreement of 1990 some 450 top civil servants from director general and above were removed from these scales and negotiations. In the following year a separate system was designed for this group, based on individual contracts. Under the new system the minister was formally responsible for determining the executive's salary. In the late 1990s, several top civil servants were removed from the new system, partly because the agencies they were heading were converted into state-owned companies, and partly because the range of positions included in the system was reduced. Thus, today some 300 executives are part of the top civil servant pay system.

Even if they are considered as civil servants, Supreme Court judges have had their salaries set by the *Storting* (Parliament) since 1962. In 1991 the other judges were also removed from the state pay system. A separate pay system for these judges was established through negotiations between the Ministry of Justice and representatives of the judges' union. Here, the salaries depended partly on the level and size of the court, and partly on their own position. Thus, the extent of leadership responsibility was seen as important, as well as recruiting and retaining qualified judges. Later on, adjustments to the system and pay increases have also been decided through negotiations between representatives of the state and the union.

The pay of MPs and cabinet ministers is decided by the *Storting*. Between 1982 and 1991, the prime minister's pay and that of the other ministers was linked to the pay of Supreme Court judges. During this period the PM earned one percent more than did the president of the Supreme Court, and ministers earned one percent more than did Supreme Court judges. Between 1970 and 1993, an MP's salary was coupled to the salary of a deputy director general of a ministry. In 1993, the salary for the prime minister, all other ministers and all MPs was set to certain steps on the general pay scale. In 1996, a commission appointed by the *Storting*, consisting of MPs from different parties, proposed that the *Storting* decide pay rises for MPs and ministers in future based on recommendations offered by an independent committee of experts. While a similar proposal from a previous commission appointed by the *Storting* was turned down in 1993, this time it went through. Since then, the expert committee has proposed specific amounts for the prime ministers, other ministers and MPs. The *Storting* has each time approved the proposed pay increases. In 2001, the *Storting* also decided that members of its Board of Presidents should have some additional salary. In 2003, a new commission appointed by the *Storting* reviewed the pay system for top politicians. While the majority argued that the real decision on pay increase still should be decided by the expert committee, a minority (representatives from the

Socialist Left Party) saw no need for this committee and wanted the *Storting* to decide the salaries itself. This majority also recommended that the arrangement of additional salary should be extended to leaders of Standing Committees. In addition, a majority (all members except the representative of the Progress Party) recommended that the president of the *Storting* now should have the same salary as the prime minister. All majority proposals were implemented in 2004. The commission appointed in 2003 also discussed whether the parliamentary leaders of the party groups should have some additional salary from the *Storting*, but no proposal was presented to the *Storting*. However, in most parties the parliamentary leader now gets an additional salary from the party group.

For pensions, civil servants are members of the Norwegian Public Service Pension Fund as well as the National Insurance Scheme. According to an arrangement existing since the National Insurance Scheme was introduced in the mid-1960s, those who have achieved full qualification (30 years) are guaranteed a total pension of 66 percent of the salary at retirement (or proportions for shorter terms of service) from the age of 67. This also applied to top civil servants, even in the new system from 1991 onwards. All civil servants contribute two percent of their salary to the Norwegian Public Service Pension Fund, in addition to the general contributions to the National Insurance Scheme.

Supreme Court judges are also members of the Norwegian Public Service Pension Fund, but have had some additional conditions since 1982. Thus, they achieve full qualification after only 15 years of service and get a pension of 57 percent of the current salary for Supreme Court judges if they remain in their position until age 67.

Until 2012, cabinet ministers and MPs were covered by separate pension schemes. For ministers, at the age of 65, they were eligible to a pension of 42 percent of the current salary for ministers if they had been a minister for at least 3 years, increasing by three steps of five percent each year to a maximum of 57 percent for tenure of 6 years or more. MPs were eligible to this retirement pension at the age of 65, or when the sum of age and tenure was 75 years, if they had met at the *Storting* for at least 6 months during 3 years. The size of the pension was proportional to their tenure, reaching a maximum of 66 percent of the current salary of MPs when having met at the *Storting* for 12 years.

Neither ministers nor MPs are entitled to receive their pensions while holding positions as a minister, a MP, or a full-time public servant. Like civil servants, ministers and MPs contribute 2 percent of their salary to their pension fund, in addition to general contributions to the National Insurance Scheme. The main aspects of the pension schemes for cabinet ministers and MPs were unchanged from (at least) the early 1980s until 2012, when the schemes were integrated into the Norwegian Public Service Pension Fund and made more equivalent to the general conditions in the National Insurance Scheme. If they are not retiring, outgoing cabinet ministers and MPs automatically get severance pay for one month, or for three months if they do not start a new job during that period.

With regard to additional supplements, these are normally low and restricted for high public office in Norway. In contrast to many other countries, Norwegian

MPs do not retain their MPs' salary in addition to their ministerial salary if appointed to the cabinet. It is also unusual for top politicians to have a large additional income from outside sources, and particularly for cabinet ministers. In 1990, a public register for MPs' financial interests was established, revealing that most MPs had modest additional incomes. The MPs had daily allowances and some other supplements added to their basic salary up to the mid-1990s, but most of this was included in increased salaries to make their remuneration more transparent. Secretarial help for MPs is covered through grants to the party groups. The prime minister and cabinet ministers have a car with a chauffeur for their disposal when in office. On duty, they also have free air travel, a supplement also given to MPs. Cabinet ministers and MPs commuting on a weekly basis from at least 40 kilometers outside Oslo are provided with a free apartment in the capital, and their travel expenses to their permanent home are also covered. Some persons in high public offices also have extra duties and assignments for which they get additional pay. In that case, they pay taxes in line with other citizens. Outside tasks like commissions have been common among Supreme Court judges. Over the past years, however, more constraints are put on the possibilities for Supreme Court judges to have additional incomes.

In contrast to the small additions to basic salaries for top public officeholders, the CEOs in private sector companies may have large supplements, such as bonuses, options and allowances in kind. These significant differences between arrangements for high public offices and top executives in private sector companies make the reward gap between leaders in the public and private sectors much bigger. Lately, bonuses and options have also become more prominent for top executives in state-owned companies.[2] Thus, the gap between CEOs of state-owned companies and other public sector top executives has also increased significantly. This trend has caused some political controversies. The incoming center-left government decided in 2006 to change the law to stop the possibility of stock options in companies where the state is involved through ownership. When the executive board of Hydro, one of the biggest partly state-owned companies in Norway, in 2007 decided to realize a previously agreed option (now amounting to 27 million NOK) for the CEO, this caused a tense public debate and eventually led to the resignation of the chairman of the executive board.

Attempts to reform the top civil servants' pay structure: more flexibility but weak on performance pay

In Norway, the NPM reform ideas constituted the basis for the new top civil servant pay system introduced in 1991. The main advocates of the reform were some agency heads, while most civil service unions were skeptical. The new pay system implied changes as to how the salary was to be determined, what was considered an equitable salary, and which criteria were to be used in determining salary levels.

In the individual contracts of top civil servants, clear and precise objectives were to be agreed upon with the secretary general and his/her minister and with directors general and the secretary general. Achieving these objectives was to be evaluated once a year, and this evaluation was to provide the basis for annual revision of the contract. The idea was that good results would lead to an increase in salary, while a poor performance could lead to a reduction in the personal supplement, or, in the worst case, transfer to another position. The leaders would, however, retain a permanent position within the civil service.

The contract system was implemented cautiously and reluctantly by the government, in order to prevent an indefensible increase in leaders' salaries. This resulted in lower increases than originally envisaged and also a less decentralized and flexible system. There was a collective transfer to the new system for all people in the relevant positions. Four salary categories were introduced, with the opportunity to award a personal supplement of up to 20 percent of the category salary. Three-quarters of the positions were placed in the lowest category and awarding personal supplements was to be very restrictive. There was also little differentiation within the same groups of positions. All secretaries general were placed in the same category. The same applied to virtually 90 percent of directors general, who comprised the largest individual group. These decisions resulted in a fairly standardized system, with the same regulations pertaining both to positions that were not exposed to market pressure, and to those state organizations which were particularly exposed, such as large financial agencies and public enterprises.

Upon entering a contract in 1991, the top civil servants received, on average, a salary increase of 14 percent, while other state salary increases were set at 4 percent that year. Since then, the pay scale has been adjusted once a year, normally according to the average pay increase in society. In Norway, the egalitarian norms are strong, and the new contract system became a part of the government's moderate incomes policy called 'the solidarity alternative.' In addition to the incentive function, the new system allowed for the granting of a personal supplement on the basis of labor market conditions or with reference to the position held, but a main objective was to keep the wage increments as low as possible. The level of salary was thus a combination of a basic salary linked to the position held, and an individual supplement. Even though the relationship between supplementary salary and performance was presented as a mainstay of the new system, the reform was still not a clear-cut 'pay for performance' system. It was a combination system designed to increase the competitiveness of the state agencies in the labor market, to improve leader mobility through more flexible salary arrangements, and to create a more active leadership policy based on performance management systems, within narrow wage supplements. The overall aim was to contribute to a more effective and efficient administration.

The majority of the Norwegian top civil servants who were transferred to the contract system in 1991, had made their careers within the state labor market and achieved their top positions through internal promotion within their own sphere. They had long records of service in the government administration and in their own ministry or agency, and few had thoughts of resigning for jobs in the private sector. At the same time, there was very little recruitment from the private sector.

Thus, one of the main goals of the reform was to recruit well-qualified leaders from outside the public sector. This mobility pattern did not change significantly in the first 5 years after the introduction of the new system, but the reform did stimulate transfers within the state sector (Lægreid and Savland 1996a). In the new millennium, internal recruitment from within one's own ministry is still the normal pattern. It has generally been very difficult to recruit candidates from the private sector, due to the enduring pay gap between top executive positions in the public and private sectors (Statskonsult 2004b).

Until the end of 1995, individual supplements or changes in salary category had been implemented for about half of all leaders covered by the system, but in most cases the amount of the supplements was very low (Lægreid and Savland 1996b). There were, however, broad differences between the ministries in the use of personal supplements. The Ministry of Finance and agencies under the Ministry of Transport and Communication were notable for having the largest and the highest number of individual supplements.

It appeared that the 'pay for performance' component was particularly difficult to operate in practice (Lægreid and Mjør 1993, Lægreid 1997). It was hard to determine precise, operational and measurable objectives and performance indicators. In a survey conducted in 1993, only 18 percent of the top civil servants covered by the new system stated that their own contract was a result of negotiations, and under one-third believed that those objectives which had been determined were, in fact, measurable. The first generation of contracts was not specific concerning the personal objectives for the individual concerned. The formulation of objectives and results was for the most part customary, general, opinionated or vague, and formulated in 'elastic' phrasing and terminology that was open to a wide range of interpretations. To the extent that more specific objective requirements did exist, these were frequently activity objectives that hardly captured the efficiency or quality aspect. The leaders were also uncertain as to whether the salary system had, in fact, contributed to increased efficiency. There was considerable doubt among top civil servants as to whether the reform had made it easier for weaker leaders to be reappointed to other posts. Thus, there were strong indications that the contract system has had little direct effect on how leaders in top positions actually functioned. Some felt that their immediate superior had increased control over their own work situation, which indicates that the contract system was one step in the direction of a control system (Lægreid 2001).

There was a growing skepticism regarding the contract system over time. A survey conducted in 1996 revealed that more than 70 percent of the leaders had put work with the performance contract aside, or regarded it as a dead ritual (Administrasjonsdepartementet 1996). The Labour government concluded, however, based on an overall assessment, that the advantages of retaining the system in a modified form were greater than the disadvantages of winding it up (Rodal 2006).

From 1997 onward there has been, within centrally determined guidelines, a certain amount of delegation to individual ministries for salary supplements and performance contracts. Flexibility was also increased through the introduction of a new fifth salary category on top, and through the establishment of three subcategories within each main category. In 2001, the limit for awarding a personal supplement by the ministry was increased from 20 percent to 30 percent of the category salary. However, supplements beyond this limit, and reclassifications of positions into a higher salary category, still must be approved by the Ministry of Government Administration (Rodal 2006).

During the review in 1996–1997, there was an intention to revitalize the performance element, but so far this wish has not given any significant results. The evaluation in 1996 concluded that there was nothing wrong with the principles behind the system, and that it was just unfortunate political and economic conditions or practical administrative problems that caused the difficulties in making the system function as intended. Failure was attributed to mismanagement and lack of political skills, management capacity or financial resources, and the suggestions from evaluators were to be patient, persevere and wait for better times. Over time, the system has been more decentralized, and the use of individual supplements has increased (Blaauw 2002). In 2004, 80 percent of top executives were in the two lowest salary categories, and 95 percent of top executives received individual supplements. On average, the individual supplement was about 10 percent of total salary (Statskonsult 2004a). When recruiting externally, the individual supplements tend to be used fully (Statskonsult 2004b). Over time, the individual supplement has been seen more as a permanent and increasing component of total pay to compensate for pay differences and unfairness than being a performance component as intended.

The system has developed towards more specified contracts regarding objectives and performance indicators, but still they are rather incomplete. The contracts work more as general steering signals than as specified tools. The rather rigid 'pay for performance' component has been modified, and there is now a softer version balancing different criteria and phasing out the annual performance assessments based on specified performance indicators formulated in detailed individual contracts. In practice, it was difficult to specify measurable individual performance indicators that could be used to assess results of individual executives. Normally, the formulations were rather elastic, allowing numerous interpretations. It is difficult to get the political executives involved in the system by formulating objectives and assessing performance and results (Christensen and Lægreid 2002). It is primarily a system used between managerial executives on different levels, and objectives are more typically formulated by managerial executives than by politicians.

In a study conducted in 2000–2001 among persons in high public office (ministers, secretaries general, and chief executives of state agencies), most ministers stated that they were not involved in pay and contracts for top civil servants to any extent (Christensen and Lægreid 2002). The goals and performance indicators in the contracts were mainly decided among secretaries general and directors general (cf. also Rodal 2006). Several top civil servants expressed skepticism about this type of formal system and its focus on quantification and efficiency. About half of the secretaries general agreed that a pragmatic and relaxed version of the systems worked reasonably well, while the other half said that it is difficult to practice the system. The performance indicators were too vague, and the discretion for setting salaries was too small. It was too difficult to move people between salary categories, and the possibilities for awarding personal pay rises were too small. It was generally regarded as difficult to use the system for subjective assessment of personal leadership qualities. A main effect of the system, according to the secretaries general, was that the system legitimized pay increases and reduced the exit of top civil servants from central government. One had, however, been reluctant to raise the salaries to meet the competition from the private sector. The most problematic component in the system was the pay for performance element. Generally, the system seemed to work in a more relaxed and less rigid version.

The chief executives in state agencies were generally more skeptical about the system than the secretaries general. Only one of ten agreed that the system had worked as intended. Many reported that the individual supplements were not rewards for individual performances, but were more used to compensate for pay differences and unfairness. Thus, according to them, it was not working as an incentive system.

Summing up, the top civil servant pay system has some intended effects, but it has been difficult to implement several parts of it. The system has symbolic features and has been implemented in a pragmatic way. On the one hand, it has enhanced flexibility and increased the pay level, making it easier to keep and reward some top civil servants and to allow greater pay differentiation. On the other hand, it is difficult to handle the subjective component, to balance the individual and the collective element in the system, to practice it as an incentive system and to implement 'pay for performance'. It appears to be cultural resistance against too large pay differences between top civil servants, and against quantification and making the system too technical. The secretaries general were most satisfied with the system, the agency executives were most skeptical and the political leaders were rather distant from the whole system.

The development of RHPOs 1992–2007

In this section we will primarily examine the development of salaries for high public offices in the period 1992–2007, but some information on the two previous decades is also presented. We will focus on changes in the level of pay in absolute and relative numbers, and make comparisons between different groups, as well as within groups.

In general, the salary level for high public office in Norway is significantly lower than the salary for CEOs in large Norwegian companies, and also much lower than for similar positions in other European countries.[3] Fifteen years after the introduction of the new top civil servant pay system, they still lagged considerably behind the salary of top executives in private sector companies.

With regard to salary in absolute numbers, Table 11.1 reveals that the salary of the prime minister in 2007 was 1,191,000 NOK. The Supreme Court president

Table 11.1 Annual salary of different types of HPO, 1992–2007 (in 1.000 NOK)

	1992	1995	1998	2001	2004	2007
Prime minister	420	457	765	925	1,022	1,191
Cabinet minister	393	428	625	760	836	969
MP*	274	291	440	520	567	654
Supreme Court president	625	630	800	950	1,022	1,450
Supreme Court judge	550	555	660	785	935	1,250
Secretary general (average)	470	498	643	779	855	1,086
Director general (average)	372	399	516	644	714	902
CEO Telenor	720	1,058	1,723	3,000	3,500	4,300
CEO Norway Post	720	730	900	1,810	2,210	2,529
CEO large companies (average)	–	746	984	1,157	1,403	2,045

Note: *In 1996, some additional allowances for MPs were included in their salary.

had a salary of 1,450,000, while cabinet ministers, MPs and top civil servants (secretaries general and directors general) had considerably less salary.

Table 11.2 shows, first, that the relative pay rise has been greatest for CEOs of state-owned companies. In the period 1990–2007 the number of state-owned companies increased from 40 to 65 partly by changing the form of affiliation for some public administration units (Lægreid *et al.* 2010).[4] Telenor and Norway Post were among the largest converted into state-owned companies during this

Table 11.2 Development of salary for different groups, 1992–2007 (1992 = 100)

	1992	1995	1998	2001	2004	2007
Prime minister	100	112	182	220	243	284
Cabinet minister	100	109	159	190	213	247
MP	100	106	161	190	207	239
Supreme Court president	100	101	128	152	164	232
Supreme Court judge	100	101	120	143	170	227
Secretary general (average)	100	106	137	166	182	231
Director general (average)	100	107	138	173	192	242
CEO Telenor	100	147	239	417	486	597
CEO Norway Post	100	101	125	251	307	351
CEO large companies (average)	–	100	132	155	188	274
Minist. exec. officer (enterprise)	100	113	138	147	158	172
Private sector employee (average)	100	107	130	151	174	203
Private sector worker (average)	100	106	126	141	156	176

period. State-owned companies are not – in contrast to ministries, state agencies and government administrative enterprises – regulated by the state budget, the state collective wage agreement, the state pension scheme, the freedom of information act, and the administrative law. These companies have a salary system more similar to private sector companies.

One argument for this devolution was to get more freedom and autonomy in pay setting for government service providing and producing units working in market competition with private sector companies. They wanted to eliminate the rather centralized, compressed and collective government pay system with low level salaries, especially for top executives. For the devolved companies, the salary increases have been very high the last 10 years. Actually, no other category in our sample has higher relative salary increases in the 1990s. The CEO for Telenor, the Norwegian telecommunication company, increased by almost 600 percent from 1992 to 2007, and for the CEO of Norway Post the increase was approximately 350 percent. Telenor changed its form of affiliation from being a government administrative enterprise to a state-owned company (limited company owned 100 percent by the state) in 1994, and was partly privatized in 2000. Norway Post was transformed from a government administrative enterprise to a state-owned company (hybrid company established by special law) in 1996, and to a limited company owned 100 percent by the state in 2000. The CEOs salaries in these two companies almost doubled soon after they became a limited company owned 100 percent by the state, and the change to a partly-privatized company for Telenor accelerated this process. This change of public administration units into state-owned companies represents the most dramatic transformation of salary system and salary level for high public offices in Norway over the last two decades not only because of the high increase of regular salary but even more because of the introduction of big additional bonuses and (in the case of partly privatized companies) options.

Second, Table 11.2 reveals that there has been a significant pay rise for political leaders, who have more than doubled their salary from 1992 to 2007. This is especially the case for the prime minister. For the MPs the jump in pay after 1995 is partly due to a change in the remuneration system, implying that different kinds of allowances were dismantled and the salary was increased to make the compensation system more transparent. This also to some extent affected the pay for ministers, because the salary for these positions was interconnected through proposals from the expert committee appointed by the *Storting* in 1996.

Third, the salary for top civil servants also increased considerably in the period. The average pay for a director general more than doubled from 1992 to 2007. After the stronger delegation of salary decisions to individual ministries in 1997, there has been an increase in pay for some top civil servants. Overall, there was a significantly greater increase for top positions than for executive officers in the ministries. The salary for academics recruited to a typical entrance position in ministries increased by 72 percent in the same period. This means that the salaries in ministries have become somewhat less compressed over time, but still they are very compressed compared to other countries. While the average pay for a secretary general was 2.7 of the entrance salary of a ministerial executive officer in 1992, it increased to 3.6 in 2007. Until 1991, the Norwegian salary system for state employees was one of the most contracted in the world (Hood and Peters 1994). It seems that the new salary system for top civil servants has made the salary differences within central government somewhat more stretched. It also means that the salary gap between top civil servants and CEOs in the private sector only increased slightly during the last decade (cf. Table 11.1): the average salary for CEOs in private sector companies with more than 250 employees has been 1.5–1.9 of the average salary of secretaries general.

Fourth, Supreme Court judges (as well as other judges) got a large salary increase in the early 1990s, but until a marked raise in 2007 the increases in their salary were lower than those of the political and the administrative executives. Supreme Court judges are not part of the salary system for top civil servants, but have their pay set by the *Storting*.

Fifth, we see from Table 11.2 that the salaries for high public offices, and especially for CEOs in state-owned companies and political executives, have increased more than the salaries for private sector employees and workers. This indicates that the egalitarian Norwegian system is under some pressure.

In a long term perspective the salary increases have been relatively parallel for the various groups of high public office: In 2007, all of them had around 10 times as much as they did in 1970 (Table 11.3).

This also implies that the relative differences are quite stable: until the mid-2000s, the secretaries general had about 85 percent of the prime minister's pay, and this did not change much after the introduction of the new salary system for top civil servants in 1991 (Table 11.4). However, in the last couple of years, the pay of secretaries general has increased more than those of the political executives. MPs have experienced a decrease in their relative pay, especially if we include their loss of allowances in 1996. The cabinet ministers also have relatively lower pay now than they had up to 1990.

Even if the new salary system for top civil servants has not changed their average pay considerably compared to other high public offices, there are significant bigger pay differences among top civil servants. Before the new system was introduced in 1991, all secretaries general had the same pay, and the same was

Table 11.3 Development of salary for different groups of high public office, 1970–2007 (1970 = 100)

	1970	1980	1990	2000	2007
Prime minister	100	236	397	814	1127
Cabinet minister	100	240	408	734	1010
MP	100	227	403	757	1011
Supreme Court president	100	201	397	862	1405
Secretary general (average)	100	241	412	844	1254

Table 11.4 Variation in salary for high public office, 1970–2007
(Prime minister = 100)

	1970	1980	1990	2000	2007
Prime minister	100	100	100	100	100
Cabinet minister	91	92	94	82	81
MP	61	59	62	57	55
Supreme Court president	97	83	98	103	122
Secretary general (average)	82	84	85	85	91

the case for the directors general. This is no longer the case. The new system has now five salary categories, and in 2007 the directors general are placed in categories 1–3, while the secretaries general are in categories 3–4. However, still 78 percent of the secretaries general are in the same category, and so is the case for 61 percent of the directors general.

Summing up, the new salary system caused a significant variation in pay for top civil servants when introduced in 1991. Over time, the salary differences within the group of secretaries general have been reduced. The same has also been the case within the whole system, but to a lesser degree.

The new salary system for top civil servants might have stopped the increase of differences between executives in the private and public sectors, but not reduced the gap as intended by the reformers. Neither have they succeeded in implementing the 'pay for performance' component in the reform. The differences in pay within the civil service have increased both between top civil servants and lower level officials and within the group of top civil servants. The relative differences between top executives and other high public offices have, however, not changed dramatically. The norms of equality in salaries for high public offices are still strong in Norway, and reduced a development towards individualized pay based on performance.

Conclusion

In this chapter we have revealed moderate changes in the rewards for high public office in Norway. This corresponds to a general tendency towards reluctant adaptation in Norwegian administrative policy, where incremental increases are made in accordance with earlier traditions (Olsen 1996). The contract reform illustrates that administrative reforms are not just a non-political struggle to achieve greater efficiency. The reform was largely a test area to see how far consensus could be stretched within the field of administrative reform, and in many cases the contracts in practice became pseudo-contracts reinforcing traditional patterns of work (cf. Bennett and Ferlie 1996). The political dilemma in which the reform resulted, prevented the use of a normal management-oriented practice as envisaged by those who initiated the reform. The process became more a process of political cooperation than of managerial planning.

The reform concepts are evidently revised, filtered, interpreted and modified through the combination of two more nationally based processes. One such process is the unique development of a national political-administrative history, a set of institutional arrangements, culture, traditions and style of governance, which proceeds in an evolutionary manner. Another such process involves the initiatives of political leaders and their instrumental actions taken through administrative design and active national administrative policy in cooperation with the interests of top civil servants and civil service unions (Olsen 1992, Olsen and Peters 1996).

This chapter shows that externally generated reform concepts and processes, when they are transferred to national political-administrative systems, are complex and have varied and ambiguous effects and implications. Contract reforms are transformed to fit the national administrative context, the government's administrative policy and external pressures, and in this way the performance contract concept keeps running, in spite of repeated disappointments and ambiguous effects.

One lesson that might be learned is the instrumental weakness of the contract reform concept. Performance contracts for this kind of position are more beautiful ex ante than ex post, and promise more than they can deliver. Another lesson is that the outcome of the new contract regimes adopted for top civil servants does not necessarily follow the intentions of the reformers (Hood 1998). It is difficult for ministers to match the demands from the contract system. The Achilles' heel in this kind of contractualism is the relation between ministers and top civil servants. Contracts may not always make it easier to dismiss or move public servants, and they have a potentially perverse effect on the accountability of top civil servants. There is a risk that the cost imposed on politicians by more formal restrictions on their ability to reach down into ministries and agencies may come without corresponding benefits (Hood 1998: 458). Hood argues that 'political re-engineering' and path dependence are important in understanding the reform processes. The argument is that path dependency based on economic features, polity structure, national administrative policy and political-administrative culture constrain the reforms.

The employment relationship, particularly at senior levels, may not be best served by too specific a listing of responsibilities and expectations. Flexibility and duty have priority over precision of job specification. In Norway, chief executives and senior managers attribute most of the improvement in government performance to the discretion given to managers, rather than to formal contracts. Few think contracts have been the main contributor to higher operational efficiency (cf. Schick 1998).

Performance pay is an appealing idea, but experiences indicate that its implementation is complex and difficult (OECD 2005a). Many performance pay schemes at the managerial level in central government organizations have failed to become key motivations for effective performance pay because performance assessment is inherently difficult in the public sector. Thus, performance-related pay is sometimes more rhetoric than reality (OECD 2005b). It is, however, a reform that does not seem to need results to march on (cf. Pollitt and Bouckaert 2004). In spite of lacking effects, it is more popular than ever. The paradox is that despite the overall consensus on the types of problems raised by performance pay, such systems continue to be introduced on a large scale in many OECD countries.

One interesting observation from this study is the parallel processes of stability and robustness on the one hand, and change and flexibility on the other hand. We have first observed a lot of path dependencies, illustrated by the strong long term stability in relative pay relations between political, administrative and judicial executives, by the strong equality in pay increases for high public office, and by the enduring gap between pay for top positions in the public and private sectors.

At the same time we have also observed radical changes in the pay conditions, particularly for many civil service organizations that have changed their form of affiliation into state-owned companies and partly privatized companies, but also to some extent by allowing greater pay differences within the same positions such as directors general and secretaries general. In addition, the salary system for central government has gradually become somewhat less compressed. Context matters, but there is also room for adaptation and adjustments, which happen in a complex combination of political design, external pressure, and cultural constraints.

One prescription for reforming the reward system for high public office is that it might be easier to obtain support and commitment for and to implement robust reform measures that are reasonable, acceptable and appropriate and that pass the compatibility test, though they may influence political and administrative practice in an ambiguous and imprecise manner (Lægreid and Roness 1999, Olsen 1997). These may be preferred to more controversial and radical reform measures that dictate more precise policy outcomes, but are more difficult to implement.

Notes

1 Earlier versions of this chapter have been presented at the workshop on 'The Rewards of High Public Office', ECPR Joint Sessions of Workshops, Nicosia 25–30 April 2006 and a book seminar in Friedrichshafen 29–31 January 2009. We wish to thank the participants at the workshop and seminar for valuable comments, and Ole Danielsen and Sturla Herfindal who have collected and systemized the data for us. Some of the material is based on Lægreid (1994).

2 Options are limited to partly privatized companies. In 2005–2006, 100 top executives in Telenor exercised about 65 million NOK in option premiums. The CEO himself realized a premium of 3.4 million NOK when he sold 1/5 of his options in February 2006 (VG 1.3. 2006).

3 CEOs in the private sector in Norway also have lower salaries than their colleagues in Europe. On average, the Norwegian CEOs earned 68 percent of the salaries of 1,700 CEOs in 233 big companies in 14 European countries. When options and bonuses are included, the gap is much bigger (VG 8.3. 2006).

4 Until the early 1990s, major public sectors such as railways, telecommunication, postal services, forestry, grain sales, airport administration and road construction were organized as integrated government services and part of the state salary systems (the general system as well as the system for top civil servants). Since then, all these have been corporatized and taken out of the state salary.

References

Administrasjonsdepartementet (1996) Statens lederlønnsordning. Rapport fra evaluering. Oslo: Administrasjonsdepartementet.

Bennett, C. and E. Ferlie (1996) Contracting in theory and practice: some evidence from the NHS. *Public Administration*, **74**(1): 49–66.

Blaauw, S.S.J. (2002) Topplederlønnssystemet i statsforvaltningen i Norge og Sverige. Bergen: Department of Administration and Organization Theory, University of Bergen, unpublished master's thesis.

Christensen, T. and P. Lægreid (2002) *Reformer og lederskap. Omstilling i den utøvende makt*. Oslo: Scandinavian University Press.

Christensen, T. and P. Lægreid (2003) Coping with modern leadership roles – the problematic redefinition of public companies. *Public Administration*, **81**(4): 803–831.

Hood, C. (1998) Individualized contracts for top public servants: copying business, path-dependent political re-engineering – or Trobrinand cricket? *Governance*, **11**(4): 443–462.

Lægreid, P. (1994) Going against the cultural grain: Norway. In C. Hood and B.G. Peters (Eds) *Rewards at the Top: A comparative study of high public office*. London: Sage.

Lægreid, P. (Ed.) (1995) *Lønnspolitikk i offentlig sector* (Pay policy in the public sector). Oslo: TANO.

Lægreid, P. (1997) Pay reform for top civil servants in Norway: towards market and performance pay or business as usual? Bergen: LOS-centre, Working Paper 9703.

Lægreid, P. (2001) Transforming top civil servants systems. In T. Christensen and P. Lægreid (Eds) *New Public Management. The transformation of ideas and practice*. Aldershot: Ashgate.

Lægreid, P. and M. Mjør (1993) Toppsjefar og leiarlønsreformer i staten. Bergen: LOS-centre, Research Report 9303.

Lægreid, P. and P.G. Roness (1999) Administrative reform as organized attention. In M. Egeberg and P. Lægreid (Eds) *Organizing Political Institutions. Essays for Johan P. Olsen*. Oslo: Scandinavian University Press.

Lægreid, P. and T.E. Savland (1996a) Lederlønnsreformer og mobilitetsmønster. Bergen: LOS-centre, Working Paper 9614.

Lægreid, P. and T.E. Savland (1996b) Individuell lederlønn i staten. Bergen: LOS-centre, Working Paper 9630.

Lægreid, P., V.W. Rolland, P.G. Roness and J.-E. Ågotnes (2010) The structural anatomy of the Norwegian State. Increased specialization or a pendulum shift? In P. Lægreid and K. Verhoest (Eds), *Governance of Public Sector Organizations, Autonomy, control and performance*. Basingstoke: Palgrave Macmillan pp. 21–43.

Norris, P. (1999) *Critical Citizens. Global Support for Democratic Governance*. Oxford: Oxford University Press.

OECD (1988) Recent trends in performance appraisal and performance related pay schemes in the public sector. *Public Management Studies*. 4, Paris: OECD.

OECD (1996) *Pay Reform in the Public Service*. Paris: OECD.

OECD (1997) Performance pay scheme for public sector managers. Occasional Papers No. 15. Paris: OECD (Puma).

OECD (2005a) *Modernizing Government. The way forward*. Paris: OECD.

OECD (2005b) *Performance-related Pay Policies for Government Employees*. Paris: OECD.

Olsen, J.P. (1992) Analyzing institutional dynamics. *Staatswissenshaften und Staatspraksis*, **3**(2): 247–271.

Olsen, J.P. (1996) Slow learner – or another triumph of the tortoise? In J.P. Olsen and B.G. Peters (Eds) *Lessons from Experience. Experimental Learning in Administrative Reforms in Eight Democracies*. Oslo: Scandinavian University Press.

Olsen, J.P. (1997) Institutional design in a democratic context. *Journal of Political Philosophy*, **5**: 203–229.

Olsen, J.P. and B.G. Peters (1996) Learning from experience? In J.P. Olsen and B.G. Peters (Eds) *Lessons from Experience. Experimental Learning in Administrative Reforms in Eight Democracies*. Oslo: Scandinavian University Press.

Pollitt, C. and G. Bouckaert (2004) *Public Management Reform. A Comparative Analysis*, 2nd edn. Oxford: Oxford University Press.

Rodal, J. (2006) Prestasjonsbasert avlønning. En studie av effektene og erfaringene med prestasjonslønnselementet i statens lederlønnsordning. Oslo: Department of Political Science, University of Oslo, unpublished master's thesis.

Schick, A. (1998) Why most developing countries should not try New Zealand's reforms. *The World Bank Research Observer*, **13**: 121–131.

Statskonsult (2004a) Evaluering av statens lederlønnsordning – innspill til fase 1, Working Paper. Oslo: Statskonsult.

Statskonsult (2004b) Toppledere i staten – Rekruttering. Report 2004:09. Oslo: Statskonsult.

12 Rewards for high public office in Sweden

Shirin Ahlbäck Öberg

Introduction

There used to be a proverb in Swedish that read that the share of the state was scanty but secure.[1] It meant that you did not choose a civil servant career because of the good money, but because you were more or less guaranteed safe employment. The proverb is hardly applicable nowadays, since the public sector underwent severe cutbacks during the 1990s and many civil servants learned that a civil servant position was no guarantee against unemployment. Furthermore, when it comes to the terms of public employment, the prerequisites have drastically changed over the last decades, thereby deviating increasingly from underlying Weberian ideals operationalized as pay grades and set initial wages.

To understand this development we need first to clarify the overall context of Sweden's wage policy. The striking feature of this policy has historically been the egalitarian tradition, which in an international comparison is manifested by a relatively low wage inequality (OECD 2008). In the beginning, strong independent central organizations negotiated independently about wage levels, and even though this bargaining has become more decentralized since the 1980s, it is still implemented without government interference and incomes policy (Sjölund 1989). The decentralized bargaining means that the agreements on the central level nowadays are framework agreements that need to be complemented with local agreements. Commentators have pointed out that decentralizing wage bargaining in the 1980s to some extent has led to a somewhat higher wage dispersion, but in an international comparison the wage inequality in Sweden is still very modest (OECD 2008).

As a striking contrast to this legacy of egalitarian wage policy, the pay policy in the public sector was changed in 1985 into a system of 'pay for performance' and market pay. The aim was to increase efficiency and effectiveness in government. There is still a central agreement, but individual pay is now decided by local negotiation between the agency as the employer and local trade unions. This development represents a shift from a solidaristic wage policy based on equity and equality to a system based on the market value of efficiency (Sjölund 1989). Thus, since this change of wage policy, a conspicuous feature of the Swedish case is the lack of set entry wages and set salary grades in the public sector, i.e. civil servants have the opportunity to negotiate higher salaries than their peers based on how they perform, or how they have performed in earlier employment. A key question here is: has this radical change had any effect on the wage dispersion within the groups analyzed here?

It should also be mentioned by way of introduction that since the 1970s an explicit official objective has been to curtail previous differences between being employed in the private and the public sector. An aim that essentially meant a change of the labor regulations for civil servants, giving them the right to negotiate their wages in collective agreements – just like everyone else – and they also gained the right to strike (with few restraints; Petersson 2007: 114f). Nowadays in principle the same labor law applies to the public sector as to others in the labor market.

Another thing to remember when analyzing the Swedish case is that the organization of the state administration differs from that of most other countries in two ways. First, since the Swedish constitution prohibits 'ministerial control' – i.e. when individual ministers influence or instruct administrative agencies – the Cabinet of Ministers act and are accountable collectively. Secondly, according to the constitution: 'No public authority, including the *Riksdag* [the Swedish Parliament] and the decision-making bodies of local authorities, may determine how an administrative authority shall decide in a particular case relating to the exercise of public authority vis-à-vis a private subject or a local authority, or relating to the application of law.'[2] Thus, the administrative agencies formally enjoy a high degree of discretion that is protected by the Swedish constitution. This independence has, among other things, resulted in recruitment practices for staff that are different from those in many other countries. In general, the government will appoint the Director General and the Deputy General Director of government agencies, but all other positions in the agency are recruited by the agency itself, including lower level managers. Hence, the recruitment to a great majority of positions in Swedish government agencies does not emanate from a pool of civil servants controlled by the ministries. However, even the small portion of appointments of senior civil servants controlled by the ministries are not exempted from frequently being questioned in the public debate, regardless of the recruitment method used (e.g. a closed or an open procedure).

One more thing that stands out in the Swedish case is that government – and municipal – agencies operate under the principle of public access, which is a principle with a long tradition (*offentlighetsprincipen*). In short, the principle of public access means that the general public and the mass media are guaranteed an unimpeded view of activities pursued by the government and local authorities. Information about wage levels and other rewards for all government employees are thereby readily accessible for everyone, and this transparency does invite coverage of rewards or perks for most high public offices (HPOs). All in all, there is no doubt that within the egalitarian tradition of the Swedish society the remuneration of high public offices has proved to be a real challenge over time. In the following sections, these debates will be presented one group at a time. We will start with the HPOs that have received a lot of public attention on this matter.

Members of Parliament

Salary and expense allowance

Sweden has, for its small population of 9.5 million people, a big parliament consisting of 349 MPs (compare to 20 Swedish members of the European parliament). For most MPs, the issue of deciding the level of their own salary is – and has been – perceived as a delicate matter. It is easy to see how the mandate of setting your own salary could become quite challenging to the general public. The MPs risk being accused of lining their pockets at the expense of the public, and thereby also risk losing legitimacy and credibility. Moreover, it is difficult to defend a wage raise for your own group, and at the same time make political decisions that may cause other groups of citizens to lose their jobs or receive a lower salary. Hence, since the 1950s there have been a number of attempts to construct a system where the level of MPs' salaries would follow the general wage trend, that is, to depoliticize wage setting.

In 1959 the salary of the MPs was linked to that of other state employees. At that time the *Riksdag* made a statement that changes in the general wage levels should influence MPs salaries, and that it was feasible to compare the salaries of MPs to that of certain civil servants.[3] A direct connection was made in 1962 when MPs' salaries were linked to specific salary grades within the civil service. In 1984 this reference to salary grades in the public sector was replaced by a reference to the wage level of specific judges and also that of certain employees in state agencies. More specifically, since then the salary of the MPs should equal that of judges of appeal, judges of the Administrative Court of Appeal and heads of divisions in state agencies. However, the reference to the latter group was taken away in 1991, since they had started to get paid by performance, and the remaining group for wage comparison, therefore, now only consisted of judges.

Ironically, linking the MPs' salary to another group's wage level did not once and for all relieve the parliamentarians from the unwanted task of setting their own salary. In the early 1990s, during the recession, the salaries of the group of comparison – the judges – increased considerably. If the MP salary had followed this increase it would have meant a conspicuous increase of 18 percent at a time when the rest of the population – especially civil servants – was urged to accept tough restraints on their own wage demands. These restraints had been negotiated by the government and the labor market actors in order to put government expenditures on a sound base again (the so-called *Rehnberg-agreement*), as a means to fight a huge public budget deficit (Sjölund 1994: 123f). The agreement implied, *inter alia*, that the pace of the wage-increase was lowered from 10 percent in 1990 to 4 percent in 1992. Understandably, under such circumstances it was politically impossible for parliamentarians to follow the wage trend of the judges, and therefore laws on deviation from the law on remuneration to members of parliament was enacted in 1990, 1991 and 1993 (SFS [Swedish Code of Statutes] 1990:1417; 1991:1876; 1993:147). These laws were, however, preceded by intense debates in Parliament, during which different opinions advanced. At the heart of these discussions were issues of how to secure the general public's trust as well as the necessity of setting a good example. The Conservative and Liberal parties, both in opposition, argued for a full increase to MPs' salaries (1991/92: KU5).

This system of letting the MPs' salaries follow a specific group ended in 1994. (1998/99: RFK3). In its place a new board was instituted under the *Riksdag* – the Board on Remuneration of MPs (*Riksdagens arvodesnämnd*) – with the sole task of deciding the size of MPs' salaries. The Board consists of three persons appointed by the Administrative Office of the Parliament. The background of these persons are, so far, chief judge positions or a higher administrative position within the *Riksdag* or the Government. Moreover, when instituting this board, legislation was also adopted that regulated the financial conditions for the MPs (SFS 1994: 1065).

Before we discuss developments of Swedish MPs' salary levels we need to say something more about another type of allowance. Until a few years ago, MPs also received a monthly *expense allowance*, which was meant to cover expenses for secretarial help, postal costs, the costs of official mobile telephone calls, expenses for newspapers, magazines and literature that are not available in the *Riksdag* Library, as well as representation costs. In the end this expense reimbursement amounted to SEK 3,743 a month and was subject to income tax. However, this allowance has been often debated over the last 20 years. The discussion has been that this specific allowance should be abolished, and salaries should in turn increase. In early 2006 the *Riksdag* Board finally presented a proposal to remove this allowance (*Framställning till riksdag*en 2005/06: RS4), a proposition accepted by the great majority of the parliament (2005/06: KU33). Since 2006 the salary has increased with approximately the amount of this allowance. Moreover, in comparison to many other countries the salary level is rather moderate, and we should also remember that the salary and the former expense allowance both are taxable.

Despite the comparatively low wage level of Swedish MPs there have been recurrent discussions about this in the media and within political parties. A typical example of the former is a young MP representing the Green Party of Sweden who, during his short term in the *Riksdag* (2002–2006), received extensive media coverage, since he persistently advocated reducing the MPs' salary by approximately one-fourth. His main argument was that of the people's trust in their elected representatives (Private member's motion 2005/06: K288). To set an example, he reduced his own salary during his *Riksdag* period, and donated the amount of the reduction to his own party and other projects on a monthly basis.

Salaries of the Swedish Members of the European Parliament (MEP) became controversial in 2009. At the time, the salary for an MP amounted to SEK 54,500, and the Swedish state had, until 2009, given the Swedish MPs and MEPs the very same salary. However, in 2005 a Statute for Members of the European Parliament was adopted in the EU, which equalized salaries within the union and adopted transparency of MEPs' pay (2005/684/EG, Euratom). The result of this statute for Swedish MPs is that a member of the national parliament initially received a much lower salary than did an MEP, as the latter receives a set basic salary of about 7,000 euros from the summer of 2009. If the informal principle of equal pay for the two representative tasks is to prevail, that would force the Board on Remuneration of MPs to give the Swedish MPs a rather drastic raise of more than 50 percent – in the midst of a deep financial crisis. In short, this emerging discrepancy between the Swedish MPs and MEPs has, as expected, created a debate in Sweden. Another factor to take into consideration is that the average age of MPs has decreased over time. Equalizing MPs' salaries with those of MEPs would also mean that fairly young members of the national parliament would get – what would be considered to be – unduly high salaries.[4] Consequently, it is very unlikely for the Board of the Remuneration of MPs to let the salary level of the MPs follow that of MEPs.

Before we proceed to other rewards for the MPs it should be added that the pay of the Speaker of the *Riksdag* amounts to 144,000 SEK/month, which is the same as the Prime Minister. This means, however, that the Speaker's salary is more than double the normal pay for an MP. The Deputy Speakers receive an increment of 30 percent of MPs' pay. The chairmen and deputy chairmen of the *Riksdag* committees receive similar increments of 20 percent and 15 percent, respectively (SFS 1994: 1065). In addition to this, MPs can earn extra income by being a board member of different Government authorities. All in all, this means that individual MPs can obtain a higher income than that presented in our figures. The scale of this extra income is, unfortunately, hard to estimate.

Other rewards

The *Riksdag* Administration provides its members with technical equipment for performing their parliamentary duties. Apart from fully equipped offices in the *Riksdag*, members receive home telephone subscriptions and portable computers, mobile phones, and printers. Further, the *Riksdag* pays the costs for telephones and mobile phones, and of broadband subscriptions. All members are entitled to an annual season-ticket on the Swedish State Railways (SJ) and, if it is economically justified, they receive a season-ticket for air travel. As a rule, journeys made by MPs within their official duties are regarded as official journeys and any expenses, such as hotel accommodation and subsistence allowances, are paid by the *Riksdag*. Members are entitled to a charge card with personal liability for payment for use only on official journeys. In order to receive money to cover the charge card bill, MPs are obliged to submit travel expenses to the *Riksdag* Administration. To promote EU-related political work a member may use up to SEK 25,000 per electoral period for travel within the EU, an option that was settled in 2006. There are also other grants available for study trips abroad. It should be noted, however, that decisions about foreign travel are not taken by the MP herself/himself, but by various bodies within the *Riksdag* (www.riksdagen.se).

The equipment and travel rewards are hardly ever up for discussion in the public debate. The one thing that might arouse attention is when a member applying for reimbursement for travel expenses, or for charge card invoices, fails to present proper specifications. For instance, the former leader of the Left party was exposed in the media in 1999 when a tabloid discovered that she had not turned in any specifications – for travel costs and costs paid by her *Riksdag* charge card – for a long period of time (*Aftonbladet* 1999). Moreover, her use of the credit card was rather extensive. In the aftermath of this disclosure, other prominent MPs were scrutinized and found guilty of the same negligence. However, in some cases the unveiled carelessness did not sum to more than SEK 3–4,000 (approximately €400).

Pensions and guaranteed income are recurring hot potatoes. The *retirement pension* paid by the *Riksdag* supplements the general pension system. All members are entitled to a retirement pension, regardless of the age at which they begin or end their term of office at the Riksdag. The qualifying period is limited to a maximum of 30 years. Moreover, the pension system also includes certain benefits for surviving family members (*Framställning till riksdagen* 2009/10: RS1; Committee on the Constitution, 2009/10: KU12).

A member who resigns before the age of 65, and after at least 3 years of continuous service, is entitled to a so-called guaranteed income. This means that the *Riksdag* guarantees a former member a certain monthly income even after the member has left the *Riksdag*, albeit with a time limit. If active as an MP less than 6 years, (s)he may receive a guaranteed income up to a year. If the MP has served for 6 years or more, the time span for the guaranteed income is judged on the basis of the former MPs age, where an age above 50 results in the possibility of a guaranteed income until the day of retirement (65 years). However, if the member receives income from other sources this reduces the guaranteed income according to certain rules, a reduction administered by the Board of Remuneration of MPs. A full guaranteed income is 66 percent of the member's monthly income and is payable to members who have served at least 12 years, except for the first year when it is 80 percent. For those who have served between six and 12 years the guaranteed income is reduced, but also in this case it is 80 percent for the first year.

On a regular basis Swedish newspapers will publish names of all former MPs receiving guaranteed income after they have left the *Riksdag*, as well as how much the income guarantee amounts to in total. The undertone is – especially in the tabloids – that this kind of benefit is unjust, and the situation of resigned MP is often compared to that of an unemployed worker who needs to support herself/ himself on a considerably more modest unemployment benefit (see e.g. *Aftonbladet* 2004, 2008a,b). This type of comparison is only possible in a society where the expectation is a small income gap and equal conditions. The aforementioned representative of the Green Party has also picked up this issue, and is advocating for a reduction of the guaranteed income (see e.g. Private Member's motion 2005/06:K29).

Table 12.1 shows the number and duration of granted guaranteed incomes after five general elections; guaranteed incomes are increasing over time, which is a result of an increasing turnover in the parliament as a whole (Ahlbäck Öberg *et al.* 2008).

As to the openness of debates on RHPOs it is important to note that information on MPs' salaries and rewards are readily available to the public. On the Swedish parliament's website a full account of all rewards (over time) can be found in Swedish as well as in English (www.riksdagen.se). The reward structure for MPs, as well as the size of the rewards, are thereby completely transparent. It should also be recognized that all MPs are obliged to register their outside engagements and financial interests (share holding, appointments as a board member, etc.) to the *Riksdag* Administration (SFS 1996: 810).[5] The explicit objective of instituting this register was to ensure the public's trust in the political system (Commissions from the *Riksdag* Administration 2005/06: URF4).

Conclusion

It is obvious that salaries are an uncomfortable issue for Swedish parliamentarians. The media coverage – and recently the discussions in the so-called blogosphere – is extensive. The Swedish public is used to seeing MPs sweat over the issue in televised interviews. However, at a comparative perspective Swedish MPs' salaries are by no means high. One should also consider that the wage level of, for instance, Swedish Directors General and chief judges in some cases are almost twice as high (see below). The uneasiness that is disclosed when the size of the MPs' salaries is discussed illustrates the difficulties in handling opposing ideals when it comes to wage setting. On the one hand, our elected representatives are expected to handle quite extensive duties, both in the parliament itself and in their constituency. To attract good people with different backgrounds to run for a place in parliament the remuneration should not be too low. On the other hand, if remuneration corresponded to that of, for instance, the former comparison group (about SEK 80,000) or to the Swedish MEPs (about SEK 84,000), MPs fear losing the trust of the public, risking public perceptions of MPs feathering their nests.

Table 12.1 Granted guaranteed incomes following the general elections to the *Riksdag* in 1994, 1998, 2002, 2006, and 2010 (numbers)

	1994	*1998*	*2002*	*2006*	*2010*
One year	48	37	36	30	27
More than a year	24	1	5	11	11
Lasting	Accounted for in the 24 above	22	57	67	52
Total	72	60	98	108	90

Source: Commissions from the *Riksdag* Administration 2004/05:URF2, and data from the *Riksdag* Administration.

Such perceptions will no doubt emerge should the Board of Remuneration for MPs decide to raise their salaries to the level set for MEPs. We will now turn to the salaries of the Prime Minister and the Cabinet Ministers.

The Prime Minister and the Cabinet Ministers

In 1990 the standing Committee on the Constitution advanced the idea of coordinating the salaries of Ministers with that of MPs (1990/91: KU18). This suggestion was well received by the Cabinet, who in a subsequent government bill declared that it was important for the Cabinet itself not to get involved in setting the salaries of its ministers (proposition 1990/91: 170). This was supported by the *Riksdag*, who enacted a law that set the salary of Cabinet Ministers at 198 percent of the salary of the MPs; for the Prime Minister the relation was 215 percent.

This coordination of wage levels meant that the ministers were also affected in the first years of the 1990s, when the *Riksdag* froze the level of MPs' salaries (see above). No increase in MPs' salaries meant no pay increase for Cabinet Ministers. This situation was perceived as unsatisfactory – especially since ministerial wages were quite low given an international perspective – and the Committee on the Constitution requested that a government commission should analyze the procedure of setting the ministerial salaries.

The conclusions of this Government Commission on the Salary of Cabinet Ministers were twofold: ministers' salaries were too low (SOU 1993: 22) and the coordination between MPs' and Cabinet Ministers' salaries should be terminated. The salaries of ministers should not be set in relation to any other group or any sort of index, but instead a Board on Remuneration of Ministers should be established under the Parliament, similar to that for MPs' salary determination. Not only should the Board handle the size of the salary, but also decide on pensions and severance pay. The Commission's proposition was followed and, in January 1994, two Boards of Remuneration were instituted under the Parliament, one for MPs and one for Cabinet Ministers (Committee on the Constitution, 1993/94:KU11). Just like the one for the MPs, the Remuneration Board of Ministers consists of three persons appointed by the Administrative Office of the Parliament. Their backgrounds are chief judge positions or a higher administrative position within the *Riksdag* or the government.

There are two salary levels considered: one for the Prime Minister (PM), which is the higher, and one for the rest of the Cabinet Ministers (in total there are usually around 20–25 ministers including the PM). No regard is paid to seniority or the relative importance of a specific portfolio. The parameters of the Board of Remuneration of Ministers to set the salary levels are supposedly (Ds 2004:27–29):

- the general wage development for chief judges, Directors General of major government agencies and comparable officials;
- wage levels of PMs and Cabinet Ministers in neighboring Nordic countries and some comparable European countries.

From Figure 2.3 in the comparative chapter, it is clear that the size of ministers' wages was positively affected by disconnecting them from other groups and making them subject to decisions of the salary board. A considerable raise takes effect in 1994, and from that point forward the ministers have benefited from an upward wage trend. Note also that the wage dispersion between the Prime Minister and the Cabinet Ministers increases considerably from 1994 onwards.[6] Today a Cabinet Minister's salary is about twice as high as that of an MP, and the PM's salary is about 2.5 times higher than an MP's, and the salaries of ministers have increased more than those of MPs.

Severance pay is paid to ministers who resign from their posts. Normally it is paid for 12 months at the same rate as the salary. The severance paid is reduced when the former minister has other income during that period. To receive severance pay, ministers must file an application to the Board on Remuneration of Ministers.[7] During the period 1994–2009, 81 ministers resigned from office, and 72 applied for and have been granted severance pay (i.e. 89 percent of the total) (figures from the Board on Remuneration of Ministers, March 2010).

As for the MPs, there have been public debates about ministers' salaries as well as their severance pay. The latter became especially delicate in connection with the general election in 2006, when a change of government in Sweden occurred. Just a few days after the bourgeois alliance government was presented by the new Prime Minister Fredrik Reinfeldt (the Conservative Party), bloggers and the media disclosed that two of the appointed ministers had neglected to pay mandatory taxes and fees. It was revealed that the Minister of Culture, Cecilia Stegö Chilò, had not paid the mandatory TV license fee for 16 years, and she had also employed illegal home cleaners. The other minister, Minister of Trade Maria Borelius, had a background of having employed illegal home cleaners and there were also problems brought to light with her own business (cf. *Dagens Nyheter* 2006). Stegö Chilò and Borelius resigned from their posts after a record-breaking short time in office, 10 days and 8 days, respectively.[8] Immediately after their resignation, a discussion started in the media about the eligibility of the resigned ministers for severance pay, despite their very short time in office. However, neither resigned minister had actually applied for severance pay at the time, and no application has been filed after the media storm passed.

These examples show, however, how alert the Swedish media, and nowadays also the blogosphere, is when it comes to issues like this. In the case of Cabinet Ministers the sensitive matter does not seem to be the size of the salary that the ministers collect, but rather the severance pay. This is to some extent connected to recurrent incidents in the public debate during the 1990s and 2000s about CEOs in major companies who, after being sacked for conducting bad – and even inappropriate – management, still received exaggerated golden parachutes. During these debates the leading political parties have often joined the critics, and this makes government representatives an obvious target for the same kind of review.

Other rewards

Nowadays ministers are not entitled to a template allowance for expenses when they are on official journeys in Sweden and abroad. Actual expenses during such journeys are reimbursed by the Government Offices only against receipts. Ministers who have their permanent residence more than 70 kilometers away from Stockholm are entitled to an allowance at the same level as employees of the government offices who permanently reside outside Stockholm. The ministers who are eligible for such an allowance are also entitled to compensation for expenses for traveling from their hometown to Stockholm and back.

Just like all Swedish citizens and civil servants of the central government administration, government ministers are covered by the National Pension System. They are also covered by a supplementary (occupational) pension system. The rules are established in a collective agreement concluded by the Swedish Agency for Government Employers and the unions of central government employees. The retirement age is 65, as for Swedish workers in general. The employees (including the Ministers) do not contribute to the costs, but they are covered by the agencies and ministries.

For Ministers who retire before they reach 65 there is also a special income guarantee scheme. To be entitled to this income a Minister must have served at least 6 years in that capacity and reached the age of 50. Earlier service as Director General in immediate connection to the Minister's portfolio is included. To be entitled to full income guarantee the minister must have served a minimum of 12 years in these functions.[9]

Ministers receive few perks. Like the MPs, they are entitled to an annual season-ticket on the Swedish State Railways, and if the distance between their home and Stockholm is far they are also entitled to a season-ticket for air travel. Ministers enjoy a chauffeured car for official use. In fact, since the murder of the former Minister of Foreign Affairs Anna Lindh in 2003, Ministers are urged to use cars for security reasons (Ds 2004: 70). The Ministers also have government aircraft at their disposal, a benefit that they share with the highest civilian and military command. In the list of perks, presented in a report in the ministerial publication series, the investigator also lists the free lunch that the Ministers are served in connection with the Cabinet meeting normally convened every Thursday, where Government decisions are made. This shows how meticulous the coverage of perks really is in Sweden.

As to housing, the Prime Minister has since 1995 access to an official residence, *Sagerska palatset*, close to Parliament, the Ministries and the Royal Palace.[10]

Just like MPs, the ministers are entitled to charge cards for which they need to present justification of expenses. In Sweden a well-known affair on this theme is the so-called Toblerone-affair. In 1995, the Deputy Prime Minister Mona Sahlin (Social Democrat), chose to resign from the Government after a scandal broke involving her spending government money for private purposes using her charge card. The private consumption amounted to about SEK 53,000, and included the purchase of two Toblerone chocolate bars (which provided the name to the scandal). She was considered as the successor to the party leadership within the Social Democratic Party, but after this scandal she chose not to run. She returned, however, as a Cabinet Minister in 1998, and was elected leader of the Social Democratic Party in 2007.

Directors General

Directors General are the professional heads of executive agencies in Sweden, that is the reference in this section is not to top officials within the ministries. There are about 200 Directors General (DGs) and other heads of central government agencies in Sweden today, including vice chancellors of universities and university colleges. The salary level is proposed by the responsible ministry – and also negotiated with the Ministry of Finance – and the final decision is made by the Cabinet collectively. Other employment conditions for central government employees, including the DGs, are established in collective agreements. Not surprisingly, the DGs is the group with the highest wage dispersion compared to the other HPOs, the range of the salary is at this time 55,000–135,000 SEK/month. In fact, the Director General of the Swedish Road Administration has currently a higher monthly wage than the Prime Minister himself. The argument for the relatively high salaries has been that it would otherwise be impossible to recruit competent persons from the private sector. But even the highest salary level is nowhere near the salaries of CEOs of large Swedish companies.

The current median salary for a DG is about 80,000 SEK/month, which is about twice as high as the level in the beginning of the 1990s. Just as for the other HPOs the DGs' salary is taxable. The development of the Directors' General salary is presented in Figure 2.3 in the comparative chapter. The median wage level does not stand out as conspicuously high when compared with other countries in this study. The type of position where salary levels really have taken off is in the state-owned enterprises. When the former Prime Minister Göran Persson (in office 1996–2006) had to step down after the 2006 election, his salary was – coincidentally – lower than his wife's (180,000 SEK/month), who was the president of the state owned *Systembolaget*, the Swedish Alcohol Retail Monopoly.[11] Another example is the CEO salary levels of enterprises that were previously state run, which now have become privatized. The former DGs' salary – currently CEOs' salary – skyrocketed overnight. For example, the base salary of the CEO of Swedish State Railways (SJ) is today almost three times as high as that of the highest paid DG (and the Prime Minister).[12]

Not so much the salary levels, but rather the appointment of DGs, has over the years generated intense political debate in Sweden. When the bourgeoisie parties were in opposition they repeatedly accused the Social Democratic government of mainly appointing former Social Democrats as Directors General, thereby circumventing the official principle of selection, namely meritocracy. The former Prime Minister Göran Persson (Social Democrat) acknowledged this accusation, and at the same time referred to the difficulties in recruiting right-wing people to higher offices in the public sector since they often were offered better terms in the private sector (2004/05: KU20, appendix B13, p. 230f). A study made in 1999 revealed that almost 90 percent of the DGs had a government background, which also illustrates well how low the mobility between the private and public sector has been historically (Statskontoret 1999: 21).

The Government makes appointments to key posts in the public sector, for example ambassadors, county governors, Directors General of government agencies, boards of state-owned companies and university and college vice-chancellors. However, appointing DGs has, until recently, been a rather closed procedure in Sweden, a government system which in many other respects praises openness and transparency. Formally, the constitution states that when making appointments to posts within the state administration attention shall be directed only to objective factors, such as merit and competence (*Instrument of Government* Ch. 11 Art. 9). Since the recruitment procedure has been closed critics have argued that it has been difficult to evaluate whether these objective factors indeed have governed the process. For instance, the position as a DG was until recently never advertised publicly, and it was thereby all up to the government to make a short-list of possible candidates, and, subsequently, to choose the candidate that was considered suitable. In fact, Transparency International Sweden concluded in an official press release in 2006 that the Swedish system of appointing DGs (and chief judges) included a clear risk for corruption (TIS 03–17–2006). In 2006 the bourgeois alliance made it part of their election platform to reform the government's appointment procedure to a more open one (*DN debatt* 2006). Today most appointments are advertised publicly, thereby making it possible for qualified candidates to state an interest for the position. Moreover, before advertising a post a demand profile is established for the position (becomes public when the recruitment process is over), which enables an evaluation of the correlation between the profile and the person who in the end gets appointed.[13] The new system is still in its infancy and, therefore, hard to evaluate. One noticeable effect is, however, that more candidates from backgrounds other than the state administration are being appointed, and, in the long run, that could mean a higher interchange between the private and the public sector.

The DGs can, in principle, not be dismissed during the period of their appointment (unless they have grossly neglected or mismanaged their work, and so far no one has ever been charged of this). In general they are appointed for a 6-year term with the possibility of a 3-year extension. After 9 years in one government agency they might, however, even get yet another 3-year term, but then for a different placement. If the DG receives signals that (s)he is not trusted by the government, and therefore chooses to resign 'voluntarily', (s)he might either be offered a new position somewhere else or get a proposition to continue the term as a DG at the government offices. The latter is referred to as 'DG at the government's disposal.' The mass media have occasionally brought to light that DGs' at the government's disposal seldom seem to have any substantial assignments, and that they nevertheless receive full pay until their term ends.

Just as for the MPs, the pension scheme for the DGs are a function of time and age. A Director General who has served for 12 years and is at least 62 years old is entitled to an 'appointment pension.' A Director General who is 55 years or younger and has served at least 6 years – and who is not offered a continuing appointment – is entitled to a reduced appointment pension. The monthly pay is equivalent to the salary. Lastly, the DGs are entitled to the supplementary retirement pension scheme applicable to all government employees. It should also be added that some of the DGs have access to perks such as a chauffeured car and the possibility of buying a fringe benefit car (the latter is a taxed benefit).

Chief judges

Sweden has two parallel court systems. The Supreme Court is the highest court of general jurisdiction and at the moment there are 16 Justices of the Supreme Court. The Supreme Administrative Court is the highest administrative court and at present there are 16 Justices of the Administrative Supreme Court. Analogous to the earlier organization of the appointment of DGs, the higher posts as justices are (still) appointed directly by the government, without being publicly advertised. This system has been criticized since the lack of transparency in the appointment procedure could cast suspicion on the judges' independence from the government. A striking fact has, at least earlier, been that the appointed chief judges to a great extent have served many years within the Government Offices. This is a comparative oddity, since the normal practice would be to try to keep the executive and the judiciary apart. After many years of discussion there seems, however, to be changes ahead. The Working Committee on Constitutional Reform presented in its extensive report from 2008 a proposition that this appointment procedure should be abolished, and that all posts as judges including the high posts should be announced as vacant. The committee suggested that matters relating to the appointment of permanent judges should be prepared by a proposals board, and thereafter the government would take the final decision based on the rankings of the board (SOU 2008: 125). The government followed the committee's suggestion and this new procedure has been in effect since 2011 (proposition 2009/10: 181 and 2010/11: 24; Committee on Justice, 2010/11: JuU3).

There is another feature that makes the case of the judiciary interesting. Court judges are the only group of public officials in Sweden who until recently have been exempted from person-based salaries. This was changed in October 2006, almost 20 years after the first steps for person-based salaries taken in the government sector, a development that is rather unique in a comparative perspective. The trade union of judges has resisted this change vigorously (cf. *Jusektidningen* 2005). Their objection is that it is unethical to differentiate their salaries based on the work in the court room, since it may cause unwanted incentives that in turn would harm the state governed by law. A position that has been supported in a resolution by the European Association of Judges:

> The EAJ is concerned about the recent proposal from the Swedish government, through the National Courts Administration to introduce remuneration for

judges based on an assessment of their individual performance. With this system the government aims to get influences to the performance of judges.

(EAJ Resolution 2005)

Obviously, the Swedish government did not respond to the resistance, and the person-based salary system has been in place for more than 2 years.

It is the Government who sets the wage for the Presidents of the Supreme Court and the Supreme Administrative Court. All other justices' wages are set through collective bargaining at the local level. For instance, central level framework agreements are settled between the Swedish National Courts Administration and the union (*Jusek*), and subsequently these agreements are complemented with local agreements. At the moment the agreement of the Justices of the Supreme Court and the Administrative Supreme Court do not, in fact, leave any room for individualization. This means that we cannot distinguish any wage dispersion for these top judge positions yet. On the lower levels in the court system individualization of wages has started, and according to the Swedish National Courts Administration the top judges are not ready yet to have their salaries individualized. Hence, the 'pay for performance' system is formally introduced for judges, but in reality pay grades are still used for the top positions in the judiciary.

In Figure 2.3 of the comparative chapter the development of chief judges' salaries is presented. As for the previous groups discussed in this chapter, the salary level of the high judges do not stand out in an international comparison. Furthermore, the judges enjoy similar pension schemes and allowances for reimbursing travel costs etc. as other employees in the government sector. Apart from that there are no other perks for this group.

Conclusion

It is obvious that remuneration of HPOs has been very closely covered in the Swedish public debate. The politicians is the group where the tolerance for high – or an increase of – salaries and other rewards is the lowest. However, in a comparative perspective the wage levels of the HPOs are modest. In practically all the figures the Swedish curve is at the bottom, together with Norway and Estonia. So given the moderate remuneration why is this such a big issue in the Swedish context? As stated earlier the Swedish political context is to a large extent characterized by egalitarian ideals. There is an expectation from the public that MPs ideally should not constitute an elite, but they should socially reflect the Swedish society. From this point of view it is permissible for the political leaders to get paid for their job, but the expectations are certainly not that MPs should be rewarded lavishly through public funding.

Moreover, one should keep in mind that Sweden in general has a compressed wage distribution compared to other advanced economies. That is, not more than approximately 10 percent of the working population earns as much or more as the HPOs under study. This means that even if the wages for the HPOs are nowhere near the CEO wages of large companies, the HPO wages can still be perceived as attractive to the best and the brightest. One should also add to this that the severance pay as well as the pension schemes are relatively generous. It seems that the substantial rewards for most high public office in Sweden comes about after the term is finished.

Sweden began early with a system of 'pay for performance' within the public sector. Despite the far-reaching reform 20 years ago we can, interestingly enough, only read small indications of a growing wage dispersion within the groups studied here. In reality the only HPOs where performance-based salaries are implemented are DGs. However, if the Swedish National Courts Administration succeeds in its ambitions the top judges will in a near future have to accept this individualization. At the moment all but the top judges have had to accept an individualization of their pay. Typically the groups that seem to have benefitted greatly from the change to a performance based system is not the HPOs within the public sector, but rather the CEOs of Swedish government enterprises.

Notes

1 I would like to thank Göran Rodin and Claes Lindgren at the Swedish Ministry of Finance, Charlotte Riberdahl from the Remuneration Board of Ministers, and Eva Lager at the *Riksdag* Administration for having generously provided me with all the information and data I have asked for. Moreover, I would like to thank the participants of the higher seminar at the Department of Government, Uppsala University for valuable comments on an earlier draft (in November 2006).
2 The Instrument of Government Ch. 12, Art. 2.
3 Committee on the Constitution no. 18, 1959.
4 Newly elected MPs had until the early 1990s an average age of 50–51 years, and in the last election in 2006 the average age had sunk to around 47 years (Ahlbäck Öberg *et al.* 2008, p. 26).
5 This law was passed in 1996, but registration became compulsory only in 2008.
6 It should here be added that in the Swedish Government there are no Deputy Ministers, which is why this category is not included.
7 Ministry of Finance, internal memo, 28 March 2006.
8 Interestingly enough the male ministers who admitted that they had either engaged illegal home cleaners or failed to pay the TV license fee did not feel pressured to resign.
9 Ministry of Finance, internal memo, 28 March 2006.
10 The official name of the building is the Sager Palace (built in the late nineteenth century). However, the Social Democratic Prime Minister Ingvar Carlsson, who was the first PM to move in, claimed it was against his political convictions to reside in a palace and the building was subsequently officially denoted to 'house'.
11 Systembolaget, Annual report for 2006.
12 SJ, Annual report for 2007.
13 There has also been a discussion on making the list of the interested candidates public, but this part will – most likely – not be carried through. The argument being that this kind of openness would prevent some qualified candidates from stepping forward and reporting their interest (SOU 2009:4).

References

Aftonbladet (1999) Inte ett kvitto från Gudrun Schyman. 24 September.
Aftonbladet (2004) Så här ska det inte vara år 2004. 20 August.

Aftonbladet (2008) De plockar ut miljoner. 12 November.

Aftonbladet (2008) Avdankade – med Sveriges bästa A-kassa. 13 November.

Ahlbäck Öberg, S. (2008) *Exit riksdagen*. Stockholm: Liber.

Commissions from the *Riksdag* Administration 2004/05: URF2, *Ekonomiska villkor för riksdagens ledamöter*.

Commissions from the *Riksdag* Administration 2005/06:URF4, *Registrering av riksd-agsledamöternas åtaganden och ekonomiska intressen*.

Dagens Nyheter (2006) Nya ministrar köpte svarthjälp. October 2007.

DN *debatt* (2006) Öppen utfrågning av tilltänkt myndighetschef. Den borgerliga alliansens förslag till ny statlig utnämningspolitik: Annonsera ut alla statliga toppjobb. 15 March.

Ds 2004:27 (Ministry Publication Series), *Ersättningar och förmåner till statsråd m.m.*

EAJ (European Association of Judges) (2005) Resolution concerning the new scheme of remuneration of judges in Sweden. Bruges: Belgium, 21–22 April.

Förslag till riksdagen 1998/99: RFK3, *Riksdagsledamöternas arvoden.*

Instrument of Government (the Swedish Constitution).

Framställning till riksdagen 2005/06: RS4, *Ändringar av ekonomiska villkor för Riksdagens ledamöter*

Framställning till riksdagen 2009/10: RS1, *Riksdagsledamöternas pensionssystem.*

Jusektidningen (2005) Kärva förhandlingar om individuella domarlöner. May 2003.

Ministry of Finance (2006) internal memo, 2 March.

OECD (2008) *Growing Unequal?: Income Distribution and Poverty in OECD*. Paris.

Petersson, O. (2007) *Den offentliga makten*. Stockholm: SNS förlag.

SFS, Svensk författningssamling [Swedish Code of Statutes].

SJ (the Swedish State Railways) (2007) Annual report 2007.

Sjölund, M. (1989) *Statens lönepolitik: 1966–1988*. Stockholm: Allmänna förlaget.

Sjölund, M. (1994) Going against the cultural grain. In C. Hood and B.G. Peters (Eds), *Rewards at the Top – A comparative study of high public office*. London: Sage.

SOU (1993) *Vad är ett statsråds arbete värt?* Betänkande av Statsrådslöneutredningen, Stockholm.

SOU (2008) *En reformerad grundlag*. Betänkande av Grundlagsutredningen, Stockholm.

SOU (2009) *Sekretess vid anställning av myndighetschefer*. Betänkande av Utredningen om sekretess i ärenden om anställning av myndighetschef, Stockholm.

Statskontoret (1999) *Det viktiga valet av verkschef*. Report 1999: 21.

Systembolaget (Swedish Alcohol Retail Monopoly) (2006) Annual report 2006.

Transparency International Sweden (TIS). 'Det svenska utnämningssystemet rymmer risker för korruption', press release, 17 March 2006.

13 Starting from scratch

Rewards for high public office in Estonia

Jane Järvalt and Tiina Randma-Liiv

Introduction

This chapter analyzes the rewards of Estonian high public officials (HPOs) in 1991–2008. Having regained independence in 1991 (Lieven's 'Year Zero'), Estonians had to build up their state and its institutions virtually from scratch.

> Whereas the East European satellites possessed at least the formal attributes of independent statehood, however theoretical they might be, the Baltic states lacked their own currencies, armed forces, border guards, diplomatic services, central or even local banks, railways, airlines, and even tourist offices.
>
> (Lieven 1993: 100).

Institution building in Estonia and the other Baltic states included introducing new reward systems at all levels of state apparatus. It was recognized soon after regaining independence that highly motivated senior public officials constitute a guarantee of reliability, professionalism and continuity in governance. However, establishing their reward systems has proved to be a lengthy process.

The development of reward mechanisms for HPOs in Estonia has been influenced by the transitional instability of the country's political and administrative systems. From 1991 to 2007, there have been five parliamentary elections and twelve changes of government. Among other things, instability has resulted in considerable changes in the public service. The first democratic government of 1992 followed through on its declared aim of 'A Clean Sweep' by replacing numerous public officials – many at the highest administrative echelons. As a result, more than 83 percent of civil servants employed in the Estonian ministries and agencies in 2003 had been in the civil service for less than 15 years (Riigikantselei 2004). After the 1992 reforms, only a very limited number of the Soviet *nomenklatura* continued working as HPOs. This led to a true transition for the Estonian state, although the side effects have included missing statistics on rewards and frequently altering reward concepts, particularly during the first decade of transition. Hence, comparable data from the first years of independence 1991–1992 are not available because rubles were used in Estonia through June 1992 and the current systems for calculating and archiving the relevant data were not in place.

According to the Constitution of 1992, Estonia is a parliamentary democracy with a unicameral parliament, the *Riigikogu*. The 101 members of the *Riigikogu* are elected for a 4-year term. The formal Head of State, the President, performs mainly a representative and ceremonial role, which is why the rewards of the presidential office are not included in this study. The Cabinet consists of the Prime Minister and up to 14 full ministers. The proposed analysis will include the gross average salaries, allowances and benefits of all ministers, with special attention to the rewards of the PM. Government institutions include ministries as well as executive agencies and inspectorates (for simplicity, we will use the collective reference 'agencies' below) that are subordinated to particular ministries. For the purposes of this chapter, top civil servants mean the Secretaries General and Deputy Secretaries General of ministries as well as Directors General of agencies. The office of State Secretary, which is the top civil service position in the country, received special attention. The rewards of State Secretary have been comparable to those of Secretaries General. In addition, the rewards of the judges at the highest level of the Estonian court system – the Supreme Court – will be analyzed with particular attention to the position of the Chief Justice. The data on the salaries of top officials is available from 1993 to 2007.

A country's economic development level limits the opportunities for creating rewards for high public officials (RHPOs). Estonia experienced negative GDP growth only in the period of 1991–1994, although the validity of these calculations is strongly contested (Aslund 2002: 135–140). Since the mid-1990s, economic growth in Estonia has been robust and, on average, well above that in West European countries. In 1995, Estonia's per capita gross domestic profit (GDP) in purchasing power adjusted terms amounted to 36.1 percent of the average in the EU27 countries, while it reached 67.9 percent of the EU27 average in 2007 (Eurostat). Despite the fast economic growth until 2007, a relatively modest average income (in 2007 GDP per capita amounted to 11,400 EUR using market exchange rates and 16,900 EUR using purchasing power parity) has not allowed the state to pay internationally competitive salaries or to introduce lucrative tangible and intangible benefits. Nevertheless, the RHPOs have gradually become more competitive within the Estonian labor market, allowing the state to recruit the nation's best to the highest positions of public office.

Base salary and regular allowances

The arrangements for determining the rewards for Estonian HPOs have varied over time but there is now a consistent movement towards unification. In recent years, the salaries of most categories of HPOs have been aligned with reference to the Estonian average gross monthly wage.[1] The salaries of members of parliament (MPs) were tied to the average wage in 1993: backbench MPs earning four times, faction and committee chairmen five times, the Parliament's Vice Presidents five and a half times and the President of the *Riigikogu* six times the average wage.[2]

The salary of Estonian MPs is further complemented by a tax-free parliamentary allowance. MPs can claim an additional amount of up to 30 percent of their monthly salary as an allowance for various expenses, which include transport, communication, business travel, secretarial and office expenses, training and representation. The actual use of this allowance has been a major source of public criticism. For instance, the widespread practice of using allowances to lease private cars has resulted in universal public cynicism concerning parliamentary ethics.

Until 2002, the salaries of Cabinet ministers and Supreme Court judges were linked to the highest rate of the civil service salary scale,[3] which was then multiplied by coefficients ranging from 1.5 to 1.8. However, the centrally set and regulated salary scale rapidly became outdated, with various ways found around it at both the organizational and the individual levels. Therefore, a reform designed to set the rewards of HPOs on a more transparent, comparable and objective basis by linking them to the average wage was implemented. Compared to the average Estonian wage, from 2001 onwards the country's ministers and judges have been better off than they were throughout the 1990s (Figure 13.1). Their purchasing power has increased 3 to 3.5 times while that of the average wage earner and MP has only increased twofold (Figure 13.2). The PM and the Chief Justice receive a base salary equivalent to that of the President of the Parliament, at six times the average wage. Other ministers and senior judges are paid the same as Vice Presidents of the *Riigikogu* (5.5 times average wages).[4] The relevant rules also entitle the ministers to an additional tax-free representation allowance of 20 percent of their monthly salary. The salary of Supreme Court judges may be topped up by up to 15 percent of the base depending on the number of years of service. Judges are also entitled to a 5 percent salary boost for supervising candidates to judicial office during the probation period.

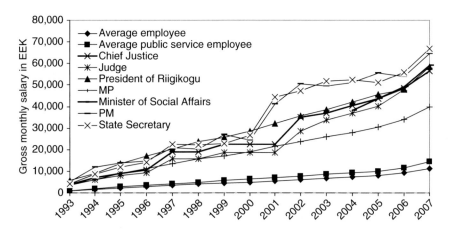

Figure 13.1 Average gross monthly salaries (fixed exchange rate 1 EUR = 15.6466 EEK).
  Source: Statistics Estonia, websites of ministries and agencies, official
  requests for information to public authorities.

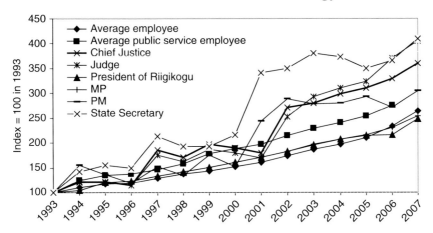

Figure 13.2 Real wages in Estonia, deflated with consumer prices, index = 100 in 1993 for
all categories.
Source: Statistics Estonia, websites of ministries and agencies, official
requests for information to public authorities.

Thus, instead of fluttering in the shifting winds of political decisions, the
RHPOs in Estonia have essentially been depoliticized by being linked to the
evolution of average wages. The egalitarian principle of striving towards a parity
of similar HPOs and keeping their rewards proportional to a standard 'popular'
level implies that the same multiple of average wages must be paid to the heads
of legislative, executive, and judicial branches of government. It could be argued
that, among other things, the established system also fulfills the performance
criterion, linking HPOs' rewards to the overall economic performance of the
country and thus making their welfare dependent on doing the job well. The
visibility of the base salary system has been guaranteed by fixing the coefficients
and calculation principles by law as well as by making the annual incomes of
the HPOs public. At the same time it also represents a clever trick: since the
salaries increase in keeping with the economy's performance, there is no need to
continually make unpopular decisions on HPO pay rise and justify them in front
of the public. However, it could be argued that RHPOs as a share of annual GDP
have not increased over time (Figure 13.3).

The salaries of HPOs caused major public debates in 2008. The issue was
raised because the HPOs' salaries had been growing rapidly and had allegedly
triggered the salary increases in the entire public sector. With the growing financial crises, freezing HPO salaries and de-linking them from the average gross
monthly wage were proposed, and a respective RHPO task force was established
at the *Riigikogu*.

The salaries of top civil servants are subject to the same regulations as those of
lower level civil servants. Under the current system, the base salaries of top civil
servants[5] are paid at a basic rate common to all staff in the grade. The salary scale

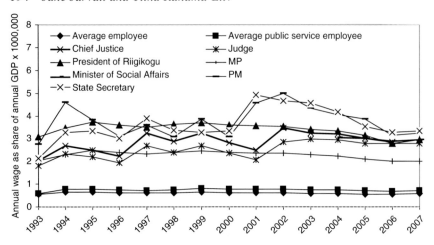

Figure 13.3 Wages as a share of gross domestic product (GDP) for different categories.
    Source: Statistics Estonia, websites of ministries and agencies, official
    requests for information to public authorities.

that was in force from 2001 to 2006 settled the highest rate for top civil servants
at 12,500 EEK (798.90 EUR; fixed exchange rate 1 EUR = 15.6466 EEK); since
2007 the highest rate has been 25,000 EEK (1597.79 EUR). As other salaries
have increased at a considerable pace during these years of fast economic growth,
the official base salaries of top civil servants have gradually been rendered
modest to the point of being something of an oddity. A number of successive
governments have been reluctant to increase the overall public service salary
levels, lacking the political will to cut top officials' salaries loose from the rest
of the civil service by linking them with average salaries in the private sector,
for instance. Therefore, as each ministry and agency is responsible for the remuneration of its staff (according to certain centrally determined statutory guidelines), individual salaries vary to a large extent due to the effects of pay
differentiation and 'add-ons', which are negotiated for each organization and
individual (Randma-Liiv 2005). As of 2006, the average salary base was worth
50 to 60 percent of top civil servants' total pay. Thus, the reward package of civil
servants may, for instance, include additional remuneration for years of service,
academic degree, handling state secrets (until 2008), or proficiency in foreign
languages. Another source of variation, in addition to differences in individual
base salaries and add-on remuneration, is performance pay. As opposed to
the period when 'pay for performance' schemes were introduced in the beginning
of the 2000s (Randma-Liiv 2005), current performance pay incentives are mostly
aimed at front-line staff rather than top civil servants, who are usually not
covered.

The growing pay differentials within the civil service and reduced transparency
of rewards drawn by top bureaucrats can be justified by the perceived need to

make the civil service more competitive and, thus, move towards a more individualized pay system in which pay varies according to the job and the incumbent's competence and performance. In order to be able to recruit good public managers at market rates, over time the heads of the civil service have exempted their posts from certain institutional rules that have continued to apply to others. The pay of civil service managers (including top civil servants) is currently closely aligned with the size of the organization managed, the salary levels in the relevant field of the private sector, performance and individual responsibilities. Meanwhile the actual remuneration is much less based on hierarchical elements, such as position rank, salary grade, or seniority. For example, these days the best-paid top officials tend to be found among those working in the highly rewarded fields of finance and telecommunications.

As a consequence of bringing public sector reward practices closer to those of the market, there has been a change in relative incomes of the country's political, judicial and administrative leaders. There are Secretaries General and Directors General who take home more than a Cabinet minister. In spite of criticism about the appropriateness of senior bureaucrats being paid more than MPs or the ministers responsible for those bureaucrats, this pattern became common by 2007. In addition, the gaps between the pay of top bureaucrats themselves have grown. For example the highest-paid agency head, the Director General of the Tax and Customs Board, earned more than 80,000 EEK (5100 EUR) a month (2005) – more than twice the average top bureaucrat's salary, five times the lowest-paid top bureaucrat's salary and well above the pay claimed by the PM.[6] Figure 13.1 shows the increase in salaries from 1993 to 2007, revealing that average salaries in the civil service have constantly topped the Estonian average by more than 20 percent. However, the salaries of top civil servants still pale when compared to private sector executives.[7]

The 'little extras'

Members of the executive, the legislature and the judiciary have traditionally been entitled to a wide range of in-kind benefits and other perks on top of their salaries and regular allowances. Thus, in accordance with the requirements of office or the functional needs of the job, they are often provided with housing, cars, travel, and so on.

Most of the MP benefits and perks are included in the regular allowance set at 30 percent of their salary, which the MPs are free to use for any of the listed purposes. In addition, a second-home allowance is payable to parliamentarians whose constituency and principal residence are outside Tallinn. Like ministers and civil servants, MPs can take a holiday of 35 calendar days. Parliamentary pensions vary between 40 and 75 percent of MPs' salary, depending on the length of service. MPs who have served for at least 3 years and have attained the statutory pensionable age receive a pension amounting to 40 percent of their salary. In order to be entitled to the maximum pension rate of 75 percent, 9 years of legislative service are required. However, currently members of the *Riigikogu* are not

entitled to the parliamentary pension since the respective changes were introduced to the MPs' Salary, Pension and Other Social Guarantees Act shortly
before the general election in 2003. As the turnover of MPs exceeded 60 percent
in 2003 and 40 percent in 2007, there is increasing agreement on the fact that the
abolition of parliamentary pensions may have an adverse effect on MPs' continuity of service and that it is increasingly difficult to attract the nation's 'best and
brightest' to politics. Additionally, MPs become entitled to severance pay
amounting to 3 months' salary in case of leaving or being replaced in
the Parliament before a full year's service and to 6 months' salary for service
exceeding one year.

The salaries of Cabinet ministers and top civil servants are further complemented by various social guarantees. Ministers who are not from Tallinn or its
surrounding municipalities can claim a rent allowance of up to 7,000 EEK
(447.38 EUR) per month. However, the real value of this allowance has declined
since 2000. A similar, second-home allowance applies to the State Secretary,
Secretaries General and County Governors, but is very rarely used. Furthermore,
all ministers are entitled to an exclusive use of a chauffeured government car. Top
civil servants either have official cars or are entitled to reimbursement of expenses
for using their private cars. Ministers who were employed in public service
before their appointment to ministerial office or held an MP's mandate have the
right to resume their mandate or previous position, or a position comparable to
the previous upon release from ministerial duties. Top civil servants are entitled
to compensation upon release from service due to the winding-up of an administrative agency or as a result of being laid off. Depending on the duration of service, that compensation ranges from 2 to 12 months' salary. This is an important
extra, since Secretaries General are appointed for 5 years with the possibility of
termination after one-year service under each new minister. The retirement
pension paid to civil servants constitutes a supplement to base national old-age
pension and is determined by the length of service. For example, retirees with
10–15 years of service draw an extra 10 percent and those with more than 30
years of service an extra 50 percent.

Among all Estonia's HPOs, the reward package of Supreme Court justices is
the most straightforward and transparent. Justices can claim an allowance for
business travel pursuant to the same regulations that apply in the civil service.
Only the Chief Justice is entitled to exclusive use of a chauffeured official car.
The right to claim a refund of mobile phone costs applies to the Chief Justice and
the Presidents of Chambers. Until 2005, Supreme Court justices used to be
provided with residence by the state but were then given an opportunity to buy
the apartments they lived in on concessionary terms. Among all HPOs justices
have the longest paid holiday – 56 calendar days. The Supreme Court's reward
policy entitles justices to a further holiday benefit of up to one month's salary,
which has become known as 13th month's pay. Justices' other benefits, for example on the occasion of the birth of a child, certain round anniversaries, marriage,
etc. can be claimed by Supreme Court employees too. All judges become entitled
to an old-age pension at 75 percent of their last salary upon reaching the statutory

pension age, provided they have held judicial office for at least 15 years or served as Chief Justice for 7 years. After being employed in judicial office for 30 years, judges can claim a length-of-service pension of 75 percent of their last salary. Unlike other HPOs, judges in Estonia are appointed for life.

In addition to their official base salaries, certain office holders have been drawing supplementary income from other sources besides the official pay. The most lucrative prospects for outside earnings are in the Estonian Parliament, where representatives can make substantial amounts of money on 'side jobs.' Thus, parliamentarians often combine public office with lecturing, media, consultancy work and the like. These types of activities include accepting international lecturing or consulting offers (for instance, in the case of MPs, to share their transitional experiences), which are presumably handsomely paid. Another source of additional income, closely linked to MPs' political role, consists of sitting on a wide array of public institutions' oversight and other bodies: official commissions, supervisory boards of state-owned enterprises (SOEs), and foundations. In supervisory boards, appointments are divided according to quotas reflecting the relative strength of political parties in Parliament and/or the coalition government. According to applicable regulations, the chairman of a supervisory board is allowed to earn up to 7,400 EEK (472.95 EUR) and a board member up to 5,550 EEK (354.71 EUR) per month. It is not uncommon for MPs to sit on several boards, enhancing their base income considerably.

As for the ministers, their opportunities for additional earnings while in office are severely restricted. They are forbidden to accept appointments or payments from outside interests during their term in office, except for teaching and research work, and must give up any previous position when appointed. Certain ministers may be board members of SOEs or foundations but will not be paid for it. Similar restrictions are also imposed by law on Supreme Court justices and all other judges. According to the regulations, they are not allowed to have side jobs extraneous to the office of the judge, except for teaching or research. Ministers and judges are supposed to dedicate themselves fully to their office.

Additional employment for top civil servants is also restricted. They are not allowed to belong to permanent oversight or control/audit bodies of companies, except as representatives of the state. This exception, however, is a major additional source of income for many Secretaries General. Besides, a top civil servant may engage in business or work for another employer, provided he or she has been authorized by the person who has appointed him or her to office and subject to the proviso that the additional job must not interfere with performance, lead to a conflict of interests or damage the reputation of the position. The rules prohibiting or restricting 'second jobs' for persons in office are closely observed.

There is no institutionalized system to guarantee income to those leaving high-level political, civil service or judicial posts. Still a widespread practice of HPOs leaving for prestigious or more lucrative positions after resigning public office is apparent. Executive branch officials appear to gain the expertise and contacts necessary to advance their future careers effectively. In many instances, the second career may be in the area of business (e.g. banking, transport, and communications) with which the individual worked while in government. The move from top public office to the private sector was particularly attractive in the mid-1990s when large-scale privatizations took place. Top bureaucrats have also provided an important supply of aspiring politicians. In addition, former HPOs stand a good chance of becoming a top civil servant or a management board member in public or private enterprises, being appointed ambassador, taking up a position as state representative to an international organization or sitting on prestigious committees. There have also been cases of 'round trips', civil servants and private sector executives moving back and forth between different offices. Ex-ministers and ex-MPs also find different openings, whether they are government posts, appointments to professorship, other political appointments, opportunities in the private sector or in different European institutions. As regards senior judges, the position of Chief Justice has served as a launching pad for high-paid careers in the European Communities court system.

There has been considerable public criticism of the 'golden handshakes' received by HPOs who are accused of nepotistic or corrupt practices. In these cases, justifications refer to the inevitable need to retain and apply the top leaders' competence in a very limited 'labor pool' of a small country (Rees *et al.* 2005).

The visible and invisible sides of transparency

In order to make RHPOs more transparent, Estonian public organizations are obliged by law to disclose the compensation of all top officials. Information about the yearly pay of the country's political, judicial and administrative leaders is made accessible to the public via the Internet each year, attracting considerable attention from the public and the press.[8] There is a statutory requirement for the HPOs to reveal their personal wealth and declare their sources of income in the *State Gazette* (Estonia's official publication for laws and related documents). In addition, the Public Information Act, which came into force in 2001, entitles any citizen or journalist to make requests for information to public authorities. The requested information may be related to the rewards of public officials. For instance, we used official information requests to various public institutions to collect data for this paper.

The requirement of making salaries public has been seen as the first step to establish a more regular process for determining rewards at the top, and to help achieve at least some consistency between the salaries paid in different institutions and to officials of similar rank. For MPs, Cabinet ministers and judges, whose reward systems are fairly transparent due to linkage to average salaries, it has been an additional measure of assuring transparency. For top civil servants, however, the public as well as the designers of reward policies at the organizational level have been especially critical about the inconsistency and opacity surrounding the setting of salaries and entitlements. Estonia, like many other countries, is moving away from a grade-related pay-system, towards a more individualized pay-system (Riigikantselei 2006).

The individualization of top civil servants' rewards is mostly achieved by means of the 'little extras' in the reward structure. This is to a large extent the result of an opaque reward system and limited central coordination in the Estonian civil service (Randma-Liiv 2005). Therefore, in order to keep up with the economic growth and salary levels most authorities have developed their own reward systems. In the most extreme cases, the formal base salary of top civil servants constitutes only about a third of the total reward. Using other available mechanisms (such as additional remuneration for extra tasks or for outstanding performance), public officials are regularly paid well above the civil service salary scale. Therefore, to understand the formation of rewards one needs to know the legal framework as well as the reward policy and structure of each individual public organization. In spite of the openness and the obligatory publishing of the total annual RHPOs, the underlying principles of top civil servants' rewards are neither transparent nor consistent.

The disclosure of compensation and economic interests is also seen as a means of preventing corruption. Its purpose is to get an overview of the sources of income of top officials and any possible conflicts between their private and public interests.[9] In the Transparency International ranking, Estonia was placed 27th in 2008,[10] one of the best among post-communist countries over the last years. However, the degree of popular trust for all public institutions has been steadily decreasing over the years.[11] Thus, increased transparency has not created more trust in public institutions. The public's trust is conditioned more by general perceptions of HPO integrity than by the availability of information about rewards.

To make RHPOs more transparent and consistent, information regarding basic HPO pay structure and rates has been made readily available. However, this has still fallen short of providing sufficient information for an objective assessment of RHPOs. Every year, after publication of the annual RHPOs, media coverage usually focuses on ranking best-paid officials, with no further analysis or explanations. The public's resulting appraisal of RHPO systems as 'cynical' could be partly explained by the fact that the perceivably 'devious' reward policies lack coordination, clarity, and consistency within the public sector itself.

RHPOs in a newly democratic state

RHPOs in Estonia have been influenced by various political, socio-economic and cultural factors that are closely intertwined and sometimes difficult to pry apart analytically. Many of these factors are in turn shaped by post-communist transitions. The analysis of these factors is complemented by a few other arguments, mainly based on the small size of Estonia.

Political factors

A country's HPO reward policies depend on how the society sees the role of government and of civil service in advancing the welfare of its citizens. A positive role of public officials cannot be taken for granted, especially in countries characterized by a lack of long-standing governance traditions and a short experience with democracy. Drechsler (2000: 267) argues that 'the fundamental challenge to Central and Eastern Europe is still a restoration or (re)creation of the positive concept of the state.' In Estonia, the development of many aspects of the state still suffers from the legacy of public estrangement from the state under the Communist regime. The missing positive concept of the state and insufficient identification with it on the part of the public leads to serious problems, including a lack of interest for public service career paths,[12] rivalries between various government units, and an absence of common administrative culture and co-operation within the public service.

Such 'anti-state' attitudes have fostered the popularity of ideas related to the minimal state. Moreover, the early years of transition coincided with the New Public Management (NPM) trend in the West (Hood 1991). The NPM ideology sat well with countries that were abolishing their one-sector economies and carrying out large-scale privatizations. Some over-idealization of the private sector (and the free market) still prevails in Estonia. As a consequence of the policies adopted by a succession of neo-liberal governments, the underlying theme of many government reform initiatives has been the 'marketization' of the state, including the 'marketization' of RHPOs. It is not unusual that the jobs and rewards of top public managers are weighed and assessed against those of their private sector counterparts. The comparison with top private sector earners has constantly pushed RHPOs upwards and served as the basis for justifying previously decided rewards. Comparing rewards in public and private sectors became a very 'practical' issue after the general elections in 1999 when Mart Laar (whom Margaret Thatcher had called her 'best student') became Prime Minister for the second time. Since the resulting government installed a number of business leaders into top political and administrative positions, RHPOs were increased markedly, as demonstrated in Figure 13.1.

Political and economic changes in Estonia have been fast and radical. This has often required fast decisions and robust action, sometimes at the price of ignoring voices that could have been heard. For more than a decade both politicians and civil servants have grown used to elaborating complicated policy proposals and drafting legislation under considerable time pressure, but there is as yet no general culture requiring serious analysis to precede the adoption of a new regulatory measure or policy. In addition, as the entire society has been undergoing sweeping changes, it has been relatively easy for all social groups to accept new initiatives without major opposition. This is partly a reason why the cornerstone of Estonian RHPOs – linking RHPOs to gross average salary – literally got lost in the overall reform debates (this general principle became a matter of public debate only in 2008). When the salary of MPs was first linked to the average gross salary in 1993, nobody questioned the principle behind multiplying the average salary by the coefficient 'four.' When the base salaries of other HPOs were linked to the average salary 9 years later, the relatively modest public debate that ensued focused exclusively on the internal parity of RHPOs, to complete neglect of possible objective reasons for justifying such high coefficients in a developing economy. Since no serious public debate over base salaries of HPOs was held until 2008, the matter has not been part of competition between political parties. The topic from the complex 'package' of RHPOs that has seen some debate is that of MPs' benefits and pensions. Yet even here, political parties have been rather reluctant to conduct reforms going beyond a mere cosmetic treatment of the underlying issues.

The political environment in Estonia has been anything but stable in the last two decades. The coalition governments have usually included at least three parties, resulting in rather unstable power relations. A high turnover of MPs[13] has been complemented by personnel changes in the ministries, especially among top civil servants. For instance, only one out of twelve Secretaries General managed to stay in office during the entire mandate of the 1999–2002 cabinet, while the cabinet that came to power in 2003 changed half of the Secretaries General. In practice, it has meant that the job of a politician or a top civil servant is perceived as a temporary appointment, contributing to 'profit maximization' during the time in office and ensuring appropriate post-public service careers (often related to the 'challenges' of privatization, particularly in the 1990s). The casting of 'marketization' as a value in itself has served as window dressing for individualist attitudes. Judges with their lifelong tenure constitute a significant exception to this general rule.

The present study of Estonian RHPOs confirms the previous finding of Hood and Lambert (1994: 37) that top salaries in the public service and the most dramatic pay raises have been secured by those who have escaped the ordinary civil service pay matrix as well as the floodlights of parliamentary scrutiny. Since the management of civil service in the Estonian administrative system is decentralized, Estonian ministries have substantial freedom in managing their (administrative) human resources. This has led to a situation where the highest rewards of all go to agency Directors as well as to Secretaries General. The individually negotiated reward packages of these officials make them the obvious winners from the 'marketization' principle. Ironically, the steepest upward leap of top civil servants' pay took place immediately after the 1999 general election (see Figure 13.1), precisely when the new government had declared the reduction of public sector expenses to be one of its main goals.

Socio-economic factors

The economic transition of Estonia provides a good testing ground for general assumptions about the correlation between economic development and the size of RHPOs. As Brans and Peters (this volume, chapter 2) argue, more affluent countries tend to pay some public employees more than they would be able to get in the private sector. However, since the base salaries of Estonian HPOs have been linked to the average gross salary for the country, Estonia's rapid economic growth has boosted both private sector salaries and HPO pay. Although it is possible to claim that as societies develop economically, it becomes easier for governments to tax and extract money for HPO rewards (Brans and Peters, this volume, chapter 2), the Estonian case demonstrates that this is not necessarily true. The relationship between GDP per capita and RHPOs has remained the same over a number of successive years of rapid economic growth with only minor fluctuations (see Figure 13.3).

Economic growth and high inflation rates (especially in the 1990s) created a situation where it took a series of trials and errors to reach the current system of RHPOs. During the 1990s the rewards of various groups of HPOs were decided independently. Only recently can the first glimmers of consensus be detected in discussions regarding different HPO sub-categories. Theoretically, the pay fluctuations within various groups of HPOs should have been larger at the beginning of transition. However, Figure 13.1 shows that this has not been the case. Instead, the growing individualization of rewards from 2000 onwards has had a clearly visible effect on increasing differentiation of pay.

Whereas fairness in RHPOs has been discussed in the media, discussion of the consistency of RHPOs with the salaries in other sectors of the economy has remained in the shadows. This is surprising in a country that is characterized by one of the highest social stratification and economic inequality rates in Europe. The Estonian Gini index was 33.0 in 2006 (Eurostat) and 19.4 percent of the population lived below the poverty line as defined as 60 percent of the median income in the same year (Statistics Estonia www.stat.ee).

Another issue that has been relatively important in the context of Estonian RHPOs is the difference of the country's living standard and those of West European countries. Already before negotiations over EU accession started in 1997, Estonian HPOs were involved in a number of working groups and committees at various EU institutions. This led to a situation where a few days' business trip to 'Europe' provided daily allowances comparable to half of the HPO's monthly salary. Especially during the 1990s, such trips were a goldmine for anyone with access to them. While relative profits accruing to HPOs from official business trips have decreased, side-employment abroad through foreign lecturing or consultancy work has remained alluring. Moreover, an HPO's job is frequently seen as a springboard onto the 'Euro-gravy-train to Brussels' (Hood and Peters 1994: 19), creating the potential of an enormous future salary increase. A number of representatives of all sub-categories of Estonia's HPOs (politicians, top civil servants and judges) have already realized that potential.

Cultural factors

Economic development has a powerful impact on cultural values: the value systems of rich countries differ systematically from those of poor countries – wealthier countries tend to emphasize self-expression related values while poorer countries emphasize survival values (Inglehart and Baker 2000). For a discussion of RHPOs, the survival element of the World Values Survey (ibid.) provides an interesting basis for further analysis by presenting a dimension in which post-communist countries clearly differ from advanced democracies. The survival values include, for instance, the following elements: 'respondent gives priority to economic and physical security over self-expression and quality of life,' 'when seeking a job, a good income and safe job are more important than a feeling of accomplishment,' 'respondent does not favour less emphasis on money and material possessions' (Inglehart and Baker 2000: 24, 27). When a country is undergoing rapid social changes and the economic base for one's survival has become uncertain, hard work, money, technological development and material possessions matter most in people's lives. Economic and physical security is emphasized above other goals. A central component of this dimension involves a polarization of respondents between materialist and postmaterialist values. Postmaterialist values focusing on leading a life of excitement and variation, leisure, and tolerance can only be espoused widely in a society where economic and physical security is taken for granted (Realo 2003). In this context, it is interesting to note that the importance of survival values in Estonia as well as in the other Central and Eastern Europe (CEE) countries (with the exception of Slovenia) *increased* during the first half of the 1990s (Inglehart and Baker 2000: 40). The negative economic growth of the early 1990s, complemented by the collapse of the poor but relatively secure socialist economic, social and political systems, contributed to the growing feeling of insecurity and the overwhelming dominance of survival (materialist) values.

These contrasting values have had an impact on shaping individual attitudes towards RHPOs. The national independence movement of the late 1980s and early 1990s clearly contributed to the development of a broadly shared feeling of collective identification. The revolutionary beginnings of the 1990s confirmed the attractions of public office felt by many of the nation's best and brightest for predominantly altruistic reasons. The excitement inherent in building an independent state coupled with a sense of duty to one's country provided a powerful motive for joining the ranks of HPOs.[14] Materialist values became more prominent in the society as a whole by the mid-1990s (Lauristin 1997). However, it could be argued that although the 'building up the state' motive started to recede in the mid-1990s, it was partly compensated for by the euphoria of looming EU accession that characterized the late-1990s. This directly involved literally all HPOs in accession negotiations and preparations. The shift in the attitudes to RHPOs started to take place at the turn of the millennium (see also Figure 13.1). From 2000 onwards, the behavior of HPOs has gradually become more and more akin to that of 'rational rent-seekers' of the Chicago theory of government (Niskanen 1971). Various groups of HPOs as well as individual officials started negotiating higher personal rewards within the constraints of institutional rules. The growing role of economic interests led to the emergence of calculating individualists rejecting ideas of 'service to the state' as its own reward. The gradual 'marketization' of RHPOs as well as HPOs' growing side-employment and the increasing importance of 'little extras' in HPO pay have been influenced by the individualist trends.

The cultural factors affecting the shaping of RHPOs are related to the attitudes held by the people vis-à-vis the public sector. The change of values manifested in

204   *Jane Järvalt and Tiina Randma-Liiv*

the course of transitional years has also caused a shift in attitudes toward RHPOs. Public perceptions of HPO jobs have gradually come to be determined by predominantly materialistic considerations. Although economic constraints have precluded very high RHPOs in absolute terms, rewards exceeding the average by a considerable margin continue to draw sarcastic commentaries by journalists and members of the public alike. That shows Estonian RHPOs following the 'tragic bias' towards cell 'four' (high and less visible RHPOs combined with a low legitimacy) in the citizen–HPO interaction matrix (Hood and Peters 1994: 9).

Small-state factor

When focusing on Estonia, there is, besides its transitional character, yet another aspect that must be taken into account. With its population of 1.344 million people (2006), Estonia is one of the smallest countries in Europe. Studies of small states (for example, Lowenthal 1987, Sutton 1987) suggest that differences between large and small states are not merely quantitative, but essential qualitative differences can also be found. Consequently, previous studies of small states may help to understand the course of development of RHPOs in Estonia.

Benedict (1966) has shown that in small societies with population figures of around one million, people grow up within an interdependent network, where each person plays several roles; thus nearly every social relationship serves many interests. In such conditions, the decisions and choices of individuals are influenced by their relationships with other individuals in many contexts. Therefore, the importance of the individual takes on a disproportionately greater significance in small societies where 'everybody knows everyone else' (Sutton 1987). Situations and decisions tend to be more personalized, which essentially permits the view of a small government apparatus as a comprehensive informal network (Sutton 1987, Bray and Packer 1993). It would be very difficult to develop 'hierarchical' values in a society where the elite are not only tightly interconnected within their own ranks, but also bound by strong informal networks to members of the larger society (Lowenthal 1987). Sutton (1987: 15) argues that in small societies, senior administrative and political office holders have more direct contact with the man in the street and, accordingly, there is less of the aloofness traditionally associated with a bureaucracy. Additionally, the high level of personification and the relative importance of individuals may contribute to the development of individualized rewards, as in the case of the leader members of Estonian administrations.

Human, financial and material resources in small states are limited. Bray and Packer (1993: 237) demonstrate that the majority of small states also have very limited natural resources. This means that, perhaps even more so than in larger states, human resources, especially those relevant for HPO recruitment, are critical for small state development. A survey by Bennell and Oxenham (1983: 27) found that all of the small countries researched ranked shortage of high-level manpower among their most serious problems. In the context of Estonian RHPOs, the shortage of potential top political and administrative leaders has contributed to the 'marketization' of rewards, especially for top administrative positions. On the other hand, this limited reserve has given young professionals great opportunities for entering the ranks of HPOs. For instance, in 1994, Estonia's Prime Minister was 33 and the Minister of Foreign Affairs only 28 years old. The average age of Secretaries General is also remarkably low (38 years in 2006). The youth of Estonian political and administrative leaders, in turn, means that there are very limited career perspectives for regular civil servants as well as for HPOs themselves. These limitations may, however, be partly compensated by higher rewards.

The importance of informal networks also influences relationships between various segments of society. First, politics and public administration are closely interconnected in small societies (Sutton 1987). There is a greater amount of mixing between politicians and civil servants and stronger personal networks beyond political ties that means that it can be difficult to maintain totally discrete roles. Sutton (1987: 15) argues that in small societies, in particular, politics may be less than a full-time job, constituting either a means to promote other interests or an avenue of mobility into other areas in a situation of limited economic opportunities. This may partially explain the tendency of Estonian MPs to 'keep all doors open' through side-employment. In extreme cases it may lead to situations where official business is discharged as a secondary activity, causing potential conflicts of interest, problems of management and accountability. Second, the web of connections spanning small societies clearly affects relationships between public and private sectors. As both public and private organizations are relatively flat, they offer a limited number of advancement opportunities. Analyses of the relevant trends in Estonia show a remarkable cross-sectoral mobility of managers (including HPOs). For instance, the careers of Secretaries Generals on average only include 3.6 years of civil service experience before becoming a top public administrator (2006), with a few directly recruited from the private sector. On the one hand, such 'in-and-outers' within HPOs present several practical and ethical problems. On the other hand, a high mobility between public and private sectors contributes to the 'marketization' of RHPOs.

Finally, it is important to note that problems of smallness can easily be confused with the specific characteristics of development (Randma 2001). These two factors may act separately from one another, or the stage of development and size of the country may interact. Consequently, there is a question yet to be answered as to whether any identifiable characteristics or consequences are associated with size or transition *per se*. As Estonia is both a country of fast development and a small state, it is difficult to separate the relative importance of the two dimensions.

Conclusion

Although the starting point for developing a reward system for Estonian HPOs was very different from those of its Western counterparts, the changes affecting RHPOs have seen similar trends and challenges in Estonia. During the period from 1991 to 2008, RHPOs could be characterized by the development of routine reward practices and stabilization of reward systems, some moves towards unification and an increasing pressure to enhance transparency. However, in spite of the governments' efforts to work more effectively and more transparently, public discontent has continued to grow. In an attempt to recruit the 'best and the brightest' to the public sector, Estonian decision-makers have implemented NPM ideas and 'marketization' principles in designing RHPOs.

The general problems of RHPO design in Estonia are complicated by specific issues related to the developing phase of the country's administration, such as the deservedly bad reputation of the state inherited from the Soviet system, rapid economic growth, sustained materialistic values of the population and the particular context of a small state. Thus, the RHPOs are not merely another set of pay and perks rules but reflect, in a way that resembles Brans and Peters's (this volume, chapter 1) approach, certain fundamental features of the given political and administrative system.

Notes

1 RHPOs are regulated by the following Republic of Estonia acts: Public Service Act, Courts Act, State Public Servants Official Titles and Salary Scale Act, Members' of Parliament Salary, Pension and Other Social Guarantees Act, Government of the Republic Act, Act of Salaries of Civil Servants Appointed by the *Riigikogu* and the President of the Republic, Anti-corruption Act, Public Information Act.
2 HPOs monthly salary = coefficient * previous year's average gross monthly wage.
3 Civil service salary scale consists of pay grades 7 to 35. The salary rate of the highest grade is set in the annual national budget with other grades' pay being provided by Cabinet Regulation.
4 The salaries of other HPOs (e.g. President of the Republic, Auditor General, Legal Chancellor, and Commander of the Defence Forces), who are not included in this study, are also related to the average wage.
5 There are about 100 top civil servants in the Estonian bureaucracy, including the State Secretary, Secretaries General (administrative heads of ministries), Deputy Secretaries General, Directors General of state agencies and County Governors.
6 As regards public companies, the Chief Executive Officer (CEO) of Eesti Energia (a state-owned energy company) earned more than 115 000 EEK (7350 EUR) in monthly salary and approximately 40 000 EEK (2556 EUR) in monthly bonus in 2005. The CEO of Eesti Post (a state-owned company engaged in providing postal services) was paid 58 000 EEK (3707 EUR) in base salary, plus 10 000 EEK (639 EUR) in bonus per month in 2005. Tallinna Sadam (Port of Tallinn, a state-owned company, which is the biggest cargo and passenger harbor in Estonia) paid its CEO a monthly salary of 70 000 EEK (4474 EUR), topped up by a monthly bonus 25 000 EEK (1598 EUR). The most highly paid CEO of a public company was the CEO of Eesti Raudtee (Estonian Railways) with a monthly base salary of 160 000 EEK (10 226 EUR) in 2007. The somewhat higher salary level in Eesti Raudtee as compared to other public companies was due to the fact that after renationalization of Eesti Raudtee in 2006, the salary levels of the previously privatized company had to be retained to a large extent (Estonian Ministry of Economic Affairs and Communications, http://www.mkm.ee).
7 For example, among the CEOs of the companies listed on the Tallinn Stock Exchange, the CEO of Ekspress Grupp (the largest publishing company in Estonia) earned 816 000 EEK (52 152 EUR) in 2006 (68 000 EEK or 4346 EUR per month) in base

salary and approximately 1 450 000 EEK (92 672 EUR) (corresponding to 121 800 EEK or 7784 EUR per month) in bonus payment. The five members of the management board of Tallink Grupp (one of the largest shipping companies in the Baltic Sea region) earned in total 31 million EEK from Sept 2005 to August 2006, including 19 million EEK in bonuses, i.e. on average 6 million EEK (383 470 EUR) per person per year in total remuneration (OMX Nordic Exchange, http://www.baltic.omxgroup.com).

 8 According to the Anti-Corruption Act, since 2004 all ministries, government agencies and SOEs have to publish the salaries and additional remuneration paid to their top officials and board members during the previous year on their web pages by April 1 each year.
 9 As required by the Anti-Corruption Act, since 1999 HPOs have been disclosing a variety of information (e.g. salary, additional remuneration and other taxable income, property, vehicles, holdings of shares, credit, other financial obligations, dividend income), all published in the *State Gazette*.
10 According to Transparency International, Estonia's CPI (corruption perceptions index) was 5.6 in 2001 and 6.4 in 2005 (www.transparency.org).
11 According to the pollster Turu-uuringute AS, popular trust in chief public offices in 2008 amounted to: the President 70 percent, Cabinet 45 percent, Judiciary 63 percent, Parliament 43 percent (www.turu-uuringute.ee).
12 For instance, the recruitment of senior civil servants (i.e. deputy secretaries general and directors general of agencies) via public competitions has not revealed great popularity of the HPO positions. In 2004, two public competitions were held and altogether eight candidates applied for these jobs with only four of the applicants being qualified for the posts. In 2005, there were three competitions with a total of 14 applicants of which 12 were deemed qualified. In 2006, four posts were advertised, 29 persons applied, but only 20 of them fulfilled the requirements for the positions. (Data obtained on request from the State Chancellery of the Republic of Estonia.) As regards the job openings for Supreme Court Judges, in which case the qualification requirements severely limit the number of potential candidates, the statistics show the following: in 2002 there were three competitions with 12 candidates, in 2003 one competition with seven applicants, in 2004 one competition with five candidates and in 2006 one competition with one candidate. (Data obtained on request from the Supreme Court of Estonia.)
13 The carry-over of MPs was 45.3 percent after general elections in 1995, 43.8 percent in 1999, 33.6 percent in 2003 and 59 percent in 2007.
14 For example, 628 persons ran as candidates in the Riigikogu elections in 1992, 1256 persons in 1995, 1901 persons in 1999, 963 persons in 2003 and 975 persons in 2007. The Riigikogu has 101 members.

References

Aslund, A. (2002) *Building Capitalism. The Transformation of the Former Soviet Bloc.* Cambridge: Cambridge University Press.
Benedict, B. (1966) Problems of smaller territories. In M. Banton (Ed.), *The Social Anthropology of Complex Societies.* London: Tavistock Publications, pp. 23–36.
Bennell, P. and J. Oxenham (1983) Skills and qualifications for small island states. *Labour and Society*, **8**(1): 13–37.
Bray, M. and S. Packer (1993) *Education in Small States. Concepts, challenges and strategies*. Oxford/New York: Pergamon Press.
Drechsler, W. (2000) Public administration in Central and Eastern Europe: considerations from the 'State Science' approach. In L. Burlamaqui, A.C. Castro and H.J. Chang (Eds) *Institutions and the Role of the State*. Cheltenham/Northampton: Edward Elgar.
Eurostat Database: http://epp.eurostat.cec.eu.int

Hood, C. (1991) A public management for all seasons? *Public Administration*, **69**: 3–19.

Hood, C. and S. Lambert (1994) Mountain tops or iceberg tips? Some comparative data on RHPOs. In C. Hood and B.G. Peters (Eds) *Rewards at the Top: A comparative study of high public office*. London: Sage, pp. 25–48.

Hood, C. and B.G. Peters (Eds) (1994) *Rewards at the Top: A comparative study of high public office*. London: Sage.

Inglehart, R. and W.E. Baker (2000) Modernization, cultural change, and the persistence of traditional values. *American Sociological Review*, **65**: 19–51.

Lauristin, M. (1997) Contexts of transition. In M. Lauristin and P. Vihalemm (Eds), *Return to the Western World*. Tartu: Tartu University Press, pp. 25–40.

Lieven, A. (1993) *The Baltic Revolution: Estonia, Latvia, Lithuania and the path to independence*. New Haven, CT: Yale University Press.

Lowenthal, D. (1987) Social features. In C. Clarke and T. Payne (Eds) *Politics, Security and Development in Small States*. London: Allen & Unwin: pp. 26–49.

Ministry of Finance of Republic of Estonia (2005) Economic prognosis in Summer 2005.

Niskanen, W.A. (1971) *Bureaucracy and Representative Government*. Chicago, IL: Aldine Atherton.

Randma, T. (2001) A small civil service in transition: the case of Estonia. *Public Administration and Development*, **21**: 41–51.

Randma-Liiv, T. (2005) Performance management in transitional administration: introduction of pay-for-performance in the Estonian civil service. *Journal of Comparative Policy Analysis*, **7**(1): 95–115.

Realo, A. (2003) Comparison of public and academic discourses: Estonian individualism and collectivism revisited. *Culture and Psychology*, **9**(1): 47–77.

Rees, C.J., J. Järvalt and B. Metcalfe (2005) Career management in transition: HRD themes from the Estonian civil service. *Journal of European Industrial Training*, **29**(7): 572–592.

Riigikantselei (2004) *Avaliku teenistuse aastaraamat 2003* (Civil Service Yearbook 2003). Tallinn, Estonia.

Riigikantselei (2006) *Eesti avaliku teenistuse personalijuhtimise uuring* (Estonian Civil Service HRM Survey) http://avalikteenistus.ee/public/Avaliku_teenistuse_personali juhtimise_uuring_2005.pdf.

Sutton, P. (1987) Political aspects. In C. Clarke and T. Payne (Eds), *Politics, Security and Development in Small States*. London: Allen & Unwin, pp. 3–25.

14 Rewards for high public offices in Hungary

Jan-Hinrik Meyer-Sahling, László Vass, and Edit Vassné Varga

Introduction

This chapter examines rewards for high public office (RHPOs) in Hungary. Hungary belongs to the first wave of post-communist countries that joined the European Union in 2004.

The development of RHPOs in Hungary is closely related to the broader context of post-communist transformation. Two features of RHPOs in Hungary are particularly striking. First, RHPOs have undergone steep increases since the early 1990s. Yet reward levels for most high public offices remain low compared to private sector salaries. Second, especially the institutional basis of RHPOs in public administration is characterized by instability, discretionary governance and large variable bonuses, which can amount to 50 percent and more of an official's take-home salary. Variable pay instruments have typically been introduced under the heading of performance-related pay (PRP). In particular, since 2004 when the businessman Ferenc Gyurcsány was appointed Prime Minister of a Socialist-Liberal government there has been a growing influence of new public management ideas on RHPOs in Hungary. The discussion will show however that the Hungarian PRP system is mistrusted by civil servants and vulnerable to politicization.

These features can be traced back to the communist legacy of the past. Studies of administrative traditions (Painter and Peters 2009) emphasize the 'stickiness' of past administrative practices, norms, values, and institutional configurations. Governance by discretion and the politicization of personnel policy were core features of the communist tradition of public administration (Goetz and Wollmann 2001, Meyer-Sahling 2009a). Marxist-Leninist ideology emphasized equality in terms of social status and material reward but the 'real-existing socialist administration' (König 1992) looked quite different. State institutions had great autonomy over rewards, leading to major differences in those rewards (Nunberg 1999). Moreover, differences in reward levels were (in)famously introduced through informal, non-monetary benefits and privileges that set apart the *nomenclature* from the rank and file of socialist systems (Pakulski 1986).

While it is difficult to deny the importance of the communist past for RHPOs in Hungary, this chapter argues that there are several additional factors that have to be considered. First, creation of the private sector economy was a main objective of the economic transformation (Åslund 2002). Yet the emerging private sector quickly challenged public sector salary systems. Salaries began rising rapidly and, in particular, high public officeholders could earn much higher salaries in the emerging private sector. Consequently, governments were forced to regularly adjust reward packages in order to offer competitive rewards that would prevent the exodus of high public officeholders, especially in public administration and the judiciary, to the private sector.

The economic transformation has also had a major influence through ideas, in that the new public management has increasingly shaped the approach to RHPOs in Hungary. The ground for the ascendance of the new public management was laid in the 1990s by integration into the global economy and privatization by foreign direct investment, both of which have heavily exposed Hungary to multi-national companies and global capitalism (Bohle and Greskovits 2007). Private sector development and the rejection of everything associated with the state and public sector further contributed to the glorification of markets. As a result, salary supplements, bonus systems and managerial discretion have often been justified by the alleged superiority of private sector methods of personnel management. In Hungary, this development gained additional momentum since the early 2000s with the rise of successful businessmen such as Prime Minister Gyurcsány and Minister of Economic Affairs, Koka, to government.

Finally, RHPOs must recognize the particularities of party-state relations in Hungary. State politicization has been endemic in post-communist Hungary, especially in areas such as the ministerial bureaucracy, executive agencies and state-owned enterprises (Meyer-Sahling 2008, Meyer-Sahling/Jáger 2008). Reliance on political appointees in public administration has fostered the 'institutional conversion' (Thelen 2003) of PRP instruments into mechanisms of political reward and control and reduced the legitimacy of PRP measures in the eyes of the wider civil service.

The role of European integration in preventing this development has been ambiguous. The European Commission made public administration reform including the establishment of fair and transparent salary systems a condition for EU membership (Dimitrova 2005, SIGMA 1998, 1999). Yet the impact of conditionality on public administration reform remains contested (Goetz 2005, Bugaric 2006). In fact, it can be argued that the accession process contributed to the emergence of discretionary bonuses, as governments needed the flexibility to reward specialists in EU affairs. In other words, the emergence of 'islands of excellence' (Goetz 2001) in public administration fostered development of a discretionary system rather than the establishment of uniform and transparent salary systems in public administration.

The remainder of this chapter examines the development of RHPOs in Hungary between 1990 and 2008. The discussion is divided into three parts. The first part outlines the institutional foundations of RHPOs. The second examines the role of salary supplements and bonuses and the third part turns to the development of actual reward levels for high public offices. The conclusion returns to the explanation of RHPO developments in post-communist Hungary.

The institutional foundations of RHPOs in Hungary

The institutional foundation of the reward system can be traced back to the regime change. New legal frameworks for the regulation of salaries and benefits were already negotiated during the Political Reconciliation Talks between the ruling communist party and the opposition in 1989 as part of the constitution-making process. Reforms sought to overcome the communist legacy and to reach Western standards of managing rewards in the public sphere. In essence, this meant introducing uniform standards to establish a transparent and predictable system of rewards regulated by law.

Many institutional changes were introduced in the first two years after the first democratic elections in 1990. The most important legal document is the Civil Service Act, adopted and implemented in 1992. The Civil Service Act regulates salaries and benefits for members of the civil service, but until recently it also defined most salary components for state secretaries and cabinet ministers. Moreover, the salary system established in the Civil Service Act represents the point of reference for the rewards of other high public offices. This part starts the discussion with the basic salary system for general civil servants and then turns to top civil servants and high ranking officials of other institutions.

The Civil Service Act has been amended several times since 1992. The main revisions occurred in 1997, 2001, and most recently in two stages in 2006 and 2007. The reforms have introduced important changes to the salary system for civil servants, and today's salary system looks significantly different from the one established in 1992. However, some fundamentals of the salary system have remained in place since 1992, for instance the logic of calculating civil servants' basic salaries.

At the most basic level, the civil service law distinguishes two general categories of civil servants, based on educational qualification. Higher civil servants must hold a university degree, while mid-level civil servants must have completed secondary school education. For each category, a classification system lists salary classes and career grades. Each salary class is assigned one multiplier. For higher civil servants seventeen salary classes are grouped in six grades. The multipliers range from 3.1 for junior civil servants to 6.0 for so-called 'senior chief counselors'.

The allocation of civil servants to individual salary classes and career grades is mainly seniority-based. Every two to four years a civil servant is automatically promoted to a higher salary class. For promotion to a higher career grade, civil servants must pass a performance appraisal. Failure delays promotion by one year, implying that seniority is dominant in determining basic salary levels for general civil servants. In order to reach the highest multiplier of 6.0, for instance, it is necessary for a civil servant to be employed for 37 years.

For the calculation of basic salary amounts, the multiplier associated with an individual salary class is multiplied with the 'salary base.' The salary base is fixed by parliament in the annual Budget Act. Civil service unions have the right to be consulted over salary matters, although their influence over civil service affairs including salary levels and benefits is generally regarded as very limited. Civil service unions were too closely involved with the former communist regime, undermining their credibility in the eyes of new center-right parties that emerged from the democratic opposition. By contrast, the successor party of the former communist party, the Hungarian Socialist Party, has tended to expect 'compliance' and subordination from the civil service unions. This has been especially important during periods of austerity in the mid 1990s and since 2006. The civil service salary base is therefore largely determined by the cabinet and by parliament in the context of budgetary policy-making.

For civil servants with managerial responsibilities basic salaries are position-based, to ensure that the basic salary of any civil service manager is higher than the basic salary of non-managing civil servants. The highest civil servants in Hungary are currently heads of departments, deputy heads of departments and heads of divisions. In their case, the Civil Service Act assigns one multiplier per position regardless of the seniority of the person holding the position. Following the hierarchy from the bottom up, the multipliers are 7.0 for heads of division, 7.5 for deputy heads of departments, and 8.0 for heads of departments. To provide an example for the calculation of basic salaries, in 2008 the salary base stood at 38,650 HUF (Hungarian Forint). The basic salary of a head of department was therefore 309,200 HUF gross, but still without guaranteed supplements and non-guaranteed bonuses, discussed below.

Before 2006 the civil service still included the position of administrative and deputy state secretary as the highest ranking civil servants. Most components of their salaries were also regulated by the Civil Service Act. A major reorganization of government after the elections of 2006 created the position of 'senior state secretary' by merging the position of administrative state secretary with that of political state secretary, which used to be part of the political leadership. Moreover, the position of deputy state secretary was re-classified as 'specialist state secretary.' Both positions were removed from the scope of the civil service and turned into political appointments whose tenure is tied to that of the government. Since 2006 the basic salary of state secretaries is defined in the Act on Members of the Government and State Secretaries but the Act also refers to the civil service salary system by establishing multipliers of 9.0 for specialist state secretaries and 12.0 for senior state secretaries.

Heads of executive agencies are usually classified as senior state secretaries, specialist state secretaries or as heads of departments. Their status and hence their salary is regulated by the legislation establishing the agency. The basic salary is typically defined by using the multiplier system and hence by relating the salary level back to the civil service salary system. Political advisors are the least regulated category of high public officeholders. Their status is regulated by the civil service law but their salary is set as a 'personal remuneration of the minister' (see also below). This means that the minister can subjectively determine the salary level of advisors. There is no precise limit on the salary level of personal advisors but ministries are required to communicate the number of advisors and their salary level to the Prime Minister's Office.

Even though ministers are members of government, their basic salary was also regulated by the Civil Service Act. Since 2006 their basic salaries are also regulated by the Act on Members of the Government and State Secretaries. The multiplier for ministers stands at 15.6, indicating that the basic salary levels are clearly associated with the hierarchical position of executive offices. The prime minister as head of government is assigned the highest basic salary. His basic salary and other benefits are regulated by yet another law, which affects the most senior positions in the Hungarian political system such as the president of the republic, the prime minister, the president of parliament, the president of the constitutional court and the president of the supreme court. The law sets the basic salary of the prime minister at 1.5 times the salary of the senior state secretary (formerly 'administrative state secretary') and hence indirectly refers to the basic civil service salary system, too.

The basic salary levels of the president of the republic as the head of state and the presidents of parliament, the constitutional court and the supreme court are subsequently defined as 'like the salary of the prime minister.' The formulation gives pre-eminence to the prime minister but it also enforces equality among the most senior positions in the Hungarian political system. This pattern neatly illustrates a basic tension in the Hungarian political system between principles of a 'majoritarian democracy,' which concentrates power in the prime minister, and principles of 'consensual democracy,' which emphasizes diffusion of power across the political system, for instance, by institutionalizing a powerful constitutional court and various opportunities for referenda (Ágh 2001, Körösenyi 1999).

The salary system of judges largely mirrors the salary system for civil servants and members of the government. The 1997 Act on Judges establishes a seniority-based classification system for judges and provides position-based allowances for senior judges. Each salary class is assigned a multiplier and an assignment to a senior position guarantees an allowance of up to 100 percent of the basic salary. Parliament sets a minimal salary that serves as the base salary for judges. As mentioned above, only the salary of the most senior judge, such as the president of the supreme court, is regulated separately. It is aligned to the basic salary levels of the prime minister and other high level offices.

Finally, the salary system for members of parliaments differs slightly from that of members of the judiciary and the executive. MPs receive a monthly base fee set by law at six times the civil service salary base. Until the late 1990s, this multiplier was located between the minister as a member of government and the administrative state secretary as the highest civil servant. Since the late 1990s, the multipliers have been lifted for ministers and state secretaries but not for members of parliament. Yet members of parliament have a different system of salary allowances. The base fee for MPs is topped up by a travel allowance depending

Table 14.1 Salary premiums for Members of Parliament, 2006

Function	Premium
Deputy President of parliament	180%
Chairman of standing committee	120%
Deputy chairman of standing committee	100%
Member of standing committee	70%
Member of second standing committee	25%
Leader of parliamentary faction	120%
Deputy leader of parliamentary faction	100%

on the distance of an MP's constituency from Budapest. MPs who live in Budapest receive an allowance of 70 percent of the base fee, while the allowance can reach up to 160 percent of the base fee for MPs who live 250 or more kilometers from Budapest. Travel allowances are paid as lump sums and no receipts are required. In addition, MPs receive premiums paid for the functions they perform inside parliament (see Table 14.1). Premiums are paid for membership in parliamentary committees, the presidency of committees, leadership of parliamentary factions, etc. The functions are differently weighted and MPs can receive premiums for up to two functions.

The logic of calculating basic salaries for all high public offices discussed so far suggests a relatively clear break with the communist tradition, in that basic salaries are regulated by law. At first glance, the fundamentals of the basic salary system have remained remarkably stable since the early 1990s. However, there have been important changes to the salary system. Some changes have occurred within the basic salary system. In particular, the multipliers for high public offices have changed every four to five years, with major consequences for basic salary levels. The multiplier for the senior state secretaries (formerly administrative state secretaries) stood initially at 5.5. In 2001, it was lifted to 9.0 and in 2006 it was raised to 12.0. Similar changes occurred for the other high public offices under study here. This implies that the stability of the salary system has been limited to its core. The impression of instability becomes more evident when looking at the frequent revision of salary supplements and bonuses.

Supplements and bonuses for Hungarian senior officials

This part examines the development of salary supplements and salary bonuses since the early 1990s. It argues that the system of supplements and bonuses has been in constant flux, being revised every few years. Moreover, it shows that for civil servants and state secretaries the size of variable, discretionary bonuses has continuously increased. In fact, the institutionalization of discretion is one main feature of the salary system for civil servants and state secretaries in Hungary. Finally, bonuses have usually been introduced in order to strengthen the performance-orientation of the salary system but performance bonuses have been vulnerable to 'institutional conversion' (Thelen 2003), in that they have been used as instruments of political reward and control by the governing political parties.

Several salary supplements were already included in the 1992 Civil Service Act. All employees of central government ministries, for instance, are guaranteed a supplement of 50 percent of their basic salary. This supplement applies also to members of the government and other high public offices discussed above. In 1997, the government introduced a special managerial supplement for heads of divisions, deputy heads of departments, heads of departments and the two types of state secretaries at the top of the ministerial hierarchy. This supplement was guaranteed, too, and has not been changed. It ranges from 25 percent of the basic salary for heads of divisions to 65 percent for administrative state secretaries. The managerial supplement also applies to members of the government and most other high ranking officials, who automatically receive the same supplement as the senior (administrative) state secretary. As a result, the 'fixed salary' of a senior state secretary (formerly administrative state secretary), to give an example, effectively consists of the basic salary plus a 50 percent salary supplement plus a 65 percent management supplement.

The salary system also includes several bonuses and allowances that are variable but non-discretionary. Since 1992, the civil service law has provided for so-called language allowances as a qualification-based bonus. The language bonus is clearly regulated by government decree. It can reach up to 100 percent of the salary base (in 2008, it stood at 38,650 HUF as defined in the annual Budget Act, see above) for proficiency in English, German, or French.[1] The language allowance system also applies to members of the government, judges and in fact also to members of parliament.

The most important bonuses have typically been both variable and discretionary. Of the three types of discretionary bonuses, the first concerns the so-called 'personal remuneration list of the minister,' introduced in 1992. The personal remuneration list of the minister has its origin in a conflict among senior officials (mainly state secretaries and department heads) during the negotiations of the 1992 civil service reform, while ministers largely accepted the compromise reached at the administrative level. One objective of the reform was the establishment of a salary system that pays equal salaries for equal job responsibilities and equal qualifications in order to overcome the substantial inequality that existed during the communist period. The multiplier solution that was proposed by the Ministry of Interior, then responsible for civil service reform, implied much greater salary increases for officials in 'poor' ministries, such as welfare, education and culture, than for 'rich' ministries, such as finance, industry, and international trade. Moreover, senior officials from the economics ministries had lucrative exit options in the emerging private sector. In order to avoid the departure of those senior officials, it was agreed to create a mechanism that made possible the negotiation of higher salaries for selected senior officials without the constraints of the standardized salary system.

The so-called personal remuneration list of the minister was originally meant to apply in exceptional circumstances only. However, by the late 1990s, it had

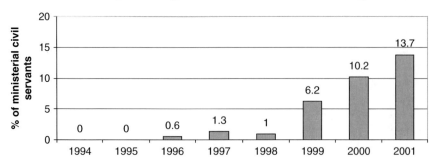

Figure 14.1 Civil servants on the 'personal remuneration list of the minister', Ministry of Transport, 1994–2001.

become an increasingly common instrument to raise salary levels of senior officials and general civil servants. The data in Figure 14.1 from the Ministry of Transport for the period from 1994 to 2001 indicates a significant increase in the application of the personal remuneration clause after the change of government in 1998 and again after the change of minister in 2000.

Personal interviews conducted with former senior officials of the Ministry of Transport suggest that the personal remuneration clause was increasingly used for political control and reward, whereby the ministers of the center-right government that took office in 1998 paid higher salaries in order to reward political appointees and to elicit loyalty from staff, bearing in mind that ministers could withdraw the personal remuneration anytime. The institution of the personal remuneration list of the ministers was thus gradually 'converted' from being an exceptional instrument to retain indispensable staff with transferable skills to an instrument of political reward and control. In 2001 the system was reformed and the personal remuneration clause became applicable to political advisors only.

The other important variable and discretionary element of the salary system in Hungary is officially labeled as PRP measures. PRP was first introduced in 1997, as part of a comprehensive administrative reform program that sought to modernize public administration and to align it with Western models. The PRP scheme created the possibility either to raise the basic salary of state secretaries and heads of departments by up to 40 percent or to lower it by up to 20 percent. For all other civil servants, the scheme allowed the salary adjustment of +/– 20 of the basic salary. By Western standards, this variable pay is very high indeed (OECD 2005). The salary increases were subject to the discretion of the minister and the administrative state secretary as the authority exercising employer's rights in the ministerial bureaucracy. The 1997 civil service reform also introduced a performance evaluation system but evaluations were conducted only when general civil servants were promoted to a higher career grade, while a link to the PRP system was not made explicit. This link was only developed in the context of the 2001 reform when a first attempt was made to strengthen the performance evaluation system.

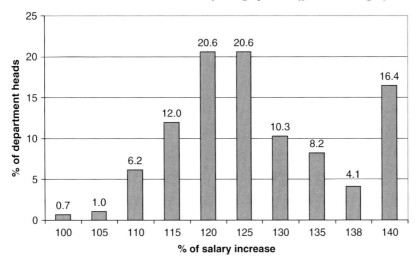

Figure 14.2 Fixed salaries for HPO, 2006.

Figure 14.2 illustrates how the +40/–20 percent rule was applied in the Ministry of Transport for heads of departments in the year 1999. The figure shows that almost all heads of departments enjoyed a salary increase, while none of them had to take a pay cut. Moreover, four in five department heads received an increase of 20 or more percent of their basic salary.

It is difficult to say what criteria were used to determine the allocation of higher or lower salary increases to senior officials. Personal interviews with senior officials then employed at the Ministry of Transport suggest that the minister was largely autonomous in allocating salary increases to state secretaries, while the administrative state secretary and the deputy state secretaries took responsibility for subordinated senior officials. Yet the methods of allocating salary increases were entirely informal and could even differ within the same ministry. Insights gained from personal interviews with representatives from other ministries, by and large, confirm this informal and discretionary method as a general method of bonus allocation at that time.

The PRR scheme that allows for the increase and decrease of basic salaries has been amended several times since 1997 but changes have not been transformative. For instance, in 2001 the performance evaluation system was strengthened, including annual evaluations, the ex ante agreement of performance objectives, and the possibility for appeal against the evaluation outcomes, and a closer link to the PRP scheme was established. The size of the proportional salary increase was adjusted several times. It currently stands at 30 percent as the maximum proportional salary increase for senior officials.

At the same time, the method of allocating performance-based salary increases has changed little. Ministers remain responsible for allocating salary increases to state secretaries while specialist state secretaries are typically in charge of setting salary increases for civil servants under their responsibility. The delegation of authority to specialist state secretaries implies that political appointees have also formally become responsible for allocating bonuses, which underlines the impression that PRP instruments have largely been converted into mechanisms of political control and reward.

The third kind of discretionary payment is a so-called annual bonus paid at the end of the year as a variable, non-guaranteed bonus. Annual bonuses existed in the 1990s. They were in fact not regulated by the civil service law but were subject to the discretion of the ministries and paid from ministerial budgets. Their size depended entirely on the wealth of individual ministries and the method of allocation was entirely subject to ministerial discretion. Estimates suggest that the annual bonus ranged up to 30 percent of the annual salary during the 1990s and early 2000s.

The bonus system was radically reformed in 2006/2007 when the Gyurcsány government introduced an ambitious PRP system, passed in 2007 and implemented in 2008. It allows the payment of bonuses of up to six monthly salaries (48 percent) for managers such as state secretaries and department heads and four salaries for non-managers. In 2008, the government adopted a decree, limiting the annual bonus to 12 percent of the annual salary. This measure largely resulted in general measures to curb government spending. The PRP system operates a forced distribution system. Managers are required to differentiate the performance of their subordinates according to quotas established by the Prime Minister's Office. For instance, the top bonus of six monthly salaries was initially limited to ten percent of the eligible officials. The evaluation is based on a revised performance evaluation system conducted annually and concentrates on civil servants' competencies and functions as specified at the beginning of the assessment period.

The first application of the new performance bonus system in 2007/2008 created considerable problems. Civil servants resented the rapid introduction of the new scheme and, in particular, the system of forced distributions. Quotas were disaggregated down to the division level, which often consisted of no more than four or five civil servants. Consequently, heads of divisions were required to cover the whole range of grades even if this did not reflect the actual performance of their subordinates. Several ministries such as the Ministry of Finance introduced compensatory bonus payments taken from internal budgetary resources in order to reduce the sense of injustice introduced by the new PRP scheme.

The ineffectiveness of the various PRP mechanisms in Hungary is reflected in the responses of ministerial civil servants to a survey conducted in the summer of 2008 (Meyer-Sahling 2009b). The survey was web-based and generated 172 responses from among ministerial civil servants. Figure 14.3 shows that civil servants doubt the link between pay and performance, in that 45 percent of the respondents disagree with the statement that good performance leads to higher salary levels, while only 29 percent agree with the statement.

The critical evaluation of the general statement is consistent with the evaluation of individual elements of the PRP system. The allocation of bonuses – at the

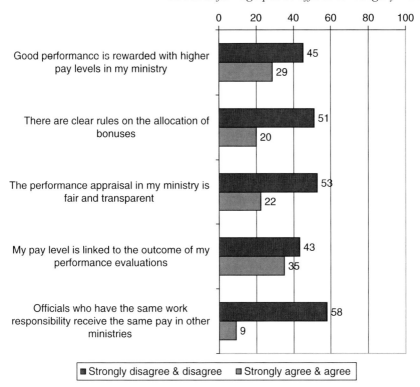

Figure 14.3 Civil servants' perception of the salary system in Hungary (% of all survey respondents).

heart of any PRP system – is seen as unclear by more than half of the respondents. The performance appraisal, which had existed since 1997 and had just undergone a major reform in 2007, is regarded as unfair and non-transparent. Even the effective link between the outcomes of the performance appraisal and civil servants' salary levels is questioned by respondents. Overall, the responses suggest that civil servants do not trust the PRP system(s) that have been applied since the late 1990s. Instead, the system is perceived as unfair and vulnerable to political favoritism and abuse.

The most recent reform of the performance related pay system was part of a wider state reform launched after the re-election of the center-left Gyurcsány government in 2006. The State Reform Commission prepared various proposals to increase public sector efficiency. In this context, the government recruited former private sector managers into the Prime Minister's Office to prepare and implement reform of human resource management in public administration. The reform was thus largely inspired by individual champions who believed private sector methods were the right medicine for public administration. The reform was clearly not a response to fiscal stress, as the budgetary situation deteriorated only after the discussion of reform measures had begun. The main initiative must therefore be related to ideological convictions of the protagonists of the center-left government at that time, Prime Minister Gyurcsány and the leader of the Free Democrats (SZDSZ) and Minister of the Economy, Koka. Both were successful businessmen before coming to government.

In sum, supplements and especially variable bonuses play an important role in the system of RHPOs, especially in public administration. Especially bonus schemes have been revised and extended several times over the last one and a half decades. The result has been the emergence of a discretionary salary system lacking transparency and unable to guarantee fair and equal salaries across state institutions (see Figure 14.3).

The development of RHPOs in Hungary

This section compares the reward levels for high public offices in 2006 and then examines the development of rewards for members of the government and senior civil servants between 1992 and 2006. It shows steep salary increases since the early 1990s for all high public offices. However, relatively low reward levels also remain a characteristic feature of RHPOs in Hungary. This salary gap between public and private sector wages exerts constant pressure on the reward system and is an important determinant of institutional instability and discretionary governance.

Table 14.2 compares basic salary levels for the most senior positions in the Hungarian political system. It shows first the equality in fixed salaries for the president of the republic, the prime minister and the presidents of parliament, the constitutional court and the supreme court. The table also shows the salary levels for ministers, state secretaries and heads of selected executive state agencies. The salary for senior state secretaries, for example, includes the basic salary resulting from the 12-fold multiplication of the salary base, the 50 percent salary supplement that all employees of central government ministries receive and the managerial supplement of 65 percent of the basic salary. This 'fixed' salary can increase if senior state secretaries are granted the full or part of the +30/–20 salary bonus, if they receive the full or part of the annual performance bonus, and if they receive guaranteed allowances such as language allowances. The average monthly salary of a given state secretary can even rise above the salary level of the prime minister if all evaluations have been awarded an 'exceeds expectations.' In practice, this could happen only in exceptional circumstances but the example also illustrates the difficulty of determining the actual salary level of senior officials.

Table 14.2 also shows that the salaries of the heads of executive agencies differ across agencies. In some cases such as the Hungarian News Agency, the salary is aligned with that of the prime minister. In the case of the Customs Authority, it is aligned with the salary of state secretaries. By contrast, the President of the National Bank stands out in that his salary is almost three times higher than that of the prime minister. The President of the National Bank may also be granted an 80 percent salary bonus, which raises his salary up to the level of private sector CEOs.

Table 14.2 Fixed salaries for HPO, 2006

High public officials	Basic salary excluding bonuses (HUF)
President of the Republic	1,435.200
President of the Parliament	1,435.200
Member of Parliament*	507.840*
President of the Constitutional Court	1,435.200
President of the Supreme Court	1,435.200
Prime Minister	1,435.200
Minister	1,234.272
Senior State Secretary	949.440
Specialist State Secretary	712.080
Head of Department	529.920
President of the Internal Revenue Service	880.000
President of the Customs Authorities	945.000
President of the National Bank	3,832.263
President of the Newscast Authorities	1,435.200
President of the National Postal Service**	2,840.000
President of the Hungarian Development Bank**	3,657.833
President of Hungarian TV (MTV)**	2,100.000

Notes:
* MPs' base fee *plus* intermediate travel allowance for MPs living between 105 and 200 km from Budapest but *without* premiums for committee membership and other functions.
** Fixed salaries for 2008, no earlier data released.

The table further indicates that managers of state-owned enterprises tend to be paid higher salaries than ministers and the prime minister. The President of the National Postal Office earns almost twice the salary of the prime minister and he may be granted a bonus of 80 percent of his annual salary. The CEO of the Hungarian Development Bank, one of the last but most important state-owned banks in Hungary also receives a salary many times higher than that of the prime minister, especially when considering that he may receive an annual bonus of 80 percent of his salary.

It is usually very difficult to compare salaries of public and private sector managers. Yet Table 14.3 indicates that salary levels for the president of the National Bank and the main state-owned enterprises are more or less aligned with comparable private sector reward levels. These institutions and senior positions are all very exposed to the private sector. By contrast, the reward levels for the prime minister, ministers and state secretaries are a good deal away from the average level of private sector CEOs. Especially ministers and senior state secretaries with an annual salary of 14.8 and 11.4 million HUF are closer to the lower quartile of the salaries earned by general private sector managers. Also, heads of

Table 14.3 Salary ranges of different types of private sector executives (Annual salaries, average of the lowest and highest quartile, values for 2006 in HUF)

Position	Total cash income (HUF)
Chief Executive Officer	27,733.841–47,770.000
Sales and marketing manager	14,329.887–24,625.656
Financial manager	13,070.246–22,314.824
Sales manager	12,357.391–19,651.000
Human resources manager	11,237.638–20,782.417
IT Manager	9,352.246–16,794.042
Purchasing manager	8,627.500–14,370.000
Marketing manager	8,064.000–17,783.250

Source: Hewitt Humán Tanácsadó Kft. (Világgazdaság online, December 2006).

departments, currently the highest ranking civil servants, earn relatively low salaries compared to private sector peers. They receive less than 7.0 million HUF per year, which is still well below the lowest paid marketing, purchasing, and HR managers in the private sector.

The relatively large gap between the RHPOs in government and managers of private sector companies indicates the importance of salary bonuses in reaching competitive salary levels in government and public administration. Once these variable pay elements are added, salary levels remain below those of private sector CEOs but they become a good deal more attractive.

One might also want to add other allowances and non-monetary benefits to the reward levels. Ministers and the prime minister, for instance, have the right to an official flat or a flat allowance, a car with a driver, a season ticket for public transport in Budapest, access to the special health care service and the use of a central governmental recreation center, and other benefits. Yet it is commonly argued that the non-monetary benefits tend to be more generous in the private sector, as private sector companies use these benefits to compete for talent.

For the civil service, non-monetary benefits have traditionally been less consistent across government institutions. They depend on the wealth of the institution and on the actual function. Civil servants of the Ministry of Transport, to give but one example, used to have the right to one free flight per year with the national airline. They could travel at reduced fares with the national railways and take advantage of one free journey by train to another European country. These privileges could add substantially to a civil servant's overall level of reward.

Over time, the number of non-monetary privileges and benefits has declined, which indicates that one main feature of the communist tradition of rewarding high public officeholders is no longer characteristic of RHPOs in Hungary. In particular, the fiscal crisis of the mid 1990s and the current crisis of the public finances have gradually led to cutting-back these privileges. By contrast, variable monetary bonuses play an important role in the system of RHPOs in Hungary.

However, even after these additions the reward levels of most top officials remain low compared to private sector earnings.

Tables 14.4 and 14.5 show the development of fixed salaries over time. The dates between 1992 and 2006 have been deliberately chosen as years after which salary reforms came into force. The 1997 reform, for instance, introduced the managerial supplement for state secretaries and other senior civil servants. The 2001 reform raised multipliers for state secretaries, senior civil servants, and government members. The 2006 reform raised the multipliers again, leading yet to another salary increase. The tables also include the fixed salaries of other officials in order to compare high public offices to junior civil servants, civil servants with many years of experience but without managerial responsibilities and the average salary for the national economy.

The steep salary increases between 1992 and 2006 are arguably the most striking feature of Tables 14.4 and 14.5. In 2006 the salaries of the prime minister and ministers were seven to eight times higher than those in 1992. To be sure, the salary increases are less steep when controlling for inflation. However, the change reflects very closely the average salary increase in the Hungarian economy during the same period of time (see Figure 14.4). Table 14.5 shows that the salaries of senior civil servants have increased at a much lower rate than the salaries of political executives and the salaries in the national economy. This indicates that senior civil servants have been relative losers during the 15 years since 1992.

The greatest losers have, however, been civil servants with many years of employment in the civil service but without assignment to a managerial position.

Table 14.4 Fixed salaries of selected members of the government and civil servants over time (in thousand HUF)

Year	1992	1998[a]	2002[a]	2006[a]
Prime Minister	187	461	958	1,435
Minister	146	254	851	1,234
State Secretary[b]	124	308	639	949
Specialist State Secretary[c]	113	260	561	712
Head of Department	101	211	475	530
Deputy Head of Department	90	177	421	469
Head of Division	79	146	370	412
Senior chief counsellors[d]	77	234	297	331
Junior civil servant	28	82	154	171
Civil service salary base	15	26	33	37
National economy average	22	68	123	171

Notes:
[a] Basic salaries without bonus.
[b] Until 2006, Administrative State Secretary.
[c] Until 2006, Deputy State Secretary.
[d] Higher civil servant after 37 years of service without managerial assignment.

Table 14.5 Fixed salaries of selected members of the government and civil servants over time (1992 = 100)

Year	1992	1998[a]	2002[a]	2006[a]
Prime Minister	100	248	516	773
Minister	100	173	582	844
State Secretary[b]	100	248	516	767
Specialist State Secretary[c]	100	231	499	633
Head of Department	100	208	469	523
Deputy Head of Department	100	196	468	521
Head of Division	100	185	469	523
Senior chief counsellor[d]	100	306	388	432
Junior civil servant	100	291	546	608
Civil service base salary	100	173	220	245
National economy average	100	304	549	769

Notes:
[a] Basic salaries without bonus.
[b] Until 2006, Administrative State Secretary.
[c] Until 2006, Deputy State Secretary.
[d] Higher civil servant after 37 years of service without managerial assignment.

Civil servants in the highest salary class, senior chief counselors with 37 years, have increased their salary by only four times since 1992. During the reforms, they have not benefited from introducing new supplements, while the multiplier was only raised once: in 1997 from 3.4 to 6.0. The salary reforms have therefore clearly discriminated against experienced civil servants.

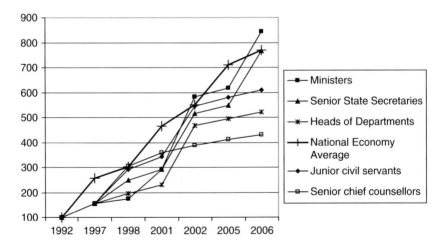

Figure 14.4 Fixed salaries of members of the government and selected civil servants over time (1992 = 100).

Table 14.5 shows that the salary position of junior civil servants also deteriorated relative to the national economy but at a lower rate than that of senior chief
counselors. It is very difficult to infer what kind of starting salary university
graduates could earn in the private economy. Personal interviews indicate that
starting salaries are higher in the private sector, especially at multi-national
companies. However, employment in the civil service often provides a good
deal for university graduates. Variable pay elements can significantly lift the
overall take-home salary, even at the junior level. Moreover, university graduates
tend to view employment in public administration as an opportunity for training
and to develop a network of contacts that can lead to a better paid job in the
private sector. The logic of 'deferred compensation' (Milgrom and Roberts 1992),
characteristic of closed career systems, does therefore also apply in the Hungarian
civil service. Ironically, young civil servants do not seem to expect the higher
level of compensation in the civil service itself but outside the public sector.

In conclusion, the features of institutional instability and discretionary governance discussed in the previous section become more understandable in light of the
constant pressure to align RHPOs with the dynamic salary development in the
private sector. Regular changes were needed in order to align salaries of high
public offices with comparable private sector salaries. The exposure of high public
offices to competitive private sector salaries has been very uneven across policy
sectors and may have increased over time. Consequently, salary reforms had to
pragmatically target some groups of top officials more than others. Variable,
discretionary bonus payments are a practical instrument under these circumstances
because their application can easily be individualized to generate selected salary
increases. However, the trade-off of this development has been the emergence of
an unstable and discretionary salary system lacking transparency. The system is
vulnerable to political favoritism and mistrusted by the general civil service.

Conclusion

This chapter has argued that RHPOs in Hungary are relatively low compared to
the private sector even though frequent attempts have been made to adjust
RHPOs with the private sector. In addition, it has shown that the institutional
basis of RHPOs in Hungary has been characterized by instability and the inclusion of discretionary bonuses, many of which are large in size and vulnerable to
politicization. Especially the many discretionary bonuses have usually been introduced under the headings of performance-related pay, setting incentives for high
public officeholders and generally modernization of rewards. The New Public
Management has therefore legitimated the continuous revision of RHPOs in
Hungary. However, the chapter has shown that the context of private sector building has provided functional pressures that have favored institutional instability
and the inclusion of discretionary bonuses into the salary system, especially in
public administration.

The Hungarian development is not unique but shares many features of the
development of RHPOs in the other Central and Eastern European countries that

have recently joined the EU (Meyer-Sahling 2009b). Especially RHPOs in public administration tend to be low compared to the private sector, bonuses are large, and managerial and political discretion are wide-ranging. RHPOs in Hungary differ from other Central and Eastern European countries in that they have been injected with a greater dose of the New Public Management of the last few years than countries such as Poland, the Czech Republic, and Slovenia. In Hungary, RHPOs have also been subject to more political meddling than in other countries, especially the three Baltic States, in which public administration is generally less politicized.

The broad similarities of RHPOs in Central and Eastern Europe suggest that specific regional characteristics are responsible for the development of RHPOs in Hungary. The legacy of the real-existing socialist administration and the context of economic transformation, in particular, private sector building, the integration into the global economy and the rejection of the state and the public sector, have had major influences on the development of RPHOs. The EU accession process sought to institutionalize transparent and predictable RHPOs in Central and Eastern Europe. Yet the features of RHPOs in the region suggest that the intended influence of the European Commission on RHPOs has been limited. Instead, it is conceivable that the EU accession process contributed to institutional instability and the entrenchment of a discretionary system of RHPOs.

With regard to the general explanations of RHPOs (Hood and Peters 1994, 2003), these findings suggest that historical institutionalist explanations and public choice explanations are more applicable than the so-called Tocquevillean explanation. Even if RHPOs have remained comparatively low, there has been no specific downward pressure from democratic competition, as suggested by the Tocquevillean explanation. Instead, political elites have been eager to continuously adjust their reward levels to the developments in the general national economy. The frequent alignment of reward packages with private sector developments and the importance of rewards as mechanisms of political control suggest that the self-interest of the politico-administrative elite has been the main driver of RHPOs in Hungary. Yet rational self-interest is not sufficient as an explanation, as the development of RHPOs requires closer attention to the opportunities and constraints that have come with the specific historical context of political and economic transformation in Central and Eastern Europe.

Note

1 Civil servants can receive a second or even third language bonus if their job description requires more than one foreign language. This provision is especially relevant for officials in the Foreign Ministry and officials of international relations departments.

References

Ágh, A. (2001) Early consolidation and performance crisis: the majoritarian-consensus democracy debate in Hungary. *West European Politics*, **24**(3): 89–112.

Åslund, A. (2002) *Building Capitalism: The transformation of the Former Soviet Bloc.* Cambridge: Cambridge University Press.

Bohle, D. and B. Greskovits (2007) Neoliberalism, embedded neoliberalism and neocorporatism: towards transnational capitalism in Central-Eastern Europe. *West European Politics*, **30**(3), 443–466.

Bugaric, B. (2006) The europeanisation of national administrations in Central and Eastern Europe: creating formal structures without substance? In W. Sadurski *et al.* (Eds) *Apres Enlargement: Legal responses in Central and Eastern Europe.* Florence: RSCAS-EUI Publications

Dimitrova, A.L. (2005) Europeanization and Civil Service Reform in Central and Eastern Europe. In F. Schimmelfennig and U. Sedelmeier (Eds), *The Europeanization of Central and Eastern Europe.* Ithaca, NY: Cornell University Press, pp. 71–90.

Goetz, K.H. (2001) Making sense of post-communist central administration: modernisation, europeanization or latinization? *Journal of European Public Policy*, **8**(6): 1032–1051.

Goetz, K.H. (2005) The new member states and the EU: responding to Europe. In S. Bulmer and C. Lequesne (Eds), *The Member States of the European Union.* Oxford: Oxford University Press, pp. 254–280.

Goetz, K.H. and H. Wollmann (2001) Governmentalizing central executives in post-communist Europe: a four-country comparison. *Journal of European Public Policy*, **8**(6): 864–887.

Hesse, J.J. (1998) Rebuilding the state: administrative reform in Central and Eastern Europe. In SIGMA (Ed.), *Preparing Public Administration for the European Administrative Space.* Paris: SIGMA Papers (23), pp. 168–179.

Hood, C. and B.G. Peters (Eds) (1994) *Rewards at the* Top: A comparative study of high public office. London: Sage.

Hood, C., and B.G. Peters (Eds) (2003) *Reward for High Public Office: Asian and Pacific Rim States.* London: Routledge.

König, K. (1992) The transformation of a 'real socialist' administrative system into a conventional West European system. *International Review of Administrative Sciences*, **58**: 147–161.

Körösenyi, A. (1999) *Government and Politics in Hungary.* Budapest: Central European University Press.

Lewis, P. (2006) Party systems in post-communist Central Europe: patterns of stability and consolidation. *Democratization*, **13**(4): 562–583.

Meyer-Sahling, J.-H. (2008) The changing colours of the post-communist state: the politicisation of the senior civil service in Hungary. *European Journal of Political Research*, **47**(1): 1–33.

Meyer-Sahling, J.-H. (2009a) Varieties of legacies: a critical review of legacy explanations of public administration reform in East Central Europe. *International Review of Administrative Science*, **75**(3): pp. 509–528.

Meyer-Sahling, J.-H. (2009b) *The Sustainability of Civil Service Reforms in Central and Eastern Europe Five Years after Accession.* Paris: SIGMA Paper (44).

Meyer-Sahling, J.-H. and K. Jáger (2008) Capturing the state: party patronage in contemporary Hungary. Florence: European University Institute, Working Paper.

Milgrom, P. and J. Roberts (1992) *Economics, Organisation and Management.* Englewood Cliffs, NJ: Prentice-Hall.

Nunberg, B. (Ed.) (1999) *The State After Communism: Administrative Transitions in Central and Eastern Europe.* Washington, DC: The World Bank.

OECD (2005) *Performance-Related Pay Policies for Government Employees*. Paris: OECD Publications.

Painter, M. and B.G. Peters (Eds) (2009) *Administrative Traditions: Inheritances and transplants in comparative perspective*. Basingstoke: Palgrave.

Pakulski, J. (1986) Bureaucracy and the Soviet System. *Studies in Comparative Communism*, **19**(1): 3–24.

SIGMA (1998) *Preparing Public Administrations for the European Administrative Space*. Paris: SIGMA Papers (23).

SIGMA (1999) *European Principles for Public Administration*. Paris: SIGMA Papers (27).

Thelen, K. (2003) How institutions evolve: insights from comparative historical analysis. In J. Mahoney and D. Rueschemeyer (Eds), *Comparative Historical Analysis in the Social Sciences*. Cambridge: Cambridge University Press, pp. 208–240.

15 Bureaucracy and rewards in Romania[1]

Katja Michalak

Introduction

The salaries of Romanian civil servants are so low that, in the absence of any bribe-taking, the bureaucrats would have the lifestyle of the lower middle class in Romania in economic terms. However, the power these bureaucrats wield is that of upper middle class Romanians. This is due to their ability to hold up approval of regulatory processes necessary for the functioning of the private sector. Civil society actors, therefore, are willing to pay bureaucrats for facilitating the processes of meeting government regulations by which the private sector is required to abide. The bureaucrats, in turn, are willing to accept bribes from the private sector so as to convert some of their power into economic gain. Such a relationship of mutual benefit between the Romanian bureaucrats and the private sector in Romania provides a solid and lasting foundation to support corruption. Second, the Romanian bureaucracy is politicized. Third, the Romanian bureaucracy is oversized in relation to other countries in the South Eastern European (SEE) region. These three forces serve to reinforce one another to produce a very substantial proportion of non-transparent activities in Romania, simply because the politicians, private-sector actors who pay bribes, and bureaucrats, all find it in their interest to keep their actions below the range of detection by the radar of transparency, to hide their illegal acts, including those of nepotism. That is what this article is about: (1) corruption and nepotism, (2) lack or transparency, and (3) inertia in implementation of civil service reforms, in Romania. The oversized character of the Romanian bureaucracy further exacerbates the problem of the very slow pace of reform.

As long as the features that constitute the foundations of corruption, nepotism, and lack of transparency remain in place, it is futile to expect anything other than inertia in civil service reform.

Romania: Problems in the bureaucracy

A continuing effort needs to be made to develop administrative capacity. Serious staff shortages in the public ministry may call for emergency measures such as a temporary re-assignment of posts. Some elements of the recruitment procedure need to be improved to attract suitably qualified recruits.

(EU Commission Report 2008)

The dictatorial nature of Romanian pre-transition history provides valuable insight into the country-specific administrative problems that preexisted before the transition to consolidated democracy started. Some significant characteristics are outlined next. It is important to note that the political transition did not coincide with bureaucratic changes, which followed a decade later.

Pre-transition aspects: The bureaucratic state under Ceausescu

Linz and Stepan characterize communist Romania as a sultanistic regime. Such regimes are unlikely to institute liberalizing reforms on their own that lead to a democratization process, as might occur in an authoritarian regime (Linz and Stepan 1996: 37). One of the major organizational obstacles was Ceausescu's bureaucratic system, filled with cronies and family members. In Romania, Ceausescu made the rules. He also decided how his political apparatus was structured. Norms and bureaucratic relations were constantly subverted by arbitrary decisions of the ruler. Ceausescu reduced his own uncertainty through the personalization of politics. Ceausescu's Romania was hence characterized as a classic sultanistic regime, with a weak bureaucratic apparatus, but a very strong personalistic form of rule. Ceausescu exercised total control over policy decision making, dismissals and recruitment of the personnel. He determined the political agenda in terms of the official ideology, which was reinterpreted by him.

Concerning the relationship between bureaucrats and politicians, Ceausescu consolidated his control not only by creating new bureaucratic structures, but also by the frequent rotation of officials between party and state bureaucracies and between national and local posts. The main objective of rotation was to enable Ceausescu to remove potential rivals to his authority before they could develop a power base. By attributing all the country's public policy problems to inept and dishonest bureaucrats intent on sabotaging his policies, Ceausescu was able to undertake the rotation measures that he deemed necessary. He called for administrative streamlining by eliminating the duplication of party and government functions, assigning responsibility for a given public policy activity to a single individual, and by holding that person accountable if the policy was not effectively administered.

In order to evaluate a bureaucrat's performance, Ceausescu introduced a salary reform, linking managers' incomes to the performance of the economic unit under their supervision. To maintain their incomes, officials falsified performance reports. As a result, aggregate production figures were grossly inflated, and annual and 5-year plan targets based on these figures became increasingly unrealistic. Ceausescu developed a tied salary-budget system. Because wages and salaries were tied to plan fulfillment and severe penalties were levied for shortfalls, managers concealed surplus operating reserves to ensure production in the event of unforeseen bottlenecks.

The structuring and re-structuring of administrative bureaucracy in the early years of post-transition Romania were marked by personalistic political party structure, rather than a pre-existing political party structure, as in the Soviet style communist party. Pre-inherited political and bureaucratic structures were very weak, especially given the fact that the main political and bureaucratic posts were filled by family members. Given that high-level bureaucrats constantly rotated in their posts between the national and local-level governments, a persistent problem that impacted the post-transition time in Romania was the absence of professionalization, especially at the top level bureaucratic apparatus.

Problems with the current Romanian bureaucracy

Given this history, the post-transition Romanian bureaucracy represents a combination of predominantly inherited structures from the past and some limited new administrative procedures initiated in the post-transition period. While Ceausescu's regime collapsed in 1989, the state administration structures and administrative practices of the Ceausescu era remained intact until 1999, as one would expect from the inertia of reforms. Evidence of this is in the retention of personnel from the earlier era, and virtually no new hiring in the bureaucracy. However, from 130,344 civil servants in Romania in 1995, the number fell by 30 percent in 2000. Thus, pre-existing employees were shed, but new hiring did not occur. The overall decrease, however, varied considerably across ministries, with the biggest drop in the number of bureaucrats from the Ministry of Agriculture.

Up to 1999, no significant administrative changes occurred. Especially conspicuous was the absence of merit-based change. This strong resistance to reform was accompanied by the fact that until 1996 a strong post-communist political party governed Romania. As already noted, towards the late 1990s, the international community (EU) expressed a need for reform.

Problems of corruption

On 23 July 2008, the European Commission (EC), in a report on monitoring the status of administrative reform in Romania, concluded:

> The National Integrity Agency will now have to demonstrate its operational capacity to effectively sanction unjustified assets and to verify incompatibilities and conflicts of interest. It has to show that it can build a strong track record in terms of cases and sanctions. Consistency and coherence in the preparation of laws and in their application needs to be ensured. There is a need for public consultation in the preparation of laws. Recourse to emergency ordinances should be reduced. More effort needs to go into applying the law consistently and uniformly. The fight against corruption needs to be

de-politicized and Romania must affirm its unequivocal commitment to fight against high-level corruption.

(European Commission Report 2008)

The European Union thus threatened to cut funds for the following years if Romania did not solve its administrative transparency problems and the problem of high-level administrative corruption. In fact, Romania has not solved these problems, nor has the EC made good on its threat (in contrast with Bulgaria, which experienced an 80 percent cut in annual EU funding, starting October 2008).

Problem of secrecy and confidentiality

Defining the Romanian administration, it can be said that it is largely based on the inherited system of 'secrecy and confidentiality.' Civil service bureaucrats are obliged to maintain confidentiality, as described in the Civil Service Law 161/2003, and are disciplined if they do not observe this obligation (articles 44 and 70). Confidentiality is inherited from the Ceausescu regime, which under Law 23/1971 defined the level of confidentiality of information and state secrecy, including the protection of the internal regulation of each ministry. In the Romanian Constitution of 1991 this law was not sufficiently adapted to the requirements of the democratic state, and only in 2002 was it finally repealed by Law 182/2002 on the protection of classified information. However, several fundamental rights are still negatively affected by this legislation, particularly the freedom of expression and uncovering corruption. Law 544/2001 on Free Access to Information of Public Interest (*Official Gazette*, 23 October 2001) presents a first step to more transparency, but it remains very restrictive. This law stipulates that 'public information is freely accessible except when it refers to classified information' (article 12-1). Classified information relates to national defense, security and public order, personal data, authorities' debates, and political and economic interests of Romania. The decisions to keep classified information secret depend on the authority holding the information. This problem is two-fold. On the one hand, authorities and higher level bureaucrats have the authority to withhold information about interactions with political appointees. On the other hand, the legislation, such as Civil Service Law 16/1996 in the National Archives, and Law 182/2002 on the protection of classified information, is highly inconsistent. As a result, the implementation process of Law 544/2001 is stagnant (see Michalak 2008). It leads to a situation in which bureaucrats are very reluctant to provide information, and 'generally opt for the negative solution in view of the possibility of facing disciplinary penalties' (SAR 2003: 16).

Politicization of the bureaucracy

In particular, as pointed out in the introduction, the problems of the Romanian bureaucracy range from the persistence of the bureaucrats from pre-transition period, including a blurred line of demarcation between bureaucrats and politicians, to an overall incomplete implementation process of the civil service law of 1999. One essential aspect that needs to be dealt with refers to the consequences of a change in political leadership because it brings with it a whole new network of nepotism and new civil servants, forcing the other ones to resign. This is a more sensitive issue as it is interconnected with the level of corruption in Romania and overall political culture. The more incentives are strengthened, first through a higher remuneration, and second, through a shift in loyalties, the less corruption there will be in the Romanian public sector. Then, as far as political culture is concerned, Romanian politicians are used to create and maintain networks of nepotism and hire their friends and families in civil servant functions (see Michalak 2008).

Moreover, as far as the legislative framework is concerned there are further problems that need to be tackled. One of the biggest problems, to which the civil service law of 1999 was responding, is a high degree of politicization of the bureaucracy reaching up to 15 years past the transition state. The main problem for the Romanian bureaucracy is that even political actors and the civil service bureaucrats realize the existence of political intrusion in the ministries. Over the time period of the 1990s, the problem of low accountability and political dependence of civil servants marked the overall characteristics of the Romanian bureaucracy. For example, the European Commission responded to the issue starting with the first candidate accession negotiation in the late 1990s referring for example, to the necessity of introducing a program of human resources management and an increase in training sessions of the civil servant bureaucrats (see European Commission Report 2000: 13).

Professionalized bureaucracy

Creation of a professional civil service is another significant problem of the Romanian bureaucracy. For providing professional training, the Romanian administration depends exclusively on the existing civil servants, who are themselves not quite professional, having been inherited from the pre-transition period. Professionalization of the bureaucracy is essential because attracting, retaining and developing new professional civil servants have been one of Romania's main problems during the civil service reform, in turn, due to the financial attractiveness of employment opportunities for highly professional young potential civil servants outside the Romanian bureaucracy, such as consulting for the EU. Table 15.1 shows that public servants' salaries (currency: Lei) are simply not competitive with salaries in the private and state-owned commercial sectors, particularly at the senior managerial level. This is especially noticeable for directors-general in public service, who earned dramatically less than directors in all three types of companies. This inability to recruit and retain professional staff in the Romanian bureaucracy continues to pose a problem to date.

With regard to the young professionals it can be said that government pay and employment policies have been stagnant. Serious problems that the Romanian

Table 15.1 Salaries in lei by type of employer, 1994

Position	Public service	Regies autonomes	State commercial company	Private commercial company
General manager	–	290,006	496,668	950,000
Economist I	–	164,708	288,793	400,000
Computer analyst	–	173,183	278,793	340,000
Judicial counselor	–	176,360	276,048	600,000
Director general	233,900	–	–	–
Advisor specialist	180,260	–	–	–

Source: World Bank 1994.

bureaucracy faces are low and compressed pay, and a major lack in the information management and forward planning of the personnel. Moreover, the World Bank found that 'links between the public service performance and fiscal or budgetary management have been negligible' (Nunberg 1999: 92).

To achieve a more egalitarian society as in the case of Norway, the Romanian public sector must undergo a process of reform. During the 1990s, civil servants earned one third or half of the salaries of private commercial employees. Hence, there was a huge gap between the public and the private sectors in Romania. As a result, the number of staff working for different ministries in the Romanian government slowly decreased after 1989. This continued in some cases, such as the Ministry of Agriculture, where the numbers decreased each year by approximately 20 percent. Such was not the case, however, with the Ministry of Education or that of Foreign Affairs. In the Ministry of Foreign Affairs, there was an increase in the number of employees, from 1058 to 1732 between 1991 and 1994, and this number grew steadily each year after that. In the case of the Ministry of Education, the numbers had doubled by 1990 and then, as with the Ministry of Agriculture, they constantly decreased. The reason for such employment fluctuations was that salaries of civil servants were considerably lower than the salaries of comparable private sector employees. For example, a general manager working for the public sector or a state-owned company earned between 290,006 and 496,668 while a general manager working for a private company earned 950,000 annually, which is two to three times as much.

Additionally, the skills of civil servants working at the Ministry of Agriculture are sector-specific and thus harder to transfer into the private sector, unlike the case of the Ministry of Education and the Ministry of Foreign Affairs. Naturally, the number of civil servants in the Agriculture Ministry constantly decreased after 1990. This partly explains why the difference in salary is still in place. Additionally, with Romania's attention focused on the industrial sectors after the 1989 revolution, agriculture and its ministry became less important to the functioning of the country.

In an interview with one of the Chamber of Deputies' interns in order to get a sense of the general perception of the job of a civil servant, the response also referred to low payment as well as the general disenchantment and apathy with regard to the job. Below is the response to the question: How do you find the Romanian rewards system?

> Experiencing the Romanian public sector reward system, it feels like one is alienated from his/her own responsibilities and co-opted into a corrupt and putrid system where connections get you anywhere and where money is all that matters. It is a sad story of moral deprivation and lack of any ethical code where it feels like a never-ending shopping experience where you have to act like you care and everybody else buys it…The reward system lacks many things among which: financial compensation, reputation and most of all, a sense of belonging. There is a sense of paranoia and ratting, while self-interest always wins the day. The day ended and I wanted to get out of the Chamber of Deputies building and run, run for a better tomorrow.
>
> (Interview Anamaria Corca 13 May 2009)

First she refers to a problem of alienation from responsibilities as well as corruption and nepotism that seem to ruin the reputation of becoming a civil servant. Then, she also mentions the lack of an ethical code of conduct and overall moral deprivation, comparing the job to a shopping experience where one only pretends to do his/her own job and wastes public money. Then, she refers to the lack of a sense of belonging and a lack of trust in the other colleagues. This interview reflects the overall problems that the public sector is faced with and is part of the explanation of why the job is no longer attractive and the incentive structure low. However, there could also be an overall economic explanation of why this is the case.

The fact that private employees earn significantly more than civil servants shows that the economic investments are booming, but at the same time, competition is not that healthy. Governmental officials earn a lot by the percent of bids they give to the companies, even if the company has the weakest material and the highest price. Bribery makes officials give the bid to a particular company, which is then empowered and creates a monopoly. In fact, the ratio of the highest- to lowest-paid employees was 4.5 in 1991, and because of the across-the-board cost of living adjustments, the ratio had fallen to 3.7 by 1994, thereby further reducing the incentive for young professionals to join the Romanian civil service (Nunberg 1999: 76).

This data indicates that in order to close the public/private salary gap and to improve the payment system, the wage incentives have to be higher. Public servants could be stimulated by bonuses and other payment schemes based on the performance and the quality of their work. This measure will translate into fewer cases of corruption because it could create a shift of loyalty from an individual-centered type of loyalty to the public sector.

Other international institutions, such as the World Bank, offer different recommendations. They refer to the recruitment procedure of civil servants, spikes in quarterly civil service turnover, annual personnel evaluations, performance criteria of acceptance into the different parts of the public sector, the reputation of the civil service, the attractiveness of a civil service career and non-discretionary remuneration. The World Bank basically suggests that as long as the selection criteria of personnel do not become more competitive and more transparent, then a civil service career cannot become any more attractive. Moreover, the less political leadership changes, the more civil servants will be able to maintain their jobs and have better career prospects. Annual performance reports on civil servants could also possibly improve the incentive structure and make the job profile more attractive. Also, non-discretionary remuneration is equally important as it would tighten the public/private sector gap and move closer to the type of reforms needed to create a more egalitarian society.

The working hours could also prove to be an important aspect in making civil servants stay on the job. The more flexible the working hours are, the stronger the incentives to stay in the job longer. Moreover, in order to establish a meritocratic system, there is a need for better accountability in place as well as more transparency. Additionally, EU conditionality could prove to have a positive impact because it would require non-discriminatory employment practices as well as the actual implementation of public sector reforms.

Thus there have been, and continue to be, serious nation-wide problems of highly inadequate civil service reform in Romania. This is, without doubt, a non-trivial issue that warrants serious political scientific examination.

Major milestones of the civil service reform: moving towards a meritocratic system

This section presents the major milestones of civil service reform with a more in-depth description of the different regulations and adjustments over time. The starting point was as early as 1991, when minor administrative reform components were part of the overall transition and consolidation process. In general, the consolidation phase includes institutional and administrative development, but does not provide specific reference to the initiation of civil service reform. This overview ranges mainly up to 2004, when major adjustments to the civil service law were made. However, since this research relies mainly on archival work, minor reform changes in recent years might have been overlooked to the extent that such changes may not have been documented yet. The major milestone of civil service reform was passing the first civil service reform law in 1999.

1999 civil service law: making the reward system more efficient

In preparation of the 1999 civil service law, an official review was conducted in order to establish a 'professional, politically neutral civil service under Law 188/1999,' followed by a 'strategy and action plan for civil service reform' (CSR) (SIGMA 2004: 9). According to the SIGMA Report (2004: 10), this plan addresses the following strategies: '(1) focusing the civil service on policy analysis functions, through capacity building; (2) ensuring an appropriate set of checks and balances in the management of the civil service; (3) ensuring both compliance and performance accountability of civil servants; and (4) providing greater managerial autonomy within the public administration, conditional on satisfaction of minimum standards of compliance and performance accountability'.

This strategy and action plan presents the first of three major strategy plans (PAL 1–3) that basically intend to present the major reform milestones, starting from the initiation strategy plan (PAL1) to implementation strategy plan (PAL3). Furthermore, the EU provided assistance as 'support to the Drafting Process of the Public Administration Reform Strategy' (reference no. RO 0106.06), which was complemented by assistance from the British Department for International Development (DFID). However, in response to international assistance, the Romanian government was to deliver the following products: (1) a review of the legal framework covering civil servants; (2) a review of pay and employment management within the central administration, to prepare two or three alternative strategic options for reforming the civil service salary structure over a 3–5 year period; and (3) a strategy plan for ensuring adequate training of civil servants in both general human capital skills, as well as Romania-specific human capital skills. The second product, the so-called options paper would consider all elements of remuneration: basic salary, seniority supplement, job position supplement, grade supplement, bonuses, and any other forms of remuneration. It would rank each of the 2–3 strategic options on at least the following criteria: '(i) competitiveness of total remuneration by type of position; (ii) wage bill sustainability (i.e. fiscal feasibility); (iii) transparency of total remuneration; (iv) the extent to which the salary structure holds out the prospect for an individual to achieve remuneration growth over time if he or she performs well and continually enhances his or her professional capacities; and (v) differentiation in remuneration across civil servants reflects differences in position demands (responsibilities, functions) and human capital requirements (skills, knowledge, experience)' (SIGMA Report 07/2004: 19).

Moving beyond the starting point of the civil service reform in 1999, major consideration has been given already to the effort of implementation. Here, the government is expected to show active steps in fulfilling these tasks (PAL 2). For example, the SIGMA report 2004 shows that overall the Romanian government meets the PAL 2 milestones for implementation of both the civil service reform plan, and the employment management reform plan. The EU expected the following objectives for reforming civil service pay: (i) competitiveness; (ii) fiscal sustainability; (iii) transparency of actual remuneration; (iv) support of career growth for civil servants who perform well and continually improve their human capital skills; and (v) matching of remuneration to work demands and human capital requirements.

At the next step, the government has to meet the criteria of PAL 3 milestones for implementation of both the civil service reform plan and the pay and employment management reform plan. Also here, at the implementation stage of civil service reform, international technical assistance was expected by the EU.

The implementation strategy plans (PAL 2–3) show quite clearly that the major source of funding came from the EU, from both support to institutional development in Eastern Europe and direct pre-accession funding. In response to international assistance, the Romanian government is required to constantly update and publish quarterly and annually newly developed measurements for the full set of monitoring indicators on civil service management practices. The monitoring indicators, including some on remuneration, are presented in the following box:

Overview of Monitoring Indicators (SIGMA Report 2004: 18)

1. Fraction of civil servants recruited and selected through transparent, competitive procedures increases over time.
2. Spikes in quarterly civil service turnover rates shortly after a change in political leadership decline over time.
3. Incidence of annual personnel performance evaluations for civil servants rises over time.
4. Summary statistics on annual civil servants performance evaluations suggest that, over time, they are doing a better job of sorting civil servants' on the basis of their performance.
5. A civil service career becomes more attractive, as measured by the average number of qualified candidates per advertised civil service position.
6. The reputation of the civil service gradually improves over time, as measured by surveys of households, businesses and public employees.
7. The non-discretionary fraction of remuneration paid to (i) general civil servants and (ii) special civil servants, rises over time.
8. Incidence of over-graded positions falls over time (based on annual independent assessments of a random sample of positions).
9. Civil service compensation becomes more competitive over time, as measured by surveys of public and private sector remuneration for prototype positions.

Law 188/1999 was thus extensively amended by Law 161/2003 on the Civil Servant Statute (published on 22 March 2004). This law was passed on 31 March 2003 under Article 113-1 of the Constitution, a provision inspired by the 1958 French Constitution (Article 49-3), which stipulated the following: 'The government assumes responsibility before Parliament, which is compelled, in a joint session of both the Chamber of Deputies and the Senate, to either endorse the government's bill without amendment or reject it in block. In the event that the bill is rejected by Parliament, the government is obliged to resign, as in a censure motion.' The Romanian government's decision to use this constitutional procedure to adopt, among others, the Civil Service Law and the legal regime of incompatibilities and conflict of interest of all public officials, raised much public controversy. Also the Venice Commission's Opinion of 18 March 2003 signaled that this procedure was detrimental to the normal distribution of powers and to the prerogatives of the Romanian Parliament, which, according to Article 58-1 of the Constitution, is the 'supreme representative body of the Romanian people and the sole legislative authority of the country.' The procedure used for passing the Civil Service Law threatened the sustainability of civil service reform: Any serious reform of the civil service as an institution of the state would require a much wider political consensus.

Law 161/2003 is a collection of different pieces of legislation – also known as the 'Anti-Corruption Package' – grouped under the title of 'Law on Certain Steps for Assuring Transparency in Performing High Official Positions, Public and Business Positions, for Preventing and Sanctioning Corruption' (Title III of Book II of this Law 161/2003), 'Regulations regarding Public Positions and Public Servants Modification and Completion of Law 188/1999 on the Status of Public Servants', together with Title IV of Book I on 'Conflict of Interest and Status of Incompatibilities in Performing High Official and Public Positions'. Book I shapes the primary civil service legislation in Romania. However, a major problem occurred when the 2004 Civil Service Law effectively reversed the provision of the 2003 Freedom of Information Act by giving broad discretion to bureaucrats regarding what was deemed confidential information, versus what was deemed public information (see Michalak 2008).

Further, government re-shuffling restructured the organization of ministries in Romania from 24 to 14. Many of the removed ministries, however, survived as central government institutions, in order to streamline government. In fact, four are the primary interest of this research. The most specific feature of legislation in the twenty-first century, to date, remains Law 544/2001, which was unfortunately voided effectively by the Law on State Secrets and Classified Information, reversing an important reform towards greater transparency.

Data and description

The ratios in Table 15.2 reflect the differences in relative statute between the various high-standing public officials. As the public officials are differentiated by the branch of government each of them serves, it is interesting to see how pay levels differ over government branches, indicating their relative power. The EU conditionality requirement for the clear separation of powers within the state should be translated in a relative level of equality of the governmental branches. If there are high levels of inequality between the branches, it may be inferred that the worst paid governmental branch is relatively subservient to the highest paid one. Moreover, the pay ratios would offer a suggestion of the levels of accountability and legitimacy of governmental branches. The pay level for administration directors has also been included for comparison purposes. Given the hierarchical model of public administration, it is useful to draw a comparison between positions filled through bureaucratic channels and the positions filled through political channels. As the bureaucratic heads of administrative institutions fall under

Table 15.2 Overview of monthly Romanian Salaries in Lei

		1998	President ratio	2003	President ratio	2005	President ratio	2006	2008	President ratio
Judge	Court of appeal judge		0.0		0.0		0.0	4,369	6,676	69.9
Judge	Constitutional ct judge	1,140.23	81.4	3,479.4	81.4	5,326.9	81.4			0.0
Judge	Constitutional ct president	1,293.11	92.3	3,945.9	92.3	6,041	92.3			0.0
Judge	Supreme court judge	885.43	63.2	3,129.5	73.2	4,791.2	73.2	5,911		0.0
Judge	Supreme court sector president	968.24	69.1	3,207.3	75.0	4,910.3	75.0	6,168		0.0
Judge	Supreme court vice president	1,140.23	81.4	3,479.4	81.4	5,326.9	81.4	6,425		0.0
Judge	Supreme court president	1,293.11	92.3	3,945.9	92.3	6,041	92.3	6,682		0.0
Government	**State secretary**	**980.98**	**70.0**	**2,993.5**	**70.0**	**4,583**	**70.0**		**6,068**	**63.5**
Government	**State secretary, member of government**	**1,025.57**	**73.2**	**3,129.5**	**73.2**	**4,791.2**	**73.2**		**6,343**	**66.4**
Government	Secretary general adjunct	980.98	70.0	2,993.5	70.0	4,791.2	73.2		6,691	70.0
Government	Secretary general	1,025.57	73.2	3,129.5	73.2	4,583	70.0		6,994	73.2
Legislative	**MP**	**1,025.57**	**73.2**	**3,129.5**	**73.2**	**4,791.2**	**73.2**		**6,343**	**66.4**
Administration	Director general	560.5	40.0		0.0	2,073	31.7		4,867	50.9
Government	Minister	1,121.12	80.0	3,421.1	80.0	5,237.5	80.0		7,643	80.0
Government	State minister	1,191.11	85.0	3,421.1	80.0	5,564.9	85.0		8,122	85.0
Government	Prime minister	1,293.11	92.3	3,945.9	92.3	6,041	92.3		8,817	92.3
Government	**President adviser**	**1,121.12**	**80.0**	**3,421.1**	**80.0**	**5,237.5**	**80.0**		**6,932**	**72.5**
Government	President	1,401.4	100.0	4,276.4	100.0	6,546.9	100.0		9,555	100.0
Private	CEOs		0.0		0.0		0.0		13,942	145.9

Source: Legea nr. 154/1998, Legea nr. 53/2003, Legea nr.571/ 2003; Legea nr. 163/2005, and Legea nr. 221/2008. available at www.gov.ro.

the direct control of senior political appointees, it is expected that the pay level of politically appointed officials are higher than the pay of senior bureaucrats. The data above confirm this theoretical expectation as the pay ratio for the highest level of the bureaucracy is 40, 31.7, and 50.9 percent of the salary of the highest paid official (i.e. president) for the years 1998, 2005, and 2008, respectively. In contrast, the salary of the lowest paid political appointee at ministerial level – the direct superior of the highest ranking bureaucrat – is 70, 73.2, and 70 percent of the head of state's salary. By separately calculating pay ratios for the level between the two positions that are in the closest hierarchical relationship – highest level bureaucrat to lowest level political appointee – the relation of subordination between administration and political institutions becomes apparent. The ratios are 57.1, 43.3, and 72.7 percent for the years 1998, 2005, and 2008, respectively and thus clearly reinforce the model of political control over the administrative institutions. Such pay discrepancies could however prove dangerous for the capacity of the state bureaucracy to retain its top officials. By contrast, for political appointees who are part of the executive, the salary discrepancies are relatively lower. The ratios between the salary of the lowest ranking political appointee (i.e. adjunct secretary general at the ministerial level) and the highest one (i.e. prime minister) are 75.8, 79.3, and 75.8 percent, respectively for the same period considered. The salary discrepancy between different political appointees may be an indicator of the political clout of each politically appointed official. Thus, if political success is to be rewarded by appointment to a higher paid position, the above ratios could be seen as different levels of rewards for the political success of political appointees. As the discrepancy between the wages of political appointees is lower than that between bureaucrats and politicians, it can be inferred that political success is better regarded, and rewarded, than bureaucratic or administrative success. This trend may again prove dangerous for the retention capacity of the state bureaucracy, as even moderate political success is rewarded better than the highest level of bureaucratic success.

Another interesting aspect of the above data is the difference between the legislative and the executive branch of government. An MP's salary is roughly the same as that of a government employee. However, wages of executive politicians are higher than those of MPs. MPs are paid only 91.5 percent of a minister's salary. This is interesting because ministers do not have to be part of the parliament. If ministerial positions were in fact restricted to MPs, then a higher salary would have been warranted, given the higher workload of ministers who are at the same time parliamentarians. However, since ministers are also recruited from outside parliament, the different salary levels show relative superiority of the executive. Legitimacy plays an important role here. The legitimacy of MPs lies with the electorate, while that of ministers lies with the prime minister, who is generally the head of the main political party. When looking at the other part of the executive branch, the issue is even more relevant, because presidential advisors are forbidden to be part of the parliament while serving the head of the state; their loyalty lies with the president. Moreover, the president has absolute power over hiring and dismissing his advisors, so the latter do not have any public legitimacy or accountability. It is thus interesting that those officials drawing their legitimacy from the people are paid less than those without any public loyalties. In the case of government ministers the issue of double legitimacy – electoral and political – could justify higher governmental salary levels, but this reasoning does not apply to presidential advisers. The overall size of the institutions concerned could provide an explanation of the relative difference between salary levels of parliamentarians and executive employees. Parliament is larger than either the government or the presidential staff, so the overall expenditure for the parliament is higher than that of either the government or the presidential cabinet.

The relative equality in the pay levels between presidential advisers and government ministers can be seen as a means of ensuring the balance between the separate executive institutions. This equality is, however, not apparent at all levels of the executive institutions, with the president having the highest salary of all the Romanian public officials. His salary is consistent with his formal position as head of state, and his powers. Moreover, as presidential advisers are supposed to be selected according to their competencies in their field, the high level of their wages could be seen as a reward for competence. Thus we can observe that in the case of the executive, the political success achieved by ministers is remunerated in the same way as the performance-based success achieved by presidential advisers.

Regarding the relative equality between the pay levels awarded to members of the different branches of government, one can observe an interesting trend in the relative power of the judicial branch. Constitutional Court judges, who are appointed by the president, the legislative, and the Supreme Judicial Council, used to be paid more than members of the Supreme Court. Over the years, however, the latter have caught up and are now, together with the Constitutional Court judges, earning similar salaries as ministers and presidential advisers. This relative equalization of salary levels occurred only in 2005 and in 2008, with the members of the Supreme Court earning much lower salaries in 1998 (the ratio of Supreme Court versus Constitutional Court judges was 77.6 in 1998 and 89 in 2008). This effect could be attributed to the strong external pressure from the EU to ensure the separation and equality between the branches of government. While there is still some discrepancy between the salaries awarded to the top judges and the salaries of political appointees in the government or the presidential staff, the gap has been significantly closed in the recent period.

Analysis

The main winner in terms of an increase in staff numbers was the Ministry of Foreign Affairs in relative terms as well as absolute numbers. The larger part of this increase, however, is due to the enlargement of the diplomatic section abroad, not included in this study. The Ministry of Education – only numbers for the national level are reported in Table 15.3 – was growing strongly, although at a smaller rate. The Ministry of Agriculture, on the other hand, was shrinking.

Table 15.3 Number of staff in pre-reform period

Ministry	1989	1990	1991	1992	1993	1994
Foreign Affairs	1,058	1,732	1,830	1,700	1,845	1,845
Education	254	411	411	353	380	356
Agriculture	1,438	1,492	1,158	1,082	936	845

The shrinking is mainly explained by a shift in needs with the transition from central planning to a market oriented system. Shedding of staff in the ministry occurred mainly through natural fluctuation and early retirement. No data is presented for the Ministry of European integration, which was founded only in 2000. Upon its founding, a large share of staff – about 40 percent – was brought in from other ministries, such that even for this ministry the 'persistence of old structures' variable – defined as the share of old timers among staff – is different from zero.

The distinct growth patterns in the ministries affect their value of the 'persistence of old structures' variable in different ways. In the Ministry of Foreign Affairs the share of old timers is 16 percent while it is 62 percent in the Ministry of Agriculture. The Ministry of European integration is in between with 39 percent old timers. As discussed in Section 5.3, the Ministry of Education poses a problem with assessing the structural variable as of 1999. It is estimated that the share of old timers in 1999 is as high as 48 percent but it has significantly decreased during the reform period due to a policy measure.

The problem of retention of capable officials is not however limited to ministerial employees. Since the legal framework of Romania views judges as civil servants, the judicial branch of government faces the same obstacles to reform as the public administration. As such, the failed implementation of a meritocratic system for the administrative system also affects the judicial system. The coupling of what is supposed to be an independent branch of government with the state administrative apparatus may prove hurtful for retaining the judiciary. As employees in this governmental branch are paid less than executive employees, judges have lower incentives to improve their competencies. Moreover, since the base wage of judges is lower, they are also more susceptible to engage in corrupt behavior to increase personal revenues.

Another issue that stands out is that the judicial branch is independent in terms of outside oversight, with only internal control mechanisms. This makes implementation of a coherent meritocratic system difficult, because the competency objectives cannot be accurately measured and interpreted from external sources. If reform is attempted towards implementing a merit-based payment method without external control, the judges would become vulnerable to suspicions of setting meaningless objectives that are designed to artificially increase salaries without any tangible increase in terms of better performance. As such, the recent trend of closing the salary gap between judges and executive employees may be viewed as an instance of successful lobbying without tangible improvements in performance.

In order to solve the issues raised by the low judicial salaries, the Romanian government faces two major options. The first would be to keep the statute of judges as public servants. If this option is preferred, then external controls on the judiciary would have to be implemented. Moreover, to cast away any doubts about a subservient position of the judicial branch, the salary base for the entire professional civil service would have to be raised so the highest paid civil servant (in this case judges) would earn the same as political appointees in the executive branch. While costly, such a move would be useful in closing the gap between professional bureaucrats and their immediate political superiors and thus may diminish the incentives for bureaucratic managers to seek private employment. The second option would be to change the legal status of judges to increase their salaries in the judiciary only and also reinforce judicial autonomy. However, external controls would still have to be put in place to ensure judicial independence. The external monitoring of the EU Commission, while accepted by the Romanian government, would not be enough in this case because the Commission simply does not have the resources to independently review the Romanian judiciary. The Commission would have to outsource the review process, and for such a process to be meaningful the legal framework would need to be changed to allow for external control of the judiciary.

Administrative capacity and Romania's struggle for better governance

The years between 2003 and 2006 were marred by obstacles to European accession, because of poor policy-making capacity and poor administration of implementation processes. Neither the incumbent nor the opposition parties were effective at proposing strategies, which explains why EU negotiations with Romania slowed down. The Romanian Academic Society has argued that there was greater reliance on ordinances because of the parliament's ineffectiveness. Due to the large number of MPs, only a small number of leaders had access to representatives of the international community which was one cause of ineffectiveness. For example, bureaucrats in the Ministry of Foreign Affairs had the greatest access to the international community, followed only by the Ministry of European Integration. Only a small number of policy materials were produced to promote reform and hence speed up the process of integration. A low level of administrative capacity and a relatively poor quality of governance was the consequence.

What is known as the 'dead law' situation in Latin America appears to have arisen in several Eastern European countries, where the laws are passed but simply not implemented. In fact, of all 2004 and 2007 accession countries, only Hungary and Estonia fully implemented civil service reform laws. Romania is no exception to this rule, where many EU-induced laws that were enacted remain dead.

In the realm of administrative capacity, the question arises as to how far Romania is from the Weberian ideal? There are indications that Romania is still quite far from it, in that the bureaucratic administration is still not 'capable of attaining the highest degree of efficiency' and is, in this sense, not formally the most rational known means of carrying out imperative control over human beings (Weber 1947: 337).

The extent of administrative capacity is also demonstrated by the extent of implementation of The Freedom of Information Act (FOIA). The FOIA was passed in 2001, requiring that access to public information by public authorities should be granted on request. In 2004 the Romanian Academic Society surveyed 500 public institutions from 96 localities, and checked how the main requirements of the law were fulfilled within the legal timeframe. Implementation is considerably lower in rural areas than in urban areas. The survey reveals that the level of compliance with FOIA decreases in cities with less than 100,000 population, and drops seriously in rural areas. Also interviews conducted by the Ministry of Agriculture and Education show that on average only 16 percent of the bureaucrats could actually show the list of public documents.

Failing implementation of the FOIA is only one out of numerous problems. It is, however, very significant and a good example of the extremely limited administrative capacity in Romania. Indeed, in 2004, and again two years later, more than 80 percent of all agencies failed to meet the level of required implementation.

Summarily, as transparency was one milestone of the process of civil service reform, the data presented here provide an example of the level of the implementation of the FOIA. The implementation of the FOIA made the data presented above available to the public. However, the secrecy and confidentiality feature of the Romanian administrative system comes into play because, while the base salaries of public officials are in the public domain, the various rewards awarded and performance criteria set for rewarding the best performing officials are still considered secret information. As such, a comprehensive study of the payment schemes practiced at various levels of the Romanian civil service is practically impossible, because the payment schemes are both decentralized (i.e. each minister has the discretion to award special bonuses in his/her department) and largely confidential.

Conclusion

There are some broad conclusions to be derived from the empirical findings on the process of civil service reform and the improvement of the quality of governance in Romania. Although Eastern Europe has experienced radical change as a consequence of the collapse of communism, inertia from initial conditions keeps several countries from radically reforming their bureaucratic structures. There are powerful forces that tend to resist reform, and, at the same time, there are forces that favor reform. No bureaucracy is completely independent of capture from politicians or from civil society actors – it is merely a matter of degree of independence.

But reform is inevitable. In a newly established democracy like Romania, the citizenry demands it, and as democratization progresses, the politicians have to comply. The bureaucrats thus have to change their behavior toward greater transparency and impartiality than customary, even though they are subject to capture from both politicians and civil society actors.

In addition to popular demands for administrative reform, Eastern European countries have the unique feature that they would rather identify with, and belong to, the club of 'modern and rich' Western European members of the EU. It would be a loss to be disassociated from the Center, the EU, and be part of the periphery, as Albania or Moldova now are. This is purely an issue of identification with those countries that are regarded as 'successful', reflecting a force for administrative reform from within the Eastern European countries. A second significant force for civil service reform, and improvement in the quality of governance is external and comes from EU's desire to include its Eastern neighbors into a greater union, to expand the EU's political and economic power, and reduce conflict in the region. These two powerful forces interact to determine the final outcome of civil service reform. There are those actors who have an incentive to reform, and will push for it, while those who stand to lose from it will resist it. Even in the presence of a powerful external reform movement, the reform process might still prove lengthy, because the confidential features of the public system in Romania can continue to protect those who resist reform.

Note

1 This chapter draws on my earlier work on civil service reform in Romania. Also, I am very grateful to Anamaria Corca and Mircea Steriu for providing expert research assistance.

References

EU Commission Report, 23 July 2008.
EU Monitoring Report (2005) EU accession. Executive Summary. Romania. Available at http://www.ec.europa.eu/enlargement/key_documents/reports/
European Parliament Resolution, 2205/2005 INI (Theme: The extent of Romanias readiness for accession to the European Union).
European Parliament Resolution, 05/2005. Topic: The extent of Romanias readiness for accession to the European Union.
Linz, J. and A. Stepan (1996) *Problems of Democratic Transition and Consolidation: Southern Europe, South America and Post-Communist Europe*. Baltimore, MD: Johns Hopkins Press.
Michalak, K. (2008) *Civil Service Reform and the Quality of Governance in Romania* (electronic form). The Ohio State University.
Nunberg, B. (1999) *The State After Communism. Administrative Transitions in Central and Eastern Europe*. Washington, DC: World Bank.
SAR Policy Warning Report (2001) *Early Warning Report Romania*. SAR – Romanian Academic Society, 02/2001, p. 13.
SAR Policy Warning Reports (12/2003) *Romania and Bulgaria Between NATO and EU*. Romanian Academic Society. Available at http://www.sar.org.ro/

SIGMA (2004) *Public Service and Administration Framework Assessment: Romania.* File: 07/2004 07 SIGMA, p. 3. Paris: SIGMA Publications. Available to all candidate countries at http://www.sigmaweb.org

Transparency International Annual Report (2000) Available online at: http://www. transparency.org.ro/publicatii/audit_si_transparenta_financiara/index_en.html

Weber, M. (1947) *The Theory of Social and Economic Organization* (translated by A.M. Henderson and Talcott Parsons). Cambridge: The Free Press and the Falcons Bring Press.

16 Into the labyrinth

The rewards for high public office in Slovakia

Katarína Staroňová and Erik Láštic

Introduction

The information on rewards to high public officials, both political and top career civil servants in Slovakia together with local officials' salaries and bonuses were made publicly available from January 2006 through the Free Access to Information Law. This was an historical moment that concluded the debate on the transparency of HPOs' rewards. Following the many questions on transparency, accountability and trust in the 15 years of transition to democracy, this amendment was part of a bigger reform that sought to redefine accountability systems to provide specific safeguards against abuses of power by either politicians or civil servants. Yet, even this change seems short-lived. In December 2007, the judge of a regional court in Bratislava, petitioned by the Ministry of Justice, asked the Constitutional Court to review the constitutionality of a 2006 'salary' amendment, arguing that free access to the salary data of public officials violates their privacy rights in the Slovak constitution.

This chapter analyzes the formal and informal mechanisms of rewarding the performance and work of the HPOs in Slovakia since independent statehood in January 1993. The research method follows the methodology developed by Brans and Peters (2006). The main question is whether the institutional arrangements for the rewards of public officials brought about the accountability mechanisms hoped for at the beginning of the transition era.

Reforms in the 1990s and 2000s

Most transition countries did not have Civil Service Laws after the fall of communism and relied upon a general labor code applicable to all employees. Delays in reforms have led to a situation where ministries in the first decade of transformation were often over-staffed, as those that remained in the administration were generally uninterested in changing jobs, while new posts were unable to attract staff. This created problems for new functions, such as policy analysis posts, project management, reform implementation, and not least civil servants dealing with EU matters.

In the first years after the fall of communism, incoming governments tried to insert their own people in all key positions, sometimes two or three layers down the hierarchy. This produced a politically dependent system with significant changes often occurring at the top and middle level positions within the administration; political affiliation was the main reason for the changes. As a result, politicization, patronage, and lack of accountability were the key features of Slovak public administration during the first decade of transition.

In order to tackle politicization, fragmentation and instability among public officials, a second decade addressed civil servants' independence from politicians to ensure that there was no ambiguity in the role division between the minister (political function) and civil servants (career functions). In this sense, the assignment of authority, responsibility and accountability for carrying out duties appropriate to departments and other offices were defined by introducing civil service legislation and a civil service training system. The Civil Service Laws were further amended several times to produce greater flexibility in the rewards system and to attract qualified people into the ranks of public service.

Civil Service and Public Service Law

The Civil Service Law was adopted in 2001 under pressure from the EU, who had warned that Slovakia's entry chances could be hurt if the reform did not pass (Regular report 2000). These long-awaited legal rules – Civil Service and Public Service Laws – took force on 1 April 2002. The main ambition of the Civil Service Law was to make the civil service more professional and to reduce the vulnerability of civil servants to changes in government. The law, as finally adopted, contained compromises between different views, but was strongly biased towards the comprehensive, labor code-oriented approach.

Since the adoption of the Civil Service Law, Slovakia managed almost a complete 180° turn: from complete political influence on public administration, through a neutral civil service guaranteed by law, to end up with a heterogeneous system of civil service regulation with no politically independent central authority. The law set the legal framework for the creation of a professional, impartial, politically neutral, efficient, and flexible civil service. It clearly distinguished between political posts (minister and state secretary) and professional posts (head of office, directors general of section, heads of units and other staff at the ministry). It also established the Civil Service Office, which is responsible for implementing the law, with functions ranging from recruitment, training, and information, to preparing secondary legislation.

The salami method applied by the center-right government to the law in 2002–2006 resulted in a slow deconstruction of the basic legal principles, with the most fundamental amendments adopted in 2003[1] and 2006.[2] Their 'Strategy of reform of employment in the public sector' was designed to increase the competitiveness of the public sector in attracting high quality candidates to government, improve remuneration of civil servants performing strategic work, and increase the efficiency and flexibility of the public sector. Thus, the amendments *removed the seniority principle* and introduced *performance-related pay*. They also *abolished tenure*. Only the specific category within the civil service, the *nominated civil service*, aiming to 'reward' a few dozens top officials with special salaries and more job protection retained tenure. A new type of civil service was introduced, the *temporary state service*, which aimed to bring people close to the ministers into government and attract young, qualified candidates into civil service. The most important change was the flexibility and discretion of individual ministries regarding the variable component of employees' salaries. This increased political appointments, but also opened the system for people from business to take up temporary positions. A last piece of salami, sliced in March 2006, definitely revoked the 2001 idea of an independent civil service guided by an independent agency. It terminated the Civil Service Office as of 1 June 2006, which changed the status of the head of the (service) office into a political position and, thus, enabled the politicization of the civil service. The powers of the Civil Service Office were transferred to the ministries, strengthening the ministers' power over civil servants. The changes were motivated by the attempt to bring the civil service closer to the business model, with more pressure on performance.

Slice by slice the country ended up once again with a civil service that is easily dismissed when a new government comes to power. The evidence suggests that the government of R. Fico, which took office in fall 2006, used the practices created by the previous one in loosening the rules on political appointments and patronage.

Remuneration of high public officials

The term *HPO* or *senior official* is not defined (and does not exist) in legislation as a formal status or an official form of appointment (Staroňová 2004). For the purpose of analyzing remuneration we therefore focus on three distinct categories of public officials as defined by the legislation: constitutional representatives, judiciary and civil servants.

The legislative framework regulating rewards for high public office (RHPOs) is a very complex set of laws, parliamentary, government and judicial council's resolutions, and of formal and informal agreements on the level and mode of remuneration. Regulations stipulated by law are easily accessible, but imprecise. These regulations usually provide a general skeleton of rules and figures (such as the base salary and fixed sum for the post held) to be further supplemented by additional regulations (lump sum allowances, business trip allowances, benefits, pensions, health care, etc.) and decisions (performance and personal bonuses). The regulations provide rather exact figures on the pay for political officials, although they remain often extremely difficult to access because of protection of personal data.

As a result, the system is fragmented (although internal linkages exist), and non-transparent, and real figures on salaries paid are difficult to find. The Civil Service Office, although formally responsible for coordination and data gathering on civil servants, did not have exact figures on remuneration of civil servants because ministries were unwilling to provide data. After the Civil Service Office was abolished in 2006, any efforts to create a central registry of data on civil servants ended, and individual ministries and agencies began to manage their own records. There are some 15 laws regulating remuneration in public administration, together with numerous opaque internal rulings of Ministries.

Constitutional Representatives

Constitutional Representatives are officials whose rights and duties are regulated by the Constitution of the Slovak Republic, such as members of the parliament, members of the government, president, constitutional and Supreme Court judges, prosecution and selected central government agencies.

Base salaries and allowances

The base salaries of MPs, members of government (Cabinet ministers), president, judges, prosecutors, and other central government agencies (such as the National Audit Office) are established by law. They are tied to the average gross monthly wage since the creation of the Slovak Republic in 1993. At the end of each year, MPs discuss the gross monthly wage changes (as calculated by the Ministry of Labor, Social Affairs and Family) and annual inflation rate, and adjust the base for formula calculations. Thus, MPs' earnings are three times the previous year's gross monthly wage and constitute the calculation base of all the other constitutional representatives' base salaries: the MPs' base salary is multiplied by 1.5 for cabinet members, by 4 for the President, and by 1.3 for constitutional judges and prosecutors. Regular judges have the same salary as MPs and the president of the Supreme Control Office has 1.5 and vice-presidents 1.3 times the MPs' base salary.

Apart from the monthly base salary in Figure 16.1. there are various additional items of pay, such as a fixed sum for the post held, allowances for various expenses (transportation, office expenses, etc.), business travel allowances and performance bonuses. The fixed sum for the post held is set by law for all major positions (speaker of the parliament, vice-chairs of the parliament, heads of the parliamentary committee, prime minister, vice-prime ministers, chief of the Constitutional court, vice-chief of the Constitutional court, heads of the court senates, chief of the Highest court, vice-chief of the Highest court, president of the Supreme Control Office). Interestingly, the total amount of the fixed sum for the post held has remained unchanged for all constitutional representatives since 1993 and, thus, its real value over time has decreased. For example, the fixed remuneration for the position of the speaker of the Parliament is 15,000 Skk, which in 1993 was close to the monthly base salary of an MP. In 2006, however, this amount is only one-third of the monthly base salary of an MP.

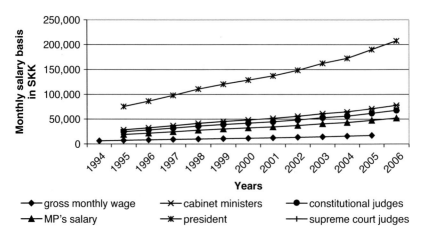

Figure 16.1 Average gross monthly salary basis for constitutional representatives.
            Source: Calculations by the authors.

The salary is further complemented by tax-free allowances for various expenses that constitutional representatives are free to use for any purposes. A lump sum is added to the base salary and further regulated by either the parliament (for MPs) or government (for Cabinet members). In fact, allowances for MPs almost equal the base salary and are tax-free (MPs can claim up to 70–80 percent of their monthly base salary depending on their permanent residence). Cabinet members and the President in turn, have a fixed lump sum allowance: the president's lump sum of 40,000 Skk is set in the law, whereas the Cabinet members' allowance is agreed by a Government Regulation. Since 2001 the Cabinet members' allowance has not changed: 22,500 Skk for the prime minister, 20,000 Skk for the vice-prime ministers and 18,000 Skk for the other Cabinet members. Thus, MPs have a more dynamic pay system that reflects the annual growth in their base salary and inflation than the president and the Cabinet members have. Should MPs be absent without explanation for more than two days in a month, all remuneration is reduced by half. Should the absence be more than four days in a month, MPs may lose the whole amount. Yet, while the media constantly presents statistics on notorious absentees, the salary of an MP was withheld only twice (Press Office of the Slovak Parliament).

Also, the President and Vice-Presidents of the Supreme Court and judges of the Constitutional Court are constitutional representatives. The Supreme Court judges receive salaries comparable to those of government ministers, fixed at 130 percent of the salary of a member of parliament. The same applies to the Constitutional Court Judges. Justices of both courts are also entitled to tax free regular allowances, decided by the resolution of the Supreme and Constitutional Court. A judge is entitled to a sum ranging from 57.8 to 64.2 percent of his/her basic salary, dependable on his/her residence status. Both chief justices are entitled to an additional fixed sum of 10,000 Skk.

Performance bonuses

There are no formal provisions on the amount of performance bonuses and no institutionalized system of performance measurement and calculation of performance bonuses for the constitutional representatives. As a result, the system is non-transparent and vulnerable to misuse. Misuse occurred in all three institutions: parliament, government, and the judiciary. In 1995, an amendment to the Law on Remuneration of Constitutional Representatives introduced a possibility for performance bonuses for the chair and vice-chairs of the parliament, which is determined by the speaker of the parliament himself for the vice-chairs and by vice-chairs for the speaker. The performance bonuses continued to be paid in 2000 and 2001 by the parliamentary speaker of the Dzurinda cabinet, Mr. Migas, on the accounts of 'heavy legislative work before the accession' (Hospodarske Noviny, 22 January 2002). The performance bonuses during this mandate amounted to between 90,000 and 180,000 Skk per speaker/vice-chairs. Two vice-chairs have refused to take performance bonuses and, when received, they immediately donated the money to charity. The amendment that allowed performance bonuses to be paid to the speaker and vice-chairs of the parliament was subsequently abolished in 2002. Table 16.1 provides the amounts paid to the speaker and vice-chairs, which were impossible to detect until the 2006 amendment of Free Access to Information Law.

Mečiar, as prime minister, provided a total of 13,815,625 Skk performance bonuses (an average of 160,000 Sk per cabinet member) during the period of his two terms (21 June 1993 to 11 March 1994 and 30 June 1995 to 9 October 1998) for Cabinet ministers. In fact, a legal analysis was conducted in 1996 by the Supreme Audit Office, which warned then-Prime Minister Vladimír Mečiar in writing that bonuses for constitutional representatives were against the law. In 1998, after the termination of Mečiar's mandate, legal steps were taken against him for the criminal act of misuse of public powers. In 2001, however, the Attorney General canceled criminal proceedings against Mečiar on the basis that the bonuses could be considered 'a means of rewarding members of the government.' The Dzurinda Cabinet (1998–2002) also provided bonuses of 134,000 Skk

Table 16.1 Bonuses paid to the Speaker and Vice-Chairs of the Parliament in Skk

	1997	1998	1999	2000	2001
Speaker of the parliament	155,000	50,000	340,000	290,000	220,000
First vice-chair	95,000	0	245,000	230,000	100,000
Vice-chair	75,000	0	205,000	140,000	160,000
Vice-chair	75,000	0	155,000	170,000	180,000
Vice-chair	–	–	185,000	160,000	90,000

Source: Request to the Parliament Office on the basis of Free Access to Information Law by the authors (Answer No. 23/195/2006/OKV from 3 May 2006).
Note: There were no bonuses paid in the years 1993–1996 and 2002 onwards.

to each Cabinet member, but all were repaid when legal experts concluded that bonuses to Cabinet members were illegal.

Media attention brought about the termination of bonuses to both Parliament and Cabinet members. *Domino*, an influential weekly newspaper, published an article in 2000 where a private lawyer pointed out that 'constitutional representatives' like Cabinet members and parliamentary chairs had no legal right to pay themselves bonuses. Following the article, the cabinet quickly assembled a group of legal experts and decided to repay all the bonuses. Mečiar was charged again for misuse of the power, while Dzurinda was not charged because he had not known he was breaking the law.

Interestingly, during the third Mečiar government (1994–1998) not a single mention of performance bonuses for MPs or Cabinet ministers occurred in the media; the first coverage started only when a case was brought to court after 1998. One possible explanation might be that the amount of performance bonuses paid to party members was of a secondary (and minor) importance when considering other 'big money and assets' that were distributed in the country. Privatization of state-owned companies had been the main showcases. The absence of checks caused the privatization process to be the quickest and most corrupt activity of government, and consequently covered by the media.

A comparable problem arose in the Supreme Court. In 2002, just a few hours before the Judicial Council was to elect a new chief justice, the incumbent Chief Justice Harabin took advantage of a legislative vacuum to award himself a performance bonus ten times the size of the ones previously awarded in Parliament and later awarded in the Judicial Council. Performance bonuses were also paid to two Supreme Court justices who were, by chance, also members of the Judicial Council. Despite massive media criticism, no justice published the sum of the bonuses awarded at that time. Four years after using the Free Access to Information Law, the authors were able to obtain data on the performance bonuses paid to the chief of the Supreme Court (see Figure 16.2). The subsequent police investigation into the Chief Justice's action did not prove any wrongdoing.

Other benefits

Constitutional officials receive other benefits, such as the use of an official car and a driver, a free flat, office, assistant, telephone, technical equipment for their term in office and others, depending on their post. They are also eligible for health insurance and pension benefits. Upon leaving office, constitutional officials are entitled to a compensation package amounting to three months' (Cabinet ministers, Constitutional and Supreme Court judges) to five months' base salary for MPs and a life pension of 40,000 Skk for the president. The five months' severance pay for MPs is, since 2006, reserved only for MPs with a minimum service in parliament of five months, following a media debate on the inappropriateness of MPs taking up the full five months' pay after very limited service.

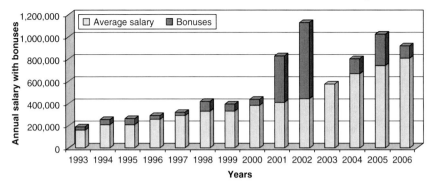

Figure 16.2 Annual base salary with bonuses paid to the Chief Justice of the Supreme Court in Skk.
    Source: Request to the Supreme Court on the basis of Free Access to Information Law by the authors (Answer No. 23-14/2006/ from 31 May 2006).
    Note: Performance bonuses to the Chief Justice were proposed in 1993–1996 by the Minister of Justice, in 1997–98 by the Chairman of the Parliament, 1998–2003 by the Chief Justice, 2004–present by the Judicial Council. In 2003 there was no Chief Justice in place.

All MPs are entitled to a fully-equipped office, including a telephone and an assistant, as well as to an allowance – 27,000 Skk per month – for the operational expenses of the office (rent, electricity, utilities, etc.). The usual practice is for offices to be on the premises of the MPs' political party, to provide the latter with an additional source of income. Furthermore, MPs are entitled to the use of a car and have free access to public transportation. Because there were no public airlines in Slovakia, the government decided in 1993 that the Interior Ministry plane would be available for MPs free of charge, a practice that was abolished in August 1999.

The law also allows MPs to keep technical equipment after leaving office. The parliamentary regulation from 1998 gives each MP a notebook and a printer for each new term in office. Additionally, the chair of the Parliament enjoys a free furnished flat, as do the vice-chairs when their permanent residence is outside Bratislava. Vacation times are not regulated, but the usual practice is to have parliamentary holidays and, thus, vacation for MPs from mid-June to the end of August, or approximately 33 days of fully paid (base salary and allowance) vacation time. The MPs and Cabinet ministers are entitled to compensation for additional costs and allowances on official business trips within Slovakia and abroad. They can travel business class in airplanes, and have no limits on accommodation and daily expenses. The budget for 2006 calculated 23 million Skk went towards allowances for business trips, which on average accounts for 133,333 Skk per MP annually.

In addition to their official base salaries, allowances, and fixed sums for the post, some constitutional officials have the right to draw a supplementary income from other sources. Many MPs are also mayors or work as attorneys, earning extra income. The new amendment to the Law on Conflict of Interests narrowed down the possibilities for extra pay. Cabinet ministers are restricted in having 'second jobs,' except for teaching and research work, and must give up any previous position when appointed. Similar constitutional restrictions apply to constitutional representatives in the judiciary (Supreme and Constitutional courts). In addition, these officials are obliged to disclose their property holdings to the chairman of the Parliament and to report any public activity connected with the state or municipal self-governance.

Judiciary

Judges are considered public servants and judicial office is a public function. Their office is incompatible with membership in parliament, in municipal self-governing authorities or any office in public administration. In practice, however, the restriction on work in public administration is commonly bypassed, as judges are routinely seconded to the Ministry of Justice to work as directors of departments. With the adoption of Act No. 385/2000 on Judges and Lay Judges, judges are expressly prohibited from becoming members or activists of any political party or movement.

Judges are not allowed to conduct any entrepreneurial activity, except for administering their own property, or scientific, pedagogical, literary, publishing, and artistic activities. These activities are allowed only provided they 'do not disrupt or otherwise impair the proper conduct of judicial function, lessen the dignity of the judge or undermine the trust of the public in the independence and impartiality of the judiciary.'

Base salaries and allowances

Generally judges' salaries are comparable to those of MPs, to which they are linked. The current average salary of judges is over three times the average salary in Slovakia. The salaries of judges are fixed by law, and are calculated at the beginning of each year according to the government decree fixing the average salary in the country. Moreover, salaries reflect inflation every half a year, provided it is higher than 10 percent. The judicial salaries ranged from 70 to 130 percent of the MPs salary (1993–2003), while a new salary scale, effective from 2003, now grants judges a base salary between 90 to 125 percent of an MP's salary. The exact salary is dependent on the level of the court and professional experience of a judge.

Allowances exceed base salaries for one judicial category only: the Special Court, created in 2004. The pay difference is related to the special tasks of this court: economic crimes, mafia prosecution and corruption. Because of its inability to attract enough judges to the court, the government raised tax-free allowances for prospective Special Court judges to six times the average nominal monthly salary. In addition, this solution reflects the negotiations with the

Ministry of Finance, which refused to increase the base salary of judges. Although the government finally managed to attract judges to the Special Court, it also created a recurrent dispute with other judges, such as the demand of Supreme Court Judges for equally high salaries. These tensions reappeared after the 2006 elections, with the new Justice Minister being highly critical of this unbalanced wage system. It was even considered to abolish the Special Court, with the special reward system cited as one of the reasons. While the proposals to abolish the Special Court failed, the Justice Ministry proposed a radical change to its salary scheme in order to equalize the reward system. Paradoxically, Prime Minister R. Fico, had proposed the special reward bonus for the Special Court as an opposition leader.

Performance bonuses

There are no formal provisions on the amount of performance bonuses for judges. The inheritance of the old regime dictates (and the law foresees this) that judges are eligible for the 13th and 14th base salary as a form of performance bonus. Naturally, this is not a genuine performance bonus but an automatic amount awarded annually. Since 2001, however, Parliament froze the performance bonuses to judges (14th base salary) to save money. Only since 2007 with Prime Minister Fico, the 14th base salary started to be paid to judges.

Other benefits

In addition to their base salary and performance bonuses, judges are entitled to a range of additional benefits, such as payments of 10–20 percent of their base salaries for court presidents and vice-presidents, overtime and anniversary bonuses. From 2003, retiring judges are entitled to a supplement to their old-age pension commensurate to their length of service, amounting to as much as 150 percent of the basic pension (3.75 percent of the basic salary for each year with a maximum of 40 years of performance). Upon retirement, a judge is also entitled to a severance payment equal to 10 months' salary.

Civil servants

Senior positions in the ministry's hierarchy may be identified only with the aid of roles and task definitions for various posts anchored in law and regulations. The law distinguishes among three top positions: political manager, manager and head of the office. The category of political managers or appointees includes *state secretaries* (deputy minister). Each ministry has one or two state secretaries, anchored in the coalition agreement. This category also includes heads of central governmental agencies. The basic salary is based on an MPs' salary, with an additional fixed sum for the post being 121 percent of tariff 11 of the civil service salary scheme. The government also approves performance bonuses for agency heads, although this data is not available.

The category of political manager is regulated by a hierarchical system of subordination for civil servants and the Civil Service Law: a ministerial department is headed by a *director general,* and further subdivided into units that are managed by *directors of units.* The final category, *head of the office,* is in charge of administrative and personal tasks in the day-to-day running of the office. This was a political appointment that has been changed by the Civil Service Law in 2002 into the highest apolitical civil service post. However, the 2006 amendment of the Civil Service Law changed this post again, into a political nomination suggested by a minister and approved by the government. Heads of the offices (ministries) have discretion over recruitment, assessment and remuneration of civil servants. Therefore, political actors may exercise political discretion over these positions *through* civil servants that have previously been appointed on political grounds.

Advisors fall between the political and apolitical appointments. While the Civil Service Law refers to politically nominated advisors, it does not regulate their remuneration, nor do official data on remuneration exist.

Base salaries and allowances

Prior to the adoption of the Civil Service Law, the base salary was based on payment classes and payment degrees with a fixed sum within each category. A civil servant was ranked to a certain class and category based on seniority, education, and responsibilities. Both the Labor Law and Civil Service Law originally recognized nine classes (responsibilities) and 12 degrees (seniority) that provided the basic scale for calculating salaries.

Pay reforms in public administration in 2003 abolished some rigid elements, such as seniority, increased employees' responsibility and obligations, and introduced innovative elements for attracting and motivating staff. The aim was to build clear distinctions between top level civil service posts and lower level posts, including a decompression of the salary system and the creation of improved conditions for top level officials. Thus, currently the Civil Service Law distinguishes 11 classes of civil servants in permanent or temporary positions based on responsibilities and education. Classes have been enlarged from 9 to 11, with the highest classes reserved for top senior civil servants (so called nominated civil service). The same reform package abolished the system of degrees based on seniority. The changes are explained by the attempt to bring the civil service closer to the business-oriented model, by putting more pressure on performance and also introducing the same flexibility in the civil service as found in the 2003 Labor Code Amendment. However, compression ratios between April 2002 and the July 2006 system have not really changed. In addition, the approximate 1:3 ratio is well below what is generally seen as desirable (1:6, used by the World Bank as a benchmark). Thus, in terms of base pay nothing has really improved, except that there are more classes and no distinction of seniority.

Top civil servants are also restricted in matters concerning 'second jobs', except for activities such as teaching, research and publications. If income from these activities exceeds 50,000 Skk per year it has to be reported to a superior. Civil servants cannot be a member of permanent oversight or control/audit bodies of companies, except as a state representative, which is not rewarded in any way. The rules prohibiting or restricting 'second jobs' for persons in office are closely observed.

Performance and other bonuses

Despite job classifications to which wages are linked, the civil service legislation provides a mechanism to 'adjust' an individual civil servant's remuneration by performance related pay, and other bonuses such as: management and deputizing bonus, personal bonus, special bonus, etc. A so-called *tariff salary* sums the salary base based on class table and performance pay increases, which are cumulative. The *service salary* is contractual for a civil servant. The determination and allocation of these bonuses to civil servants is 'soft,' which means that formalized procedures and standards are vague and it is extremely difficult to get concrete data in this area.

The performance bonus was introduced in 2003, together with job evaluation and appraisal by a 'performance based points system.' Each year, civil servants are evaluated by their superior on the basis of a point system established in the Civil Service Law: 4 points lead to a 3 percent increase, 3 points to 2 percent increase, 1 and 0 points to no increase. At face value, it is a rudimentary performance management system, departing from individual objectives and targets for the appraisal. However, evidence from an evaluation of the scheme by the Civil Service Office in 2004 (Information on Service Assessment 2004) suggests that the mechanism has not been used for genuine performance evaluation, but rather as a substitute for annual salary increases: 45 percent of civil servants received the available maximum of a 3 percent increase, followed by 41 percent of civil servants with a 2 percent increase.

The management bonus, in turn, is regulated by Civil Service Law and constitutes percentage ranges of the tariff salary, depending on the managerial category of the post held. The personal bonus may be as high as 100 percent of the monetary salary base for quality fulfillment of service tasks. It is negotiated in the contract, and failure to fulfill the tasks results in cuts. In addition to the personal bonus, targeted output or high quality work also can be rewarded. Each ministry decides on the amount and mechanism for paying both personal and reward bonuses, and this information is not publicly available on the grounds of data protection. Nevertheless, the budget for remunerating civil servants in some ministries does not allow for very high personal and reward bonuses. The 2003 amendment introduced greater flexibility and opportunities for creating funds for paying these bonuses. The variable segment can be increased by each ministry when pruning its staff or not filling planned vacancies. In this way, no additional finances are needed for bonuses and ministries are motivated to slim their offices to have money for bonuses. Reorganization to gain bonus money, however, has not proved to be possible in all ministries, as they differ in the number of staff and stage of reorganization. Relatively small ministries simply do not have the opportunity to downsize. Moreover, this informal system is not sustainable, as ministries tend to deliberately overestimate the number of posts needed in annual budget discussions with the Ministry of Finance in order to keep the unspent finances for remuneration.

Personal bonuses and rewards for political appointees were gradually abolished – from 1998 onwards for the Cabinet ministers and from 2003 for state secretaries. Yet in 2006, Fico's new government reintroduced personal bonuses and rewards to state secretaries.

The 2003 reform introduced two distinctive posts with *permanent special bonuses*: the nominated civil service and posts of 'superior significance.' The first rewards top officials with an automatic 50 percent pay increase. Posts of superior significance get a permanent special bonus of 50–100 percent of their tariff salary, but they are obliged to disclose their and their family's assets. These posts are designated by the minister and head of office for tasks and priorities stemming from the Cabinet Memorandum (including EU tasks) and used to be approved by the Civil Service Office and government, but only when additional finances were required. Permanent special bonuses from ministries able to provide them from their own budgets are exempted from government approval. In addition, there are posts of superior significance with a *permanent special salary*. These posts were designated by ministers and heads of office in a Ministry and approved together with the proposed salary by the government. The salary is calculated on the basis of private sector comparisons. Under Dzurinda's government in 2002–2006, four posts were designated with a competitive salary, such as head of state treasury, head of debt management agency, chief economist, head of anti-corruption unit at the Government Office and head of programing of structural funds at the Ministry of Construction and Regional Development. Posts of superior significance are intended to attract and remunerate civil servants in posts that were difficult to fill or posts where good salaries should reduce corruption. These measures have been evaluated very positively: highly qualified staff was attracted and pressures to increase base salaries were reduced.

Although differences exist across the ministries on average personal bonuses paid, we were able to get some data based on the Free Access to Information Law, on the basis of which we calculated the trends in civil service remuneration (Figure 16.3). Figure 16.3 clearly shows the changes produced by various remuneration laws. First, bonuses for political appointees were gradually abolished – from 1998 onwards for the Cabinet ministers and from 2003 for state secretaries (although these were reintroduced in 2006), which brought the average remuneration of political appointees closer to the top apolitical civil servants (in some cases directors general actually began earning more than political appointees from 2003 onwards). Second, the liberalization of the Civil Service Law in 2003 enabled ministries to provide higher bonuses to top civil servants, which increases the compression ratio and brings it to the EU level.

In 2003 the government approved statements on 'Successful Integration of Slovakia into the EU and its Structural Funds.' This material identified a specific

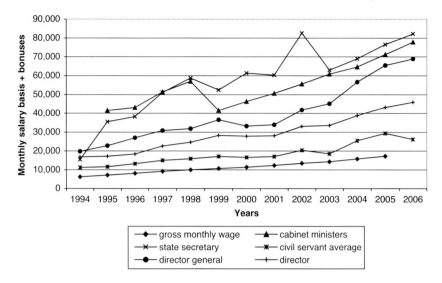

Figure 16.3 Average monthly salary basis + bonuses for civil servants in Skk.
   Source: Calculations by the authors on the basis of data provided by
   individual Ministries on the Request for Free Access to Information.
   Note: The years 1994, 1995, 1998, and 2002 are the election years when the
   changes in the political nominations can distort data by extra bonuses paid
   to the outgoing officials.

problem connected to the country's accession into the EU: a lack of qualified EU
experts in ministries and central agencies. Several changes in the civil service
were made to attract such people, especially through the creation of separate
salary scales, the increase in personal bonuses or a combination of both – which
on average increased the basic salary by 7,017 Skk for 968 posts (the average
civil service salary in 2004 was approximately 23,000 Skk). These posts were
identified by individual ministries and approved by the Ministry of Finance. Even
so, this measure seems to be insufficient to retain EU qualified civil servants,
mostly due to better career opportunities in Brussels and the private sector.
Moreover, ministries report that such large pay differentials gave rise to tensions
among EU and non-EU staff.

Other benefits

All political managers and heads of agencies are entitled to the exclusive use of
a chauffeured government car and cellular phone (the limit is set by the
Government Office). However, the lack of clear rules facilitates improper use. In
addition, political managers are entitled to a tax-free allowance for various
expenses, to use at their discretion. It is a lump sum added to their base salary –
121 percent of the highest salary class.
   Apolitical civil servants and managers are not tenured since the 2003 reforms,
nor do they have secure pensions or health insurance; they are considered regular

employees in this regard. Only the nominated civil service described above enjoys the security of tenure.

Comparing rewards among high public officials

Pay structures center on the distinction between base – so-called functional salary – and additional allowances and various kinds of bonuses, including management (or fixed sums for a certain position) and performance bonuses (see Figure 16.4 and Table 16.2). From the discussion above, we see that the base salary of constitutional representatives is linked to the average gross monthly salary in Slovakia from the previous year. In practice this means that every year, when the state budget is being approved, the average gross monthly salary has to be determined as well as the percentage for the annual linkage to salaries. The base salary of civil servants is linked to the payment classes, which are extremely low and, in practice, do not differentiate between managerial categories. However, the availability and flexibility in various personal and performance bonuses allow salaries for top civil servants to reach a level comparable with the private sector. This is usually done automatically and negotiated prior to beginning employment.

The data shown in Figure 16.5, calculated by the authors from various provisions in the laws and government and parliamentary regulations, only provide a partial picture of the relative differences and similarities among rewards for HPOs. The figures show the formal remuneration as anchored in the official documents (salary base for all categories of public officials and allowance for expenses and fixed sums for posts held for constitutional representatives). Personal and performance bonuses have not occured with constitutional representatives (see above) since the early 2000s. Data on personal and performance

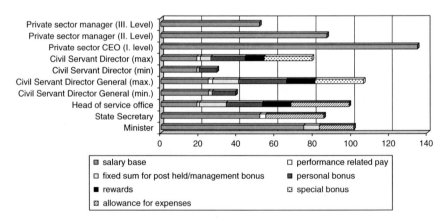

Figure 16.4 Ratio between fixed and variable part of remuneration, 2006.
Source: Authors' calculations.

Table 16.2 Ratio between fixed and variable parts of remuneration, 2006

Tariff salary

Service salary

	Salary base	Performance related pay (cumulative on annual basis)	Management bonus (fixed sum for post held)	Personal bonus	Special bonus	Rewards	Allowance for expenses (non-taxable)
Minister	1.5 MP's salary (74,550–)	–	8.000*	–	–	Abolished since 1998	18,000–**
State Secretary (manager Level 1)	1 MP's salary (51,900)	0–3%	–	–	–	Abolished in 2003–2006	121% of salary tariff of the eleventh salary class
Head of Service Office (manager Level 2)	Salary classes	0–3%	17–75% of the tariff salary	Up to 100%	–	Determined individually on recommendation of immediate superior and approved by head of the office and minister usually on annual basis	121% of salary tariff of the eleventh salary class
Civil servant manager (Level 3)		0–3%	8–55% of the tariff salary	Up to 100%	50–100% for posts of superior importance and/ or 50% for nominated civil service		–
Civil servant manager (level 4)		0–3%	5.5–40% of the tariff salary	Up to 100%	–		–
Civil servant		0–3%	–	Up to 100%	–		–
Private sector CEO	135,000–					n/a	n/a
Private sector manager (Level 2)	87,000–					n/a	n/a
Private sector manager (Level 3)	52,000–					n/a	n/a

Source: Authors on the basis of Civil Service Law, salaries in the private sector (industrial production) as published by Trexima, s.r.o. in Profit.

Notes:

* The total amount of the fixed sum for the post held has remained unchanged for all constitutional representatives since 1993 and thus its real value over time has decreased.

** Cabinet members' allowance is agreed by a Government Regulation from April 2001.

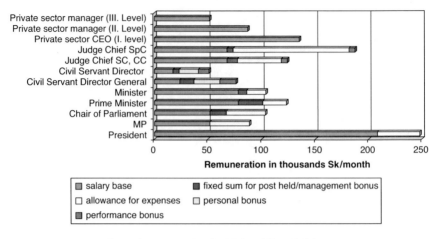

Figure 16.5 Comparison of remuneration for high public officials, 2005.
    Source: Calculations by the authors based on data gathered from legislation,
    Free Access to Information Law. Private sector data are from Trexima, s.r.o
    published in Profit on 18 October 2005, p. 17.
    Note: SpC = Special Court, SC = Supreme Court, CC = Constitutional Court,
    MP = Member of Parliament.

bonuses of the civil servants are calculated on the basis of averages given by
individual ministries requested by the Free Access to Information Law by the
authors.

The Slovakian President does not have a dominant role either over government
or over parliament. His role as Head of State is more ceremonial than functional.
Therefore, it is quite surprising to see (see Figure 16.5 for more detail) that the
fixed rewards to the President, as set by the law, are significantly higher than
those of the Prime Minister, Cabinet members, MPs or judges. This difference
was even more visible 10 years ago when the fixed allowance of the President and
the salary base tripled the rewards of all the others (at that time Special courts
were nonexistent).

Transparency and accountability in remuneration mechanisms

In the last four years, the government adopted measures such as free access to the
Corporate Register, the court management project (electronic file distribution),
enlarged powers of the Supreme Audit Office, better access to information on
judicial activities and the introduction of zero tolerance in law professions. A
2006 report from the TIS (SITA 2006) also confirmed that the perception of
corruption is changing, with political party funding and public procurement being
areas where corruption in Slovakia is most rampant. Eighty-two percent
of Slovak citizens presume that corruption is present in public procurement.

Another problem with the freedom of information legislation was caused by a decision made by the National Security Office (No. 432/2001), which, after the government's request, decided to conceal all personal data on ministers (including salaries). This removed all data on salaries at the governmental level (2001–2005) from the public eye.

Despite a constitutional law on conflict of interests, the law is only partly enforceable due to technicalities. The former law from 1995 was largely ineffective, since no public official has been fined for violating it. There were several attempts to amend the law, but these failed due to the alleged 'lack of political will.' After 2002, the new law on conflict of interest became a priority for the new government, supported once again by a massive non-governmental organization (NGO) campaign for transparency. After initial withdrawals, a new draft was prepared and was finally approved by the Parliament, effective from October 2005.

The new law obliged public officials to publish their property declarations on the website of the Slovak Parliament, with the strictest sanction for repeated violation being loss of mandate or office. The law also extended the range of functions, positions and activities incompatible with functions of public officials. Officials must submit property statements of their spouses and children. The new bill applies to the president, ministers, MPs, state secretaries, heads of central state administration agencies, judges of the Constitutional Court, president and vice-president of Supreme Court and Special Court, members of the Judiciary Council, general prosecutor, army chief of staff, ombudsman, head of the intelligence service (SIS), members of the Bank Board of the National Bank of Slovakia, and rectors of state universities. It also applies to municipal officials, leading positions in public service institutions and to managers of state-owned companies.

The law's implementation is cumbersome. The main problem lies in the form of reports and their content. The parliamentary commission on conflict of interests approved a form making it actually impossible to find out the property increase of a public official while in office. Indeed, officials do not need to report the exact value of their assets prior to their election or appointment. For example, the Chief Justice of the Supreme Court M. Karabín declared in 2005 that he earned 991,000 Skk in 2004 and his property included an apartment, a garden, and a garden house, without any value estimation.[3]

Conclusion

It was possible to broadly reconstruct the reward structure of Slovak HPOs, by using a range of separate laws, regulations, documents, some of which were declared as confidential (because of the protection of personal data), some public. The Slovak reward structure is characterized by its extreme fragmentation, and one has to make various calculations from secondary data to get an actual idea of how much high officials really get. One possible explanation is that the whole Slovak reward structure is meant to be so complicated in order not to be easily understood.

The changes to the Civil Service Law and related rules on civil service management in 2003 aimed to introduce flexibility into the payment and recruitment system to strengthen the capacity to attract and retain high caliber staff at all levels. They included measures to reduce the emphasis on seniority to make the system more open for the young; changes to the grading system to increase pay at middle and senior levels; and informal arrangements to allow ministries to pay bonuses from special funds created by reducing staff numbers. The flexibility is welcomed, but in the absence of central direction it carries with it significant dangers; bonuses granted at the discretion of local managers have become a major part of take-home pay, and some ministries are in a better position to make use of the flexibility than others. The changes have also introduced a number of major uncertainties into the system, not least the removal of job security for civil servants. In spite of the innovations introduced in 2003, the Slovak system has major weaknesses that are mostly related to the absence of human resource strategies in individual ministries and an incoherent performance appraisal system.

Notes

1 Act No. 551/2003 Coll., coming into effect as of 1 January 2004.
2 Act No. 231/2006 Coll. of 15 March 2006, coming into effect as of 1 June 2006.
3 http://www.nrsr.sk/appbin/net/exeit.nrsr.vnf.web.public/oznamenie. aspx?UserId=Kara Mila, accessed 24 April 2006.

References

Act No. 120/1993 Coll. on Remuneration of Constitutional Representatives [Zákon č. 120/1993 Z. z. o platových pomeroch niektorých ústavných činitel'ov].
Act No. 143/1992 Coll. on Salary and Remuneration [Zákon č. 143/1992 Z. z. o plate a odmene za pracovnú pohotovost' v rozpočtových a v niektorých d'alších organizáciach a orgánoch].
Act No. 154/2001 Coll. on Prosecutors and Lay prosecutors [Zákon č. 154/2001 Z. z. o prokurátoroch a právnych čakatel'och prokuratúry].
Act No. 200/1998 Coll. on Civil Service of Customs Officers [Zákon č. 200/1998 Z. z. o štátnej službe colníkov].
Act No. 312/2001 Coll. on State Service [Zákon č. 312/2001 Z.z. o štátnej službe].
Act No. 313/2001 Coll. on Public Service [Zákon č. 313/2001 Z.z. o verejnej službe].
Act No. 315/2001 Coll. on Fire Service [Zákon č. 315/2001 Z.z. o hasičskom a záchrannom zbore].
Act No. 328/2002 Coll. on social coverage of police and army [Zákon č. 328/2002 Z. z. o sociálnom zabezpečení policajtov a vojakov].
Act No. 346/2005 Coll. on Professional Army [Zákon č. 346/2005 Z.z. o štátnej službe profesionálnych vojakov ozbrojených síl SR].
Act No. 385/2000 Coll. on Judges and Lay Judges [Zákon č. 385/2000 Z.z. o sudcoch a prísediacich].
Act No. 391/2004 Coll. on Salary of European Parliament Members [Zákon č. 391/2004 Z. z. o plate poslanca Európskeho parlamentu].

Act No. 458/2003 Coll. on Special Court and Special Prosecutor Office Establishment [Zákon č. 458/2003 Z.z. o zriadení Špeciálneho súdu a Úradu špeciálnej prokuratúry].

Act No. 515/2003 Coll. on Regional and Area Offices [Zákon č. 515/2003 o krajských úradoch a obecných úradoch].

Act No. 552/2003 Coll. on performing work in public interest [Zákon č. 552/2003 Z.z. o výkone práce vo verejnom záujme].

Act No. 553/2003 Coll. on remuneration of some employees performing work in public interest [Zákon č. 553/2003 Z.z. o odmeňovaní niektorých zamestnancov pri vykonávaní práce vo verejnom záujme].

Act No. 73/1998 Coll. on Civil Service of Police Force, Intelligence service, Corps of Prison and Judicial Guard and Railway police [Zákon č. 73/1998 Z.z. o štátnej službe príslušníkov Policajného zboru, Slovenskej informačnej služby, Zboru väzenskej a justičnej stráže Slovenskej republiky a Železničnej polície].

Act No. 369/2004 amending the Act No. 369/1990 on Municipalities [Zákon č. 369/2004 o obecnom zriadení].

Beblavý, M. (2002) Management of civil service reform in Central Europe. In G. Péteri (Ed.), *Mastering Decentralization and Public Administration Reforms in Central and Eastern Europe.* Budapest: OSI – LGI, pp. 55–72.

Brans, M. and B.G. Peters (2006) Rewards of High Public Office: Continuing developments. Framework paper presented for the Workshop #4: Rewards of High Public Office the ECPR Joint Sessions of Workshops, Nicosia, 25–30 April.

Constitutional Act No. 357/2004 Coll. on Protection of Public Interest during Performance of Public Function Officials [Zákon č. 357/2004 Z.z. o ochrane verejného záujmu pri výkone funkcií verejných funkcionárov].

Hood, C. and B.G. Peters (1994) *Rewards at the Top: A comparative study of high public office.* London: Sage.

Labour Code No. 311/2001 Coll.[Zákon č. 311/2001 Zákonník práce].

Lesná, L. (2001) *Únos demokracie (Democracy kidnapping).* Bratislava, Inštitút pre verejné otázky.

Malová, D. (2002) Organized Interests. In G. Mesežnikov (Ed.), *Slovakia: Global Report.* Bratislava: IVO.

Resolution of the Government No. 487/2003 on Strategy of reform on employment in public sector [Stratégia reformy zamestnávania vo verejnom sektore schválená uznesením vlády Slovenskej republiky č. 487/2003].

Resolution of the Government No. 702/2001 on analysis of administrative capacities and needs related to the implementation of EU law [Analýza požiadaviek na zabezpečenie administratívnych potrieb súvisiacich s implementáciou práva EÚ].

Resolution of the Government No. 849 of 10 September 2003 to draft on improving remuneration status of civil servants and employees in public interest working in the sector of pre-accession funds and structural and Cohesion Fund 2009 [Uznesenie vlády SR č. 849 z 10. septembra 2003 k návrhu na zlepšenie odmeňovania zamestnancov štátnej a verejnej služby pracujúcich v oblasti predvstupových fondov a prípravy na čerpanie prostriedkov zo štrukturálnych fondov a Kohézneho fondu 2009].

Resolution of the Government No. 947/2002 on the analysis of administrative capacities and needs and new institutions related to the implementation of EU law in 2003 (creation of new 718 posts in EU affairs). [Uznesenie vlády č. 947/2002 k analýze požiadaviek na zabezpečenie administratívnych potrieb a nových inštitúcií súvisiacich s implementáciou práva EÚ].

Resolution of the Government No. 974/2003 on Systemization for 2004 as a part of state budget [Uznesenie vlády č. 974 zo 14. októbra 2003 k návrhu systemizácie na rok 2004 ako súčasť návrhu štátneho rozpočtu na rok 2004].

Rozhodnutie predsedu NR SR č. 646 o neospravedlnení neúčasti poslanca Národnej rady Slovenskej republiky na 22. schôdzi Národnej rady Slovenskej republiky za mesiac marec 2004.

SITA, 21.04.2006, 14:02, TIS Notes Corruption in Politics and Public Procurement.

Staroňová, K. and L. Malíková (2005) Politico-Administrative Relations under Coalition Politics in Slovakia. In B. G. Peters, T. Verheijen and L. Vass (Eds), *Coalitions of the Unwilling? Politicians and Civil Servants in Coalition Governments.* Bratislava: NISPAcee, pp. 178–203.

Staroňová, K. (2004) Roles and perceptions of senior officials in coalition governments in Slovakia. In B. Michael, R. Kattel and W. Drechsler (Eds), *Enhancing the Capacities to Govern: Challenges Facing the Central and Eastern European Countries.* Bratislava: NISPAcee, pp. 67–83.

Uznesenie NRSR č. 1222/2000 k Zákonu č. 120/1993 o ustanovení podmienok o úhrade výdavkov na prevádzku poslaneckej kancelárie a o zabezpečení služieb asistenta a odmeňovaní asistenta poslanca.

Uznesenie NRSR č. 73/1998 k Zákonu č. 120/1993.

Uznesenie NRSR č. 92/1995 k Zákonu č. 120/1993 o uskutočňovaní zahraničných pracovných ciest poslancov Národnej rady Slovenskej republiky.

Verheijen, T. (2002) The European Union and public administration development in Central and Eastern Europe. In R. Baker (Ed.), *Transitions from Authoritarianism – The Role of the Bureaucracy.* Praeger: Westport.

17 Rewards at the top

The European Union

Dionyssis Dimitrakopoulos and
Edward C. Page

Europe-wide administrative systems have had a strong track record of innovation. The Frankish Empire, above all under Charlemagne, is generally considered the cradle of feudalism – a system that directly grew out of the dominant arrangements for paying imperial officials. Napoleon's integration of Europe left a legacy of national and local institutions that appears to remain today. The administrative system of the EU is an exception to this tradition. Certainly Monnet's conception of a European administration consisting of just a few hundred European civil servants who would, in turn, set thousands of national experts to work, and make firms and governments serve the aims of the Schuman Plan (Monnet 1976) was in many ways revolutionary. Yet the methods used to establish the independence of the EU civil service from national interests involved the elaboration of a system of rewards for officials that reflects more closely the philosophy of the nineteenth-century national *Rechtsstaat* than the pay schemes of many member states.

As a supranational organization the EU and its predecessors have sought to limit the degree to which 'national interests' exercise an influence outside the Councils. This basic principle can be found in the oath of office according to which Commissioners can 'neither solicit nor accept instructions from any action incompatible with the supranational character of his tasks.' The supranationality of the whole European civil service is enshrined in the Protocol on the Privileges and Immunities of the European Economic Community appended to the Treaty of Rome. This protocol gave the newly established institutions all the formal trappings of the diplomatic representations of a state, such as inviolability of premises and free movement of representatives, and sought to seclude European civil servants from national governments by ensuring that they are paid by the European level of government, exempting their salaries from national income taxes and providing them with a series of financial benefits. The pay system that subsequently emerged has come to resemble the traditional Hegelian principle according to which the official is

> deliberately insulated from the changing state of the economy so that he can devote himself entirely to the service of the state and serve its purposes.

The measurement of pay takes place on the basis of what is required to maintain his lifestyle [...] if there is a rise in prices or a general rise in living conditions, then salaries too must be increased, but the regulation of pay is not in the form of struggles over wages and all that goes with them as in the private sector, but through legislative acts of state.

(Hintze 1964: 75–6)

Paying the people who run Europe

Many HPOs (in the sense used in this book) are not on the EU's payroll. The salaries of the hundreds of members of the Council of Ministers (i.e. national government ministers) and the 27 of the 29 members[1] of the European Council (i.e. the Heads of State or Government) as well as the heads of the national permanent representations to the EU are paid from national public funds that are subjected to national taxation. For many years the same applied to MEPs, even after (and despite) the direct elections that first took place in 1979, thus leading to vast disparities between them, with Hungarian MEPs receiving 6.76 percent of the Italian parliamentary allowance in 2005.[2] However, as a result of a reform adopted in 2005 (European Parliament 2005), as of June 2009 all (751)[3] MEPs receive the same salary – set at 38.5 percent of the salary of a member of the European Court of Justice (ECJ), i.e. approximately €7,665 monthly – and will pay income taxes to the EU budget, though individual member states retain the right to impose additional taxation. The Statute for MEPs also stipulates that during the transitional period (which may not exceed the length of two EP terms, i.e. a total of 10 years) each member state may apply different rules (in relation to salary, transitional allowance, and pension) to the MEPs who are elected by its citizens. The transitional arrangements may not be less favorable than those applied to national MPs of the country in question and all payments will be made from the budget of that country (Art. 29).

High public office holders in Europe also include: the President of the European Council (since 2010), the 27 Commissioners, including the High Representative for Common and Security Policy, their respective 27 *chefs de cabinet*, the Secretary General and her two deputies along with the 272 Directors General and their deputies in charge of 32 Directorates General within the Commission, the 27 judges, 8 advocates general and one registrar of the ECJ, the 27 judges of the Court of First Instance and the seven judges of the Civil Service Tribunal, the 27 members of the European Court of Auditors, the Secretary General and the 11 Directors General within the EP's Secretariat, the Council's Secretary General, his deputy, and the nine Directors General within the Council, the Heads of the agencies set up in the context of the EU's common foreign and security policy, or police and judicial co-operation matters, the six members of the European Central Bank's (ECB) Executive Board and the Heads of the 11 Directorates General within the ECB, the nine members of the Management Board of the European Investment Bank, the European Ombudsman[4], the European Data

Protection Supervisor and his deputy, the Heads of the Community, and other executive agencies, the Director of the European Administrative School.

Thus, whereas in the early 1990s only a minority of top EU officials received salaries from the EU (Page and Wouters 1994), now the obverse is true. Two factors – one procedural and one substantive – appear to explain the delay[5] in this change. First, the adoption of the reform required the unanimous support of (a) the Council as well as (b) the majority of MEPs, some of whom had much to lose from it.[6] Second, although the growth in the EP's powers since the mid-1980s has turned it into a co-legislator, the institution needed time to mature in terms of this key aspect of its operation, which risked affecting its credibility.

As the 2011 budget indicates (Official Journal L 68, 15 March 2011), in addition to a total of €67,755,185 that corresponds to their salaries (i.e. €90,219.95 or $128,789 per MEP)[7], MEPs also receive significant sums in various kinds of allowances (title I, budget chapter 10) to the tune of €123,123,220[8] (i.e. €163,945.699, or $234,032 per MEP)[9].

The single largest amount in that category was devoted to MEPs' travel and subsistence expenses in connection with traveling to and from their places of work and other travel related to their duties (€75,396,756). Reforms adopted in 2005 replaced the flat-rate travel allowance (which meant that some MEPs used economy class tickets but received refunds for more expensive ones) with the reimbursement of actual costs incurred (BBC News online, 23 June 2005). The second largest amount (€38,330,147) is allocated to the 'general expenditure allowance' that covers expenses resulting from the parliamentary activities of MEPs in the member state where they are elected. Finally, MEPs also receive €9,396,317 for 'other travel expenses' (i.e. travel expenses incurred in the member state of election and repatriation expenses). In addition, MEPs receive a sum used for the staff that they employ. Under the 'parliamentary assistance' heading, this amounted to €176,043,709,[10] i.e. approximately €243,412 (or $347,471) per MEP in 2011. The assistants to MEPs perform important and extremely varied roles and the improvement of their precarious status has been a longstanding issue within the EP. In the past, MEPs had almost complete freedom in that aspect of their work. As a result, problems arose, including the employment of relatives, tax avoidance and the non-payment of pension-related and social security contributions. As of June 2009, assistants who are based in Brussels (where most of the EP's work is done) are covered by the statute that covers EU contract staff.[11] The contracts of other assistants are managed by certified paying agents with whom the EP concludes model contracts. These agents are responsible for compliance with the corresponding national legislation regarding social security and tax. Though MEPs remain free to choose their assistants, define the duration of their contract and allocate tasks to them, they are not allowed to employ their close relatives and the EP's services handle the contracts of and salary payments to assistants (up to €16,914 per month per MEP in 2008 figures, including travel expenses, social security contributions and tax paid upon presentation of invoices). MEPs have the right to utilize up to a quarter of their parliamentary assistance allowance for research studies and other advisory work (Euractiv, 14 July 2008, http://www.euractiv.com/en/future-eu/meps-set-stricter-rules-assistant-payment-scandal/article-174207).

The EU also contributes to the pension schemes of MEPs – an appropriation of €14,664,889 in 2011 that includes €11,131,000 for retirement pensions (i.e. approximately €14,822 or \$21,158 per MEP)[12], €406,742 for invalidity pensions, and €3,072,147 for survivors' pensions.

Furthermore, the sum of €3,477,040 has been allocated for accident insurance, the reimbursement of medical expenses for MEPs and loss and theft of their personal effects and €800,000 for language and computer courses. Though there are other EU-funded activities that facilitate the work (and life) of MEPs, they are indirect and cannot be ascribed to individual MEPs. These include current administrative expenditures and expenditures relating to the political and information activities of the political groups and non-attached MEPs (€54,850,000), contributions to European political parties (€17,400,000)[13] as well as €569,844,235 for the remuneration and social security insurance of permanent and temporary staff of the EP.

How do these sums compare to those made to other relevant categories? It has been argued that under the previous arrangements 'MEP payments were around two thirds *below* top salary levels in 1973, they were more or less equal to them in the middle of the 1980s, and they are currently around one half *above* them in 1993 because these expenses could (at the time) be used in part as supplementary income' (Page and Wouters 1994: 203). Given the introduction of the aforementioned reforms, it would now be more apposite to compare the basic gross salary of an MEP (€7,665 per month under the new statute) with the highest salary of a European Commission official (in December 2010 this was set at €18,370.84). After the European elections of 2009, the former corresponds to 41.72 percent of the latter.

Is EU service attractive?

The pay of EU civil servants at first appeared extremely attractive in the early 1990s since 'a newly-appointed junior professor at the European University Institute, for example, on an A5 step 1 salary would be earning £51,067 gross, before allowances and adjustments for local cost of living' (Page and Wouters 1994: 204), a strong incentive to attract high caliber officials from across the Union.

Although Monnet's intention was to establish a civil service devoid of emphasis on nationality and national quotas (Monnet 1976: 450), the avoidance of major imbalances has been historically a major expressed objective of recruitment policy (Page 1997: Ch. 3; Page and Wouters 1994). Just as shares of seats in Parliament and numbers of commissioners supplied by member states are related to population size, the system of recruitment and pay has also sought to secure fair shares in the senior ranks of the administration. However, the enlargement of the EU has led to a new balance within each of the relevant institutions. The two institutions where the most significant changes have been observed are the College of Commissioners and the ECJ. In the EP and the senior civil service, the size of the population remains an important determinant of the distribution of seats and posts (especially in the EP). In the EU of 27 member states, each member state has the right to nominate just one Commissioner and judge, irrespective of the size of its population. As a result, the more populous member states (Germany, France, Italy, Britain, and Spain) have lost the right to nominate a second Commissioner each. In the administrative echelon of the Commission, smaller countries used to have one Director General each, while larger ones had two or three (Page and Wouters 1994: 204).

In the past, officials fell into one of five major pay categories (A, B, C, and D and the LA grade for translators), a series of divisions within each grade (from A1 to A8 and so on) with a series of steps within each grade division. Staff regulations currently divide officials into two groups: Assistants (AST) and Administrators (AD) (Art. 5). The former is comprised of 11 grades, corresponding to executive, technical and clerical duties. The latter is comprised of 12 grades, corresponding to administrative, advisory, linguistic, and scientific duties. Since 2006 they are placed on a single pay scale that is composed of 16 grades, each of which is sub-divided into five seniority steps[14] with officials moving up one step every two years. Assistants occupy grades 1–11 while Administrators occupy grades 5–16. Each grade and step is represented on the EU servants' pay matrix. The pay grading system for EU employees applies uniformly to all nationalities and all major posts.

In the early 1990s Germany, Britain, Italy, and Spain were underrepresented with only 63 percent, 70 percent, 76 percent, and 87 percent, respectively of the employees that one would expect on the basis of population. In contrast, Belgium and Luxembourg, that is, the main host countries, were overrepresented among grade A employees (421 and 1,095 percent, respectively) and the same applied to other smaller countries, such as Ireland (320 percent), Denmark (191 percent), and Greece (191 percent) (Page and Wouters 1994: 205).

Two decades later, in April 2011[15] – i.e. after both the 'big bang enlargement' of 2004 and the Kinnock reforms of the early 2000s that involved the introduction of new staff regulations that enshrined merit as the main criterion for promotion (Kassim 2008) – Germany, Britain, Italy, Spain, and Poland were underrepresented with only 51 percent, 39 percent, 84 percent, 76 percent, and 66 percent of the AD and AST Commission employees that one would expect on the basis of population, having been joined by Denmark and Belgium (58 and 86 percent, respectively). In contrast, Luxembourg remains overrepresented among these employees (858 percent) and the same applies to other small countries, such as Slovenia (228 percent), Ireland (226 percent), and Greece (163 percent). As regards the top two tiers (AD16 and AD15) of the European Commission's officialdom, Germany, Italy, and France remain underrepresented – 75 percent, 81 percent, and 88 percent, respectively – and have been joined by Poland (28 percent), but Britain's rate has increased to 95 percent. In contrast, Belgium, Denmark, Ireland, Greece, Luxembourg, and Slovenia are overrepresented

(371 percent, 306 percent, 379 percent, 206 percent, 842 percent, and 207 percent) while another small country, the Czech Republic, is severely underrepresented with its nationals holding a quarter (26 percent) of the top posts one would expect on the basis of the country's population.

Although levels of remuneration provide a common set of incentives so as to attract EU citizens from all member states, the disincentives that they must counterbalance vary along national lines. There are numerous causes of variation but the most important are national differences in pay for civil servants, the costs of relocation and the inability to speak the language of the country where EU posts are located.

Although the expatriate allowance (see below) is not paid to EU officials who live and work in their country of origin (thus leading to discrepancies between officials on the same salary point), the intensity of the incentives varies along national lines. A system that is designed to attract candidates from states amongst which pay and the cost of living are unevenly distributed, inevitably creates much stronger incentives for candidates from countries where pay and costs are lower. Moreover, the same system is likely to provide greater incentives, even in sectors where there is no shortage of candidates. Thus, to the extent that shortages play a role in determining the overall rate of adjustment of the matrix, they are likely to lead to pay rates that are clearly above those required to attract candidates from many member states and sectors or specializations. In other words, the allocation of financial rewards is bound to be inefficient when construed exclusively on the basis of recruitment from across the EU, since varying rewards on the basis of nationality or sector or not varying them on the basis of hierarchy is as inconceivable in the EU as it is in its member states.

If nationality were not an issue, it might be argued that pay is above the level required to attract candidates. This is due to a number of reasons. As survey evidence has suggested in the past, commitment to European integration is an important motive for (especially senior) EU officials (Page and Wouters 1994, Shore and Black 1992). More recent research indicates that top Commission officials have a slight preference for supranationalism, but there is also considerable support for intergovernmentalism (Hooghe 2001). Since senior posts (Directors General, Deputy Directors General and, to some extent, Directors) were traditionally filled by *parachutistes* – i.e. people who have made their careers outside of the EU civil service – it cannot be argued that the matrix was designed to encourage the recruitment of officials to junior posts so that they can subsequently be promoted to top jobs. Between 1975 and 1995, 81.8 percent of A1 and 65.7 percent of A2 officials had parachuted into the Commission (Page 1997). In the late 1990s, the job in the Commission was the first job for only 18 percent of top Commission officials and close to 45 percent had extensive experience outside the public sector (Hooghe 2001). In 2011 only 19 percent of the Directors General had at least one year's experience outside the public sector and its duration varies from one (one case) to five years (half, or three, of the cases – all British).[16]

The matrix, supplements, and deductions

The matrix is central to the rewards of top EU officials since it directly determines their gross pay. A series of weightings reflecting local costs of living are used so as to make the matrix applicable to all EU officials throughout the Union, including Commissioners, Judges, and other top officials, since their basic salaries are related to the top step of the top grade (third step of grade 16). Changes in the matrix directly affect changes in supplements to and deductions from income (see below).

The basic monthly salary of senior EU officials is equal to an amount resulting from the application of the following percentages to that basic salary: 138 percent for the Presidents of the European Council, the Commission and the ECJ, 130 percent for the High Representative for Common and Security Policy, 125 percent for the Vice-Presidents of the Commission, 112.5 percent for other Commissioners, ECJ Judges, and Advocates General, 101 percent for the ECJ's Registrar and 104, 100, and 90 percent, respectively for the President, the members and the Registrar of the EU Civil Service Tribunal.

The supplements to officials' income take various forms and appear in the staff regulations (Council of Ministers [EEC & EURATOM], 1962 as amended in 2008). Officials receive an *expatriation allowance* equal[17] to 16 percent of the total of the basic salary, and they are also entitled to a household allowance and dependent child allowance. The *household allowance* (whose payment is subject to status) is equal to €159.49 plus two percent of an official's basic salary. The *dependent child allowance* is equal to €348.50 per month for each dependent child automatically for children under 18 years of age and by application for children between 18 and 26 who are attending university or are receiving vocational training. The *education allowance* is equal to the actual education costs[18] incurred up to a maximum of €236.46 per month for each dependent child who is at least five years old and in regular full-time attendance at a primary or secondary school[19] that charges fees or at an establishment of higher education. An *installation allowance* (equal to two months' basic salary in the case of an official who is entitled to the household allowance or equal to one month's basic salary in other cases) is paid to an official for whom a change in the place of residence is required. It is weighted at the rate fixed for the place where the official is employed. On termination of service, officials who provide evidence of a change in address are entitled to a *resettlement allowance* (equal to two months' basic salary in the case of an official who is entitled to the household allowance or to one month's basic salary in other cases), provided that they have completed four years of service and do not receive a similar allowance through their new job. Furthermore, officials are entitled to be paid in each calendar year a sum equivalent to the cost of travel from their place of employment to their place of origin for themselves and, if they are entitled to the household allowance, for their spouse and dependents.

EU officials who live and work in a third country receive an allowance for living conditions that is fixed, according to the official's place of employment, as a percentage of a reference amount that is comprised of their total basic salary, plus the expatriation allowance, household allowance, and dependent child allowance, less any compulsory deductions. This allowance rises as a function of distance. A supplement is added to it depending on the distance by train between the place of employment and the place of origin.[20]

Commissioners and ECJ Judges receive a *residence allowance* equal to 15 percent of their basic salary as well as a monthly entertainment allowance. They are also entitled to (a) an *installation allowance* equal to two months' basic salary on taking up their duties and a resettlement allowance equal to one month's basic salary on ceasing to hold office and (b) the reimbursement of *travel expenses* incurred by themselves and for members of their family, and (c) reimbursement of the *cost of removal* of their personal effects and furniture, including insurance against ordinary risks (theft, breakage, fire) upon taking office.

The remuneration of the officials and other servants of the Communities are reviewed annually by the Council of Ministers (on the basis of qualified majority voting) in light of a report by the Commission based on a joint index prepared by Eurostat in agreement with the national statistical offices of the Member States. In the context of the review the Council considers whether remuneration should be adjusted, taking particular account 'of any increases in salaries in the public service and the needs of recruitment' (Art. 65 of Staff Regulations). Eurostat's report focused on 'changes in the cost of living in Brussels [the Brussels International Index], the economic parities between Brussels and certain places in the Member States, and changes in the purchasing power of salaries in national civil services in central government' (Art. 1, Annex XI, Staff Regulations). The adjustment is presented in net terms as a 'uniform across-the-board percentage.' The updated tables take effect in July, but the matrix can be upgraded more than once a year and even retrospectively in order to correct mistakes or when more information on the cost of living and salaries paid in national administrations becomes available.

As Page and Wouters note (1994: 210–211), the Council, which actually makes the pay awards, is bound by its own regulation to accept the pay increases calculated on the basis of the formula. In 1981 it sought to implement the 3.3 percent increase recommended by the Commission only for the lowest paid officials while paying the other grades a flat rate increase bringing the average pay increase to just 1.5 percent. It justified this decision on the grounds that (a) the regulation that sets the mechanisms used to update the matrix referred to two additional criteria, the recruitment needs of the institutions and the 'economic and social situation' of the Community, and (b) there was a serious crisis in Community finances. The Commission challenged the legality of this decision in the ECJ and won (Case 59/81). However, the revised staff regulations currently in force after the Kinnock reforms stipulate that 'if there is a serious and sudden deterioration in the economic and social situation within the Community, assessed in the light of objective data supplied for this purpose by the Commission, the latter shall submit appropriate proposals on which the Council shall act' (Art. 10, Annex XI, Staff Regulations). These arrangements are applicable between July 2004 and December 2012 and are meant to be reviewed on the basis of a report and, where appropriate, a proposal by the Commission (Art. 15). The Commission will conduct a review of the formula in 2012.

In November 2009, the Commission proposed an increase of 3.7 percent for staff salaries and pensions, which was amended by the Council to be an increase of just 1.85 percent so as to take account of the economic and financial crisis but without invoking the special procedure provided for by the Staff Regulations in case of a serious and sudden deterioration in economic conditions. The Commission took the Council to court, arguing that by doing so the Council had exceeded the powers conferred on it by the Staff Regulations, a view with which the Council disagreed. The Court found in the Commission's favor and annulled the corresponding parts of the Council's decision (C-40/10, European Commission v. Council of the European Union, *Official Journal*, C30, 29 January 2011, p. 10).

It is widely and erroneously believed that EU officials do not pay taxes. Although they do not pay income taxes on their salaries in their native country or in their country of residence, they are liable to pay all provincial and local taxes as well as, of course, taxes on what they buy, on what they earn apart from their salaries, and they must pay estate duties and other such taxes. In addition they pay a Community tax and a 'crisis levy' or 'temporary contribution' (Page and Wouters 1994).

The Community Tax is progressive. For each band of income a differential percentage is paid, initially rising from 8 percent in the first to 10 percent in the second, then ten further steps increasing by 2.5 percent each to 35 percent, a penultimate step of 40 percent and anything earned over the top rate of this band is taxed at 45 percent. Since the budget crisis of 1981 there has been a second tax. The 'crisis levy' was introduced from July 1981 for a period of 10 years. After 1991, and substantial industrial action by EU civil servants, it was replaced by a 'temporary contribution,' again for a period of 10 years, and was set at a standard rate of 5.8 percent. Since May 2004 a 'special levy' has been applied (until the end of 2012) on the basic salary minus (a) social security and pension contributions and the tax, before special levy, payable by an official in the same grade and step without dependents, and (b) an amount equal to the basic salary of an official in grade 1, step 1. The rate rises from 2.50 percent in 2004 to 5.50 percent in 2011 (Council of Ministers 1968). The same applies to the President and Members of the Commission, the President, Judges, Advocates General and Registrar of the Court of Justice and the President, Members and Registrar of the Court of First Instance (Council Regulation [EEC, Euratom, ECSC] No. 1084/92 of 28 April 1992, OJ L 117, 1 May 1992).

Commissioners and Judges are entitled to a pension from the age of 65. The amount of the pension is 4.275 percent of the basic salary last received for each full year in office and one-twelfth of that sum for each complete month, the maximum being 70 percent of the basic salary last received (Council Regulation [EC, Euratom] No. 1292/2004 of 30 April 2004 L 243, 15 July 2004).

Officials who have completed at least 10 years in service are entitled to a pension[21] of up to 70 percent of the final basic salary carried by the last grade in which the official was classified for at least one year. Officials contribute one third of the cost of this pension scheme to the tune of 10.25 percent of their basic salary – up from 8.25 in 1993 (Page and Wouters 1994: 208). Moreover, social security arrangements cover between 80 and 100 percent of the expenditure incurred by sickness.

Officials who travel in the course of their duties receive a daily subsistence allowance that is comprised of a flat-rate sum that covers 'all expenses incurred by the person on mission: breakfast, two main meals, and incidental expenses, including local travel.' Accommodation costs, including local taxes, are reimbursed up to a maximum fixed for each country, on production of supporting documents (Art. 10, Annex VII, Staff Regulations). Commissioners and Judges receive 105 percent of that amount for the same purposes, in addition to travel and accommodation expenses. Also, officials who, because of their duties, regularly incur entertainment expenses may be granted a fixed rate allowance determined by the appointing authority. In addition, senior management staff (i.e. Directors General or their equivalents in grade AD 16 or AD 15 and Directors or their equivalents in grade AD 15 or AD 14) who do not have an official car at their disposal may receive a fixed allowance not exceeding €892.42 a year to cover normal travel within the boundaries of the town where they are employed (Art. 15, Annex VII, Staff Regulations).

A monthly entertainment allowance is also paid to Commissioners, ECJ Judges, Advocates General and Registrar. This amounts to €1,418 for the Presidents of the Commission and ECJ, €911 for the Vice-Presidents of the Commission, €607 for other Commissioners, €608 for ECJ judges and Advocates-General and €554 for the ECJ's Registrar. Presiding Judges of Chambers of the Court and the First Advocate-General also receive during their term of office a special duty allowance of €811 per month. These allowances are increased annually by the Council (Council Regulation [EC, ECSC, Euratom] No. 2778/98 of 17 December 1998 L 347, 23 December 1998).

While in post, Commissioners are banned by the Treaty of Rome from any paid work. However, the *potential* for rewards after a career as a Commissioner is undoubtedly significant. For example, as Page and Wouters point out (1994: 209–210), Sir Christopher Tugendhat, Commissioner between 1977 and 1985,

> went on to become, among other things, a Director of the National Westminster Bank, of Commercial Union Assurance as well as Chairman of the Civil Aviation Authority and the Royal Institute for International Affairs. There can be little doubt that the prestige and experience associated with having been a senior Commissioner makes former office holders attractive candidates for such positions. Precisely how much value was added to Tugendhat's career by his appointment in the Commission is not easy to determine since his qualities were obviously appreciated before he went to Brussels. He was a director of Sunningdale Oils and Phillips Petroleum International (UK) in the early 1970s. Moreover a rewarding position in the

private sector is not, as far as can be ascertained, the destination of most ex-commissioners. Of the 59 ex-commissioners, the subsequent careers of only 36 could be traced – the remainder died (3), disappeared without trace from the standard biographical references (15) or departed office too recently to be included in them (5). Of the 36, 16 went back to positions in domestic politics (at positions ranging from mayor of a small town through MP to President or Prime Minister), a further six went back into law (3) or teaching (3), six became eminent members of public organisations (such as Victor Bodson who became President of the International Association of French Speaking Parliamentarians) and eight went into private industry, usually in a directorial or managerial capacity. Of these four were British, two were Belgian, one was Luxembourgeois and one was French (the latter going into a semi-public rather than a private business).

Arrangements have been in place at least since the early 1970s to facilitate the life of Judges and Commissioners after the end of their service for these two institutions. For three years, from the first day of the month following that in which they cease to hold office, they receive a monthly *transitional allowance*. The amount depends on their length of service. It rises from 40 percent of their last basic salary when they were in office if their period of service is less than two years, to 60 percent if it is between 10 and 15 years and to more than 65 percent of the same salary in other cases (Regulation [ECSC, EEC, Euratom] No. 1546/73 of the Council of 4 June 1973, OJ L 155, 11 June 1973). These generous arrangements can be seen as an attempt to ensure that these HPOs are under no financial pressure to rush into new jobs that might conflict with their former EU role. In addition, Art. 213 of the Treaty stipulates *inter alia* that (a) Commissioners have, upon leaving office, 'a duty to behave with integrity and discretion as regards the acceptance […] of certain appointments or benefits' and (b) the Council or the Commission have the right to take legal action against breaches.

However, what became known as the (infamous) 'Bangemann case' in 1999 led to the adoption of rules whose aim is to ensure that problems of this kind are less likely to occur. Martin Bangemann – a lawyer, former MEP, federal MP, leader of Germany's Liberals (FDP) and economics minister in successive German governments led by Helmut Kohl – served as a Commissioner (under Jacques Delors and Jacques Santer) between 1989 and 1999, initially in charge of the internal market and, since 1995, responsible for industrial affairs, IT and telecommunications. In June 1999 – that is, *prior* to the completion of his term of office – he decided to leave the Commission and, with immediate effect, take up a lucrative offer to join the board of Telefónica,[22] a major company that was active in the policy domain (telecommunications) covered by his portfolio (*Financial Times*, 1 July 1999, p. 26). His decision was vehemently opposed by the EP, the Commission, the Council (*Financial Times*, 23 July 1999, p. 2), other politicians (including the leader of his own party) and the German government, though he maintained that he had breached no rules. As a result, the Council took legal action against him at the ECJ that aimed to deprive him of his pension rights for the breach of Art. 213 of the Treaty.

Following this embarrassing controversy, Romano Prodi, then-president of the Commission, introduced a Code of Conduct for Commissioners stipulating that

> Whenever Commissioners intend to engage in an occupation during the year after they have ceased to hold office, whether this be at the end of their term or upon resignation, they shall inform the Commission in good time. The Commission shall examine the nature of the planned occupation. If it is related to the content of the portfolio of the Commissioner during his/her full term of office, the Commission shall seek the opinion of an ad hoc ethics committee. In the light of the committee's findings it will decide whether the planned occupation is compatible with the last paragraph of Article 213(2) of the Treaty.

The Council subsequently decided to drop the case in the ECJ once Bangemann agreed in writing to delay taking up his new job by a year, in line with the Commission's new Code of Conduct for Commissioners, not to work for another telecommunications company during this period, not to represent any third party in dealings with EU institutions for two years after his departure from Brussels and to 'permanently continue to safeguard' any confidential information he may have become aware of as a Commissioner (Council of Ministers [ECSC/EC/ EURATOM], 1999).

In August 2010 the Commission's ad hoc ethics committee forced Charlie McCreevy (internal market and financial services Commissioner between 2004 and 2009) to resign from the board of a London-based investment bank due to a conflict of interest. This was the first case of its kind (http:// euobserver.com/?aid=30996, 26 April 2011, accessed on 11 May 2011). In an effort to force the Commission to enhance its code of conduct (in line with President Barroso's earlier promise) the European Parliament voted in October 2010 to withhold some of the monies that had been earmarked for former Commissioners (http://euobserver.com/?aid=31101, 22 October 2010, accessed on 11 May 2011). The revised code of conduct was adopted by the Commission in April 2011, i.e. after former industrial affairs Commissioner Günter Verheugen had set up a lobbying consultancy firm and former maritime affairs Commissioner Joe Borg had joined a PR consultancy firm 'actively lobby-ing on maritime issues' (http://euobserver.com/?aid=31248, 11 November 2010, accessed on 11 May 2011).

The revised code extends the remit of the ethics committee (which obtains the power, if requested by the President of the Commission, to issue opinions 'on any general ethical question' concerning the interpretation of the code), introduces guiding criteria for its assessments and, for the first time, compels it to make public both its findings and its reasoning. It extends from 12 to 18 months the period during which former Commissioners 'shall not lobby nor advocate with members of the Commission and their staff for her/his business, client or employer on matters for which they have been responsible within their portfolio.' It also introduces a clear procedure whereby the President of the Commission may re-allocate responsibility for a dossier in case of potential conflicts of interest while a Commissioner is still in office, explicitly bans Commissioners from recruiting spouses, partners or direct family members in their *cabinet*, enhances existing restrictions regarding gifts in the form of hospitality and obliges Commissioners to update their declaration of interests on an annual basis (European Commission 2011).

Conclusion

Despite significant reforms in how the European Union works, in how its officials are recruited and promoted and how its politicians are paid in the last 15 years, its image as a 'gravy train' has hardly improved. Indeed, with the fiscal austerity following the 2008 financial crisis, the central philosophy of ensuring independence from member states and making European service attractive to officials from 27 member states seems almost guaranteed to enhance the impression of a gravy train. Yet the expenses involved in living (possibly temporarily) in a city like Brussels and the financial incentives needed to make people want to do it do not come cheap. Commission pay shows the difficulty, if not impossibility, of paying enough to make employment in the EU attractive while not outraging member state electorates. In the UK, with a comparatively Eurosceptic electorate and a highly Eurosceptic press, a pay rise in 2010 was condemned in the *Daily Mail* as, in the words of a Conservative MP, a case of 'self-serving Eurocrats [yet again] handing large amounts of our money to other self-serving Eurocrats.' Yet the Commission and the British Government had for some time been concerned that the number of UK applicants to join the Commission's civil service was far too low, since those with the necessary qualifications (the critical shortage in the UK being with language qualifications) were believed to be attracted to better paid jobs elsewhere.

Answers to the question of whether salaries are 'too high' will always vary according to the perspective of the person giving the answer as well as the factors taken into account and left out. However, given the importance of the objective of recruiting officials of the right caliber from the right countries, and given the constraints of a common pay scale for all nationalities that has to maintain hierarchical distinctions in pay differentials, the argument for wages that appear generous by many national standards is not to be explained simply as EC officials having been successful in the pursuit of self-interest. Rather the pay system is a result of the current level of development of European integration, where supranational sentiments are not fully matched by the dropping of national interests. While a worthy ideal, member states are only likely to tolerate true supranationality in recruitment in the lower echelons of the EC where 56 percent of the employees come from Belgium, Luxembourg, or Italy. Among judges, MEPs and Commissioners formal national quotas determine the nationality of incumbents.

In between this, where official as well as unofficial quotas are illegal, member states appear to prefer to pay for a system that formally recognizes the principle of supranationality in the senior ranks but at the same time ensures that the top rank of the civil service contains acceptable numbers of their own citizens.

Notes

1 The President of the European Council and the President of the European Commission are also members of the European Council and their salaries are paid out of the EU budget.
2 Euractiv, 23 June 2005, http://www.euractiv.com/en/opinion/meps-agree-reform-salaries-travel-expenses/article-141439.
3 This is the number specified by the Treaty of Lisbon, which entered into force in December 2009.
4 The Ombudsman has the same rank in terms of remuneration, allowances and pension as a judge of the ECJ (European Parliament, 1994, Art. 10).
5 This reform was adopted 26 years after the first direct European elections.
6 This explains the fact that the politicians who were MEPs prior to the entry into force of the Statute and were since re-elected 'may opt for the national system applicable hitherto in respect of the salary, transitional allowance and pensions for the entire duration of their membership of the European Parliament' (Art. 25 (1)).
7 All conversions in this chapter are made at a rate of €1=$1.4275 (April 2011).
8 This figure does not include €179,000 intended for flat-rate subsistence and representation allowances in connection with the duties of the EP's President.
9 In addition to the cost of carbon offsets, these include ordinary travel expenses (i.e. travel and subsistence expenses in connection with travelling to and from the places of work and with other duty travel), other travel expenses (i.e. travel expenses incurred in the member state of election and repatriation expenses), general expenditure allowance (i.e. expenses resulting from the parliamentary activities of MEPs in the member state where they are elected).
10 This includes €250,000 for 'exchange losses' which is understandable since MEPs need to employ (and, consequently, remunerate) staff in the country where they are elected at a time when 10 of the 27 members of the EU do not use the euro.
11 This is subject to the amendment of the Staff Regulations of officials of the European Communities and the conditions of employment of other servants of the European Communities (OJ L56, 4 March 1968, pp. 1–7), which requires the unanimous agreement of the Council.
12 Page and Wouters reported that in 1993 the EC's contribution to the pension schemes of MEPs amounted to 7.7 million ECU or 14,882 ECU per MEP (Page and Wouters 1994, p. 203).
13 This corresponds to €23,169 approximately (i.e. $33,074) per MEP.
14 The top grade (AD16) is an exception: it has three steps.
15 For these calculations we have used Eurostat's population estimates for 2010 (EURO-STAT 2011) and the European Commission's official staff figures (European Commission/Human Resources and Security DG, 2011a, b).
16 This calculation is based on the 31 CVs found on the European Commission's web site (http://ec.europa.eu/civil_service/about/who/dg_en.htm accessed on 19 April 2011) from which the CVs of five Directors General were missing.
17 It is at least €472.70 per month.
18 Children may be educated in the European School free of charge.

19 For each dependent child who is less than five years old or is not yet in regular full-time attendance at a primary or secondary school, the amount of this allowance is fixed at €8,514.
20 It amounts to €177.22 if the distance is between 725 km and 1450 km, and €354.41 if it is greater than 1,450 km.
21 This entitlement also applies irrespective of length of service, if an official is over the age of 63, if it has not been possible to reinstate him during a period of non-active status or in the event of retirement in the interests of the service.
22 His links to that company go way back. In the early 1990s he created a high level group to outline the EU's strategy on information highways. Candido Velazquez, then president of Telefonica, was a member of the group (*Financial Times*, 2 July 1999, p. 2).

References

Council of Ministers (1968) Regulation (EEC, Euratom, ECSC) No. 260/68 of the Council of 29 February 1968 laying down the conditions and procedure for applying the tax for the benefit of the European Communities. *Official Journal of the European Communities* L 56, 4 March, 8–10 as last amended by Regulation (EC, Euratom) No. 1750/2002 (OJ L 264, 2 October 2002, p. 15).

Council of Ministers (ECSC/EC/EURATOM) (1999) Council Decision 2000/44 of 17 December 1999 on the settlement of the Bangemann case. *Official Journal of the European Communities*, L 016, 21 January 2000, p. 0073.

Council of Ministers (EEC & EURATOM) (1962) Regulation No. 31 (EEC), 11 (EAEC) laying down the Staff Regulations of Officials and the Conditions of Employment of Other Servants of the European Economic Community and the European Atomic Energy Community. *Official Journal of the European Communities*, P 45, 14 June, as amended.

European Commission (2011) Code of conduct for Commissioners C (2011) 2904. Brussels: European Commission.

European Commission/Human Resources and Security DG (2011a) Distribution of active contract agents by nationality (all budgets). Brussels: European Commission.

European Commission/Human Resources and Security DG (2011b) Distribution of officials and temporary agents by gender, nationality, function groups and grades (all budgets). Brussels: European Commission.

European Parliament (1994) Decision of the European Parliament on the regulations and general conditions governing the performance of the Ombudsman's duties. *Official Journal of the European Union*, L113, 4 May; 15.

European Parliament (2005) Decision of the European Parliament of 28 September 2005 adopting the Statute for Members of the European Parliament. *Official Journal of the European Union*, L262, 7 October.

EUROSTAT (2011) Total population statistics.

Hintze, O. (1964) Der Beamtenstand. In *Soziologie und Geschichte.* Göttingen: Vandenhoeck und Ruprecht, pp. 66–125.

Hooghe, L. (2001) *The European Commission and the Integration of Europe: Images of Governance.* Cambridge: Cambridge University Press.

Kassim, H. (2008) Mission impossible, but mission accomplished: the Kinnock reforms and the European Commission. *Journal of European Public Policy*, **5**(5): pp. 648–668 (special issue edited by Michael Bauer).

Monnet, J. (1976) *Mémoires.* Paris: Fayard.

Page, E.C. (1997) *People Who Run Europe.* Oxford: Clarendon Press.

Page, E.C. and L. Wouters (1994) Paying the top people in Europe. In C. Hood and
   B. G. Peters (Eds) *Rewards at the Top: A comparative study of high public office.*
   London: Sage.
Shore, C. and A. Black (1992) The European Communities and the construction of
   Europe. *Anthropology Today,* **8**(3), 10–11.

18 Conclusion

Choosing public sector rewards

B. Guy Peters and Marleen Brans

Most studies of comparative politics involve identifying both similarities and differences among the cases being investigated. There are also important comparisons to be made across time, with continuity and change providing important information about the political systems being studied. The present study of the rewards for high public office is not different. Many of the expectations we had when we began the research were fulfilled, and the research reinforced the findings that came from an earlier study of these rewards in Europe and North America (Hood and Peters 1994). Many of the countries that had offered high rewards for public officials continue to do so. Likewise, the tendency to reward members of parliament somewhat less than other members of the political and administrative elite has persisted from the 1980s until the present and has to some extent accelerated.

At the same time that there was some continuity in the findings, there also were a number of significant changes in the politics of public sector rewards[1] and in the willingness of governments to reward their employees, especially their higher civil servants. Perhaps most importantly, the ideas of the New Public Management (NPM) have emphasized the need to attract high quality managers to the public sector, and hence those salaries have markedly increased (see Moon 2000). Further, the collapse of the Soviet Union has freed a number of countries to make their own decisions about rewards, and has increased the degree of variation among countries in the level and the structure of rewards. We were not able to include those countries in the earlier study but have been fortunate enough to include several in this volume.

There are a number of points that could be made concerning the similarities and differences among the versions of the politics of pay in the countries included in this study. We will develop a number of these points below. This discussion includes several comparative points, as well as several points about the theoretical implications of our findings for public governance. Further, some of our findings about the rewards of high public office have implications for the actors in government who must make decisions about how they will reward themselves and other public officials and about how to hold those officials accountable for the rewards they receive. As we have already pointed out, the rewards offered to high public officials may be considered to be a rather arcane subject, but it offers a great deal of insight into the functioning of the public sector. Therefore, these findings help to understand general issues of governing as well as specific political characteristics of some of the individual countries. Additionally, they have both theoretical and practical significance.

Shifting relative level of rewards

In many of the countries considered in this book, rewards in the public sector have tended to decline relative to those offered in the private sector. This decline is especially apparent when we compare the rewards offered to top officials in government to those offered to top managers in the private sector. The pay and perquisites of bankers and other financial executives is often in the millions of euros or pounds per year, while even the most well compensated in the public sector may make several hundred thousand.[2] The financial crisis of 2008 and 2009 made the rewards available in the private sector all too apparent to the public, but this does not appear to have eased the pressures to keep public sector rewards low.

As well as some general movements in rewards for officials in the public sector, there are movements in the relative rewards offered to different types of officials. In the 1994 study, the most obvious losers were the members of parliament and other legislatures. As the most visible public officials in most democratic societies, these officials are under substantial popular pressure not to increase their own salaries. In the last two decades, MPs in several countries have been able to modestly raise their base salaries, but the pay gap with other officials remains, and has even widened related to senior public servants. Moreover, in most countries, MPs had to trade in their allowances for salary raises. The net effect of salary increases was hence mostly neutralized. Despite some modest increases, we therefore conclude that the constraints for MPs to raise their salaries persist.

While populist pressures to maintain low salaries for members of parliament are perhaps understandable, they may have some negative implications for governing. The most important of these is that it potentially will become more difficult to recruit well-qualified people to be parliamentarians and by extension ministers, since in most systems, members of parliament are also future ministers.[3] Further, restricting the level of rewards offered to MPs may mean that only the affluent, or those with close connections to moneyed interests in the society, will be able to serve in parliament. The debate about the need to offer reasonable levels of compensation for politicians has been going on for centuries, but the answer to the question can have substantial relevance for the nature of democracy.

Finally, restricting the official rewards offered to members of parliament and also to ministers may mean that they will attempt to find other, more hidden, sources of income and further undermine the legitimacy of these crucial democratic institutions. The political crisis arising from the abuses of parliamentary expenses in the United Kingdom have demonstrated that utilizing those suspect sources of income can undermine the already fragile legitimacy of politicians.

Even in countries with public sectors that are widely regarded as transparent and honest the use of irregular benefits for politicians can provoke substantial concern among the public (Parry 2009).

Managerialism and rewards

As implied above, changing values about the public sector and the role of civil servants and public managers are influencing the rewards offered to these officials. The NPM (Christensen and Lægreid 2001) has emphasized the importance of public managers as a source of governance, and with that the relative unimportance of political executives. Thus, the acceptance of NPM has tended to push civil service salaries higher, and to match those salaries more closely to those in the private sector. The major exception to that movement has been in the United States, where civil service salaries are not permitted to exceed those of Congress and therefore remain substantially lower than even many middle managers.

Another of the consequences of adopting the tenets of the NPM was to use a variety of non-departmental bodies to supply public services (Pollitt and Talbot 2004). Especially for organizations such as public corporations, and even for agencies and quangos, the use of a variety of organizational formats has tended to remove rewards from formal pay systems to more individualized contractual arrangements. Further, as these contracts are personal they may be protected from public disclosure. Many of these managers, and the members of boards of corporations (often composed of other sitting or retired public officials) receive substantial rewards, but it is difficult to ascertain exactly what those rewards may be.

The secondary consequence of the emphasis on managerial salaries is that the political managers in government – the ministers – have not kept pace in many instances with their nominal subordinates. Such an inversion of rewards would generally be unacceptable in the private sector and it may produce important management problems within public sector organizations as well. If nothing else, these relative rewards emphasize the point from the NPM about the relative importance of managers as compared to politicians in making government work effectively.

Another secondary consequence of managerialism in the reward structures of government has been that the implicit incentive structure in the public sector has been altered. Most of the available evidence on the attitudes and behavior of civil servants had argued that purposive and solidary rewards were more important than material rewards (see Peters in this volume). With the large scale increases in rewards coming at least in part from the NPM, the apparent logic is that the best way to attract highly skilled people to work for government is to pay them more.

Pay for ethics

One option for dealing with the use of corrupt, or apparently corrupt, sources of income for high public officials has been to make explicit or implicit deals of 'pay for ethics'. That is, rewards for public office may be increased in exchange for increased transparency about other sources of income and reduced use of unofficial income. Further, in such arrangements the sanctions imposed for accepting unauthorized income or perquisites may be stiffened so that the public officials would be even more careful about any potential outside income.

The term 'pay for ethics' was coined with respect to an explicit arrangement limiting the outside income of Congressmen in the United States in the early 1990s. The logic has, however, been used in several other countries contained in this volume. For example, several of the Eastern European cases have been attempting to increase the rewards offered to public officials in order to ensure their more complete involvement with the public sector. Likewise, the scandals over the use of parliamentary allowances in the United Kingdom provoked some discussion of higher salaries in order to prevent what was perceived by so many citizens as the abuse of the rewards system in Parliament.

Making rewards automatic

The pressure on rewards offered to members of parliament makes the political difficulties of making decisions about pay and perquisites very apparent. These problems have led to some political systems to implement mechanisms for making rewards automatic. The automatic rewards systems function in two ways. One is to relate the rewards for public officials to changes in the economy, especially to changes in average wages in the economy. In Estonia, for example, the salary of a member of parliament is four times the average salary, and that of Prime Minister six times that salary. In other cases, for example the United States, changes in the salary of members of Congress change automatically in response to changes in price levels, unless the Congress acts to deny themselves those increases.

As well as linkages to changes in the economy, reward levels for one set of officials may be pegged to those for other officials. For example, in the United States the rewards for executive officials (other than the President and the Vice-President) are linked to Congressional salaries. Likewise, as noted in Estonia, the salaries for most important public officials are set relative to the salaries of MPs, and those in turn reflect average wages in the economy. This pattern of reward determination obviously maintains relativities among the various actors within government.

This use of automatic movements in pay may enable the public sector to maintain its position relative to basic levels of reward in the economy, although certainly not with the rapid movements of salaries for very high earners. The relatively low level of reward is true even though public officials may be managing some of the largest organizations in their economies. Part of the logic of administrative reforms over the past several decades has been to open the public sector to more managers from the private sector. This attempt to improve management in government will, however, be very unlikely to produce any real changes if the rewards offered in government are substantially lower than those in the private sector.[4]

The automatic pattern of pay determination is very important for removing this function from more open politics. The determination of the initial relative pay for the various actors, and the initial linkage of public sector rewards to the economy are themselves important political decisions, and may be a way in which current elites can lock in future elites to particular positions in the economy. Future attempts to alter those positions will be more visible and accentuate the politics of rewards.

Lifetime earnings versus the short-term

Most of the public discussion of rewards for high public office appears premised on the rewards that officials earn while in office. That rather short-term perspective may, however, be contrasted with a perspective of rewards while in office merely being one component of total earnings over a career in and out of government. Thus, accepting relatively low rewards for a public office can be considered an investment in some cases for much greater rewards after leaving government. Or, in less frequent cases, accepting a public job, for example a judgeship may offer intangible rewards after a legal career with much higher monetary rewards.

In some cases the lifetime earnings derived from public employment have become almost institutionalized, and to some extent are a strategic element of governing. This governance style is clearest in the *pantouflage* arrangements in France, with many talented people trained for the public sector moving into high paying positions in the private sector. This enhances the earnings of these individuals, but also enables the State to recruit the best and brightest, and to have them in government for at least part of their career. Further the continuing personal linkages through the *grands corps* also help to integrate state and the economy and to provide alternative mechanisms for steering.

In other settings, the lifetime earning model may be considered almost corrupt. Most governments now have some restrictions on civil servants leaving office and then going to work for the same industries that they may have contracted with, or regulated, while they were in official positions. The 'revolving door' in government appears to be a continuing problem for some of the newer democracies such as Slovakia, and remains a problem for other countries despite attempts to regulate this movement. Even in more established democracies, however, the movement from government to the private sector may appear corrupt, and may in reality be corrupt (Babcock 2006).

The lifetime earnings model is clearly applicable to the specialized careers within the civil service, but is perhaps less clearly applicable to most legislative bodies. Former members of parliaments may have continuing contacts with their former colleagues and hence may be useful as lobbyists. In the parliamentary systems contained in this volume the potential for such earnings may be relatively modest, given the importance of political parties and their ideologies in shaping policy decisions. The major exception to this generalization would be the Congress of the United States in which members are both more independent and many during their careers specialize and develop substantial policy expertise (Parker and Parker 2009).

Accountability and transparency

The final set of comments about the rewards of high public office concern the transparency of the reward systems and the accountability of public officials. Several of the chapters have pointed to the importance of transparency and particularly to the deleterious effects on public confidence in government of having reward systems that are not transparent. The absence of transparency may permit higher rewards in the short-run, but in the longer term it may undermine public confidence and in time undermine rewards.

Further, the recent events in the United Kingdom have demonstrated that if rewards that have been hidden from the public become known, the reaction will likely be intense. Therefore, although transparency may limit rewards in the short-term if the public resists high levels of rewards for their high public officials, the political dangers of hidden rewards may be substantial, especially in countries that have some element of populism. More elitist, or cynical, political systems may be able to accept the revelation of disguised rewards.

We attempted to assess the level of transparency of reward structures in the appendices supplied by each of the authors, and we found marked variations in that transparency. As might be expected, the Nordic countries and the United States were the most open about rewards. At the other end of this dimension France and Belgium were less than open about rewards and the authors of these chapters displayed remarkable persistence and creativity in developing the data that they have presented.[5] In the group of Central and Eastern Europe (CEE) countries, Estonia and Hungary have displayed relatively high levels of transparency of rewards, while in Slovakia and Romania opacity remains the rule. The differences across countries reflect long-established patterns within administrative and political cultures that in some cases have persisted in an era of marked increases in the openness of government (see Painter and Peters 2010). But the division of CEE cases along the transparency dimension of rewards also demonstrates how polities have designed the reward system to break with past legacies.

One of the more remarkable findings, given the general improvement in levels of transparency in many governments, is that in some ways there is perhaps less openness about public sector rewards than in previous eras. This is especially true for the often substantial rewards offered to the leaders of public corporations and other business activities in the public sector. Further, the ideas of the NPM and the desire to recruit more senior managers, often from outside government on individual contracts, has meant that a number of public officials have pay and perquisites that are not visible to the public. While this practice may be considered necessary to recruit the 'best and brightest,' it does not sit comfortably in the public sectors of the industrial democracies.

The development of agencies and public corporations to provide public services provides another barrier to the transparency of these rewards systems. The rewards for corporate officials in the public system may have to approximate those in the private sector, in order to be able to compete for managers. But those salaries are sufficiently high to be a political embarrassment to the elected officials to whom they are nominally responsible, so that they are best kept out of the public eye. Hence, like those of many higher civil servants, the salaries of officials in public corporations may not be open and transparent. It does therefore not come as a surprise that most of the authors who contributed data to this volume failed to provide consistent time series on rewards for CEOs of public corporations.

Even when it may be possible to obtain salaries of public officials as a matter of law or policy, it does not mean that this information is readily available. Therefore we need to distinguish between active and passive forms of transparency. In most of the cases reported here the researchers had to engage in some substantial effort to uncover the level of rewards, although the information was not nominally secret. That passive transparency is in contrast to the more active publication of reward levels and active efforts on the part of some countries to make rewards known to their citizens (and to researchers).

Even when the rewards system is not open and transparent the public may be better informed, or at least think they are better informed, than in the past. The growing 'blogosphere' about these rewards has become an alternative to more traditional forms of spreading information. While these sources of information are unmediated, tend to exaggerate some of the real or perceived problems in public rewards, and may lead to various forms of populism, they have helped to make the public aware of what is happening in government.

Conclusions

This book has demonstrated the utility of the rewards of high public office for the comparative analysis of political systems. The various country chapters have revealed a great deal about the internal politics of these systems, and about the ways in which the important questions about how to reward public officials are resolved. Further, when we consider this evidence across time we can understand how major structural and ideational changes in the public sector have altered the ways in which rewards are determined.

These studies also demonstrate the practical importance of rewards for governing. The level and the nature of rewards are important for recruiting officials and for the internal management of public organizations. Individuals may choose to work in the public sector for a number of reasons, but certainly rewards are part of that equation. Further, the level of rewards and their visibility to the public will affect the manner in which citizens consider their political and administrative leaders, and may therefore affect the legitimacy of the political system. Any number of factors influences the legitimacy and authority of a government, but these rewards are certainly an important part of the story.

Notes

1 The British chapter reflects the beginning of a major political debate over rewards. The exposure of a number of apparent abuses in the perquisites enjoyed by Members of Parliament produced a firestorm in British politics that led to a number of sitting

members to decline from standing at the next election. It further has undermined the respect that members of the public have for government, emphasizing the argument we have made that attempts to hide rewards often backfire.
2 This is true for the European and North American countries in this book (the US president earns $400,000 per year), but the political and administrative leadership in Singapore (see Quah 2003) may earn over $1 million (US) per year.
3 A number of parliamentary systems permit recruitment of ministers from outside parliament, but the majority will come from people sitting in parliament.
4 The whole attempt to rely on financial rewards for public service managers may, however, be misguided. Substantial evidence has demonstrated that individuals who choose public service careers tend to do so for reasons other than money (Perry and Hondeghem 2008). Further, as Allison (1979) has famously argued, public and private management may be so different that the skills are not necessarily transferrable.
5 None of these systems was as opaque as that of the People's Republic of China (see Burns 2003).

References

Allison, G.T. (1979) *Public and Private Management: Are They Fundamentally Alike in All Unimportant Respects?* Proceedings for the Public Management Research Conference, 19–20 November. Washington, DC: Office of Personnel Management, pp. 27–38.

Babcock, C.R. (2006) Defense contractors offensive maneuvers. *The Washington Post*, 20 March.

Burns, J. (2003) Rewarding comrades at the top in China. In C. Hood, B.G. Peters and G.O.M. Lee (Eds) *Rewards for High Public Office in Asia and the Pacific.* London: Routledge, pp. 49–69.

Christensen, T. and P. Lægreid (2001) *New Public Management: The transformation of ideas and practice.* Aldershot: Ashgate.

Hood, C. and B.G. Peters (1994) *Rewards at the Top: A comparative study of high public office.* London: Sage.

Moon, M.J. (2000) Organizational commitment revisited in the New Public Management. *Public Performance and Management Review*, **24**: 177–194.

Painter, M.A. and B.G. Peters (2010) *Administrative Traditions and Administrative Reforms.* London: Macmillan.

Parker, G.R. and S.L. Parker (2009) Earning through learning in legislatures. *Public Choice*, 141: 319–333.

Parry, M. (2009) Ministers enjoy subsidized rents thanks to wealthy contacts. *Helsinki Times*, 26 November.

Perry, J.L. and A. Hondeghem (2008) *Motivation in Public Management. The call of public service.* Oxford: Oxford University Press.

Peters, B.G. (2009) *The Politics of Bureaucracy.* 6th edn. London: Routledge.

Pollitt, C. and C. Talbot (2004) *Unbundled Government: A critical analysis of the global trend to agencies, quangos and contractualisation.* London: Routledge.

Quah, J.S.T. (2003) Paying for the 'best and brightest': rewards for high public office in Singapore. In C. Hood, B.G. Peters and G.O.M. Lee (Eds) *Rewards for High Public Office in Asia and the Pacific.* London: Routledge, pp. 145–162.

Appendix – Basic data on RHPO in 15 countries and the EU institutions[1]

The figures presented in Tables A.1–A.5, as in Chapter 2, are for basic annual salary without bonuses, allowances, etc. unless otherwise indicated. The limits of the data are explained in Chapter 2: 'add-ons', which often vary on an individual basis, can significantly alter the actual amounts that high public officials (HPOs) take home, as can taxation.

With respect to the development of salaries of the 15 countries plus EU institutions, original data were received in different monetary units. All non-members of the euro zone, with the exception of Ireland, submitted their data in national currency units (NCU) while all euro zone members submitted their data in euros (EUR). Data from non-euro zone countries – except for Ireland – were converted into euros using European Central Bank exchange rates (http://www.ecb.int/stats/exchange/eurofxref/html/index.en.html). For the actual pre-euro era (1992 to 1997), fixed exchange rates based on the European currency unit (XEU) were used.

For the figures in the Appendix, data were first converted into purchasing power parities in dollar terms (PPP$); for the tables in Chapter 2, these were then deflated at 2000 consumer prices (CPI) using the International Monetary Fund's (IMF) World Economic Database http://www.imf.org/external/pubs/ft/weo/2008/02/weodata/index.aspx, using the following formula:

$$\text{Real Value} = \frac{\text{Nominal Value}}{\text{Price Index (decimal form)}}$$

or more specifically

$$\text{Real Value} = \frac{\text{Income Year (i)}}{\text{CPI Year}\dfrac{(i)}{100}}$$

For all countries, data in their original currency were used to conduct these transformations except for Ireland. In order to be able to use the IMF's PPP$ and CPI values, the Irish values had to be reconverted into Irish pounds. The Romanian EUR exchange rate in 2003 is calculated by averaging the closest available exchange rates of respectively 1998 and 2005, due to the lack of exchange rates for the new Romanian lei.

Data on gross domestic product (GDP, in PPP$) (see Chapter 2) were obtained from the IMF World Indicators Outlook Data 2010 http://www.imf.org/external/ns/cs.aspx?id=28 and were also deflated at 2000-level prices using the same formula as for national salaries. While the data were complete in 2000, this was not the case for 1992 and 2008. In order to minimize the number of missing data points in 1992 and 2008, their value was replaced by the closest available value to them. The Chief Executives' salaries of Estonia and the US in 1992 were replaced by their respective values of 1993 and 1994. For the same position, the 2007 salaries of the Chief Executives of Hungary and the UK were used instead of their 2008 values.

Note

1 The authors wish to thank all contributors to this volume for supplying the original data. Anna Christensen Meyer of Ceps/Instead, Luxembourg, supplied the data for Denmark. The authors are also grateful to Bart Verbelen and Jesse Stroobants of the Public Management Institute of the Katholieke Universiteit Leuven, for their help with the PPP$, CPI and GDP calculations.

A.1 Chief Executives – annual nominal base salaries 1992–2008 (in PPP $)

	Belgium	Denmark	Estonia	France	Hungary	Ireland	Italy	Netherlands	Norway	Romania	Slovak Republic	Spain	Sweden	UK	US	EU
1992	118.016	80.734			56.802	94.173	218.193	110.831	59.247			108.761	59.466	123.157		220.821
1993	119.269	82.851	23.964		57.501	94.401	225.725	115.708	63.695			105.378	60.406	122.366		225.958
1994	122.990	84.164	40.022		49.145	98.239	230.088	117.655	65.186			103.764	80.049	126.277	200.000	228.235
1995	128.829	86.075	35.497		40.335	100.322	227.982	116.079	65.446		49.670	106.096	78.804	131.626	200.000	235.657
1996	127.020	87.537	30.896		37.687	101.963	227.146	117.350	90.947		52.112	104.360	91.855	160.185	200.000	234.904
1997	181.713	89.216	40.283		37.839	103.868	235.038	116.990	96.859		53.937	107.373	98.089	224.431	200.000	239.746
1998	183.515	90.780	36.821		54.094	117.112	242.142	119.428	107.868	54.067	56.123	108.188	102.311	228.111	200.000	242.646
1999	185.714	93.236	46.809		50.613	119.102	242.390	121.875	102.629		56.006	108.863	109.035	236.483	200.000	250.220
2000	189.842	142.578	41.578		64.599	118.819	249.809	123.002	101.932		54.746	109.617	116.032	245.601	200.000	257.537
2001	194.491	147.493	68.286		66.300	129.047	255.999	125.696	110.356		55.759	109.931	121.136	253.755	400.000	264.099
2002	198.153	149.761	82.055		67.486	149.478	250.274	127.559	120.489		57.725	109.372	127.540	262.717	400.000	274.105
2003	203.005	152.762	78.196		93.039	164.621	258.661	128.188	119.515	40.714	59.746	109.319	132.777	266.182	400.000	280.818
2004	207.751	156.108	81.141		119.011	173.598	265.271	134.039	121.696		60.433	110.033	141.491	273.163	400.000	294.183
2005	213.569	160.601	85.295		127.463	179.728	276.462	135.979	121.154		65.422	110.626	150.600	283.408	400.000	298.549
2006	220.525	163.954	79.714		133.187	195.446	272.857	140.744	120.151	47.505	70.216	113.116	159.211	288.017	400.000	308.896
2007	227.240	168.924	89.473	92.905	129.784	208.994	244.021	147.003	129.710		75.693	114.933	165.156	297.854	400.000	319.236
2008	223.677	169.021	97.534	252.143		217.472	243.745	148.410	128.724	58.070	79.483	116.580	169.781		400.000	317.374

A.2 Cabinet Ministers or equivalent – annual nominal base salaries 1992–2008 (in PPP $)

	Belgium	Denmark	Estonia	France	Hungary	Ireland	Italy	Netherlands	Norway	Romania	Slovak Republic	Spain	Sweden	UK	US	EU
1992	118.016	80.734			49.229	74.904	186.646	110.831	55.437			95.958	54.790	101.853		180.017
1993	119.269	82.851			49.834	75.101	194.664	115.708	59.528			92.974	55.747	101.199		184.205
1994	122.990	84.164			42.592	78.096	198.986	117.655	60.921			91.550	67.734	104.434	148.400	186.061
1995	128.829	86.075			34.957	80.020	197.445	116.079	61.187		27.692	93.607	66.680	108.859	148.400	192.111
1996	127.020	87.537			32.662	81.330	196.760	117.350	76.955		30.755	92.075	73.484	137.210	148.400	191.498
1997	181.713	89.216			32.794	82.848	202.564	116.990	78.871		33.455	94.734	79.698	162.028	148.400	195.445
1998	183.515	90.780			46.881	93.581	208.080	119.428	88.127	46.876	36.407	95.426	82.589	164.685	151.800	197.810
1999	185.714	93.236			43.864	95.051	208.154	121.875	83.848		37.378	96.049	87.971	170.729	151.800	203.984
2000	189.842	114.062			42.989	94.825	214.780	123.002	83.561		37.348	96.714	93.575	177.311	157.000	209.948
2001	194.491	117.994			44.121	102.987	220.226	125.696	90.670		38.794	96.990	97.409	183.197	161.200	215.298
2002	198.153	119.809			82.911	118.323	217.192	127.559	98.863		41.106	96.498	102.532	191.392	166.700	223.455
2003	203.005	122.209			80.013	129.695	225.016	128.188	98.063	35.299	43.627	96.451	106.472	193.917	171.900	228.928
2004	207.751	124.886	60.887		78.730	137.483	231.239	134.039	99.548		44.831	97.081	113.448	199.003	175.700	239.823
2005	213.569	128.481	67.105		84.322	142.338	241.151	135.979	98.756	44.229	49.721	97.604	120.740	206.467	180.100	243.382
2006	220.525	131.163	72.893		114.541	154.118	236.215	140.744	97.737		54.472	99.801	127.632	209.825	183.500	251.818
2007	227.240	135.139	81.873		111.615	164.801	217.180	147.003	105.533		59.701	101.404	132.387	216.991	186.600	260.247
2008	223.677	135.216	89.538	141.991		171.486	216.617	148.410	104.626	50.338	63.692	102.858	136.084		196.700	258.729

A.3 Members of Parliament or equivalent – annual nominal base salaries 1992–2008 (in PPP $)

	Belgium	Denmark	Estonia	France	Hungary	Ireland	Italy	Netherlands	Norway	Romania	Slovak Republic	Spain	Sweden	UK	US
1992	62.663	38.425			28.307	36.362	123.548	69.145	38.680				27.776	49.845	
1993	65.794	39.433	17.825		23.879	57.949	132.541	80.485	38.685				29.003	50.862	
1994	67.812	40.058	20.124		20.409	60.021	136.782	80.390	41.456				30.788	53.531	133.600
1995	70.834	40.968	23.166		20.101	62.578	136.374	79.680	41.574		18.462		32.128	54.711	133.600
1996	69.839	41.664	23.907		22.047	63.602	135.988	81.152	55.968		20.503		33.680	67.823	133.600
1997	72.093	42.463	26.176		24.596	64.791	137.614	85.199	56.732		22.303		36.170	68.424	133.600
1998	72.428	43.207	28.852		22.078	63.739	139.954	86.643	62.042	42.881	24.272		37.350	69.546	136.673
1999	74.749	44.376	29.869		23.541	64.673	139.684	88.848	59.029		24.919		44.605	72.098	136.673
2000	76.492	54.788	32.452		35.376	64.521	144.722	87.301	58.078		24.899		47.411	74.878	141.300
2001	79.420	56.677	35.587		36.307	70.074	148.681	92.189	62.038		25.862		49.953	77.363	141.300
2002	79.872	57.549	38.641		36.956	81.185	151.028	93.535	67.350		27.404		51.891	78.282	150.000
2003	85.778	58.702	41.212		42.798	91.127	157.726	93.589	66.806	32.291	29.085		54.113	85.520	154.700
2004	87.745	60.216	44.736		42.111	99.583	163.176	95.233	67.516		29.887		57.361	87.763	158.100
2005	90.235	61.950	46.740		45.102	103.100	170.528	97.322	66.629	40.461	33.147		60.240	91.055	162.100
2006	93.127	63.243	50.510		47.128	108.859	162.928	101.837	65.948		36.315	82.817	65.789	92.536	165.200
2007	94.267	66.101	55.279		45.924	116.404	163.497	107.945	71.226		39.801	85.457	67.111	95.697	168.000
2008	92.789	66.139	69.210	70.996		121.126	162.363	110.344	70.666	41.776	42.461	87.081	68.560		172.200

A.4 Top judges – annual nominal base salaries 1992–2008 (in PPP $)

	Belgium	Denmark	Estonia	France	Hungary	Ireland	Italy	Netherlands	Norway	Romania	Slovak Republic	Spain	Sweden	UK	US	EU
1992	98.637					94.178	159.600	110.831	88.202			90.048	51.229	169.225		178.544
1993	103.791		17.774			94.404	157.135	115.708	88.215			87.247	50.764	179.909		192.443
1994	105.988		23.327			98.109	163.585	117.655	91.001			85.911	59.113	180.779	164.100	196.958
1995	112.596		23.321			107.250	163.872	116.079	90.129		24.000	106.051	58.194	194.396	164.100	198.372
1996	113.214	78.265	22.156			117.515	164.143	117.350	101.441		26.654	104.315	67.361	200.658	164.100	202.730
1997	116.224	79.829	36.463			119.711	173.080	116.990	103.778		28.994	107.396	69.889	211.320	164.100	198.510
1998	102.683	88.552	34.615			116.821	176.828	119.428	112.803	54.067	31.553	108.175	70.262	221.420	164.100	199.721
1999	105.154	89.131	39.221			119.102	183.015	121.875	111.350		32.395	173.593	73.103	233.413	167.900	211.326
2000	106.974	89.196	38.380			118.822	188.496	123.002	105.488		32.368	174.886	89.832	243.825	173.600	216.795
2001	110.056	94.251	37.339		66.300	129.053	193.652	125.696	113.338		33.621	175.350	96.160	256.615	178.300	216.290
2002	113.991	95.139	57.002		67.486	149.484	196.709	130.243	123.085		35.625	174.454	96.280	262.443	184.400	225.483
2003	123.036	97.645	58.414		93.039	162.990	205.434	130.243	122.089	40.714	37.810	174.431	102.714	269.416	191.300	236.374
2004	129.786	102.651	64.224		119.011	168.539	212.532	136.187	121.696		38.854	175.561	104.525	305.704	194.300	243.075
2005	135.069	105.019	67.153		127.463	174.492	222.107	138.158	121.154	51.015	43.091	176.432	97.371	316.243	199.200	247.461
2006	139.011	113.209	71.742		133.187	192.873	235.788	140.188	120.151	52.545	47.209	179.974	104.605	348.837	203.000	260.311
2007	142.532	117.302	78.328		129.784	206.242	242.723	146.070	157.918		51.741	182.883	117.968	356.656	205.800	265.175
2008	145.625	117.349	89.002	89.478		225.339	252.310	150.931	156.584		55.199	185.425			208.100	268.677

A.5 Top civil servants – annual nominal base salaries 1992–2008 (in PPP $)

	Belgium	Denmark	Estonia	France	Hungary	Ireland	Italy	Netherlands	Norway	Romania	Slovak Republic	Spain	Sweden	UK	US	EU
1992	79.623				41.655	72.165	104.221	97.442	66.289			75.114	80.578	136.107		160.015
1993	83.389		18.476		42.168		106.297	101.729	71.013			73.905	82.831	140.642		163.738
1994	84.928		28.395		36.039		110.690	103.435	71.073			73.574	77.586	145.400	133.600	165.388
1995	89.215		31.097		29.579		100.006	102.054	71.188		19.808	74.820	115.175	152.570		170.766
1996	89.719	96.581	29.910		27.637	91.510	94.415	102.654	69.810		21.155	75.687	116.350	157.727	133.600	170.221
1997	90.596	98.713	43.511		27.749		113.352	102.852	77.549		23.007	76.134	118.320	171.605	133.600	173.729
1998	91.227	103.259	40.330		39.669		114.767	105.001	90.647	42.881	23.638	76.459	118.952	177.468	136.673	175.831
1999	94.168	105.642	39.831		37.116		122.558	107.145	90.499		22.711	77.092	126.381	184.048	136.673	181.319
2000	96.385	111.338	45.267		36.376	100.290	145.087	108.137	86.604		21.980	77.724	127.261	201.237	141.300	186.621
2001	98.740	116.480	73.482		37.333	102.111	173.863	110.612	92.880		22.248	78.068	137.371	209.626	141.300	191.376
2002	217.106	117.347	76.607		62.183	115.033	176.827	112.236	105.081		23.347	78.007	137.543	214.394	150.000	198.627
2003	218.180	122.560	82.114		60.010	122.242	162.398	112.809	103.881	32.291	24.876	78.578	139.666	220.029	154.700	203.491
2004	215.417	128.358	83.623		59.048	126.403	165.146	117.949	101.868		31.059	79.704	147.228	229.006	158.100	213.176
2005	217.095	133.746	78.514		63.241	130.867	169.799	119.656	103.275		34.994	80.752	154.495	246.532	162.100	216.340
2006	219.887	136.195	82.624		88.108	144.651	191.646	123.845	109.140	36.039	37.513	82.604	165.000	263.564	165.200	223.838
2007	222.169	147.392	92.614		85.857	154.678	201.863	129.526	118.220			85.127	169.612	263.156	168.000	231.331
2008	219.089	153.470	92.371	78.691		168.999		130.773		46.064		86.248	167.707		172.200	229.981

A.6 Annotations to tables A.1–A.5 of the Appendix

Country	Office				
	Chief Executive	Ministers	MPs	Civil Servants	Judges
Belgium	Prime Minister: salary, including end of year premium and holiday pay	Minister: salary, including end of year premium and holiday pay	Member of the Chamber of Representatives: salary, including end of year premium and holiday pay	Chairs of Direction Committee of Federal Government Services: salaries, including end of year premium and holiday pay without correction downward	First President of the Court of Cassation: salaries, including end of year premium and holiday pay; the data from 1992 until 1997 were provided from a different source than the 1997–2008 data
Denmark	Prime Minister	Minister	Member of Parliament	Permanent Secretary	Supreme Court Judges
Estonia	Prime Minister	Minister of Social Affairs	Member of the unicameral *Riigikogu*	State Secretary: salary highest civil servant, comparable to that of Secretaries-General	Chief Justice, Supreme Court
France	President: salary before tax but after deduction of social security contributions	Minister: double MP's basic allowance, salary before tax and deduction of social security contributions	Members of the Chamber of Representatives: salary before tax and social security contributions; average of HE1 A1 and HE G of *hors échelle scale*	Director or Director General of HE E2 Scale: salary before tax and deduction of social security contributions	President of Court of Cassation: salary before tax and deduction of social security contributions
Hungary	Prime Minister	Minister	Member of Parliament: fixed salary, includes travel allowances for MPs living 100–200 km from Budapest	Senior State Secretary	President of the Supreme Court
Ireland	Prime Minister, Taoisigh: includes PM salary plus MP's base salary	Minister: includes ministerial salary plus MP's base salary	Members of the Dáil	Secretary General	Chief Justice

Country					
Italy	Prime Minister	Minister	Member of Chamber of Representatives	Director General Grade 1: base salary plus supplementary salary	First President of the Supreme Court
The Netherlands	Prime Minister	Minister	MP: member of Second Chamber	Civil Servants: Secretary-General: average 30% bonus excluded	President of and Attorney-General of the Supreme Court
Norway	Prime Minister	Cabinet Minister	Members of the *Storting*	Secretary-General: average base salaries	President of the Supreme Court
Romania	Prime Minister	Minister	MP	Secretary-General	President of the Supreme Court
Slovak Republic	PM: base salary including fixed function allowance	Minister: base salary including fixed function allowance	MP: base salary, not including regular allowances of about 70 to 80 percent of base.	Director-General in Ministries – average base salary	Constitutional Court Judge: base salary plus maximum fixed function allowance of 120,000 SKK
Spain	Prime Minister	Cabinet Minister	Member of Chamber of Representatives	Level 30 Civil Servant	President of the Supreme Court
Sweden	Prime Minister	Cabinet Minister	Members of the *Rikstag*	Directors-General of Executive Agencies	President of the Supreme Administrative Court
UK	Prime Minister	Cabinet Minister	Members of the House of Commons	Permanent Secretaries	Lord Chief Justice
US	President	Cabinet Officer	Member of Congress	Highest Senior Executive Service: salaries excluding bonuses	Supreme Court Justices
EU	President of the European Commission	Member of the European Commission	Until 2009, MEPs were paid the same as member states' MPs	Staff officials AD 16(3) or A1(6)	President of the European Court of Justice

Note: The figures presented in the Appendix are for basic annual salary, before tax, without variable bonuses, allowances, etc. In some cases, as indicated in this table, some fixed salary supplements are included. The offices are as indicated by country experts.

Index